Despoilers of Democracy

Despoilers of Democracy

By CLARK R. MOLLENHOFF

The real story of what Washington propagandists, arrogant bureaucrats, mismanagers, influence peddlers, and outright corrupters are doing to our federal government.

DOUBLEDAY & COMPANY, INC.
Garden City, New York, 1965

Library of Congress Catalog Card Number 65–17224
Copyright © 1965 by Clark R. Mollenhoff
All Rights Reserved
Printed in the United States of America
First Edition

To Georgia

CONTENTS

Despoilers of Democracy

CHAPTER 1

Capital Corrosion

Not long ago, a newspaper editor chided a wealthy and powerful United States Senator about activities of his that seemed to be misuse of public power for private gain. The editor expected a flat denial or some kind of rationalization. He was completely taken aback when the Senator said bluntly that of course he had used his position to add to his multimillion-dollar fortune.

"What do you think I spent all that money getting elected for if I didn't expect to get more back?" the Senator is quoted as saying.

Amazed at such an attitude on the part of a major public figure, the editor passed on the story to a number of other editors. Few were really surprised that this Senator would sell out the public trust. They were surprised, however, that he would admit it and dismiss it in such cavalier fashion. The usual ploy is for accused officials—even when caught with conclusive evidence—to deny everything.

Is this official's behavior an isolated blemish on the body politic? Unfortunately, it is not. Though an extreme example, it is nevertheless symptomatic of the creeping corruption and cynicism that afflict our society today.

One must return to the language of muckraking to describe what is happening. Fraud and favoritism are sapping the strength of America's democracy. Politics and plunder are wasting billions of tax dollars. Unwarranted secrecy combined with superficial press coverage distort or hide many vital government decisions.

Big Government and the Big Lie threaten and too often over-whelm those men who seek no more than honest government and truth.

I am not so naïve that I believe we can eliminate all corruption in government. This is as impossible as abolishing sin. There will always be people seeking to take advantage of friendships, of po-litical or cash payoffs, to win large government contracts or other-wise increase their personal estate. The point, however, is that we must not begin to *accept* corruption or mismanagement as the normal way of doing things, or it will destroy us.

In the past, when corruption or foolishness in government was discovered and exposed, a wave of angry public reaction and re-form usually followed. It was not total exposure, nor was it total reform, but usually it served to demonstrate that politicians who are caught tampering with the public trust often pay with public disgrace. Such wrath has caused resignations from posts as high as the Cabinet and the White House.[1]

I hope our federal government will continue to be strong enough to recover from the sicknesses of dishonesty and undue favoritism. I hope our citizens always will react with sufficient anger to force reform. There are ominous signs that they will not.

What happens to citizen concern when more attention is paid to party labels than principles? When there is too much parroting of slogans, and not enough work on and study of the important de-tails of government? When there are too many mass movements by pressure groups? When there is too much worship of the syn-thetic image of the public man, and too little effort to determine what lies behind the carefully concocted image?

I fear that we are in real danger of losing the enlightened con-cern needed to save ourselves. I fear that most citizens are con-fused by the bigness and complexity of governmental operations and fail to distinguish between good government and clever public relations. I fear that there is too much debilitating cynicism in the land and too little understanding of the importance of honest government.

One needs only to consider the government corruption in parts of Africa, the Middle East and Asia to appreciate the importance of integrity in government. In many of the nations in these areas, the payoff and the bribe are the accepted way of life. Highly placed officials engage in business operations that are directly and indirectly aided by government funds. Under such circumstances, public office is not a public trust. It is simply an opportunity for public plunder.

When integrity and idealism die, so does the hope of solving a nation's social and economic problems. Misuse and waste of American foreign-aid funds in Korea, Laos, Cambodia, Turkey, Iran, Peru and other places have dramatized how corruption can kill or stifle progress. The difficulty of obtaining anything but paper reforms in personal taxation in Latin-American countries has hampered the Alliance for Progress from its birth.

Isolated outbreaks abroad and at home can become epidemic. What chance is there for integrity to survive at the lower levels of government if high public officials flagrantly misuse public money and public power to enrich themselves? Businessmen who lose out to corrupt colleagues begin to believe it is necessary to cheat and to "fix" to prosper. Manufacturers who lose contracts because of political deals may start giving less attention to efficiency and technical progress and more attention to political bonuses. Contractors who see shoddy work accepted on government projects may come to believe it is more important to pour money into political campaign chests than to pour honest concrete into government buildings or government highways.

If corruption becomes the norm, then all who deal with government—businessmen, labor organizations, farmers, doctors, housewives, journalists—will start to question whether honesty really counts. Such an attitude could destroy our government and our society.

Fortunately, we are not yet dominated by the philosophy that it is right and it is smart to swindle the government. But the belief spreads that the skillful lie and the glib denial, aided and abetted by well-oiled public relations, can convince the public—and three-fourths of the press—that wrong is right.

For more than twenty years as a working newspaperman, I have spent most of my time exposing government corruption on the city, county, state and federal government levels. I have always tried to do more than expose a scandal for the sake of the story of the moment; I have tried to understand the causes and the subtle elements of corruption. I have tried to recognize *all* of the corrupters—not merely the obvious fellows involved in personal perjury or crude thievery. Some of the worst corrupters do not break the laws, but hire others to break or circumvent the laws. And some have become quite adept at obtaining distorted interpretations of the law that benefit them.

I have no doubt that the vast majority of Americans would still rise up in anger if confronted with evidence of an obvious bribe or a ruthless theft of government property. The new danger lies in the more complex forms of corruption, which do not come to light until they have done severe damage to our system of government.

Once the American people recognize all the corrupters—the genteel as well as the brazen, the efficient as well as the careless and slipshod—and once it becomes fully understood how the corrupters threaten our way of life, I hope they will react with vigor and remove them from public life. I am writing this book to try to give average citizens some concept of the many forms of corruption, intentional and otherwise, and to remind them what happens when wrongdoing in government persists and scoundrels are permitted to remain on the public payroll.

Who are the Washington despoilers? There are many:

They are the glib political lawyers who condemned the Dixon-Yates contract in the Eisenhower administration, but defended the conflicts of interest that developed under the Kennedy and Johnson administrations.

They are the United States Senators and Representatives who fumed about tax scandals and R.F.C. scandals in the Truman administration, but excused similar scandals under Eisenhower.

They are the partisan journalists whose judgment wobbles with the wind. They are caustic in their criticism of political influences on the Federal Communications Commission when the Eisenhower administration is in power. But they can find little even to question when a Democratic President's wife holds a multimillion-dollar interest in a government-regulated radio and television business.

They are the men who seek high office denouncing their opponents' corruption and pledging honest government. But later they excuse perjury and plunder when these involve their own political pets.

They are the members of Congress who bargain away their responsibility to examine and investigate government operations, and accept political deals or personal profits from their relations with regulatory agencies or government departments which they should be policing.

They are the self-styled free enterprisers who milk government contracts for exorbitant profits and use political deals rather than fair competition as a major business tool.

They are the self-styled liberals who prattle of "equal rights"—then railroad an obscure government clerk to a mental institution without a hearing, for the crime of objecting to seizure of the files of her boss.

They are the foreign-aid administrators who talk of fighting Communism, then fire the conscientious employee who tries to report waste and misuse of foreign-aid funds.

They are the military officers who talk of the honor of the career service, then order subordinates to violate the laws on contracts and destroy the records of the law violations.

They are the authoritarian bureaucrats. They conspire to crush the honest dissenters who dare inform Congress of examples of bad government or dishonesty.

They are the slick government public-relations operators, clever in their use of editorial connections, and vindictive in smearing civil servants who threaten to shadow the projected bright image of the government with the truth.

They are the political appointees who boast of carefully documented decisions and efficiency, then make arbitrary judgments on multimillion-dollar contracts that just happen to favor former business associates and political friends.

The corrupters also include the unprincipled pseudo-sophisticates who excuse dishonesty in government as acceptable, and treat angry indignation as an emotion of the naïve.

And the corrupters' greatest bulwark is the legion of citizens who are too unconcerned or too lazy to seek accurate information, or too partisan to be objective in viewing candidates of their own political party.

Most of our Presidents have talked of the importance of honest government in campaigning for office, as well as after election.

When General Dwight D. Eisenhower campaigned in 1952, he lashed out at the scandals of the Truman administration. The General pledged himself "to put an end to corruption, to oust the crooks and grafters, to administer tax laws fairly and impartially, and to restore honest government to the people."

In Des Moines, Iowa, on September 18, 1952, General Eisenhower asserted: "We are going to cast out the crooks and their cronies. And when it comes to casting out the crooks and their cronies, I can promise you that we won't wait for Congressional prodding and investigations. The prodding this time will start from the top."

Somehow President Eisenhower forgot his pledge—or just did not understand the dubious activities of some of his appointees. It was necessary for the Congress and the press to do considerable prodding to persuade the President that certain officials should be forced to resign.

There was no indication that President Eisenhower was involved in any of the "conflicts of interest" or other improprieties that plagued his administration. Indeed, the evidence indicates he did not know the facts in some of the cases of corruption and mismanagement until long after the newspapers were saturated with the details. But by his refusal to utter a critical word, he put himself in the position of appearing to condone the activities of some of those who resigned. And in some instances the General actually commended those who had betrayed or been loose with the public trust.

Candidate John F. Kennedy appeared to be a man with a realistic view of the problem of corruption and mismanagement in government. He showed a will to impose the highest ethical standards on his administration.

"Experience has shown that such promises . . . are not enough," Senator Kennedy told a crowd at Wittenberg College, in Springfield, Ohio, on October 17, 1960. "For ours is a government of men, not of promises—and some men yield to temptation—other men lack discrimination—and other men see no wrong in pursuing their private interest in their public capacities."

"The problem is not merely one of vicuña coats or deep freezes," the Senator said. "Less flamboyant but at least equally flagrant are the cases of those who use their office to obtain contracts for firms in which they have a financial interest—those who use their position to repay political or financial debts—those who extract profits from the information they receive or the power they wield."

Senator Kennedy went on to say: "If we are successful this fall, such a program will be accomplished only with a government that is honest, a government that is efficient, a government that is dedicated solely to the public interest. I pledge that kind of government to the American people."

He emphasized the need for appointing good men to high public office, and said it would be "improper to confine Presidential appointments to the members of one political party."

"History teaches us," the candidate said, "that no party has a monopoly on honesty.

"Both parties attract their share of crooks and weaklings. But that does not mean that these problems are incapable of solution. That does not mean that a campaign promise is enough. A new administration must screen out those who regard Government service as the door to power or wealth, those who cannot distinguish between private gains and public trust, and those who believe that old-fashioned honesty with the public's money is both old and out of fashion."

Mr. Kennedy declared that the next President had to "set the moral tone—and I refer not to his language but to his actions in office.

"For the Presidency, as Franklin Roosevelt observed, 'is pre-eminently a place of moral leadership'—and I intend to restore that kind of leadership and atmosphere beginning in 1961."

Mr. Kennedy promised that he would bring into government men "with a single-minded loyalty to the national interest—men who would regard 'public office as a public trust' " and he pledged:

"It would further be my intention, at the earliest opportunity, to submit to the Congress a single, comprehensive code on con-flicts of interest, aimed at eliminating duplications, inadvertencies and gaps, at drawing a clearer line between propriety and impro-priety, at protecting the public against unethical behavior without making it impossible for able and conscientious citizens to accept public service."

In April, 1961, three months after becoming President, John F. Kennedy again told the nation of the importance of the highest ethical standards in government.

"No President can excuse or pardon the slightest deviation from irreproachable standards of behavior on the part of any member of the executive branch," President Kennedy said. "For his firm-ness and determination is the ultimate source of public confidence in the government of the United States. And there is no considera-tion that can justify the undermining of that confidence."*

President Kennedy, born to great wealth and never compromised by a need or desire for money, seemed ideally suited to set an ex-ample and enforce the highest standards of ethics in government.

---

*In a Special Message to the Congress on conflict-of-interest legislation and on problems of ethics in government, President Kennedy said: "There can be no dissent from the principle that all officials must act with unwaver-ing integrity, absolute impartiality and complete devotion to the public in-terest. This principle must be followed not only in reality but in appearance. For the basis of effective government is public confidence, and that confi-dence is endangered when ethical standards falter or appear to falter."

His words indicated a realistic understanding of the constant problem of corruption in government. He seemed, by his own words, a man determined to pursue aggressive action in removing from public office any and all who deviated from the highest principles of integrity.

But as the new President spoke, some of his own political appointees were becoming involved in actions that were to violate the spirit of his words in a dozen different government agencies. Even in those first few months of the Kennedy-Johnson administration, some officials were asserting more power over their subordinates in the name of "greater economy and efficiency." Others were pushing "reform measures" to make it easier to fire career government employees. Within a year, several Congressional investigations were under way.

In any study of the anatomy of corruption, it is essential to point out that there are many kinds of corrupting acts and many degrees of responsibility for them. They range from careless nonfeasance to knowing criminal acts from faulty or indifferent supervision to outright collusion. Some of the men we will deal with were premeditated in their efforts to misuse political influence or governmental power for their own ends. However, many were simply slipshod in their associations, lax in examining facts presented to them for official action, or blindly partisan in defending political supporters.

It is virtually impossible to draw a simple, clear line of distinction between the aggressively corrupt and the careless. There is no known way to delve into the minds of men to fully prove motivations and the existence of guilty knowledge. One can judge each man only on the basis of documents and statements presented under oath against him, balanced by the explanations given under oath in the same forum. For this reason, I have for the most part restricted myself to testimony given under oath in official investigations by Congress. I have done this because Congress, with all its admitted imperfections, represents the best and often the only means for discovering the truth about the decisions and actions of government officials.

Certainly we cannot rely upon the self-serving declarations of our highest or lowest officials when great personal or political stakes are involved. This sort of declaration becomes as unreliable as a public-relations handout under these conditions.

The committees of Congress have the subpoena power and the authority to force the production of records and testimony from high government officials, and to challenge the decisions of the executive branch. Though these committees are made up of partisan political figures, they do represent a diversity of viewpoint. All committees include both Democrats and Republicans. Indeed, most committees include every shade of political belief from extreme liberal to extreme conservative.

The individual members of Congressional committees may be motivated by political considerations or personal malice, but there are balancing factors within the committee membership. Also, there is the additional safeguard in the fact that what is done usually takes place in the open, where the actions of all members are subject to scrutiny and criticism. (If national security or fairness requires a closed hearing, a nearly complete text of the proceedings becomes available in a few days or a few weeks.)

In the cases we will deal with, most of the persons who are subject to critical analysis have been given the opportunity to make their explanations under oath. Some men, such as Billie Sol Estes and Robert G. (Bobby) Baker, have taken the Fifth Amendment and have contended that they might incriminate themselves if forced to give testimony. In other instances officials have testified, but have given testimony that was sharply contradicted by other witnesses and documentary evidence. In the absence of any corroborative evidence, some cases reduce to the word of one man against another.

Some of the investigations have led to criminal prosecutions and convictions. Others have yielded reports by Congressional committees, with official findings of fact and conclusions of law.

Where the reports represent the unanimous or nearly unanimous views of Democrats and Republicans, this is stated, and I give considerable weight to such findings. Where there have been divided views or no official reports, I report that the views were not unanimous and try to give sufficient detail for the reader to arrive at his own judgment as to the logic and fairness of the criticism.

The Congressional investigating committee has come in for its own share of criticism, and it has been subjected to its share of misusers. To many minds, the term "Congressional investigation" recalls the irresponsible acts of the late Senator Joseph R. McCarthy or the questionable conduct by some members of the House Un-American Activities Committee. But year in, year out, other responsible, reliable committees do their work, sometimes publicized, sometimes not. The abuses of the system do not discredit it; they emphasize the value of conscientious Senators and Congressmen who actually do serve as watchdogs guarding the public trust.

CHAPTER 2

Foreign Aid or Foreign Charade

From the time the Truman doctrine and the Marshall Plan were announced in 1947, the idea of helping nations help themselves has had considerable appeal to many Congressmen as a means of fighting international Communism. But from the outset it has been difficult to make sure that the funds given are actually used to strengthen the economies and better the lot of poverty-stricken masses in other nations.

The $12 billion the United States poured into Western Europe from 1947 through 1950 is credited with restoring the economic health of that area and stopping the Western march of Communism. Problems arose in administering this aid, of course. But they were infinitesimal compared with those that accompanied the next wave of aid billions to dozens of underdeveloped and politically immature countries. Careless and corrupt foreign officials in many of these areas operated on standards that sometimes embraced the bribe and the rake-off as part of normal operations. Corruption and loose handling of U.S. foreign-aid funds often only made the rich richer—and the poor poorer.

Perhaps it is unrealistic to expect that U.S. aid would be administered in Africa or Asia with the same standard of honesty we expect in state administration of federal-aid programs in this country. However, there is no doubt that we should strive for this goal. U.S. foreign aid is not appropriated by Congress and paid for by American taxpayers for the purpose of filling the pockets of corrupt monarchs or dictators. Nor is it intended to help the

Russian or Chinese Communists build monuments to their system.

For this reason, the foreign-aid agency—known at different times as the Foreign Operations Administration, the International Cooperation Administration, and now the Agency for International Development—has had hundreds of "end-use" investigators spread about the world. Investigators try to determine whether the funds are being used properly. The end-use investigator travels out of the capital city of the recipient country, often far away from the U.S. foreign-aid headquarters. He makes sure that the roads have been constructed, the schools built and housing projects completed.

One such investigator was a man named Jerry M. Jackis, of Charleston, South Carolina. The case history of Jerry Jackis demonstrates that sometimes the real hazards in a man's life are not encountered among strangers in remote parts of the world. Sometimes they are met at home when a man simply tries to do a conscientious job in a bureaucracy so large it hides incompetents and their spoilage. For Jackis, a Congressional committee was able—partially, at least—to right a wrong. Others, it seems safe to assume, have not been so fortunate.

Jackis, who went to work for the F.O.A. in 1954, first won recognition in 1956 in Korea. There he exposed a $750,000 scandal, followed shortly by one involving $2 million.[1]

In Korea, Jerry Jackis felt he had found his niche. His work had been remarkably effective. It had resulted in reforms of supply procurement, warehousing and end-use utilization, and had brought him a promotion of two grades. In urging the promotion, his superior in Korea had written: "Mr. Jackis has initiative and is performing with a minimum of supervision. The net savings to the program, as a result of his findings, in itself justifies the promotion to the level requested."

Jackis, son of a Greek immigrant barber, was proud of his achievement. It was the most solid accomplishment of his life up to that time. He had been an enlisted man with Patton's Third Army in Europe, and later worked his way through college. He was thirty when, in 1950, he was graduated from The Citadel, in Charleston, South Carolina, with a bachelor's degree in English. After a brief period as a civilian employee with the Marines, he went to work for the National Security Agency. He remained there until 1954, when he transferred to the aid agency.

In February, 1957, shortly after his investigative success in Korea, Jackis was transferred, under the rotational system, to Cambodia. In the jungles of northern Cambodia, Jackis rode elephants and hiked with small groups of soldiers to find out, for example, how effective a U.S. well-digging program had been. No trek was too difficult for Jackis, because he was buoyed by his success in Korea.

His first fifteen months in Cambodia were relatively pleasant. His efficiency rating was "good," and he was promoted within the first year. But on June 10, 1958, his life changed. It has never really been the same since.

On that day, Jerry Jackis drove by a Russian-sponsored hospital under construction in Phnom Penh. He noticed some steel rods on the ground that bore markings indicating they were purchased with U.S. aid. The basic laws, regulations and policies of foreign aid were aimed at stopping or minimizing the possibility of any mingling of U.S. and Russian aid. Particularly, it was not intended that the United States government would provide material to be used in a Communist showpiece in Cambodia.

Jackis jumped from his jeep to get a better look. He found not only the rods but cement bearing the U.S.-aid handclasp emblem. A Fiat tractor bore the same marking. In addition, there were drums of asphalt showing splotches of paint that appeared to Jackis to have been put on in an attempt to cover I.C.A. emblems. Other possibly I.C.A.-financed material was nearby.

This evidence indicated to him a need for an immediate and thorough investigation. He hurried back to I.C.A. headquarters to report what he had found. There he wrote a memorandum to his superior, Marlin F. Haas, controller for the U. S. Operating Mission for I.C.A., telling Haas he believed the cement, steel and asphalt were being used by the Cambodians in violation of the agreement between the royal government and the U.S. He said that he believed this use violated the Mutual Security Act declaration that "the U.S. foreign-aid program does not, of course, have as its objectives the fostering and implementing of Soviet economic aid projects."

Jackis recommended that Haas have all I.C.A. commodities removed from the Soviet hospital site immediately. If this failed, he believed the only alternative for the I.C.A. mission would be to initiate refund action against the Cambodian government, as provided by U.S. regulations.

Jackis did not report a completed investigation, but only reported circumstances which he believed required further investigation immediately. He expected a quick follow-through by Haas, whose responsibility it was to make sure the aid operation was carried out in accordance with the laws, regulations, policies and agreements.

Haas did move quickly. The aid controller summoned Jackis to his office. The reaction, however, was hardly what Jackis expected. The investigator was told he had overstepped his bounds and that he should not have gone to the Soviet hospital because it was not his duty to do so.

Haas appeared angry because the investigator had written the memorandum, Jackis said later. He also showed irritation at Jackis for sending a copy of the memorandum to the chief of the I.C.A. Public Health Division before clearing it with Haas.

Haas criticized Jackis for making the report and then declined to investigate the matter. The controller discussed the report with Alvin E. Roseman, I.C.A. director in Cambodia. The two agreed, without benefit of an investigation, that no goods mentioned by Jackis had been sent into Cambodia over which the U.S. had end-use control. Therefore, they decided there could be no violation of the foreign-aid agreements by the Cambodian government. If they checked their suppositions, it is not so recorded.

Haas explained later to a Congressional committee that he "knew" Jackis's report could not constitute violation of U.S.-aid agreements with Cambodia. He distinguished between what he called "project aid," which is earmarked for a specific project, and "nonproject commodities," which are given to aid the general economy of a nation. He explained that U.S.-financed nonproject commodities might be sold and indirectly find their way into a Communist propaganda project without violating U.S. agreements with the Cambodian government, even though this violated U.S. policy aimed at preventing such commingling of U.S. and Communist foreign aid.

Haas testified that, without investigating, he assumed that the Jackis report involved nonproject commodities because "I know for a fact that we did not finance any cement under project assistance."

It sounded convincing. But Haas's contention was squarely contradicted when Congressional investigators discovered information in foreign-aid files. These disclosed that, in the three-month period preceding the Jackis report, the U.S. had financed $58,000 worth of cement for Cambodia.

Though Haas failed to check this fact, he did initiate a series of actions against Jackis. On July 2, 1958, less than a month after he had filed the memorandum on the Soviet hospital, Jackis received an "unsatisfactory" efficiency rating. He was shocked. It was the first such rating in his career. He decided to fight it and within three weeks filed an appeal.

In September, 1958, Jackis was transferred out of his job as an end-use investigator and assigned to straightening out the I.C.A. warehouse in Phnom Penh. Though his salary and classification remained the same, he regarded the new job as a demotion. The work was little different from that of a janitor. He was being humiliated because he had displeased his superior with an aggressive investigation. Jackis was nevertheless convinced he was right and that his appeal would eventually correct the record and permit him to resume his job as an investigator.

For eight months, Jackis worked in the warehouse. He shoved boxes around, pushed a broom and waited—and hoped—for action on his appeal. It did not come. In May, 1959, Jerry Jackis returned to the United States for home leave. On July 9, he reported to the Washington I.C.A. office for further assignment.

Jackis made several efforts to find out what had happened to his appeal. Each time the personnel division told him there was no record of his appeal on file. Finally, he made a direct inquiry to Haas's superior, John E. DeWilde, the director of the audit division in Washington, D.C.

On July 21, 1959, DeWilde wrote Haas, asking for an immediate report on the work of Jackis, including the details on the Russian-sponsored hospital.

On August 12th, DeWilde repeated his request to Haas, but it was not until September 16th that Haas replied. In regard to the Russian hospital, he wrote:

"Mr. Jackis sent a copy of subject memo to the Chief, Public Health Division, USOM, prior to clearing it with the Controller.

"No action was contemplated by the Controller's office on the basis of Mr. Jackis' erroneous conclusions.

"Mr. Haas, USOM Controller, had previously explained to Mr. Jackis a policy approved by the USOM Director, that is to say, commodities purchased through I.C.A. commercial aid by private importers can be sold to any end-user in Cambodia. Further, for example, if a Cambodian construction company had purchased equipment or commodities from local importers, such equipment or commodities could be used for any undertaking.

"Current status: Closed on basis of disposition cited above."

By inquiring of Haas's superior, Jackis assumed he finally had set the bureaucratic machinery in operation and that in a few months his record would be cleared. It didn't happen that way. No official action was taken until nearly a year later, on August 11, 1960. Then, after Jackis had complained further of lack of action, he was granted a hearing on the "unsatisfactory" efficiency rating and the whole appeal matter.

On October 10, 1960, Jackis received a letter from J. T. Walden, Acting Director of Personnel for I.C.A., that he regarded as the long-sought vindication. "The derogatory implications of the [unsatisfactory] efficiency rating mentioned have been overcome by subsequent documentation," the personnel office notified Jackis. The letter stated that it was proper for the agency to assign Jackis to Washington, and that no further action on the appeal would be taken.

Jackis was elated, and believed his persistence had finally cleared his record, even though it appeared that no action would be taken against Haas, whose conduct had caused the trouble in the first place. This he could not understand, but he did not complain.

Through 1961, Jackis continued to work for the foreign-aid agency. He received four efficiency ratings—two satisfactory and two superior. Things seemed bright.

On November 1, 1961, Jackis was dealt a major blow. He received a letter from Fowler Hamilton, at that time the new head of the agency, which had been revamped again—from I.C.A. to the Agency for International Development (A.I.D.). The letter notified Jackis that, as of December 1st, he was fired. A Foreign Service "evaluation panel" had rated Jackis as "marginal." He was to be dropped under a provision of the reorganization law.

Jackis could not believe it. In his seven years in foreign-aid administration his efficiency rating had ranged from "satisfactory" to "superior," with the exception of the one "unsatisfactory" rating.

As Jackis understood it, that one "unsatisfactory" rating had been wiped out by a finding of the personnel office that this rating was "unnecessarily harsh" and that Jackis, in fact, had performed in a creditable manner in Cambodia.

Jackis appealed the notice of termination, but it was useless. On January 5, 1962, Jackis was advised by A.I.D. director Hamilton that he had personally examined the evaluation and regretted to inform Jackis that his employment would be terminated on January 15, 1962.

Jerry Jackis was bitter over his plight. He became even more bitter when he learned that Marlin Haas had been promoted to Foreign Service Reserve Officer, Class 2, at a salary of $13,000 a year.

There was only one appeal left, and Jackis used it. He went to the Capitol and told his story to John T. Reddan, Chief Counsel for Representative Porter Hardy's (Democrat, Virginia) Government Operations Subcommittee on Foreign Operations and Monetary Affairs.

Some Congressmen and Senators might have dismissed the complaints by Jackis. The rank injustice he described was so extreme that many might have regarded it as unbelievable. But Chairman Hardy and Counsel Reddan had had experience with similar injustices in the federal bureaucracy.

Reddan, along with Investigators Walton Woods and Charles Rothenberg, went to work to see if the story Jackis told could be documented. The State Department declined to give the Hardy subcommittee some of the personnel folders the investigators sought. But through other records and interviews the investigators were able to prove that the facts were essentially as Jackis had presented them.

On March 15, 1962, Jackis appeared in an open hearing and testified that I.C.A.-financed supplies were used in construction of a Communist-sponsored hospital. Unidentified A.I.D. officials told wire-service reporters it was "quite possible" the supplies originally came from the United States. However, they denied that this was a misuse of the foreign-assistance program, as Chairman Hardy indicated it was.

Chairman Hardy was openly furious at the published statements by these anonymous officials, indicating approval of the use of I.C.A.-financed material in a Communist propaganda project.

Three A.I.D. information officers—Joseph L. Newman, John F. Kane and Edgar A. Comee—were called to testify the next day. Newman, Deputy Director of the Public Affairs Office, explained that all three were new employees, with no personal knowledge of the Cambodian incident. He admitted that they had given out the story that use of U.S.-financed material on a Russian hospital was not a misuse of foreign aid.

Newman was unable to identify any A.I.D. official who had told him that the diversion of U.S. material to the Red project was not improper. He said only that it was "the consensus" of persons with whom he had talked that these U.S.-financed goods could flow through regular commercial channels and into the Russian hospital.

Newman admitted he had talked to only three A.I.D. officials. Chairman Hardy was incensed that such superficial "research" was peddled to the press as "policy."

A.I.D. director Hamilton testified he had no knowledge of the statement attributed to "foreign-aid officials." He said his views did not coincide with what his spokesmen had said, and he declared that every possible means should be used to avoid commingling U.S. and Russian aid.

Despite the testimony by Hamilton, news stories appeared a day later indicating that more unidentified State Department "officials" were explaining away the mingling of U.S. and Russian aid. These stories said that the unnamed officials were basing their stand on the assumption that the commodities involved were "nonproject" aid. As the phantom spokesmen explained it: once the I.C.A.-financed cement entered the free market in Cambodia, there was nothing to prevent it from being bought by a contractor and used in the Soviet-sponsored hospital.

Deputy Assistant Secretary of State Avery F. Peterson said he had no knowledge of, or responsibility for, the news story. In fact, he said he was in total disagreement with the position it quoted.

Chairman Hardy and members of his committee were irked by this continuing backfire of anonymous stories. Hardy asked:

"Who speaks for the Department of State and for A.I.D.?

"To what extent is the public given nonauthoritative, slanted stories?

"To what extent do subordinate apologists issue or release to the news media statements contrary to the position, understanding, and views of responsible Department or Agency officials?"

And, significantly, Chairman Hardy and his colleagues added: "No one had ever investigated Jackis's complaints to establish the facts."

Hardy and his subcommittee declared that some A.I.D. officials had sought to hide "dereliction of A.I.D. officials," to "confuse or mislead the public." The purpose of this was to "disparage the efforts of the subcommittee."

The subcommittee further pointed out that, in order to investigate the Jackis case properly, it was necessary for it to obtain A.I.D.'s personnel records. But even after A.I.D. director Hamilton agreed to deliver all records on the Jackis case to Hardy's subcommittee, the actual delivery was blocked by State Department Counsel Abram Chayes.

Chairman Hardy complained of the cover-ups by Chayes, and on March 22, 1962, President Kennedy was asked about it at his press conference. Under pressure, Mr. Kennedy said a solution would be found for the problem. Within an hour after the press conference, Undersecretary of State George Ball delivered the bundle of previously withheld records to Chairman Hardy.

These records proved even more convincingly that Jerry Jackis was the victim of a grave injustice. They documented the fact that Haas had given an inaccurate account of the handling of the Jackis case. Hardy accused the State Department spokesmen of hiding the facts, and of giving the impression that they think "it is a good idea" to be using U.S. aid for Communist projects.

In addition to the blasts from the Hardy subcommittee, a barrage of criticism was fired by high-ranking Republicans—Representative Ben F. Jensen, of Iowa, who had a key position on the House Appropriations Committee, and Representative H. R. Gross, of Iowa, one of the highest-ranking Republicans on the House Post Office and Civil Service Committee. Representative George Meader, of Michigan, condemned the "cover-up" by the State Department and also the practice of using American foreign aid for "monuments" to the Communists.

Finally, Haas was called before the subcommittee. He was questioned about his failure to follow through on the Jackis report that U.S.-financed concrete, asphalt and steel were finding their way into the Russian hospital.

Haas testified he had assumed the concrete and other materials were "nonproject" aid material. He took the position that the U.S. had put it into the Cambodian economy for the Cambodians to use as they pleased and not on any specific project. He assumed this, he said, because he knew of no other type of concrete that had come to Cambodia.

Hardy contradicted Haas and pointed out he had a letter verifying that U.S.-purchased concrete from Japan had been brought into Cambodia in large quantities and for specific projects during that period. The chairman, indignant about the injustice of the whole case, characterized Haas as "the kind of individual this country should not have representing it."

After the record had been established, A.I.D. chief Hamilton expressed his personal view that Jackis had been "improperly dismissed." He had not been aware of all the details, he said.

On May 30, 1962, A.I.D. reported that Jackis had been rehired. He was to serve as an administrative assistant in the international training division. His grade would be GS-9, and his salary $7,425 —a drop of two grades and $1,230. Jackis reluctantly accepted. Having been worn down by the frustrations of the four-year fight, he was satisfied with being rehired and being vindicated. He hoped he again would be able to find a niche for himself where he would find satisfaction in his work and reasonable opportunity for promotion.

There also was satisfaction for Jackis in the report of the Hardy subcommittee, which said he had been the victim of the unfair tactics of his superior, Marlin Haas.

The case was a classic example of the dangers of a bureaucracy and of the need for Congressional checks on the executive branch of the government. The Hardy subcommittee had to force the issue to obtain the personnel folders. It was only under protest that A.I.D. Administrator Hamilton made the personnel information available to Chairman Hardy on a "confidential" basis.

"Without access to the documents," the subcommittee report stated, "the subcommittee probably would have been precluded from ascertaining that Haas took steps to remove Jackis from his position as end-use investigator in . . . Cambodia, in refutation of Haas's sworn testimony to the contrary."

The Hardy subcommittee report recommended that the Department of State and A.I.D. take these immediate steps:

"1. Devise regulations and establish procedures to insure that U.S. foreign aid is not employed to further foreign aid activities of the Communist bloc countries.

"2. Insure that foreign aid agreements committing the United States to dollar expenditures be drawn with precision as to objectives and scope. . . .

"3. Accelerate the investigation, consideration and determination of employee grievances, particularly those challenging poor efficiency ratings.

"4. Insure that no punitive action is taken against employees as a result of their reporting possible misuses of foreign aid; and that where aid officials have engaged in such punitive action or have ignored or sought to cover up reported abuses of the aid program, this fact shall be made a part of their personnel record for appropriate administrative action."

"To the extent that U.S. aid dollars are used," wrote the Hardy subcommittee, "either directly or indirectly, to promote or carry out projects or programs identified in the minds of the people of the host country as Sino-Soviet, the U.S. taxpayers are financing the cause of Communism."

In addition to the misuse of aid pointed out by Jackis, the subcommittee found evidence of other bungling in Cambodia. The power plant the Russians had supplied for the 500-bed hospital was inadequate, and it was necessary to install a large transformer to supply electricity from a local power company.

"This transformer and connecting cable were purchased with [$520,000] U.S. foreign aid dollars, but . . . I.C.A. . . . and the Department of State were unaware of their use for the Russian project for approximately 1 year," the Hardy subcommittee reported. "No evidence was produced to show that the people of Cambodia were ever informed that it was U.S. aid that enabled the hospital to function."

A.I.D. director Hamilton agreed with Porter Hardy that strong disciplinary action should be taken against Haas. In addition to his part in the unjust treatment of Jackis, Haas had disregarded a report by another investigator calling attention to the need for an investigation of the Soviet-sponsored hospital. Hamilton and Hardy also agreed that Haas initially had misrepresented the facts in the Jackis matter to the subcommittee and to A.I.D. officials.

Ironically, even while A.I.D. director Hamilton was contemplating disciplinary action against Haas, he inadvertently signed an order promoting the former Cambodia controller. He soon rectified the error. Haas was dropped two grades.

It would be reassuring to report that Jerry Jackis was put to work by A.I.D. in the area of his demonstrated competence—tracking down evidence of misuse of foreign-aid money. He was, unfortunately, shuttled about in the agency in Washington. Jackis received no investigative duties, no promotions. His efforts to obtain overseas assignments were always met with the stock explanation that no suitable post could be found to utilize his talents.

On September 20, 1963, Jackis quit in disgust. In a letter to the new A.I.D. Administrator, David Bell, Jackis reviewed his record as an investigator in Korea and Cambodia, and told of the "freeze" he had received after being restored to duty in Washington.

"I have been informed that no suitable overseas position exists in which my talents can be utilized at present," Jackis wrote Bell. "I am aware of a number of administrative and investigative positions that I could fill successfully."

Representative Gross told the House it was unfortunate that A.I.D. was able to find rather high positions for defeated Democratic Congressmen with no particular talent in its kind of work but "is unable to find a place for a man who has demonstrated some effectiveness as an investigator."

By contrast, the A.I.D. agency did manage to find a plush assignment for Marlin Haas in Paris. At the time Jackis quit, Haas, the man who had started all his troubles, was moving forward again. His career had been set back only temporarily by the demotion forced by Representative Hardy's subcommittee. By June, 1964, Haas was receiving a salary of more than $17,000 a year.

The five-year struggle of Jerry Jackis was over. Bureaucracy had triumphed over the career government employee who challenged his superiors and gave Congress the facts on government mismanagement. Because the A.I.D. agency did not initiate the timely investigation recommended by Jackis, it was impossible to determine the precise source of the concrete that went into the Communist-sponsored hospital in Cambodia. It was not a story to encourage other investigators to pursue the facts on corruption and bungling in our foreign-aid program. It was not a story to give taxpayers confidence in the top men administering our foreign-aid billions.

The damage to Jerry Jackis was direct and personal, but there was broader damage to the whole concept of fair play in our American system of government. The wrongs were never fully righted, and the responsibility for the unsatisfactory conclusion to the Jackis case rests squarely on the shoulders of A.I.D. Administrator David Bell. It was hardly an example of "the high moral tone" that President Kennedy had called on his officials to set.

CHAPTER 3

Lying in State (and Defense)

When he took office in January, 1961, President John F. Kennedy offered the hope of a man who was determined not to tolerate conditions which bred corruption in Washington.

He seemed aware of the mismanagement in the multibillion-dollar foreign-aid program. He acted as if he was going to break the grip of the State Department's Foreign Service clique, that tight little inner circle which shielded the administration of the foreign-aid program from any charges of wrongdoing.

Yet the echo of his inauguration oath had hardly ended when President Kennedy began finding it difficult to run the government in a goldfish bowl. The new President was hamstrung by government career officials and by some of his highest appointees.

For years under the Eisenhower administration, major foreign-aid scandals in Laos and Peru had been kept hidden.[1] President Eisenhower had allowed subordinates to claim "executive privilege"—i.e., a flat refusal to give information to Congress or other investigative agencies—on several occasions. This had the effect of barring Congress as well as the General Accounting Office (G.A.O.) from obtaining evidence. But, through an investigation of sources outside the I.C.A., the agency then administering foreign aid, Chairman Hardy, the Virginia Democrat who headed the House Government Operations subcommittee, was able to break the secrecy surrounding the Laos program. The outside sources revealed a shocking network of bribery, incompetence and fraud.

Despite this exposure, the secrecy lid was still clamped tightly on files of the foreign-aid operations in Peru. In late December, 1960, as President-elect Kennedy was preparing to take office, Hardy spoke with him about it. Kennedy promised that Hardy's subcommittee would be given the records on Peru foreign aid. He said further that use of "executive privilege" by officials or employees of the executive branch would not be tolerated in this instance.[2]

In his State of the Union message, delivered to Congress on January 30, 1961, President Kennedy said: "Our Constitution wisely assigns both joint and separate roles to each branch of the Government; and a President and a Congress who hold each other in mutual respect will neither permit nor attempt any trespass. For my part, I shall withhold from neither the Congress nor the people any fact or report, past, present, or future, which is necessary for an informed judgment of our conduct or hazards. I shall neither shift the burden of executive decisions to the Congress, nor avoid responsibility for the outcome of those decisions."

The President's clear words failed to move his State Department aides. In March, Chairman Hardy was still being denied the records, despite his persistent efforts to get them. Late that month, State Department witnesses appeared before the Hardy subcommittee, armed with identical letters from Secretary of State Rusk prepared by Abram Chayes, the State Department counsel. The letters instructed them to use the "executive privilege" claim in refusing to give testimony on Peru.

This was too much for Hardy. He called President Kennedy. The President overruled Secretary of State Rusk and ordered the records delivered to Hardy.

When made public, the records disclosed that John R. Neale, while director of the U. S. Operations Mission in Peru, had acquired a $200,000 interest in a ranching corporation that received aid under the American program. Although Neale had since resigned, there were indications that I.C.A. and State Department personnel had protected him for months. There also were widespread irregularities in the $14 million drought-relief program. As much as 60 per cent of the "relief" had gone into unauthorized channels.

The documented records showed that the first disclosures of fraud were disregarded by high-ranking aid officials. Instead of taking action against the dishonest officials, they began investigations to discredit the conscientious I.C.A. employees who had first tried to stimulate an investigation into the Peru shenanigans. Only direct action by the President ended this cover-up in Peru.

Even as President Kennedy was clearing the air at the State Department, a storm was blowing up in the Defense Department. In April, 1961, Defense Secretary Robert S. McNamara made a closed-door appearance before the Senate Committee on Armed Services. His testimony, released later, seemed to indicate that McNamara favored less information for the public and *mis*information on our military posture when it suited his purpose.

"Why should we tell Russia that the Zeus [guided missile] development may not be satisfactory?" McNamara argued to the committee members. "What we ought to be saying is that we have the most perfect anti-ICBM system that the human mind will ever devise. Instead the public domain is already full of statements that the Zeus may not be satisfactory, that it has deficiencies. . . ."[3]

In the public furor that followed, it was a Democrat, Representative John E. Moss of California, who first took McNamara to task. Chairman Moss pointed out that McNamara's dubious defense of meritorious mendacity was not in accord with President Kennedy's rules of the game. Declaring that the McNamara viewpoint was "most alarming," he said:

". . . Advocacy of a program of misinformation constitutes a grave disservice to a nation already confused and suffering from informational malnutrition. . . . To claim perfection in a weapon system, thereby creating a false sense of security, only results in complacency complained about by the very officials who would further feed it."

The Defense Secretary beat a fast retreat to a more tenable position. "In a democratic society, the public must be kept informed of the major issues in our national defense policy," McNamara said later. The second time around, he merely pointed to the need for avoiding disclosure of information that might aid an enemy.

By this time other complaints about the Pentagon were being heard. The *Navy Times,* a private publication, fired a broadside against arbitrary secrecy not justified on grounds of National security:

"Americans generally ought to be having some misgivings over the current trend at the Pentagon." There had been an air of secrecy, of censorship, of arbitrary rulings, it said.

As if to prove the magazine's point, the Defense Department tried to invoke the "executive privilege" claim to bar two committees from records in an investigation of shipments of strategic materials to various Iron Curtain countries. These studies were being conducted by the Internal Security Subcommittee of the Senate and a House Select Committee on Export Control. The Defense Department appealed to the Justice Department for a ruling. Attorney General Robert Kennedy ruled against the Defense Department, and it was forced to yield the records.

Next in the assault on the good intentions of the Kennedys came a memorandum written by Frederick G. Dutton, Special Assistant to the President. It contained instructions on government information that "shocked" Chairman Moss. Dated July 20, 1961, it was attached to a Civil Service Commission statement on standards of conduct for government employees. It stated:

"Employees may not disclose official information without either appropriate general or specific authority under agency regulations."

This amounted to a White House order to hide all records from the public unless there was a specific order to do otherwise. Congressman Moss, who was "shocked" by the statement, asked the White House for a "complete reversal," plus a "positive directive to all employees to honor the people's right to know as a routine matter in the conduct of government business."[4]

To its credit, the White House immediately withdrew the directive. At the same time, it asserted the right of the public and the press to information about the government, unless there was a specific need for withholding such information.

On the "Meet the Press" television show of September 24, 1961, Attorney General Kennedy again indicated where he stood. James Reston, Washington Bureau Chief for the *New York Times,* observed to him:

"In the field of 'executive privilege' . . . you seem more willing than previous Presidents and administrations to give information sought by Congress."

Kennedy responded: "I think it is terribly important to insure that the executive branch of the government is not corrupt and that they [sic] are efficient, that the legislative branch of the government has the ability to check on what we are doing in the executive branch of the government.

"So, in every instance that has been brought to our attention in the Department of Justice so far by various departments of the executive branch where this question has been raised, we have suggested and recommended that they make the information available to Congress. We will continue to do that.

"I don't say there might not be an instance where executive privilege might be used. But I think it is terribly important that the executive branch of the government—as powerful and strong as it is—that there be some check and balance on it, and in the last analysis the group that can best check and insure that it is handling its affairs properly is the Congress of the United States. So we will lean over backwards to make sure that they [sic] get the information they request."

There was every reason to believe in the youthful Attorney General's sincerity. His considerable experience as a Congressional-committee counsel had made him aware of the arbitrary bureaucratic cover-up in cases where the President and top officers probably were unaware of what their subordinates were hiding.

This enlightened view on open records was made easier, perhaps, because the Kennedy administration had no need to cover up. The particular incidents of mismanagement and corruption that were Congressional targets in 1961 dated from the Eisenhower era. There was every practical political reason for the Kennedy administration to cooperate in any exposé.

The first sign that the President might be forgetting his pledge to bring to government only those with a "single-minded loyalty to the national interest" came in September, 1961. Kennedy let it be known that he intended to appoint George D. Woods, a New York investment banker, as head of the newly reorganized foreign-aid agency. The selection of Woods brought an immediate outcry from several powerful Democrats, including the late Senator Estes Kefauver, of Tennessee, and Senator Wayne Morse, of Oregon. Woods had been an important figure in the controversial Dixon-Yates investigation, involving a conflict of interest in an Atomic Energy Commission contract for electric power.[5] Senators Kefauver and Morse, who had led the fight against Dixon-Yates, regarded the proposal of Woods as a direct kick in the teeth.

Senator Kefauver reminded the White House that Woods was identified in the Senate hearings as the man who had arranged for Adolphe Wenzell, vice-president of the First Boston Corporation, to be a government consultant on the Dixon-Yates contract.

Kefauver did not feel it was necessary to spell out details of the "conflict of interest." He believed every Democrat was aware of the evidence involving Wenzell. Wenzell had been exposed in a dual role as adviser to the Bureau of the Budget on the Dixon-Yates contract and as financial adviser to the Dixon-Yates power combine. Just about the time of President Kennedy's inauguration, the Supreme Court finally had ruled on a legal aspect of the contract, and had declared Wenzell was involved in a conflict of interest in his Dixon-Yates role.[6]

For a while, President Kennedy continued his firm support of Woods, a Republican, despite the powerful objections. Then, abruptly, he dropped the idea of naming Woods as foreign-aid administrator. Later he appointed Woods as president of the World Bank, a position that does not require Senate confirmation.

Another major fight between the Defense Department and the Congress now raised some serious questions as to just what the

Kennedy administration's long-range policy on "executive privilege" really was. Pentagon and State Department censors, operating jointly, had deleted some phrases from the speeches of high-ranking military officers, and had thus given rise to a charge by Senator Strom Thurmond, the conservative South Carolina Democrat, that a "no-win" philosophy was being injected into the speeches. The Senator contended that our high military officers were being "muzzled" by the Defense Department and State Department censors. An investigation was authorized by the Preparedness Subcommittee of the Senate Committee on Armed Services. The chairman was Senator John Stennis (Democrat, Mississippi).[7]

The subcommittee called witnesses, obtained documents, and heard testimony without causing major internal controversy. It was a properly authorized committee, operating within its jurisdiction and headed by a responsible chairman. Members of the subcommittee were orderly in their conduct, and there was no abuse of witnesses. The Stennis subcommittee had been given copies of the speeches, had the record of the censored passages, and was interested in questioning the censors themselves to determine why they had made the questionable deletions.

But Defense Secretary McNamara flatly refused to allow the censors to testify. And President Kennedy gave him the green light to mask his reasons for the refusal by claiming "executive privilege."

The redoubtable Defense Secretary told the Senators that he was responsible for running his department. If he thought explanations were necessary, he was the one who would make them. McNamara's position was that the subcommittee would have to content itself, in this case, with what he chose to tell, and that the Senators could not go beyond his statements.

His reasoning was interesting. He did not make the usual claim that national security was involved in the "muzzling" investigation or that he was protecting defense secrets. Instead, McNamara presented a letter from President Kennedy, dated February 8, 1962, which set forth a claim that the national interest was at stake. The letter from the President read: "I have concluded that it would be contrary to the public interest to make available any information which would enable the subcommittee to identify and hold accountable any individual with respect to any particular speech that he has reviewed. I therefore direct you, and all personnel under jurisdiction of your department, not to give any testimony or produce any documents which would disclose such information; I am issuing parallel instructions to the Secretary of State.

"The principle which is at stake here cannot be automatically applied to every request for information. Each case must be judged on its own merits. But I do not intend to permit subordinate officials of our career service to bear the brunt of congressional inquiry into policies which are the responsibilities of their superiors."

The letter seemed to claim an absolute right for the executive branch to bar testimony before Congress by any subordinate career officials. This concept was attacked by various Senators as a "dangerous" precedent that would have barred Congress from investigating the Pearl Harbor disaster or obtaining information on a wide variety of scandals.

President Eisenhower's earlier letter on "executive privilege" (March 17, 1954) had claimed the right to bar testimony or records of communications or actions of "high level" officials of the government. Kennedy extended it to cover the activities of lower-level officials of the government. If Congress could be denied access to testimony by both high-level and low-level officials, it would be powerless to get any information, except what the executive branch sanctioned.

Representative Moss said he believed the Senate subcommittee had the legal right to ask questions to determine which censors had blue-penciled which speeches. In a letter to President Kennedy, he expressed his concern over the possibility of wide use of the precedent set out in his letter of February 8.

On March 7, 1962, President Kennedy assured Representative Moss that "executive privilege . . . will not be used without specific Presidential approval." However, the use of the gag in the muzzling hearings was a bad omen for the future. What was denied Congress was also denied the press and the American people.

While this new threat to the freedom of the press developed, what was the response of the nation's press? Most of the press disregarded the fact that a duly authorized committee of Congress was conducting the investigation, conducting it properly, and that it was entitled to ask pertinent questions of all witnesses who had direct knowledge of the issue under study.

The press also disregarded evidence which showed that the Pentagon censorship operations were bogged down in confusion and maladministration. McNamara's stand won overwhelming support from the nation's editorial pages. Why? The Defense Secretary was cheered because he defied Senator Strom Thurmond, a conservative Southerner who had little popularity outside his home state of South Carolina.

In addition to Senator Thurmond's "no-win" claim, he was also charging that the whole censorship procedure was inconsistent, badly managed, and susceptible to being perverted by persons who wanted to take the steel out of the voices of our military men.

The question of whether Senator Thurmond was right or wrong in his views was not the important issue. He had the right to be wrong, as long as he conducted himself in a proper manner. He had the right to be wrong, as long as he asked questions pertinent to the issue before the committee.

However, the principle of the right to make proper inquiry was forgotten for the moment, in the interest of abusing a Senator whose views on other, unrelated subjects were unpopular. Many segments of the press completely lost sight of their long-standing self-interest in freedom of the press and thereby endorsed the broadest possible interpretation of "executive privilege." An undiscriminating public went along.

So Defense Secretary McNamara, who was arbitrary, defiant of Congress, and opposed to the very principle the editorial writers should have been defending, was crowned a hero by the press. Secretary McNamara had made a landing on the beachhead and had extended the perimeter of "executive privilege." He did so with the approval or at the orders of the White House. Before long, there were to be more assaults on the public's right to know the facts, more attempts by the roughriders of the New Frontier to let the public know only as much as they thought the public ought to know. Thus began the decline of the new administration's initial avowal of high standards and open government, and thus the new administration began to reveal that it, too, had feet of clay.

CHAPTER 4

The "Honor Code" in Practice

It is a basic rule of military indoctrination that a military man automatically and instinctively obeys commands from a superior officer. That's the way it is, and that's the way it ought to be. Without discipline, a military organization rapidly breaks down into anarchy.

The chain-of-command principle, however, never was meant—in war or in peace—to perpetuate lying, cheating and defiance of a military regulation or a law of the land. That, unfortunately, is what takes place today in some parts of the U.S. military system.

Here is how it works:

A superior officer—for various reasons, usually because he wants something for himself, for his unit or his base that he is not entitled to—chooses to disregard the existence of a regulation or a law. He issues orders that put the men under his command in a spot where they must either disobey him—or break the law.

What do they do? Given the "system," they usually "go along" and break the law. By so doing, they avoid bad fitness reports or reassignment to distasteful duties which the law-flouting commanding officer can give them.

The extent to which this flouting of the law exists in the U.S. armed forces is not fully known—and never will be. From time to time, however, a fully documented instance comes to light and is exposed. One such case, involving the building of an airplane-landing strip at Fort Lee, Virginia, was rooted out by the General Accounting Office (G.A.O.), "watchdog" for Congress on the expenditure of public funds. It was followed up and thoroughly aired by the Executive and Legislative Reorganization Subcommittee of the House Government Operations Committee.[1]

No one went to jail. But before it was over, the Congressional investigating committee had spread on the record the full story of what it called a case of "falsification and deception . . . indeed a sorry record for the Army and for the nation." By the time it was uncovered, the statute of limitations had run out and prosecution was barred.

The story began in 1956, during the Eisenhower administration, and continued into the first year of the Kennedy administration. Thus, it is not a scandal to be blamed on Republicans or Democrats. It is, rather, a scandal that is symptomatic of what happens whenever a bureaucracy—whether it be military or civilian—comes to regard the fulfillment of its whims as a standard larger than the law.

The importance of the Fort Lee affair is that it could happen in any military service or civilian agency where fear of displeasing superior officials is so deep that it permeates every major decision. In the official report of the Government Operations subcommittee, the story is permanently recorded as a warning of the police-state attitudes that can grow up in a large organization when men abuse the "chain of command" philosophy.

High-ranking officers lied, contradicted each other and contradicted their own records. After the G.A.O. first uncovered the illegal act, the responsible military officers destroyed records and made every effort to play down the seriousness of the offenses and to avoid enforcing the laws. A colonel told the Congressional investigators that he believed violation of the law was justified if an Army man was obeying a superior officer, and when he was finally caught and trapped in his own evasions, the commanding general wept in the witness chair.

This shabby little mess had powerful support. It was actually aided by the Quartermaster General's office and the office of the General Counsel of the Army. The Quartermaster General did eventually reprimand the post commander, Major General Alfred

B. Denniston, an officer with thirty-nine years of service. But the subcommittee found that the Q.M.G. disregarded the flagrant nature of the illegal spending, and paid no attention to the law concerning false statements. The Army attributed the unlawful actions to mere "overzealousness" and sought to excuse the officers involved.

Fort Lee is an Army Quartermaster Training Command near Petersburg, Virginia. The Petersburg Airport, twelve miles from Fort Lee, and Camp Pickett Blackstone Airport, forty-one miles away, were available for all necessary training purposes. High-ranking officers at Fort Lee twice requested permission to build a concrete airstrip to replace a grass landing field for aircraft. Twice, the Department of the Army turned down the request, saying that the concrete strip was not necessary. But the Fort Lee officers, disregarding the laws and the regulations, decided they would have their airstrip anyhow.

Some of the junior officers complained that it was an "illegal project" that could send them to the penitentiary. They balked at signing their names to phony bills and reports. In the end, they took their orders, and the airstrip took shape.

It was not a large job, as U.S. military projects go, but more than half a million had been spent on this illegal strip when General Accounting Office auditors discovered the evidence of false bills and rigged files, and called a halt.

As early as February, 1956, officers at Fort Lee asked approval for construction of an airstrip that was to cost about $876,000. After the Pentagon twice rejected the project, the Fort Lee officers started experimenting with fiscal procedures in an effort to get the strip built anyway. They resorted to laws setting up less restrictive requirements for minor projects in cases where construction is "urgently needed."

The law plainly said that these "urgently needed" projects should not include any that could have been reasonably included in the regular military construction program. And the law specifically limited spending on such projects to $25,000, over and above material and labor which a post already had on hand.

In September, 1957, Fort Lee made its third try on the airstrip. It attempted to get the Quartermaster General's approval for construction of a 1,500-foot flexible-pavement landing strip. The estimate for the whole project was $110,095, of which $73,086 represented the value of labor and supplies on hand and $37,009 would be required in new funds. The project was submitted by Lieutenant Colonel William H. Jarrett, the post engineer, and approved by Colonel Louis H. Shirley, the deputy post commander. But this request, too, was rejected by Washington on several grounds. It exceeded the $25,000 maximum on supplemental money, the runway was too short, and the pavement was too thin.

Two months later, Colonel Shirley and Colonel Jarrett submitted revised project estimates. They lengthened the runway 2,500 feet and increased the thickness of the concrete to two inches. And they estimated the total project cost at $141,537, of which $116,589 now was figured to be labor and supplies on hand. By the sheerest of coincidences, this brought the amount of new funds needed down to $24,948—just under the $25,000 maximum, and low enough to start building.

Colonel Jarrett admitted later that the estimates "were arbitrary and were merely put down to meet the requirement of lowering the funds requested below $25,000." Colonel Shirley admitted that he made no effort to determine if the figures were realistic. Nor did he question the incongruity of enlarging the project while decreasing the cost.

The fact that the estimates were baseless was apparent as the project progressed. The basic cost of the project rose to $508,305, or $366,000 more than the authorized figure. Actually, the total cost was a great deal more. For one thing, $28,000 was spent on a building listed as "a warehouse." It really was a hangar, and should have been included in the airstrip project. Another $84,121 came out of operation and maintenance funds for transportation and per-diem pay for engineer troop labor from Fort Belvoir, Virginia.

When the officers at Fort Lee learned that the G.A.O. planned to audit the construction-work papers, hasty instructions went out to the assistant post engineer. He was ordered to get rid of any material in his files which might embarrass the command.

The G.A.O. investigators, to whom this sort of thing is an old story, began putting embarrassing questions to Army headquarters. After considerable prodding, the Army sent a report to Congress that didn't mention falsification of documents or removal and destruction of files.

Eventually, it was revealed that General Denniston had taken disciplinary action against his subordinates who took the initiative on the airstrip. He wrote a reprimand and gave them a lecture in which he told them, in effect, that they had been bad boys and were not to do it again. The Army's General Counsel in Washington, it was established, went along with this "disciplinary action."

The G.A.O. persisted in its investigation, however, and work on the airstrip was halted.

Meanwhile the Government Operations committee, under Chairman William L. Dawson (Democrat, Illinois), began probing the case. It was only then that the full sordidness of the "system" was revealed. Most disturbing to the committee members was the evidence showing how officers were forced to lie and cover up for their superiors.

When they were called before the committee in March, 1962, the officers told conflicting stories relating to the destruction of records. Major Thomas S. Swartz, the former assistant post engineer at Fort Lee, had retired by the time he testified. He admitted that he removed documents from the files and destroyed them. He said he had objected when Colonel Jarrett ordered him to remove the papers from the files. But Jarrett, Swartz said, had told him that someone even superior to him wanted it done. Major Swartz told the committee that Colonel Jarrett later came down to his office to determine if he had followed instructions to destroy the papers. The materials removed and destroyed, Swartz testified, were copies of purchase requests and some project working estimates.

Colonel Jarrett testified that he, in turn, had been ordered by Colonel Shirley to have the files "cleansed." Subsequently, he said, Colonel Shirley asked him whether this had been done. He said he told Colonel Shirley that the files had been "cleansed" so the G.A.O. auditors would find no evidence of false billing.

Colonel James W. Connor was subordinate to Colonel Shirley at the time the records were destroyed. He testified that he had understood Colonel Shirley's order to mean that embarrassing documents should be removed from the files. Colonel Connor stated that he had told Colonel Shirley a day or two after the orders were issued that he would not be a party to the removal and concealment of documents from the G.A.O.

Colonel Shirley, stern-faced and defiant, admitted calling Colonel Jarrett and Colonel Connor to his office. However, he denied that he had ordered files removed and destroyed. He told the committee he had merely instructed Colonel Jarrett to put the files in order for the G.A.O. men.

Colonel Shirley also testified that he didn't remember Colonel Connor protesting to him about the removal and concealment of documents. "I don't recall that," Shirley said, "but he could have done that."

This was not the end of conflicting testimony and bad memory. Colonel James C. Pennington testified he had informed Colonel Shirley that the Pentagon had denied the request for waiving certain requirements on the airstrip construction. Shirley testified that Pennington never told him the waivers had been denied.

Colonel Walter R. Ridlehuber, the project officer, and Colonel Shirley testified they had told General Denniston that both material and services for the airfield were being falsely billed to other projects. But General Denniston denied that either officer had informed him of the false billings.

Another direct conflict of testimony arose after Lieutenant Colonel Julian E. Pylant testified that Colonel Ridlehuber had told him to charge the airfield expenses to other projects. Colonel Pylant said that he had replied to Ridlehuber: "I am not going to the pen for this." Later, Ridlehuber denied that Pylant had made this remark.

In an effort to solve the conflict, Chairman Dawson recalled Pylant, who pointed to Ridlehuber and repeated the statement. In a direct confrontation with his accuser, Colonel Ridlehuber stated only that he did not recall the incident.

The House subcommittee declared it was unable to determine "which officers were telling the truth in these instances and which were not." It added: "We do, however, regard the existence of these conflicts as a serious reflection on the standards of conduct of the officer corps of the Army."

William A. Newman, chief of the G.A.O.'s defense accounting division, testified that the highest officials at Fort Lee not only had spent $536,373 on the illegal airstrip but were ready to spend a million more at the time the accounting office moved in and stopped the project.

The House subcommittee was told that the grass airstrip at Fort Lee was used by the light planes stationed there. Also available for any necessary training purposes were the Camp Pickett Blackstone Airport and the one at Petersburg, only twelve miles distant.

"While the building of a new airfield might have seemed desirable to the responsible officials at Fort Lee," said the committee, "it must be concluded that there was no real urgency for the project, as required by law."

Through two weeks of hearings, the House subcommittee documented the subterfuge through which the Army officers at Fort Lee had concealed the costs of material going into the airfield. Obviously, the files had not been cleansed quite well enough.

One incriminating note from Major Swartz was found in the files. On a purchase order for 2,150 tons of stone, this notation appeared: "This order will be followed by additional orders and I will have to keep a record of them. Actually, although charged to road maintenance, this material will be used for the airfield."

Another false purchase request for stone for "maintenance of roads" was accompanied by a memorandum that flatly admitted the material was actually to be used for "the construction of the airfield facilities by Company A, 87th Engineer Battalion."

From the Fort Lee files came a memorandum of a telephone conversation between Colonel Ridlehuber and Colonel Pennington on the problem of how to acquire an airplane hangar without calling it a hangar. Colonel Ridlehuber's memo stated:

"The immediate problem is the purchase of a metal hangar building for erection by troop labor at a later date. I asked Colonel Pennington to assure the Quartermaster General that we would not recommend anything that would put him in an embarrassing position. In the case of the hangar, it will be procured, if the purchase is approved and the . . . funds are available, for the aerial detachment and not directly associated with the airfield.

"In the case of a physical inspection by the Department of the Army representatives at some later date, it can be explained that this is a temporary building which will be moved to meet other storage requirements if and when no longer required at the airfield site."

The most revealing insight into the system came from Colonel Jarrett. In explaining his failure to make more than routine objections to the illegal actions, he told the Congressmen:

"Of course, I feel that an officer does not have to blindly follow orders, but I think that my following these orders was predicated only on personal feeling in the matter, having been in it from the beginning, that this whole operation was known within the command."

Colonel Jarrett said there had been discussions with the Chief of Engineers, visits by the Deputy Chief of Staff of Logistics, and continuous discussion of an airstrip at Fort Lee.

"In other words, even though it was illegal . . . everybody was doing it," Representative John Anderson (Republican, Illinois) commented.

"That is right, sir," Jarrett replied.

"Regulations notwithstanding," Anderson noted.

"I think," Jarrett replied, "that if the committee were to check with my associates overseas and other post camping stations

I have been in, you would find I have been a stickler for regulations and had a reputation for it. However, I was burned in Austria when I made reports too factual and was given a verbal reprimand and told I would be relieved immediately if I ever wrote such a letter.

"The letter happened to be truthful, but it did not please the post commander," Colonel Jarrett went on. "He [the area commander] rewrote the letter and got the other letter back. He was the area commander in Salzburg, Austria."

"What suggestions would you have to make in view of your experiences there in Salzburg, Austria, where you were threatened with removal from command if you complained about something?" Representative Anderson asked. "What do you think the Congress can do, and should do, to make sure that things like this do not happen?"

"There is too much flexibility allowed at station level, in my opinion, for interpretation of what the regulation means," Colonel Jarrett replied.

"I do not care how flexible these regulations were," Representative Anderson said. "They just did not bend them, they broke them."

"That is right, sir," Colonel Jarrett answered. "Certainly after we got the bear by the tail we knew what we were doing, at least I knew what I was doing. We were evading the regulations as they were written."

When General Denniston, a much-decorated veteran, was called to testify on the airstrip project, he fumbled for answers and quibbled. Finally, he broke into tears. The General admitted he had "failed in leadership."

In answer to questions by Representative Neal Smith (Democrat, Iowa), General Denniston said he did not know the cost of the project would exceed $25,000. He said he had delegated most of the responsibility to subordinates.

"And . . . among these persons then was Colonel Shirley?" Representative Smith asked.

"That is correct," General Denniston replied. "He was my deputy, and I had known him longer and better than any of the rest."

Representative Smith, through his next questions to Denniston, recalled the fact that the General's trusted deputy, Colonel Shirley, had been the subject of a critical report by the Senate Permanent Investigating Subcommittee a few years earlier. At that time, the subcommittee was investigating Army procurement scandals in New York. The investigation resulted in the indictment and conviction of several officials. Colonel Shirley had been a witness before the Senate group and, in his testimony, had suffered a lack of memory on many points.

"You were his superior officer at another time when procurement scandals were investigated by a committee of Congress, were you not?" Smith asked.

"I knew it after the fact," Denniston replied. "I followed the hearings. I was completely out of the Quartermaster procurement at that time."

"In view of these previous procurement problems involving Colonel Shirley, should you not have been . . . a little bit hesitant about delegating all of these or some of these financial matters here?" Smith asked.

"Colonel Shirley, in turn, delegated almost as much as I did in this particular case," General Denniston replied.

Admitting that he was "lacking in leadership," the General told his questioners he had failed to notice that the $25,000 limit on spending was being violated. He also acknowledged that false statements were filed to circumvent the law.

Under intensive questioning by Chairman Dawson and Representative Clarence Brown (Republican, Ohio), General Denninston admitted that even after he found the conspiracy to destroy "embarrassing" records, he did no more than issue letters of reprimand.

On hearing this admission from the General, Representative Brown addressed him at some length.

"This has been a terribly distressing investigation," Brown said. "There is something wrong with our military system when . . . men who have . . . served their country in war ably . . . will come in here and . . . admit they had advised superior officers that they did not want to sign certain papers . . . to do something that was a direct violation of the law.

"They had advised these superior officers they did not want to go to the penitentiary by signing such a thing, and yet they said they signed . . . because they were afraid of the system.

"It is a pretty sorry mess," Representative Brown added, then asked:

"Now, the only thing that worries me, General, and it rather hurts me to ask this question—did you know all of those things were going on?"

"No, sir, I did not," General Denniston answered. "I should have."

Reminding the General that an enlisted man would have been court-martialed for a petty theft, Brown demanded to know:

"How can we, as members of Congress, go out and tell the country that we do have a fair system . . . that we have the same law and the same demand for a respect for morality, honesty, and decency for officers as we do for enlisted men?"

"It was not my final decision," General Denniston answered. He said he left the way open for the Army Department in Washington or the Justice Department to take criminal action, but none was taken.

Representative Anderson said he was sure that the prime interest of the committee was to see "that there is no repetition of the tawdry and sordid series of events."

"Our concern," Anderson commented, "is whether or not a reprimand . . . is anything more than just a slap on the wrist, or whether it is of sufficient import to drive home to the Army and to the people involved that this kind of thing is not going to be countenanced?"

"I can promise you that it hurt me," General Denniston replied. "It hurt me more than going to jail, that after thirty-nine years of service with nothing but commendations on my record, I don't like that reprimand. I deserved it and that is what hurts."

Denniston added another example of how it hurt. "I cannot run into a general that I have not seen for a while that does not make some remark . . . needling me. . . . Behind it, there is a consciousness . . . [that] he sure is glad he is not in my shoes.

"I went through a receiving line, and the Vice Chief looked at me and said: 'My God, Danny, I thought you were in jail.' And I said: 'No, I don't go until day after tomorrow.'

"Now there, right at the top, is an indication that when he sees me, the first thing he thinks about is the Fort Lee airfield and why I am not already in jail for it. Now I am not being facetious, Mr. Anderson."

When the hearing was concluded, the House Government Operations subcommittee wrote a scathing official report.

Published as a House document on June 20, 1962, the report said:

"This particular incident . . . furnishes an almost unbelievable example of the workings of the military and bureaucratic mind. A change in nomenclature, clever gimmick and an easy acceptance of a subterfuge cannot change a fact, no matter how much the military mind wants them [sic] to do so. There can be no doubt that despite the testimony of the officers and other personnel involved, the building at the Fort Lee airstrip is a hangar, was a hangar when it was built, and had always been planned and intended to be a hangar.

"The amazing thing to the committee is not only that the laws were evaded and violated, but also that, having failed in their scheme to disguise the nature of the building and to deceive any future inspectors of the installation, the personnel involved still persist in the attempted deception. . . . It was conceived in violation of the law and applicable Army regulation. Falsification and deception accompanied every step of this construction; and in the end when all attempts to cover up the record and destroy relevant papers had failed, the actions of the officers responsible were condoned and excused by their superiors. This is indeed a sorry record for the Army and for the nation.

"When confronted with illegality . . . subordinate officers

either did not protest or made weak protests which they soon swallowed," the report continued. "These officers indicated by their testimony that they were only too conscious of the traditional techniques for indirect reprisal against a subordinate officer who stands on principle against the desire of his superiors—such techniques as unfavorable fitness reports, delayed promotion, undesirable assignments, early retirement and social ostracism. . . . The committee knows that the officers at Fort Lee, who protested the illegal actions which they felt required to take, were not without courage and conviction. Nevertheless, none, obviously, thought he could have survived an attempt to expose the illegal actions in which he later participated."

The report went on:

"The operation of the 'system' was further demonstrated by the failure of responsible officers to bring court-martial proceedings against those guilty of the offenses, by their failure to investigate the matter except under extreme pressure, by their general reluctance to take disciplinary action, and by their attempts to cover up and excuse the offense rather than to get to the bottom of the whole affair."

General Denniston was blamed for sanctioning the revised report on the airstrip project. The committee called this report an "attempt to excuse, condone and cover up." Characterizing the entire Fort Lee affair as a "public disgrace," the committee concluded:

"The concealment of wrongdoing is itself an insidious corruptive influence which spreads its decay far beyond the immediate wrongful act."

Again, it would be gratifying to report that the work of Congressman Dawson's committee and the G.A.O. touched off a series of prosecutions of those persons involved in the active violation of the law and the destruction of records. However, by the time the investigations were concluded and the reports made, the three-year statute of limitations had barred prosecution on what the subcommittee concluded was violation of eighteen different criminal laws. The only action taken by the Defense Department was to place simple reprimands in the files of the officers. Some in government would heed the warning. Some would not.

The Fort Lee incident is another demonstration of the need for Congressional checks on bureaucracy. But it also points up the inherent danger of too tight an administration, whether it be military or civilian. No man is perfect, and when any man arrogates to himself complete, or nearly complete, power, he too often becomes ruthless. He disregards dissent to the point that laws and regulations are set aside. Even reason is ignored.

CHAPTER 5

Stockpile of Scandal

At a press conference on January 31, 1962, President Kennedy announced that federal investigators had been studying the government's multibillion-dollar stockpile of strategic materials. He said he considered this stockpile "a source of excessive and unconscionable profits."

Thus Mr. Kennedy set in motion a Congressional study that, for the first time, shed a strong light on aspects of the stockpiling program never before known to the public.[1]

So much money—taxpayers' money—was involved that it was almost too much for the average mind to grasp. The investigation assumed an importance that far exceeded all previous probes of the nation's stockpile.

President Kennedy had been in office only a few months when aides called his attention to what they believed was a major scandal in the handling of the giant program. The stockpiles had been authorized during the early part of the Korean War to ensure the U.S. an adequate supply of strategic material. Kennedy's aides had been examining the secret records and concluded that the stockpiling authority had been abused and misused by both the Truman and Eisenhower administrations.

The Congressional acts and administrative regulations governing the stockpile clearly stated that minerals and other raw materials were to be bought for one purpose only—to provide for the nation's strategic needs. But the preliminary study indicated that the program had been put to other uses. It had been used to prop up ailing mining companies, to support the price of minerals, as an economic gimmick to help shore up foreign aid, and even as a weapon in the political campaign of a former Cabinet officer in the Eisenhower administration.

In news-conference remarks, President Kennedy was relatively circumspect. "It was apparent to me," he said, "that this excessive storage of costly materials was a questionable burden on public funds and in addition a potential source of excessive and unconscionable profits. Last spring a detailed check was ordered, and our information to date has convinced me that a thorough investigation is warranted. The cloak of secrecy which has surrounded this program may have been justified originally to conceal our shortages, but this is no longer the case, and secrecy now is only an invitation to mismanagement."

The President said he had discussed the matter with Senator W. Stuart Symington, the Missouri Democrat who headed the Senate Armed Services Subcommittee on stockpiling. "He agrees that the program should be completely explored, and without delay. I have assured him that we will make available . . . all the material we have already discovered and that the executive branch will cooperate fully with any investigation."

How serious was the problem? The President said that the accumulation of strategic materials to be used in time of war had been built up far beyond the nation's needs. He said he was astonished to learn that the $7.7 billion worth of material—a figure that surpassed the value of the nation's surplus farm products—actually exceeded the stockpile needs by nearly $3.4 billion.

"The value of the aluminum in the stockpile exceeds the amounts we would need for three years in the event of war by $347 million," the President said. "The excess supply of nickel is $103 million."

When a reporter asked if President Kennedy's statement carried "implications of wrongdoing by an individual," the President retreated a bit:

"No, I am not making any implication. The only thing is I think a large amount of money has been invested. I think the whole matter should be carefully looked into, contracts and all the rest, profits and so on.

"I am very much aware of the intricate and interrelated problems involved in this area, including the difficulties experienced by certain mineral industries, the impact of world markets and the heavy reliance of certain countries on producing one or more of these minerals," the President went on. "And I can say that we will take no action which will disrupt commodity prices. All of these factors and a careful review of the program will be taken into account, but the cold facts on this matter must be open to the public."

The political implications of the proposed Symington investigation did not elude the President. Nor did they escape the Republicans, either. Many Republicans regarded Kennedy's move primarily as an attempt to discredit the Eisenhower administration.

One Republican who did speak out for the investigation was Senator John J. Williams of Delaware. An indefatigable investigator in his own right, Williams had been making speeches about the stockpile program for six years—with little results. Now Senator Williams welcomed Kennedy and the Democrats to the fray. But, with a sly wielding of the political scalpel, he observed that he could not understand how Kennedy could be "astonished" at the stockpile program in the light of Williams' many speeches on the subject. There also had been periodic reports filed by the Joint Committee on the Reduction of Nonessential Federal Expenditures.

"Mr. Kennedy," Senator Williams pointed out, "as a member of the United States Senate was furnished with copies of all these reports."

Williams also produced the record of votes for continuing and expanding stockpile subsidies. This showed, he said, that Kennedy had voted against the subsidies on the first roll-call but had been recorded in favor of the subsidies on eight successive votes.

Most of what was known about the stockpile's shady past had already been brought out by Williams. He told the Senate: "The record is well documented that there have been millions of dol-

lars in windfall profits in this field. . . . If the administration
wants some facts to start with, they can come to me."

As early as May 27, 1955, Williams had brought out that the
Office of Defense Mobilization (O.D.M.), which set the program's
policy at the time, had agreed to the cancellation of contracts
with the Miami Copper Company, the Copper Range Company
and the Howe Sound Company. The cancellation resulted in windfall profits of an estimated $400,000.[2] A few days later, Williams
charged in another speech that the General Services Administration (G.S.A.), operating agency for the program, had permitted
a similar windfall profit of $250,000 for the Banner Mining Com-
pany, of Tucson, Arizona.[3]

These and a few other examples brought to the Senate's attention by Williams were only the visible part of the iceberg. The
problem was vast and deep.

Although it might be argued that President Kennedy was slow
in recognizing the problem, there was no doubt of his interest in
it in 1962. In a move calculated to facilitate the investigation of
stockpiling, Edward McDermott, a forty-one-year-old lawyer
from Dubuque, Iowa, was named as director of the Office of
Emergency Planning (O.E.P.). This was the agency that had
taken over the chores of O.D.M. McDermott, former chief counsel for a Senate investigating committee, was given the assistance
of Carmine Bellino, generally recognized as the most astute investigative accountant in the U.S. Bellino had had a role in exposing frauds of General Benny Meyers, Teamster bosses Dave
Beck and James R. Hoffa, and many others.

"Stu" Symington, a genial Missouri politician, was not a lawyer. He did not have the bulldog instinct and the ability to grasp
facts that made the late Senator Kefauver and Senator John Mc-
Clellan so effective as investigative chairmen. He needed strong
legal and investigative support—and President Kennedy tried to
give it to him. As a special assistant to President Kennedy, Carmine Bellino was available to help Senator Symington. In addition,
Timothy J. May, another White House staff member, joined the
Symington investigating subcommittee as assistant counsel.

For his chief counsel, Chairman Symington selected Richmond C. Coburn, a tall, impressive-looking trial lawyer from St. Louis. This selection displeased some high-ranking White House figures, for Coburn was a former Republican finance chairman for the State of Missouri. He had been an admirer and supporter of President Eisenhower. Coburn carried out his assignment in an impartial, nonpolitical fashion.

The new counsel had little knowledge of Congressional investigations and less knowledge of the strategic and critical material stockpiles. But he plunged into the work with enthusiasm. Even before the stockpile figures were declassified, Coburn asked the largest producers to estimate government inventories on hand. To his great surprise, all knew approximately how much the government had at the time, despite the fact that stockpile figures supposedly were a closely guarded secret.

The producers tolerantly explained to Coburn that it was easy to figure. By watching published figures of domestic production and consumption, as well as figures of exports, they could make an informed estimate of how much was in the government inventory at any one time. The Soviets, of course, were equally capable of making such calculations.

Coburn was shocked. It seemed to him that the secrecy surrounding the stockpile was worse than useless. It prevented the American public from knowing how huge sums of their money were spent. But it hid nothing from potential enemies.

Before the public hearings had started, Coburn was convinced that the broad-scale secrecy regulations were not justified. The secrecy created the very atmosphere that would permit mismanagement, corruption and the "unconscionable profits" to which President Kennedy had alluded. Decisions to spend hundreds of millions of dollars could be made in secret on the dubious justification that national security was involved. It wasn't difficult to see how political pressures easily could get into the act.

Public hearings started in late March, 1962. Politics filled the air from the start. Some Republicans sought to justify the bungling in the stockpiling decisions, or to blame it on Democrats. Chairman Symington and his Democratic colleagues tried to dump the stockpile scandals at the feet of the Eisenhower administration. In truth, both parties shared in the blame.

According to statistics developed at the hearings, the cost to the government of all stockpiled materials on December 31, 1961, was $8,909,917,935. But the value placed on them by G.S.A. was only $7,723,229,700. In addition, the subcommittee was warned that even this value was suspect because of the lack of a ready market for many of the items. But assuming the materials could be sold, the paper loss was still $1,186,688,235.

The subcommittee also found that surpluses over and above stockpile objectives existed in all but three items, and the value of these surpluses came to $3,390,866,000. The surplus problem was further aggravated by the fact that more unneeded materials, principally nickel and aluminum, were being dumped on the stockpiles every day, under terms of contracts still in force. The government still had an obligation to purchase $9,987,000 worth of nickel from the Hanna Nickel Smelting Company, and $23,081,-000 worth of aluminum from the Harvey Aluminum Company.

The subcommittee heard witnesses describe how the stockpile program was manipulated over and over again in an effort to convert it into a price-support program for the lead and zinc mines. To accomplish this, the uniform methods of establishing stockpile objectives were scuttled. Originally, objectives were established by scaling requirements to the estimated war period. The stockpilers were supposed to take into account (a) what was on hand, (b) what could be counted on from domestic production, and (c) what could be reasonably counted on from overseas sources.

In 1954, it was found that application of this standard to the lead and zinc programs would have stopped the buying. In short, we had enough. However, under the secrecy created by the phony "national security" label, the administrators found it easy to juggle the requirements by ignoring arbitrarily the possibility of supplies from overseas. This doubled the amount of material that had to be stockpiled, and buying continued.

Even with this juggling, lead and zinc prices kept slipping. So another gimmick was introduced behind the closed doors of the O.D.M. An arbitrary "one-year rule" was set. This boosted the objectives to having on hand enough for a full year's consumption regardless of amounts available from domestic production or from other sources in this hemisphere.

The result of this secret decision was that $200 million was spent from 1954 to 1958 to purchase unneeded lead and zinc. The Symington subcommittee called these manipulations "devices employed to permit additional purchases of material as a subsidy to mining interests and unrelated to our national defense needs."

There was more juggling of standards in the O.D.M. on the rubber stockpile program. The result again was wasted millions in tax money for unneeded materials. By 1956, the United States had become a strong producer of synthetic rubber. Leaders in the American rubber industry were urging the Government to reduce the stockpiling objectives for this product since we rapidly were becoming self-sufficient.

"Despite this fact, Dr. [Arthur] Flemming [head of O.D.M.] refused to reduce the rubber objective of 1,230,000 tons, although his staff, after having balanced requirement against supplies, recommended a considerable reduction," the committee report stated.

The only reason given for overruling staff experts was that reducing the objectives might have a serious impact upon rubber-producing friends in southeast Asia.

"Although it has for some years been stockpile policy to avoid adverse effects on international interests of the United States in the disposal of surplus materials," the Senate subcommittee found, "there is nothing in the Stockpiling Act or in any executive order that justifies a consideration of foreign relations in the acquisition of material."

Chairman Symington said the U.S. "got stuck" with about $1 billion in natural rubber while the British and others were able to sell theirs on the world market when prices were high. Symington and Counsel Coburn contended that Flemming had disregarded the law. But Flemming argued that he had simply adopted a general policy of opposition to sale of any materials that were still on the critical and strategic materials lists.

The stockpile program was based on the assumption that it would be needed for a five-year war. But as early as August, 1955, the Joint Chiefs of Staff had begun using a three-year-war planning period. At that time, Assistant Secretary of Defense T. P. Pike wrote Dr. Flemming and strongly recommended a reduction of the stockpiling from a five- to a three-year basis. Pike argued that the policy assumptions exaggerated the needs and the size of the stockpile. He added that he felt the funds could be better spent on more direct military objectives than for a raw materials stockpile. Continued reliance on the five-year concept would cost at least an extra $220 million.

Assistant Secretary of Interior Felix Wormser, who had charge of mineral resources, argued on the other hand that to cut the stockpile from a five- to a three-year concept would be "a breach of faith" with the mining industry. "I think the miners would have strong justification for resentment over the sudden change in policy," Wormser wrote. "The most important declaration in the report of the Cabinet Committee [on Mineral Policy] was its emphasis upon a strong, vigorous, and efficient domestic mining industry being essential to the prosperity of the Nation.

"Therefore, unless we are prepared at the time any curtailment of stockpiling is contemplated to propose an alternate means of sustaining our mobilization base and to foster a healthy mining industry, this administration is apt to find itself in unpleasant and, I may say, well-deserved political difficulties."

Dr. Flemming recommended to the National Security Council that the five-year planning concept be continued for the stockpile, and President Eisenhower approved the continuation of the five-year program. It was not until June 30, 1958, when Gordon Gray had succeeded Dr. Flemming as Director of O.D.M., that it was reduced to three years.

"Failure to revise this factor in mobilization and stockpile planning from 1954 through 1958 led to inflated stockpile requirements not in keeping with our true needs," the Symington subcommittee report concluded. "This failure had the effect of shifting funds from defense needs of a higher priority for national security to the procurement of raw materials . . . based on obsolete strategic assumptions."

The subcommittee report characterized the stockpile secrecy as an example of the "inclination in Government to immediately classify as secret all matters that relate to the military. There is no doubt that inventories, objectives in most materials, and management of the stockpile remained classified when there was no need for such secrecy," the report stated. "Certainly the American public is entitled to know as much about the stockpile as the contractors who are selling the material to the Government. Certainly the American taxpayer is entitled to know how much money is being spent."

LEAD AND ZINC

As it investigated the various commodities, the Symington subcommittee accumulated massive evidence concerning mismanagement of the stockpiling program. Some of the worst abuses centered around the purchase of lead and zinc. It was clearly established that the basic strategic purpose of the program was ignored in order to create price supports for lead and zinc. And as the record built up, it was revealed that high among those responsible for making stockpiling something it wasn't meant to be was Assistant Secretary Wormser, mineral-resources chief for the Department of the Interior.

Wormser had been a vice-president of the St. Joseph Lead Company, of New York, the nation's largest lead producer, and he returned to that same post when he concluded his government service. St. Joseph Lead was one of the largest beneficiaries of the policies that Wormser pushed for the lead and zinc industry.

"It seems clear that Assistant Secretary of the Interior Wormser used all his influence with Government officials to assist the industry with which he was identified before and after his Government service," the Symington subcommittee stated.

In June, 1954, the O.D.M. had launched a monthly cash stockpile-purchase program for lead and zinc. It was a program that was to last until 1958. "The primary object of this unique purchase program was to raise and maintain prices of lead and zinc at a time when prices were depressed," said the subcommittee. "This was not within the purpose of the Stock Piling Act."

The purchases added 293,665 tons of lead, costing $86,800,697, and 457,718 tons of zinc, valued at $117,239,698. These were only a beginning. The policy-makers also used the government's barter program, under which U.S. goods (usually farm products) are traded for foreign-produced goods (usually minerals). The barter program added another 221,245 tons of lead, costing $60,-188,794, and 323,168 tons of zinc, valued at $86,933,655, to the stockpile. Actually, the barter program was another part of the price-support program for American producers, because most of the barter lead and zinc came from foreign subsidiaries of large U.S. producers.

Despite the help, the industry continued to have troubles. Various legislative maneuvers, designed to bolster the industry by stemming low-cost competitive imports, failed in 1957. The industry's friends in the Eisenhower administration decided that the monthly purchase program had to be continued. Thus, as the subcommittee Democrats said in their report, the stockpile approach became a "continuous trough through which the taxpayers' funds flowed directly to a small group of large lead and zinc producers."

When the O.D.M.'s time had about run out, and there seemed no possible justification for buying more lead and zinc, Flemming brought up the new idea of a stockpile to contain "no less than one year's normal U.S. use." President Eisenhower adopted the rule even though this criterion for acquiring materials was to be used for no materials other than lead and zinc. It was a desperate move, however, and it backfired.

The Flemming device created an artificially high price for lead and zinc as long as it continued. But it also caused foreign imports to flood the U.S. market. The government's shortsighted action merely resulted in high profits for lead and zinc for a brief period. In the end, it did not provide a stable mobilization base.

The massive effort for the industry was a failure in the end, despite all of the extralegal—if not illegal—manipulations in its behalf. The stockpiling program could not be used forever to support the companies, and purchases finally were stopped. Prices immediately dropped to low levels that prevailed throughout the Senate investigation. When the entire program came to an end, most of the small producers went bankrupt.

Assistant Interior Secretary Wormser unabashedly admitted to the Symington subcommittee that he used all the persuasion he possessed, urging his fellow government officials to consider the plight of the lead and zinc miners. All of his recommendations and the resulting actions were hidden from the public. As the subcommittee noted: "The specific techniques of this price support program were buried deep in files stamped 'secret.' This secrecy barred the true facts; but these files show that the primary purpose of the program was an attempt to accommodate the economic needs of the lead and zinc industry to the standards of a statute based on the national security."

In his testimony, Dr. Flemming had made an effort to shift the responsibility for what was done to President Eisenhower. He said, in effect, that the President set the long-term objectives in the lead and zinc programs. The hearing record, however, shows that Flemming and Wormser were primarily responsible for the policy.

The subcommittee Democrats concluded:

"Regardless of the question of responsibility, the evil of the price support program was that it loaded the stockpile with greater quantities of unneeded materials at a time when the Defense Department was seeking funds for more urgent defense needs.

"This was done without public knowledge under a cloak of secrecy imposed because of the supposed demands of national security. Perhaps the primary lesson to be learned from this unfortunate stockpiling episode is that stockpile operations should be conducted with the full knowledge of the American taxpayer."

COPPER

The subcommittee found a problem of a different sort when it looked into the copper-stockpiling program. Strikes in Southern Rhodesia in 1954 had caused a temporary shortage in the world copper market. To help alleviate the shortage, the U. S. Department of Commerce recommended that copper ordered for the stockpile, as well as some of it already delivered, be sold to industrial consumers.

Under the stockpile contracts, the government had been paying between 27 and 32 cents a pound. But because of the shortage, the price on the market jumped from 30 to 46 cents a pound.

"Since the market price of copper went as high as 16 cents per pound above the contract price," the Symington subcommittee found, "the contractors received a windfall profit when they were permitted to sell copper on the market rather than delivering it to the stockpile."

The stockpile goals were not being met, and opposition arose to the costly deferrals and cancellations of deliveries. The first to complain outside the O.D.M. itself was the General Accounting Office. The G.A.O. reported that, in one instance, the O.D.M. had forfeited its right to the difference of $400,000 between the market and the contract price. On May 27, 1955, Dr. Flemming acknowledged that his cancellation of the contract had been a mistake. But, mistake or not, he continued to defer deliveries, and the industry again reaped profits.

A General Service Administration memorandum of April 25, 1955, stated that the copper policy was "established by Secretary [Sinclair] Weeks of the Commerce Department and Secretary [George M.] Humphrey of the Treasury Department; and therefore there was nothing that the G.S.A. could do about it."

There were protests from Johnston Russell, director of financial analyses at G.S.A. Russell noted that besides providing windfalls to the industry, the policy put the whole burden of the fluctuating market on the government. He suggested that the government should take the material into inventory and resell it, enjoying the profit itself. Otherwise, it should allow the contractor to act as agent in the sales to industry.

"In either case, the Government would have had the profit, and a windfall to the contractor would have been prevented," the Symington subcommittee found. However, because of the great secrecy enveloping the stockpiling operations, the ranking officials of the Eisenhower administration were able to override the G.A.O. and the G.S.A.

The amounts lost to the taxpayers were considerable. Excluding one large contract with the Calumet & Hecla Co., a total of 84,748,000 pounds of copper was diverted from the stockpile between 1955 and 1958. The contract value was $26,093,314. But producers were able to sell it on the market for about $29,086,616 and pocket profits of $2,993,302.

In the handling of the Calumet & Hecla contract, the Symington subcommittee found "a clear instance of special treatment and high-level official interference to the advantage of the contractor and the substantial disadvantage of the Government." The report stated that Commerce Secretary Weeks and Treasury Secretary Humphrey were the Cabinet officers who took part in Dr. Flemming's decision "to give special consideration" to Calumet & Hecla.

Here is how the special consideration came about: The Truman administration signed a stockpile contract with the company on January 6, 1953, just prior to the Eisenhower inaugural. It provided for delivery of a minimum of 146 million pounds of copper by December 31, 1955. The price was fixed at 27½ cents a pound —three cents above the existing ceiling price for copper. The purpose was to keep a marginal mine in operation by assuring market plus premium price for its output. The delivery schedule called for 46 million pounds in 1953; 50 million pounds in 1954, and 50 million pounds in 1955.

When the copper shortage developed in mid-1954, Calumet & Hecla decided to use its production for its own fabricating division, rather than deliver it to the government, as required under the contract. By the end of 1954, it had defaulted on deliveries of 8,035,000 pounds and got O.D.M. authority to defer delivery on an additional 4,434,000 pounds.

The copper shortage continued, and Calumet & Hecla was given authority for deferral of deliveries of another 25 million pounds in 1955, bringing the total deferrals to 37,465,000 pounds. The firm could sell the copper in the market for up to 43 cents in 1955, rather than fulfill a contract to deliver to the government at 28½ cents a pound.

All good things must come to an end. Late in 1955, Calumet & Hecla was faced with the obligation to deliver 37,500,000 pounds of copper to the stockpile—and at an unfavorable price. However, the firm decided to see whether the end had really arrived. It petitioned friends in the administration to see what could be done.

The problem was solved for the Calumet & Hecla Co. in a series of closed meetings on July 11, 12, and 13, 1955. The meetings were attended by Dr. Flemming, Commerce Secretary Weeks, and Treasury Secretary Humphrey. The copper firm was permitted to postpone *all* deliveries during 1955. The defaults on deliveries were forgiven. An additional three years was to be given for delivery. The firm was to agree to pay the government all profits it received on the copper sales above two cents a pound.

The decision was worth approximately $5 million to Calumet & Hecla, for that would have been the cost if the firm had been required to deliver the 37.5 million pounds of copper. Louis Brooks, of the G.S.A. Comptroller's office, protested vainly against the decision, on grounds that the revised contract permitted windfall profits to the copper firm and shifted the risk of future fluctuation to the government.

But the tender, loving care for Calumet & Hecla was not over by any means. Copper prices remained as high as 46 cents a pound during early 1956, and it appeared that, despite a questionable contract, the government might obtain about $1,700,000 from the profit-sharing clause of the contract. Thereupon, Calumet & Hecla, in March, 1956, came up with a proposal to cancel the whole contract. It offered the government $197,000 to eliminate the profit-sharing provision!

G.S.A. turned this offer down since, according to its estimates, over $1 million of the government's share of the profits had already accrued on copper sales by Calumet.

On October 26, 1956, Calumet & Hecla upped the offer to $500,000 for complete cancellation of the contract. Again it was turned down. It would cost the government an additional $2.7 million to obtain the same copper that Calumet & Hecla was obliged to deliver.

But the company tried again. On November 8, 1956, a meeting was held among G.S.A. officials, including Administrator Franklin Floete, at which it was decided that the Calumet & Hecla offer would be rejected and the government would insist on the contract with the profits that had accumulated.

The following day—without explanation—Floete reversed his position. Floete allowed the copper firm to cancel the profit-sharing provisions, abandoned $1 million in accrued profits, forgave all prior defaults and extended the contract at a higher price of 31 cents a pound. Calumet & Hecla received this deal from Floete for agreeing to pay the government the same $197,000 figure that had been rejected eight months earlier.

Not only did Calumet & Hecla enjoy a windfall of $5.5 million, but the United States spent almost $900,000 more than it otherwise would have for the copper delivered to it by Calumet.

To this day there has been no satisfactory explanation of why Calumet & Hecla was given this favored treatment.

CHROMITE

When it got into its investigation of chromite stockpiling, the Symington subcommittee turned up an unsavory fact: politics and the stockpiling program went hand in hand.

Political pressure, the Senate investigators found, was almost constantly being exerted on those who administered the stockpile program. Sometimes it came from presidential appointees, Democrats as well as Republicans; sometimes from members of Congress.

In 1954, President Eisenhower issued a directive that purchases above the minimum stockpile objectives "must be at advantageous prices." He meant advantageous to the government, of course, but judging from what the Symington subcommittee learned, one wonders whether the President's chief aides understood him. In line with Eisenhower's directive, W. S. Floyd, Assistant Director of O.D.M. for materials, called attention to the fact that a proposed contract for the purchase of chromite was far from "advantageous" to the government. The minimum stockpile objective, he noted, had already been achieved. Floyd pointed out to O.D.M. Chief Flemming that a proposed purchase of chromite from the depot at Grants Pass, Oregon, was at $110 a ton. At that time, the world price was $45 a ton.

Even the lead and zinc industry's friend, Assistant Interior Secretary Wormser, recommended that the chromite program be halted. On March 19, 1956, he said that further purchases made no contribution to the mobilization base because production would stop as soon as the purchase program stopped.

However, Dr. Flemming saw it differently. He wrote Wormser two months later, asking for further consideration of the chromite program. Wormser promptly did an about-face and recommended an extension. Later, he told the Symington subcommittee he had changed his position because of pressure from Western Congressmen.

The most significant political pressure, however, seemed to come from another direction. Republican Douglas McKay had resigned as Secretary of the Interior and was challenging Wayne Morse for the Democrat's Senate seat in Oregon. McKay wrote Flemming, recommending that the chromite purchase program be extended to aid an Oregon industry and that an announcement be made when it was done. A few days later, Dr. Flemming wired McKay at his political-campaign headquarters:

"In reply to your letter of June 18, in testimony today before the House Committee on Insular Affairs I will make the following statement relative to metallurgical chromite.

" 'The Department of Interior has advised us that continuation of the program until the entire quota of 200,000 tons has been purchased may serve to develop a significant mobilization base. Therefore, I have authorized the General Services Administration to extend the program until June 30, 1959.' "

This reasoning was diametrically opposed to the department's initial view that extending the program would make no contribution to the mobilization base. Separated from the facts by a curtain of secrecy, the public did not know that a political decision had set the stage for a waste of $11,519,000 in tax money.

"Total purchases under the Grants Pass domestic chromite program were 199,961 long dry tons at a total price of $18,588,036," the Symington subcommittee reported. "Prices paid for the material at all times during the program ranged from two to two and one-half times the world market price. The paper loss to the Government under the program as of the date of the hearing on December 13, 1962, was $11,519,000."

During the Korean War, the government made a contract, under the Defense Production Act, with the American Chrome Company. It called for the production and delivery of low-grade chromite from a deposit in the high mountains of southwestern Montana. The government agreed to pay more than the market price. This was for the purpose of developing production within the United States, and giving a boost to a domestic industry.

The American Chrome Company was organized as a corporation only a few days before its application for the government contract in January, 1951. It proposed a nine-year contract for delivery of 900,000 short tons of chromite.

The government obligated itself to spend $3 million in capital improvements to put the mine into operation. Further, the government agreed to pay the contractor $34.67 a short ton for low-grade 38.5-per-cent chrome. The market price then for high-grade 44-per-cent chromite was only $27 a ton.

The entire 900,000 short tons were produced, and as soon as the contract was performed the mine was closed down.

The total cost to the government was $32 million, and in the end this stockpile of chromite was useless for commercial purposes. It was low-grade material and it was not economically feasible to upgrade or refine it, according to expert testimony.

MOLYBDENUM

The United States produces about 90 per cent of the free-world supply of molybdenum, an alloying additive for steel in certain high-temperature applications.

A government contract with the Climax Molybdenum Company was not a fixed price agreement. It provided for payment of the actual cost of producing the molybdenum ore, plus a fixed amortization of cost, plus a fixed profit of 18 cents a pound. A $1.07 ceiling was placed on the production cost. The contract would run from 1954 through June 30, 1962, or until 50 million pounds of molybdenum were delivered.

At the time the contract was signed, the price of molybdenum was $1 a pound. In July, 1956, the market price advanced to a point that was higher than the government contract price. In 1957 Climax asked to be permitted to cancel the contract.

The G.S.A. staff estimated that if the contract was canceled, Climax would realize profits in excess of $4.5 million. Despite this, G.S.A. Administrator Floete negotiated a settlement with Arthur H. Bunker, president of Climax. Climax was to pay only $1.2 million for the privilege of ending the contract.

This secret deal cost the taxpayers even more than the $3.3 million the initial G.S.A. estimates indicated, said the Symington subcommittee. Since the market price of molybdenum eventually rose to $1.40 a pound, Climax's windfall was in excess of $4.5 million. The subcommittee also learned that Climax had previously accumulated windfall profits of $835,000 when the government permitted it to defer deliveries to the stockpile.

"Climax was permitted to sell on the market rather than deliver to the stockpile on the ground that it was more vital to national defense to relieve domestic shortages than to meet the stockpile goal," the subcommittee said. "The fact is, however, that Climax was using some of the diverted molybdenum to fill overseas orders.

"Not only did Climax reap windfalls at the expense of the Government, but the contract was finally canceled for a sum substantially less than the windfall profits accruing to the contractor by such cancellation."

CRYOLITE

Thirteen million dollars spent for a material that really wasn't needed—that's the story of cryolite.

This waste by the stockpilers and the bureaucrats began under the Truman administration and extended into the days of President Eisenhower. The public would have had no knowledge of it had not the unnecessary wraps been stripped from the stockpiling program by the Symington subcommittee.

Cryolite is a material used in the manufacture of aluminum. It was a low-priority item that never made the list of strategic and critical materials. It became, nevertheless, a blue chip in the stockpile game.

During the Truman administration, the G.S.A., following a directive from Administrator Jess Larson, signed a "letter of intent" with the Aluminum Ore Company for the purchase of synthetic cryolite. It provided for delivery of 42,600 short tons by 1957, and it had an unusual feature—the government was permitted to terminate the contract upon payment of a specified penalty to the contractor.

Only a small amount of synthetic cryolite had been delivered by January, 1954, and Johnston Russell, of G.S.A., wrote a memorandum recommending that the contract be terminated. He noted that the only aluminum producer who needed cryolite had stopped buying it from the government. The other aluminum companies produced their own. The government could have terminated the contract at that time for only $268,000. The savings in storage costs alone would have amounted to more than $1 million.

Despite these good reasons for cancelling the contract, O.D.M. rejected Russell's recommendation. The reason given was that there "might be" a future need for listing cryolite as a "strategic and critical material."

A few months later, Russell again recommended termination, calling attention to the fact that cryolite had not yet been declared strategic and critical. The G.S.A. wrote to the O.D.M., asking for authority to exercise its option and stop buying cryolite. At that time, this could have been done for $240,000. The government would have saved $6 million over the life of the contract in the cost of purchasing undelivered material, as well as the shipping and storage costs. O.D.M. refused to give the authorization. But it still did not put cryolite on the "strategic and critical" list.

The contract went on, deliveries continued, and storage costs mounted. In the end, a total of $11,776,836 of unneeded cryolite was purchased. Transportation and storage costs brought the government's expenditures to well over $13 million.

The Senate investigators wrote an epitaph:

"This was a clear case of lack of coordination between the two agencies that were responsible for the operations of the stockpile. The right to terminate a contract for the purchase of material not needed by the Government was nullified by inaction in O.D.M. As a result, the Government spent $13 million, most of which expense could have been avoided."

TUNGSTEN

Tungsten—a nonmagnetic metal, used principally as an alloy to produce a hard, highly heat-resistant steel—was found to be over-stockpiled on a colossal scale. The most the government ever said it wanted of tungsten was 50 million pounds. But by 1962 the government's stockpile inventories somehow had climbed to 161,464,-000 pounds! That was enough surplus, the subcommittee figured, to provide for all the needs of the country for at least ten years.

Quality tungsten in the stockpile cost the government $550,-900,000. Since tungsten supplies were plentiful, the stockpiled amount had a market value of only $236 million. In addition, the government inventory contained 43,475,000 pounds of below-specification tungsten, costing another $160,369,000. The initial cost on the tungsten contracts was $63 a ton. It was reduced to $55 a ton in 1958, but this was still two or three times higher than the world-market price.

The Symington subcommittee singled out the government's tungsten contract with the Wah Chang Corporation, of New York, as one that resulted in a particularly heavy loss to the taxpayers. Wah Chang had a tungsten-mining property in Brazil called Inhandjara, and the government had been led to expect that this mine would be opened for the purpose of fulfilling the contract. The agreement required the government to take no less than 393,-000 tons of tungsten, and the contractor could sell the government as much as 787,000 tons.

The cost was to be the average published market price at the time of delivery, plus $4 per ton for initial processing of the ore at the Wah Chang plant in New York State. However, this figure was deceptive, for the contract also provided that under no circumstances should the price drop below $55 per ton. This turned out to be two or three times the market price during most of the seven-year contract period, because of a sharp drop in world prices.

The government paid Wah Chang $35,138,419 for delivery of 636,189 tons—$22 million more than the world-market price at the time of deliveries.

Although it was understood that Wah Chang was to bring into operation a new mine at Inhandjara, the contract did not specify that the product should come from that mine. Accordingly, only

15 per cent of the tungsten delivered came from the new mine.

How was this done? "Evidence showed," said Symington's committee, that the contractor had purchased tungsten in Brazil during most of the contract at $17 a short ton unit, and then delivered it to the government at $55. . . ."

MANGANESE, MICA—AND ALUMINUM

The Symington subcommittee, in its delvings, found that the government had spent $106,345,000 for manganese, and $35,-381,000 for mica. At the time of the hearings in 1962, the values of these materials had declined, respectively, to $23,715,000 and $5,241,000.

But these were small chips compared to the big aluminum stakes. Once again, a major political figure enters the picture. Here is the story of how O.D.M. Chief Flemming bought $100 million worth of aluminum that he knew the government didn't need:

On May 19, 1953, the government signed a letter of intent with the Harvey Aluminum Company, of Torrance, California, for the purchase of as much as 270,000 tons of primary aluminum pig metal over a five-year period, to begin in 1955.

Even at the time the letter was signed, the necessity for increasing aluminum production was doubtful because of the expansion of primary aluminum facilities in Canada and the United States. However, the letter of intent required the Harvey Company to begin building a new aluminum plant in 1953. Accordingly, an option was taken by the company for a site in Oregon, and a contract for power was signed with the government's Bonneville Power Administration.

Between 1953 and mid-1955, there was so much expansion of aluminum-supply facilities in the U.S. and Canada that the Harvey plant "was unnecessary for national defense purposes," Symington subcommittee Democrats concluded. Flemming later admitted to the Senate investigators that, at the time he signed the Harvey letter of intent, he would not have signed a contract to buy more aluminum for the government. Yet later he signed a contract to buy aluminum from the new Harvey plant.

How did this come about? The subcommittee traced the background.

Through 1953, 1954 and early 1955, Harvey officials had tried to persuade the government to proceed with the contract. In May, 1955, the New York law firm of Dewey, Ballentine, Bushby, Palmer & Wood wrote to Dr. Flemming's office, stating that it had been retained by Harvey to push a damage claim against the government for not signing a contract.

The first member of the firm to call on Dr. Flemming was Thomas E. Dewey, the former Governor of New York and the former G.O.P. Presidential candidate. Dewey urged Flemming to sign the contract or face a damage suit.

Mr. Dewey then advised Dr. Flemming that James B. Nickerson, of his law firm, would continue the negotiations. Mr. Nickerson prepared the Harvey case against the government, and presented a complaint asking $70 million in damages.

Faced with the threat of a law suit, Dr. Flemming said, he signed the contract. At the time of the hearings, Harvey had delivered 165,138 short tons of aluminum at a cost of $82,069,000, and still had the option to deliver another $16,132,000 worth of aluminum.

In support of his action, Dr. Flemming stated that he felt "a moral duty" on the part of the government to live up to its agreement, even though there was probably no legal obligation to sign the contract. He told the committee there was no suggestion that the government settle with Harvey by paying out-of-pocket expenses plus a fair profit. This meant that the government, with aluminum running out of its ears, was obligated to spend many millions in tax money after Governor Dewey's law firm threatened suit.

The Symington subcommittee closed its recital of the incident with a not-quite-rhetorical question:

"Should the government have negotiated a settlement with Harvey . . . or should the government spend some $94,000,000 for unneeded materials?"

Perhaps the taxpayers could answer that one.

CHAPTER 6

Humphrey of Hanna

The Symington subcommittee saved until last the stockpile investigation that was dearest to President Kennedy's heart—the nickel contracts negotiated with the M. A. Hanna Company, of Cleveland, Ohio, and its subsidiaries. That investigation was to put the spotlight squarely on George M. Humphrey, who had been Secretary of the Treasury from the outset of the Eisenhower administration until 1957, and was widely regarded as the strong man of the Eisenhower Cabinet.

George Magoffin Humphrey, frequent host to President Eisenhower at quail-shooting parties on his Georgia plantation, had been chairman of the board of the parent M. A. Hanna Company until he resigned to enter the Eisenhower Cabinet in January, 1953. When he left the Cabinet four years later, he returned to the company as honorary board chairman and director of the M. A. Hanna Company.

George Humphrey's name was synonymous with the Hanna Company, and to President Kennedy and many of his closest associates it was synonymous with Republicanism. If there was going to be any real political pay dirt in the stockpile investigation, the Hanna-Humphrey investigation was most likely to yield it.

The Hanna-Humphrey probe revolved around whether "unconscionable profits" were made off the U.S. government by the former Secretary of the Treasury's company. Humphrey said the profits were reasonable. President Kennedy and Democratic subcommittee members contended the profits were unreasonable, and that the Hanna Company had taken the taxpayers for an expensive ride. They said a Comptroller General's report proved it.[1]

The Hanna-Humphrey nickel affair spanned three administrations. The stockpile contracts were signed under Truman, administered under Eisenhower, and investigated under Kennedy. The contracts were signed hurriedly in the last days of the Truman administration in January, 1953, but the terms of the contracts and its operation were unknown to the public because of the cloak of secrecy that covered nearly all of the activities in the multibillion-dollar stockpile program. It was claimed that national security required this great secrecy, but it provided a convenient curtain to hide mistakes or political favoritism. For years, Senator John J. Williams, the Delaware Republican, and others had raised questions about what was taking place in the secret stockpile deals. Williams had been curious about the Hanna Company's nickel contracts, but hard facts were difficult to obtain until President Kennedy ordered the records opened for the Symington investigations and hearings.

As traced by the Senate investigating subcommittee, part of the Hanna story goes back to 1943, when the Hanna group acquired mineral rights on Nickel Mountain, in Douglas County, near Riddle, Oregon. This acquisition and subsequent exploration and planning cost the Hanna group about $440,000. Following the outbreak of the Korean War, there was a nickel shortage. Hanna officials, under the general supervision of George Humphrey, went to the Office of Defense Mobilization, told officials the Hanna Company had proven quantities of nickel-bearing ore in Oregon, and submitted a proposal for development of the mines and the erection of a smelting plant. It was reported to be the only nickel deposit in the United States with sufficient quantities for defense purposes.

The government started to negotiate at once, but ran into unusual demands by Hanna officials. Instead of the standard single contract, the Hanna officials came up with a proposal for two contracts. Under the first, the Hanna Mining Company proposed to

sell nickel ore to the government for $6 a ton. Hanna was to pro-
vide the capital of about $4 million for the mining operation.

The second contract proposal called for the government to sell
the ore it bought from Hanna Mining to Hanna Smelting for the
same $6 a ton for processing. After refining the ore to ferronickel,
Hanna Smelting was to sell the nickel back to the government at
the smelting company's cost. This was not to exceed 62.5 cents
per pound, with some modification to keep the cost in line with the
published market price.

Career government specialists found these Hanna demands unbelievable, but that wasn't all. The government was to agree to
pay the Hanna Smelting Company $22 million. This was to pro-
vide for construction of the smelting plant, plus working capital.
Hanna Smelting was to have the right to cancel its contract if the
smelting process should not prove feasible. If either Hanna Smelting or the government cancelled, the government was to reimburse
the Hanna Mining Company for its capital investment in the mine,
plus damages for the profits it would lose by *not* selling the nickel
to be processed by its affiliate. In addition, the government would
take back the smelter and Hanna Smelting would be relieved of
any responsibility for capital advances made by the government.

Government negotiators considered the Hanna proposal preposterous. They felt the $6-a-ton price for the raw ore was too
high, and Hanna produced no valid figures to support it.[2] The
principal government negotiator, M. C. Robinson, of the Defense
Materials Procurement Agency (D.M.P.A.), opposed the government's financing the smelter for $22 million and then, in effect,
giving it to Hanna. Also, the formula for damage on the contract
was totally favorable to Hanna, with no protection for the government.

It was reported to Robinson that George Humphrey, then head
of Hanna, would not agree to changes more favorable to the government. In late July, 1952, the Hanna Company told the government it had no interest in the smelting operation, and was only
interested in selling its ore.

However, inside the Hanna Company the technical advisers predicted a large market for production from a ferronickel plant they wanted the government to finance for them. On September 11, 1952, D. M. Vedensky, a Hanna metallurgist, wrote an optimistic internal memorandum to other Hanna executives, concluding that "the important point here is that we are certain to have a peacetime market in the steel industry and that the Government contract will give us time to develop fully this market."

(Democrats on the Symington subcommittee concluded later that "Vedensky's thinking was contrary to all representations by Hanna that it was not interested in smelting the ore and that there would be no usefulness to the smelter, other than scrap, at the end of the contract.")[3]

On September 25, 1952, John Ford, another government negotiator, wrote a report criticizing "the extortionate demand of the [Hanna] company regarding liquidated damages." Ford pointed out that the provisions were "substantially in excess of consideration granted under any other contract negotiated by this office."[4]

In a memorandum of October 7, 1952, Johnston Russell, Director of Financial Analysis for G.S.A., summarized the objections:[5]

". . . I feel that this proposed contract represents a degree of unilateral consideration in favor of the contractor [Hanna] which is entirely too unreasonable from the standpoint of the Government's interest."

He added: "Provisions have been included largely at the insistence of the contractor, which are designed to shift the maximum risk to the Government, place the contractor's obligation at the irreducible minimum and avoid potential tax liability by questionable means. . . .

"The contracts are to be so rigged that all profits accrue to the mining company and none to the smelting company, although the great bulk of the capital investment is required for the smelter.

"The contractor magnanimously points to the nominal management fee which he will draw from operating the smelter, but the fact is that the price to be paid the mining company for the ore is set so high that the potential profits of the mining company will be quite liberal for both companies combined."

The government financial analyst also pointed out that, "with all the concessions," the Hanna group still was asking the government to supply all the working capital required for the smelter.

There followed a period of tough bickering between the G.S.A. and the Hanna interests. The G.S.A. hoped to win agreement to more reasonable terms, but Hanna held firm.

In December, 1952, after it had been announced that Humphrey would be Secretary of the Treasury but before he had taken office, he told one G.S.A. official that the nickel contract "had better be signed" before he took office.[6]

Finally, despite all the provisions in the proposal that were unfavorable to the government, G.S.A. Administrator Jess Larson approved the twin Hanna contracts on January 16, 1953. He said he felt he had no choice if he wanted the nickel for the stockpile.

Less than a week later, Humphrey was confirmed as Secretary of the Treasury in the Eisenhower administration, where he was to become a symbol of big-business leadership in government. He was lauded by many as a fellow who had met a payroll and knew how to guard the public till.

While Secretary Humphrey was enjoying his buildup, profits from the two Hanna contracts rolled right along. Unlike some public officials who severed their business connections when they entered government service, Humphrey and his family, according to the subcommittee, retained a 14-per-cent interest in the Hanna firm.[7] Thus throughout his tenure as Secretary of the Treasury, the nickel contracts were pouring millions into the personal bank accounts of the Secretary of the Treasury and members of his family. At the time, the public had no way of learning how much.

Republican Senator John J. Williams and Comptroller General Joseph Campbell were highly critical of the Hanna nickel contracts. Senator Williams did not like to be critical of a Republican administration, but he had enough information to make him question whether this and other contracts were an efficient use of tax money.

Campbell, an Eisenhower appointee, filed an official report to Congress on April 26, 1961, which made these points:

"The sale of ore to the government at fixed prices without provision for price redetermination [in the event profits were too high] does not appear to be appropriate for these contracts.

"The terms of the contracts resulted in limited financial risks on the part of the Hanna companies.

"The terms of one of the contracts permit Hanna to acquire clear title to a smelter constructed with government funds of over $22,000,000 by paying the government the estimated salvage value of the facilities, about $1,700,000."

The G.A.O. chief also called attention to an unusual clause in one of the contracts that barred the government from examining the company's records on profits. This was secrecy beyond the normal secrecy for national security, and Campbell noted:

"The contract with the Hanna Mining Company, under which most of Hanna's profits are earned . . . does not contain an adequate examination of records clause."

More than $100 million in government funds was involved in the Hanna contracts, and the G.A.O. report touched off more public criticism. Representative Charles Vanik, an Ohio Democrat, charged, in a speech on the House floor on May 17, 1961, that the Hanna Company "parlayed a $440,000 investment into a $50,000,000 profit—much of it tax free—at practically no risk."

No figures on the profits were available at that time, and Vanik's estimate on the profit was later proved to be highly inflated.

The price of $6 a ton for the nickel-bearing ore was double or nearly triple what some government experts felt should have been paid. The government needed nickel badly for the stockpiling, but career experts felt there were limits that should not be exceeded. Humphrey's company, which had the nickel to sell, insisted on the high price and also on the questionable contract provisions.

The G.A.O. report certainly supported Representative Vanik's claim that Humphrey's Hanna companies had "practically no risk" in this multimillion-dollar venture. The G.A.O. report stated:

"Under the contract, the government guaranteed virtually all the contractor's capital investment and provided a market for all the contractor's production at prices which virtually precluded operating loss."

When President Kennedy launched the stockpile investigation in late January, 1962, he did not know how much profit the Humphrey family had received. He knew only that it had been substantial. Kennedy knew that G.S.A. subordinates had objected to the "extortionate" terms. He knew that Comptroller General Campbell, an Eisenhower appointee, had been highly critical of the general contract terms.

G.S.A. officials said former Administrator Larson had pushed to get the Hanna contracts signed before the inauguration of President Eisenhower because he "didn't want to embarrass the new Secretary of Treasury."

From the time the Symington investigation of the Hanna Company started, it was a two-ring political circus. The Kennedy administration felt it had found a prime scandal in the alleged "unconscionable profits," and Chairman Symington and other Democrats on the subcommittee obliged the White House by banging away at the ex-Secretary. With equal spirit, a number of Republicans came to Humphrey's defense. "A personal vendetta against me," thundered Humphrey.

"They are after political pay dirt—I don't believe there is any," said ex-Commerce Secretary Sinclair Weeks.

Eisenhower issued a statement attesting his complete faith in Humphrey. Humphrey, he said, never would engage in profiteering at the expense of the taxpayers. "If Secretary Humphrey ever did a dishonest thing in his life I'm ready to mount the cross and you can put the nails and spear in me," said the former President. "I will never believe he did a dishonest thing in his life."

On the same day, Symington stated that stockpiling mismanagement had resulted in losses of more than $1 billion, and termed them "far greater than any I have seen in the Billie Sol Estes case."

President Kennedy and the Democrats showed no signs of relenting. While hearings on other stockpile problems proceeded,

the committee's best investigators probed into all the details of
Humphrey's role in the development of the Hanna contracts.
Gradually, they shaped up the story, which was unfolded at the
later public hearings.

It was established that Hanna Mining had delivered 108,696,-
000 pounds of ferronickel, for which the government paid it
$71,404,000. In addition, the government had advanced Hanna
$22,223,000 to build the smelter, and in March, 1960, the com-
pany had taken over ownership of the smelter for the bargain price
of $1,722,000, as the contract provided.

Investigators found that Hanna had taken full advantage of the
secrecy on the contract. It also had invoked the contract provision
that gave the company the sole right to determine "feasibility" of
the production, and to demand a higher price for the nickel under
a threat of termination of the contract.

Investigators revealed that in November, 1956, Hanna decided
that the 65.77-cent-a-pound ceiling for nickel was not enough to
meet actual costs. The company wanted 84.5 cents a pound.[8]

The government engineer who inspected the plant reported he
felt the higher figure did not represent actual operating costs. The
engineer suggested ceilings of from 69 cents to 71 cents maximum.
However, the G.S.A. disregarded the government engineer and
granted a temporary ceiling-price increase to 86.75 cents per
pound—more than two cents a pound above what Hanna was
asking.[9]

The Symington-subcommittee investigators found no records
that explained why Hanna was given even a higher price than it
requested. But they did find a rather astonishing memorandum,
dated December 19, 1956—from one Hanna official, R. C. Fish,
to another, Earl S. Mollard—in the company files.

Fish said he had just gone over the G.S.A. engineer's report.
The government man's figures were "well within reason and I
agree with you that we should better his costs of 70 cents for 1958
and 69 cents for 1959."[10]

"In other words," the Senate investigators noted, "at the same
time Hanna was demanding of the Government an increase in the

ceiling price to 84.5 cents, its own staff was concurring with the conclusions of the government engineers that Hanna's actual operating costs would show a decline to 69 or 70 cents."

The subcommittee investigators checked the correspondence files of the two Hanna subsidiaries. They found that in April, 1957, the companies started charging off large capital expenditures to "expenses." These improperly charged items, the investigators found, included ducts, Dutch ovens, dust-collecting equipment, and a slag-conveyor system for the smelter. "This policy increased operating costs of Hanna Smelting and lent justification to its demand for a permanent increase in the ceiling price," the investigators reported.

"Once Hanna Smelting secured its new permanent ceiling price . . . a steep decline in operating costs occurred," the investigators reported to Symington.

General Accounting Office auditors made a preliminary examination of Hanna's books for the years 1958 and 1959, and concluded that an additional $383,000 had been improperly charged to expenses during that period. Symington was informed that the G.A.O. auditors also found that numerous other capital items had been completely charged off in 1960. These included items such as a scoopmobile (a large tractorlike vehicle used for moving ore and fuel), machinery for casting ingots, and such office equipment as typewriters and air-conditioners.

The investigators learned that G.S.A. officials had no knowledge that Hanna was charging these items—which should have been paid for out of the contract's capital-construction account—to expense. The result was that the former Treasury Secretary's company was overstating costs to the government, and the G.S.A. accountants were not conducting their own investigations, which would have been standard operating procedure on most contracts. They were simply forced to accept the word of Hanna officials because of secrecy provisions in the contract.

"The procedures in this case," the investigators found, "expressly violated the internal audit regulations of G.S.A., because the regulations of that Government agency did not permit the substitution of an outside accounting-firm audit for a Government audit."[11]

A more thorough audit by the G.A.O. later resulted in the charge that more than $1 million was charged improperly to expenses by the Hanna Company. (This figure later was placed even higher by the G.S.A.)

"Through this improper expensing of capital items Hanna was able to (1) acquire at least $1,030,000 more from the Government than proper under the terms of the contract; (2) reduce by $77,200 the amount of the residual payment Hanna had to make to obtain ownership of the smelter; and (3) achieve the tax advantage of having expensed out $1 million of capital items that should have been depreciated for tax purposes as capital expenditures," the G.A.O. auditors found.

In response to an inquiry from the Symington subcommittee, Mortimer Caplin, then the Commissioner of Internal Revenue, advised that the Hanna Company should not have deducted these items as expense. Hanna officials defended their actions on the ground that the decision was made by Ernst & Ernst, their accountants. But the subcommittee's investigators countered:

"The record is clear . . . that the original decision was made by Hanna officials, and then subsequently referred to Ernst & Ernst for approval."

Hassel Tippit, the managing partner of Ernst & Ernst, supported the Hanna officials in their contention that it was proper to deduct the questionable items as expenses.[12] However, his own company's field man, who had examined the Hanna operations, had written on the work papers:

". . . it was noted that many items of capital nature had been written off to expense . . . which the writer feels should have been capitalized."

When Tippit continued to side with Hanna, it was pointed out to him that everyone—including the Commissioner of Internal Revenue, the G.S.A., the G.A.O., his client's chief accountant, and his own field man—disagreed with him.

Walter Henson, a G.A.O. auditor, testified that Hanna Mining had earned $15,096,446, before taxes. The profits of Hanna Mining, after taxes, were $10,206,337. These figures represented a fat 57.4-per-cent profit on sales over a six-year period. If figured on cost, Hanna Mining's profit was even higher—135 per cent. And if figured on capital investment, the auditor said, it was higher still—457 per cent.

A final audit by the G.S.A. concluded that, through improper handling of expenses, Hanna had "improperly overcharged the Government $1,816,958."[13] (When Hanna refused to pay the bill presented by the G.S.A., the matter was turned over to the Justice Department and suit was filed to collect the nearly $2 million.) *

Thus the stage was set for the much-awaited appearance of former Secretary Humphrey before Senate investigators. The millionaire industrialist, balding and well-groomed, was aggressively self-confident as he appeared before the subcommittee. He had the air of a man who was donating some of his valuable time to straighten out some not-very-bright inquisitors. His attitude was one of total confidence.

Senator Clair Engle (Democrat, of California) brought up the G.A.O. auditor's figures "on which it is claimed that Hanna, based upon invested capital of $4.5 million, made these huge and excessive profits.[14] "It seems to me," he said, "that here are the essentials of the case . . . whether or not, in fact, the Hanna Company did make unconscionable profits on material necessary and vital to the defense of the country. I would like to have your comment on each of those items."

"Now, Senator, I am sorry to say this, but the fact is that it has got so mixed up that you are just all confused here," Humphrey replied. "On $27 million of sales, we made a profit of about $7½ million after we had paid a tax to the Government of $5,920,000. Now that is our entire transaction with the Government. Every-

---

*The filing of the suit was announced by the Justice Department in a press release dated Friday, November 8, 1963, indicating the suit was filed that day in Portland, Oregon. There is still no settlement.

thing else we did for the Government was done at cost, and the only other thing that comes into the picture at all is that we bought a plant which to you was worthless at the time, because you did not have any ore.

"Now, that is the whole story," Humphrey insisted. "All of the rest of this stuff is just thrown in here to confuse it. Our whole being involved $27 million of sales on which we made a net profit of $7 million, $7.5 million in seven years. Now if that is unconscionable profit, I would like to know where it comes from. The rest of this is just baloney."

Senator Strom Thurmond (Democrat, of South Carolina) asked Humphrey if he felt it was proper for a company to push for such tremendous profits on a contract involving national defense.

"Well, now, Senator, I think you also are confused in this situation," Humphrey lectured. He dismissed the contracts involving expenditures of $100 million in government funds as relatively small, and characterized the nickel division of Hanna as "a tag end of our business."

The subcommittee explained later in its report that Hanna Mining Company has three mining divisions: the nickel division, the Minnesota division, and the Michigan division. It disclosed that Hanna's 1957 tax returns revealed that the Minnesota division earned 6 per cent profit on costs; the Michigan division earned 30 per cent; and the nickel division—described by Humphrey as the "tag end of the business"—earned 135 per cent.

"For the seven years during which the government nickel contracts were operating—1954 through 1960—the Minnesota division, on costs of $207 million, had profits before taxes of $22 million; the Michigan division, on costs of $44 million, profits of $6,455,000; and the nickel division, on costs of $11 million, profits of $15 million," the Symington subcommittee stated.[15]

Humphrey dismissed $22 million in government financing on the smelter as unimportant. "We did not need $25 million from the Government," he scoffed. "We could write a check for it ourselves . . . that is small potatoes for the business that we are conducting."

However, a memorandum from D.M.P.A.'s Robinson stated that Hanna declined to finance the smelter because it claimed it needed all its resources for other purposes. The company said at the time it was heavily extended in a Labrador operation, Robinson testified. And the subcommittee pointed out:

"According to another G.S.A. memorandum of the negotiations . . . it was George Humphrey who refused to allow Hanna to finance the smelter, insisting the Government finance it."

Humphrey bridled at any questions suggesting that he and his family had made a great deal of money from the Hanna Company nickel contracts.

"Now, when you try to develop that I make money or that this is an important item of increase in . . . my assets, you are comparing the $22 million with $450 million and I am a very small percentage stockholder of both," Humphrey said in one of the more modest disclaimers of our time. "Never at any time were the earnings from this more than 5 per cent of the total earnings that my stock interest applied to."[16]

Humphrey testified that the Humphrey-family interest in the M. A. Hanna Company "approximated just a little under or a little over 10 per cent of the total stock outstanding."

By the subcommittee's computation, the Humphrey family owned 14 per cent of Hanna Smelting and Hanna Mining.

"Whatever profits or windfalls that Hanna Mining and Hanna Smelting enjoyed, the Humphrey family received 14 per cent of those profits and windfalls," the subcommittee stated.

The Senatorial investigators found that the smelting company obtained an $18 million windfall on the purchase of the smelter. Both companies together, the subcommittee estimated, received windfalls and profits of $30 million. And, the way the subcommittee's accountants figured it, the Humphrey family's share of this total was $4,159,321.[17]

Under questioning by Committee Counsel Coburn, Humphrey

admitted that he made the final decisions on all of the principal features of the contracts.

Gilbert Humphrey, son of George Humphrey and chairman of the board of the M. A. Hanna Company, also was a witness. He admitted that the company had insisted on a "take it or leave it" basis in its nickel contracts with the government. The company's attitude, he said, was that if the government wanted the nickel, it could pay Hanna's price.

There was much ground still to be covered when the public hearing came to an abrupt end in a fantastic blowup between Chairman Symington and the former Treasury Secretary. Throughout the hearing, the chairman and the witness had bickered with each other, with barely disguised political overtones apparent in their exchanges. . . .

The Senate had once cleared the Hanna contracts, Senator Glenn Beall, the Maryland Republican, said in defending Humphrey.

"A Senate subcommittee headed by the now Vice President Lyndon Johnson held nickel hearings in 1957," Senator Beall said. "The then Senator Johnson approved of the contracts . . . never did we have anything about this until right now."

Chairman Symington resented a "bitter attack" on him by Humphrey, because Humphrey "disputed nearly every fact that had been developed by the accounting team . . . after a five-month audit." Symington indicated he would adjourn the hearing for further investigation.

"Did you make the statement . . . that this was a personal vendetta against you?" Symington asked Humphrey.

"I did, and I believe it," Humphrey replied. "The statement you just read is ample proof of the extremely prejudicial atmosphere. . . ."

Both men tried to talk, and a shouting match erupted. Humphrey stormed, "It is my turn now." Symington yelled, "Let me interrupt," and nothing made sense for a time.

"You cannot stop me from making a statement and adjourn this," Humphrey challenged. "You don't dare . . ."

"This hearing is adjourned," Symington snapped as he banged down the gavel. "Don't ever tell me as a U.S. Senator and chairman of the committee what I dare or dare not do."

The anger, the shouting, and the pounding gavel provided a colorful if confusing end to Humphrey's testimony. The scene, carried widely on radio and television, did nothing to help the image of the Symington investigation. The detailed work of subcommittee accountants was lost in the din of temper and politics. Humphrey was quite possibly delighted to be gaveled off the witness stand, for he was never called again.

In its own probing, after the Humphrey-Symington episode, the subcommittee's professional staff, guided by Counsel Coburn and the ace accountant, Carmine Bellino, dug further into the records. The staff's purpose was to determine exactly how George Humphrey arrived at that $7.5-million-dollar "profit after taxes" figure he had handed the subcommittee. The way the staff interpreted the figures, the Hanna Mining Company's books showed $10,-469,814 in profits after taxes. As it turned out, the Hanna Mining Company's income-tax returns substantiated the higher figure.

The investigators finally concluded that special figures were worked up for use in Humphrey's testimony. Said the subcommittee's official report:

"In arriving at the $7,500,000 figure, Hanna Mining reallocated to the nickel division expenses previously attributed to the other two mining divisions. In this connection, Hanna charged to the nickel division $2,173,000 for exploration, research and ore reserves. None of this exploration expense was actually incurred by the nickel division but was incurred by other divisions of the company. . . . In an effort to reduce the net profit on the nickel contract just prior to the hearings, these subsequent reallocations were made."[18]

If it was the purpose of the former Secretary of the Treasury or anyone else to confuse the reporters covering the hearings, and, through them, to confuse the public about how much Hanna and the Humphrey family really earned, the performance was successful. Most reporters and editorial writers did not seem able to figure out whether it was $7.5 million profit or $10.4 million profit.

An irate President Kennedy wanted to make the "unconscionable profit" charge stick against Humphrey of Hanna. At a press conference on August 22, the President said that the Hanna Mining Company had made "extremely large [profits] . . . with very little risk to the company." He directed the attention of reporters to a Senate speech by Senator Clair Engle, the California Democrat, which he said "everyone should read."

Senator Engle charged that the M. A. Hanna Company had made "deliberate misrepresentations" to the government during the contract negotiations in estimating the cost of producing ore. He said documents found in the Hanna files showed "misrepresentations" of 48 to 68 cents a ton, or a total of more than $2.1 million on the whole contract.[19]

Chairman Symington, Senator Engle and Senator Howard W. Cannon, the Nevada Democrat, signed the report prepared by Chief Counsel Richmond C. Coburn and his staff. Three members of the subcommittee did not sign the report. Senator Strom Thurmond submitted individual views that were fully as critical of the administration of the stockpile program as those set out in the report signed by the other three Democrats. He declared the investigation of abuses of the stockpile program was "most decidedly in the public interest."

"Too long have these matters been shrouded in secrecy, immune from the public scrutiny which can insure the desired degree of responsibility in the administration of public funds," Senator Thurmond stated. "If it accomplishes nothing else, this investigation of the stockpile programs should result in more responsible and careful handling of these programs as a result of the glare of the public spotlight being focused on its conduct."[20]

The South Carolina Democrat was equally critical of the Congress for writing loose legislation that gave the executive branch great discretion in administering a program in secret.

"It should be noted that this excessive grant of discretion to the Executive Branch falls in an area of activity which is subject to the application of strict classification on information dealing with the stockpile program and such information was classified until very recently," he said.

"Both Congress and the public were at a disadvantage, to say the least, in attempting to learn of the manner in which this broad discretion was exercised."

Thurmond pointed out that "secrecy has contributed substantially to the problems experienced with the stockpiles."

"Prior to the beginning of the hearings, the administration declassified much information of the stockpiles," he said, and warned: "In the event this or any other administration chose to follow a course of secrecy in the future, however, there is nothing in the law to prevent it. This statutory deficiency should be remedied."[21]

Senator Clifford Case, the New Jersey Republican, and Senator J. Glenn Beall, the Maryland Republican, voted against adoption of the report. They characterized it as "inadequate and unfair" to the Eisenhower administration. Senator Case submitted a letter from former President Eisenhower on the stockpile which observed that "while in such matters hindsight is often desirable and even enjoyable, foresight is always a necessity."

The former President did not argue with the facts in the report, but compared the stockpile to investment in an insurance policy. "If an emergency does not arise, there are always those who can consider the investment a waste," former President Eisenhower said. He did not touch on the subjects of "profiteering" or "political" influence in stockpile decisions.[22]

Senator Beall's brief dissent was a general charge that the Symington-subcommittee report was "slanted in its approach, lacking in objectivity, and unwarranted in the attacks it makes on former government officials."

The Maryland Republican made no effort to challenge the factual information cited in the report signed by the three Democrats, but simply expressed his shock that "respected officials of the Eisenhower Administration are made the objects of unjustified charges through the use of distortions, omissions, and misinterpretations."[23]

Senator Beall made no effort to detail his complaint, but he added: "It is unconscionable that the charges in this statement are proposed to be published without first giving to those individuals who are unjustly maligned the opportunity to answer these politically motivated charges."

Chairman Symington said that George Humphrey and all persons who were criticized were given an opportunity to testify, and to explain their actions.

The comments of President Kennedy, the Senate speech by Senator Engle and the Symington-subcommittee report never did put full public focus on the details of the Hanna nickel contracts and the profits. This was particularly irritating to President Kennedy and his closest associates, who viewed the press as too protective of the Eisenhower administration. The irritation was accentuated by the fact that at the very moment the Hanna investigation was under way, and George Humphrey was getting off comparatively lightly, the Kennedy administration was being blasted by newspapers all over the country. The criticism was the result of investigations of a man named Billie Sol Estes by other committees of Congress.

CHAPTER 7

A Texas Sunburst —
Billie Sol Estes

In the Spanish language, which is spoken widely in his native West Texas, the middle name of Billie Sol Estes means "sun." Billie Sol's sun certainly rose in a burst of glory. It went down behind a mountain of debt and fraud and disgrace.[1]

The meteoric career of the boy financier from Pecos peaked in January, 1963. Then, at the age of 37, Billie Sol seemed to have almost unlimited power and influence in the business and political worlds. By his skillful grasp of the government's incredibly complex agricultural programs, he had parlayed a small investment into a multimillion-dollar empire. The boy wonder gave the impression he was well on his way to becoming as rich as any of the big wheelers and dealers in Texas land and oil.

Billie Sol's financial career began during the Eisenhower administration. Politically, he began to roam the range as soon as the New Frontier, with its heavy Texas backing, took over. Billie Sol knew all too well that a little charm and a lot of money, spread in the right places, could do him no harm.

By January, 1962, when the New Frontier was a year old, Billie Sol was wheeling strong. In addition to affluence, he had earned honors. He had been appointed to a national committee to advise the Department of Agriculture on its cotton-program policies, and he was planning a trip to Washington to help his political friends celebrate the New Frontier's first birthday.

Billie Sol's financial empire was built on the government's grain-storage program. He collected $8 million from the government for storing grain from 1959 through 1961; $5 million of it he got in 1961 alone. At one time, he had 50 million bushels of grain in storage.

Billie Sol was also selling farmers anhydrous ammonia, an easily applied liquid fertilizer that achieves amazing results in increasing crop production. While this fertilizer usually sold for more than $90 a ton wholesale and at least $100 a ton retail, Billie Sol was selling it to Texas farmers for as little as $40 to $60 a ton. His aim was to corner the fertilizer market.

To get the money to manufacture the tanks to hold the fertilizer, Billie Sol resorted to a complicated mortgage scheme. He first sold fertilizer tanks to farmers and West Texas businessmen, promising them big profits and guaranteeing to relieve them of financial responsibility if anything went wrong. Estes took the mortgages for the tanks and sold them at a discount to a dozen finance companies. Then he used that money to buy tanks from the Superior Manufacturing Company of Amarillo, Texas.

Billie Sol was taking a loss on the anhydrous ammonia, which he bought from the Commercial Solvent Company, of New York. But that didn't faze him a bit. He made it up on the money he got from the government for storing grain. Once he had the fertilizer market cornered in West Texas, he could recoup.[2] That, at least, was his plan.

There also was good money to be made in growing crops, especially at government-guaranteed prices. Billie Sol had the land on which to grow cotton. But he couldn't get government-supported prices without a qualifying acreage allotment from the government. Since he never had grown cotton on much of the land, he had no allotment. This technicality could not stop a fellow of Estes' enterprise. He went about acquiring some allotments.

Under normal circumstances, the Agriculture Department bars the transfer of cotton-acreage allotments from one farm to another. The allotment remains attached to the land on which it was first granted. However, exceptions are made for farmers whose land is claimed under the doctrine of eminent domain for some public use. In such cases, a displaced farmer has the right to transfer his allotment to any new land he might buy within a three-year period.

Billie Sol and his agents scoured the countryside of the South and Southwest, coming up with 3,000 acres in Alabama, Georgia, Oklahoma and Texas owned by farmers whose cotton land was about to be taken over by the government.[3] Estes contracted to "sell" his land to the displaced farmers to make them eligible to transfer their allotments. But the "sales" were made with the understanding that the farmers would default on the contracts and that Billie Sol would take over both the mortgages and the cotton allotments, for which, of course, he paid the farmers.

This, in brief, was the dubious foundation of the Billie Sol Estes empire. It was an "illegal scheme and device," according to Agriculture Department reports later filed by cotton-allotment experts. But Billie Sol, it must be remembered, had friends in high places, and he was confident that if complications arose he could work things out. If there was anything Billie Sol wasn't lacking— as one could see from his demeanor at his subsequent trial and in his appearances before Congressional investigating committees —it was confidence.

In the summer of 1961, when Secretary of Agriculture Orville Freeman named Estes to the National Cotton Advisory Committee, Billie Sol's support came from Under-Secretary of Agriculture Charles S. Murphy. Murphy, who had worked at the White House under Harry Truman, headed the Johnson-for-President drive in the District of Columbia. When Lyndon Johnson became Vice-President, Murphy got the No. 2 job at Agriculture.

Murphy extended himself to push through the Estes appointment to the advisory committee. There were derogatory reports from both the F.B.I. and from Agriculture Department officials who were familiar with Billie Sol's activities. John E. Francis, chief of review for Agriculture's personnel office, and George Gould, also of the personnel office, both argued against it. They cited evidence supporting their belief that Estes was involved in illegal manipulations of cotton-acreage allotments. Francis concluded in his report that their findings were "sufficiently derogatory in nature that I recommend against subject's [Estes'] appointment." A memorandum added the damning information that "since the matter has been referred for consideration of prosecution, it appeared advisable to drop his name from consideration until the matter is cleared up."[4]

A summary report of the F.B.I. investigation told of an informant who said that Estes had obtained false and inflated financial statements from a number of farmers. Then, the informant alleged, Billie Sol had used the credit of these farmers to purchase fertilizer tanks. The F.B.I. memorandum said the office of the U.S. Attorney in Dallas had examined the case but had concluded there was insufficient evidence to warrant federal prosecution.

The Agriculture Department reports were submitted to the office of Secretary Freeman, but Freeman himself did not examine them. Nor did Murphy bother to tell his boss about the allegations against Estes. Instead, instructions went down from Murphy's office to Francis and Gould to "clean up" the derogatory reports.

The personnel office refused to remove the critical information. Murphy went ahead with the appointment anyway. The official papers carried a scrawled note that it should be done "notwithstanding" the reports about Billie Sol.

The public, of course, was unaware of the confidential reports at the time Estes was honored with this appointment. Nor did the public know about other help Billie Sol was about to receive. On Saturday morning, January 6, 1962, Under-Secretary Murphy called a meeting in his office.[5] Certain employees in the Commodity Stabilization Service (C.S.S.) took a dim view of Billie Sol's complicated allotment deals and were considering canceling the allotments pending further investigation.

On the other hand there were high-level political appointees eager to be helpful to the young millionaire from Texas. A Saturday-morning meeting was arranged by Murphy so that Billie Sol and his attorney, John Dennison, could have a chance to talk to the balky officials.

It didn't take much talking. On the following Monday, January 8th, Murphy and Emery E. (Red) Jacobs, the Agricultural Stabilization and Conservation Service deputy administrator for production adjustment, directed three subordinates to travel to Texas and restudy the Estes cotton allotments. The three were Thomas H. Miller, acting Southwest-area director of the C.S.S.; Thomas Gaschet, of the Agriculture Department's cotton division; and Howard Rooney, a staff member.

Factual reports by Gaschet and Rooney were consistent with prior studies opposing the allotment transfers. But it was brought out at subsequent Congressional hearings that Miller, acting under direct orders from Jacobs, wrote a report on January 12th which was favorable to Estes. In it, Miller recommended "that the allotment acreage transfers be allowed to stand for 1961 and subsequent years."

In later testimony, Miller conceded that he believed his report was contrary to law as well as to the facts. But, he said, he had slanted the report because he felt compelled to do so under instructions given to him by Red Jacobs, his superior.[6] He also indicated that Jacobs had given the impression that Murphy had given the orders for a report favorable to Estes. Murphy said he had no contact with Miller in the investigation and had left the matter up to Jacobs.

What was the secret of Billie Sol's success? He had a shrewd mind and a glib line of talk. He made friends easily. He also was a prolific name-dropper—and not without reason. Billie Sol, quick on the draw with his billfold, had contributed to the campaigns of such Texas Democrats as Senator Ralph Yarborough and Representative J. T. Rutherford, who represented the Pecos district. His billfold also opened to government officials who weren't campaigning. He was free with gifts of clothing, and even cash. Once Billie Sol gave $1,000 to Assistant Labor Secretary Jerry R. Holleman, the former president of the Texas A.F.L.-C.I.O. and a Johnson man. Holleman admitted receiving the gift. He rationalized that it was necessary to supplement his $20,000-a-year salary to keep up with the high expense of living in Washington.

Probably Billie Sol's most extravagant display of affection for his political friends took place during that January, 1962, trip to Washington. He withdrew $40,000 from the First National Bank of Pecos before he left. Just how—or if—he spent all of it has not been officially established. However, the McClellan-committee investigation showed he spent $6,000 on 60 tickets for the $100-a-seat birthday party of the New Frontier.[7]

Billie Sol also entertained liberally. The big spender was reportedly rebuffed, however, on one of his efforts to be hospitable. He had offered to pick up the tab for a lavish dinner for Vice-President Johnson that was being given by the then Secretary of Labor, Arthur Goldberg. Estes made the offer through his good friend Jerry Holleman. But Goldberg, later a Supreme Court Justice, told the press that he rejected the offer and paid for the Johnson dinner out of his own pocket.

The birthday party for the New Frontier may well have been the last occasion for celebration in Billie Sol's career. For around the end of January, 1962, dust was beginning to blow on the Estes empire. Stirring it up were the owners of the Pecos *Independent & Enterprise,* a small twice-weekly newspaper in Billie Sol's home town. These men were Alan Propp, the 38-year-old business manager; Dr. Harlow F. Avery, a physician; and Dr. Charles R. Sullivan, a dentist. Their editor was 29-year-old Oscar Griffin, who was later awarded a Pulitzer Prize for his work on the Estes case.

The owners were suspicious of the booming Estes fortune, being aware of his cozy relationship with liberal Democrats in Washington and having heard some disturbing reports about his dealings in mortgages on liquid-fertilizer tanks. When they started to research the mortgage records, they had no idea they were about to expose a national scandal. Though the number of mortgages placed on storage tanks for anhydrous ammonia was close to unbelievable, Griffin did not rush into print with the information. He let the data accumulate for more detailed study. Finally, he put together this picture: Estes had placed mortgages on more than 33,000 liquid-fertilizer storage tanks in eleven counties. That was enough anhydrous-ammonia fertilizer to take care of the whole state of Texas.[8] The total amount of money acquired through these mortgages exceeded $30 million.

Clearly, something was wrong. There were still a lot of unanswered questions in Griffin's mind as he put together the first articles. Why would there be 33,000 storage tanks in West Texas when 300 or 400 tanks would more than take care of local needs? Did this fantastic number of tanks really exist? If not, the mortgage complex could be a multimillion-dollar scandal and might ruin a good many people in the Pecos area.

The reaction to the stories in the *Independent & Enterprise* was not immediately explosive, for it was a small paper with almost no readers outside of Pecos. Also, the stories made no flat accusations of wrongdoing against government officials or against Billie Sol. They simply set out the facts, and set the stage for further investigations by local, state or federal officials.

Although the reaction was slow, the stories did have the desired impact. Local farmers and businessmen became concerned. The financial institutions that had lent millions of dollars to Estes became uneasy about their security. Initially, there was no panic. The lenders had mortgages on specific liquid-fertilizer tanks. If there was some problem, it could be handled best with a careful and sensible investigation. The representatives of the financial houses from New York to Los Angeles, eager to retain Billie Sol's good will, approached the whole investigation gingerly and diplomatically. If anything was a little out of line, they wanted to sit down with Billie Sol and work it out.

The financial men just couldn't believe that the affable young man from Pecos could have swindled them. Hadn't they dispatched their own representatives to examine the serial numbers of the fertilizer tanks pledged as security? They had, but they didn't know Billie Sol had tricked them the way the old Texas cattlemen used to outsmart the city slickers in cattle mortgaging.

The truth was there weren't 33,000 fertilizer tanks; there were only a few hundred. When the mortgagees' representatives came around to check up on them, Estes simply switched the serial numbers on the tanks he did have, to make them correspond with the numbers on whatever mortgage was being investigated.

One of Billie Sol's associates, J. S. (Mutt) Wheeler, operator of the Wheeler Fertilizer Company, in Pecos, caught on early in the game to what Estes was doing. He later told a Texas court of inquiry it was such an easy scheme to see through, it made him nervous. Since he had most of his money tied up with the fertilizer operations, he approached Billie Sol about it. Estes reassured him:

"Oh, they'll never catch up with you. These [financial] people are stupid."

Estes went on to tell him a story about a man who once borrowed a lot of money from a Kansas City bank, putting up cattle as security. When the "city boys" came out to inspect their security, the man drove them around in circles to several water holes, and each time showed them the same cattle, so eventually their "count" tallied with the number of cattle that had been mortgaged.

"We can do the same with tanks, and we'll starve them to death looking for equipment," Wheeler quoted Estes as saying.

Wheeler told this story under oath before the special court of inquiry directed by Texas Attorney General Will Wilson. He related that Estes had a special room in his Pecos office where he kept extra sets of serial numbers. When the agents of the financial houses began coming around to check up on the banks, Billie Sol would send tag-switching crews out ahead of them, directing their movements by shortwave radio. Back at the office, Billie Sol would detain the investigators with true Texas-style hospitality while his men romped around the countryside changing serial numbers. The investigators never seemed to catch on that they were counting the same tanks.

The fertilizer tanks were supposed to have been made at the Superior Manufacturing Company, in nearby Amarillo. It was operated by two friends of Billie Sol's. Actually, they manufactured relatively few tanks, but they made lots of extra serial-number plates. Plates are usually welded to a tank, but these were made with special brackets, so they could be simply and easily switched.

Estes dutifully kept up the monthly rentals and the monthly mortgage payments on the largely nonexistent tanks. This made everything look fine, for what sort of businessman would be putting out good money for rent and mortgage payments on something he knew wasn't there? He paid about $500,000 in rentals, and about the same amount on the mortgages.

The scheme went along quite well as long as only one mortgagee at a time sent investigators. But when the Pecos *Independent & Enterprise* dug up the records on the number of tanks, the mortgagees ganged up on Billie Sol. The investigators came faster than Billie Sol's radio-directed crews could switch the numbers.

The real trouble started when Frank Cain, a Dallas lawyer for the Pacific Finance Company, of Los Angeles, arrived in Pecos. His visit was unannounced. Cain was unable to find any fertilizer tanks carrying his firm's serial numbers. Then he visited the Superior Manufacturing Company and concluded it was "utterly impossible" for this small plant to have manufactured the 3,376 tanks that supposedly were fabricated there in January, 1962.

Cain told the Texas court of inquiry that he confronted Billie Sol with his suspicions, and Estes admitted that "there just aren't any tanks."

"You realize that you are subject to criminal penalties . . . as well as civil?" Cain said he told Estes.

Estes replied that he knew the money he raised by mortgaging the phantom tanks was "penitentiary money." Then he took the offensive. He told Cain that Pacific and the other finance companies would have to work with him if they expected to salvage anything on what he owed them.

Billie Sol spelled out the details of his big operation in the storage of government-owned grain. He boasted that it had brought him nearly $5 million in 1961. Then he began name-dropping. He had the "political connections" to keep this grain business, Billie Sol told Cain. He said he even had a card showing that he contributed $100,000 to the Democratic Party. He also pointed out that through his price cutting he had been able to obtain a virtual monopoly on the anhydrous-ammonia fertilizer business in West Texas.

For once, Billie Sol's pitch was not good enough. The creditors decided to lower the boom. They called him to a Dallas hotel on March 27, 1962. Unknown to Billie Sol, an F.B.I. agent was sitting in on the meeting. Estes reportedly made the same admissions about the fraudulent mortgages, and confidently suggested that the creditors had no choice but to go along with him.

In a conversation with Cain that day, Estes bragged he could call off an F.B.I. investigation by talking to Vice-President Lyndon B. Johnson. And later in the day he boasted that he actually had made a call and had been assured that the investigation would be killed, Cain related.

The F.B.I. agent present at the meeting had previously reported the essence of the case to the U. S. District Attorney in Dallas. The F.B.I. also informed the U. S. District Attorney that Estes had made some statements that indicated he might try to gather up all his available cash and skip to Brazil, as Ben Jack Cage, a Texas insurance swindler, had done a few years earlier.

Two days later, on March 29, 1962, the U. S. Attorney filed *an information* charging Estes with illegal interstate shipment of fraudulent chattel mortgages on the nonexistent fertilizer tanks.[9] That night, the F.B.I. arrested Estes at his $150,000 home in Pecos, and took him to jail. The government asked a $500,000 bond, but the court let Billie Sol go free on $100,000 bond.

On April 1st, Estes wired his resignation as a member of the National Cotton Advisory Committee. The resignation was accepted on April 6th—one day after his indictment by a federal grand jury. Billie Sol Estes had become too hot a potato for his political friends to handle. The Pecos newspaper had produced the evidence, the creditors and the F.B.I. had followed through, and

Billie Sol was on the skids. Once it started, the collapse took only a few weeks.

However, there remained many unanswered questions about where the national Democratic political administration had stood in regard to the Pecos manipulator. Will Wilson, the Attorney General of the State of Texas, a Democrat, said he believed the Agriculture Department in Washington had engaged in political "favoritism" toward Estes in a number of ways. First, he asked, why had Estes been named as a member of the National Cotton Advisory Committee? Second, why were Estes' grain-storage facilities expanded so rapidly? Third, why had there been no action against Estes for "illegal" purchases of cotton allotments from other farmers?

Although Attorney General Wilson was a Democrat, he had no love for the Kennedy-Johnson administration. Vice-President Johnson was regarded as the man behind the decision of John B. Connally to resign as Navy Secretary to seek the Texas Democratic gubernatorial candidacy in 1962. Will Wilson had wanted that nomination himself. He disliked Johnson intensely, and made statements indicating his belief that Johnson had influenced the Agriculture Department to favor Billie Sol.

Billie Sol's indictment was followed by Attorney General Wilson's announcement that he would convene a court of inquiry to investigate the Estes operations. While Agriculture Secretary Freeman contended the Estes matter had been handled without favoritism in his department, Wilson started delving into the earlier relationships between Estes and officials of the Kennedy administration. Initially, Freeman thought so little of the Estes matter that he permitted it to be handled by Under-Secretary Murphy—the man who had overruled personnel-office recommendations to appoint Estes to the advisory committee.

However, Freeman was forced to take notice when Will Wilson produced evidence that three officials of the Agriculture Department had accepted gifts of clothing or other favors from Estes.

The men named were Emery Jacobs, who had ordered the report on cotton allotments favorable to Estes; Dr. James T. Ralph, then an Assistant Secretary of Agriculture; and William E. Morris, an assistant to Dr. Ralph.[10]

Wilson's hearings in Texas produced testimony that Jacobs once had been on a shopping expedition with Billie Sol at the well-known Nieman-Marcus store in Dallas. According to testimony, Jacobs selected more than $1,000 worth of suits, shoes and shirts. He went into a dressing room with Billie Sol, came out with $1,000 cash in his hand, and paid for the clothing, Nieman-Marcus clerks testified. Under oath, Jacobs denied that he had received any money from Estes.

The Secretary of Agriculture said that Jacobs insisted he paid for the clothing with his own funds. Freeman said he was inclined to believe him and to disregard testimony produced by "that wild man, Will Wilson," who, Freeman said, was simply trying to embarrass the Kennedy administration. However, Secretary Freeman said that, in view of the doubts raised and the admissions, Jacobs had to go. Jacobs resigned on April 13, 1962.

Assistant Secretary Ralph and Morris had also gone on shopping trips with Estes. Morris had received a $100 cowboy hat. Ralph was measured for two expensive suits at a Dallas department store, but he denied the suits were ever delivered to him. Ralph and Morris each received $200 in money orders from Estes, but both said that they were embarrassed by the money and turned it over to the Democratic National Committee. Ralph had also charged some long-distance calls to Estes' account.

Freeman forced both men to resign. Though Freeman had described Jacobs as the type of friendly "political animal" that he liked, he hadn't liked Ralph. And Morris was a former administrative assistant to Representative H. Carl Anderson, a Minnesota Republican, so two of the firings were not so painful for Freeman.

By mid-April, 1962, the Texas court of inquiry had created an embarrassing situation for the Kennedy administration. The Billie Sol Estes scandal was being billed by Republicans as another Teapot Dome. The image-conscious President and Attorney General wanted the Estes matter handled aggressively, in a way that would demonstrate they meant what they said in the 1960 campaign about clean government. So orders went from the White House and from Attorney General Robert F. Kennedy to Secretary Freeman; he was to dig into the Estes case and to act immediately against anyone involved in favoritism or impropriety.

Freeman examined the facts briefly in consultation with Under-Secretary Murphy and other subordinates, who insisted there had been no favoritism for Estes. The testimony involving gifts for three Agriculture Department employees, Murphy and his associates said, represented the only dubious area. A preliminary investigation, Freeman said, indicated there was no shortage of grain in the Estes facilities.

He voiced the opinion that the entire Billie Sol Estes case was "ballooned out of proportion" by Republican critics and the Republican press. He advised the White House there was no "favoritism." President Kennedy accepted that assurance.

CHAPTER 8

The Lies of Texas
Are upon Us

In that same month of April, 1962, N. Battle Hales, a veteran career employee of the Department of Agriculture, faced a difficult problem. He knew that some of the papers in the Billie Sol Estes cotton allotments, which appeared to be based on improper transfers, had come across his desk in the fall of 1961. Hales, a lawyer in the Agricultural Stabilization and Conservation Service, believed that some of his superiors had let political favoritism influence their actions. He particularly suspected his immediate superior, Emery (Red) Jacobs, who seemed proud of his contacts with Billie Sol. It also appeared to Hales that Horace Godfrey, administrator of the A.S.C.S., and Under-Secretary of Agriculture Charles S. Murphy, were overly solicitous in regard to the Estes cotton-allotment matter.[1]

In October, 1961, Hales was present at meetings where the Estes cotton-allotment problem had been discussed. It was his personal view that the allotments should have been canceled and civil action instituted to try to recover several hundred thousand dollars from the Pecos millionaire. Hales also believed that the Agriculture Department should send the Estes file to the Justice Department with a recommendation for criminal prosecution.

The tough course of action against Estes that Hales advocated was rejected. He believed his appraisal of Billie Sol was vindicated, however, when the F.B.I. arrested Estes on March 29, 1962, and again when a federal grand jury indicted him and three associates on eight counts of fraud, conspiracy, and interstate shipment of fraudulent chattel mortgages.

None of the fraud charges involved the cotton-allotment transfers, but Hales now expected there would be a thorough probe of them. Certainly the ax would fall on his superiors who had let favoritism for Estes influence their decisions.

But as weeks went by, there were no signs of the housecleaning in Agriculture that Hales felt was necessary. Instead of a vigorous investigation, President Kennedy and Agriculture Secretary Freeman insisted there had been no favoritism for Billie Sol in the Agriculture Department. The President was willing to admit that there had been some questionable activity by a few New Frontier appointees who accepted gifts or money from the Texas millionaire. But he stuck to the claim that political contributions, entertainment and gift-giving by Estes had not resulted in wrong government decisions.

Hales wanted to warn President Kennedy and Freeman that a close examination of the files would demonstrate the very favoritism they were denying. But such action presented a troublesome problem for a career official schooled in "chain of command" thinking. The customary procedure would have been to report to Red Jacobs. Jacobs then would report to Horace Godfrey, Godfrey would report to Under-Secretary Murphy, and Murphy could carry it up to Freeman.

After some soul-searching, which he later described at official hearings, Hales decided it would be necessary for him to go straight to Secretary Freeman. He delayed going to the Secretary, for it was a dangerous step for a career civil servant. In addition, he hoped that the revelations coming out of Attorney General Will Wilson's State Court of Inquiry in Texas would prod Freeman to start asking his key political appointees more questions.

Attorney General Wilson's investigation brought only louder denials from Freeman and President Kennedy. They admitted "minor" errors. But it was plain that they resented the way the press treated the affair as a "national scandal." It also was obvious that they resented Wilson's inquiry.

It seemed to many White House correspondents that President Kennedy regarded the Billie Sol Estes affair as the sort of embarrassment that could happen to any administration. He also seemed to believe that his administration was taking perfectly reasonable steps to deal with the mess left on his doorstep. The President took the attitude that the newspapers weren't quite fair in not realizing this. One highly critical newspaper, the New York *Herald Tribune,* was even dropped from the President's reading list.

The President further seemed to feel that the papers were playing along with Attorney General Wilson. Wilson, of course, was charging the Kennedy administration with "favoritism" toward Billie Sol. He was saying specifically that his fellow Texan, Vice-President Lyndon B. Johnson, was a key man in keeping Billie Sol in a favored spot.

The administration, to its embarrassment, could not explain away one piece of evidence. It was a memorandum to Secretary Freeman from John Bagwell, Department of Agriculture counsel. It stated that "Vice President Johnson requested information on behalf of a representative of Billie Sol Estes" on the cotton-allotment problem.

Estes had wanted to get the farmers, who were transferring cotton allotments to his land, excused from appearing before the local agriculture committees. An earlier letter from Freeman to Vice-President Johnson had explained that it was possible in hardship cases to "excuse a displaced owner from such personal appearances" in cotton allotment transfers.

The Bagwell memorandum, dated April 11, 1962, also said: "We understand that the Vice President has recently discussed this matter with the Under Secretary [Murphy]."[2] There were no details on the nature of the discussions.

Those were the only official records showing that Vice-President Johnson had been in touch with the Agriculture Department about the Estes cotton-allotment transfers. There was later testimony involving two of Johnson's assistants in contacts for Estes. Kennedy-administration officials, including Freeman and Murphy, stoutly defended Vice-President Johnson against insinuations that Billie Sol might be his protégé. Johnson, as he had done before when unpleasant allegations came up that needed explaining, simply made himself unavailable for questioning by the press.

But rampaging Will Wilson, in a television speech on April 27th, pointed out the connection between Estes and one of Johnson's chief advisers. He called attention to a memorandum to Estes from Cliff Carter, personal assistant to Johnson. Carter, who specialized in Texas political matters, noted a recommendation from Estes that William (Bill) Mattox, of Pecos, be appointed to a state Agricultural Stabilization and Conservation committee in Texas. Carter promised to put Billie Sol's "fine" letter about Mattox "in the proper hands." Mattox never did get the state A.S.C. appointment, but he was elected to a county A.S.C. committee in the Pecos area and had a role in the initial cotton-allotment decisions that were favorable to Estes.

Carter admitted Estes gave him at least ten of his sixty tickets for the $100-a-plate party in January, 1962, celebrating the anniversary of the inauguration of President Kennedy. Carter told investigators he had distributed Billie Sol's tickets to "stenographers, typists, doorkeepers, and others." Additional testimony brought the name of Walter Jenkins into the record of administration contacts with Estes.

Will Wilson charged that Billie Sol's close relationship with high government officials, his contributions to political campaigns, and his purchase of tickets for Democratic fund-raising affairs had set the stage for his "favored" treatment at the Agriculture Department. When Freeman and other high officials kept insisting that Estes had received no special treatment, Wilson, though a Democrat, emphatically charged that the Kennedy administration was covering up the facts.

The Republicans joined in enthusiastically.

Meanwhile, N. Battle Hales felt he could wait no longer to let the Secretary of Agriculture know of his suspicions about Estes and the favoritism he felt the Texan was getting from some of Freeman's subordinates.[3] On April 20th, he went to Freeman's office.

He did not get in to see the Secretary. Instead, he was sidetracked to Freeman's administrative assistant, Tom Hughes. Hughes first indicated that Hales could talk with Freeman. Then he changed his mind and shunted him to F.B.I. agents who were investigating the Estes case. Hales later told the McClellan-subcommittee investigator that as he unfolded his story to Hughes, the Freeman aide began treating him as if he were the culprit, rather than the accuser.

Then, after agreeing to talk with the F.B.I. agents, Hales related, he suddenly found that orders had been issued by the Agriculture Department, barring him from access to his office files and from his office. He had wanted to take certain reports from his files that would corroborate his charges of favoritism for Estes. The Department flatly refused to let him go through his own files—even with the F.B.I. present.

What happened next reflects no credit on the Department of Agriculture, the United States government, or the processes of justice and fair play as we expect them to be carried out in a democracy. It is an incident that one would expect to happen in a Communist police state, not in the United States of America.

On April 24th, Hales had a talk with his secretary, Mary Kimbrough Jones, a fifty-one-year-old woman who had been an employee of the Department for twenty-five years. He confided to her the troubles he was having about his office files since he had voiced his suspicions to Secretary Freeman's aide.

Next day after Hales had been locked out, some of Freeman's staff members came to his office to take custody of the files containing the Estes reports. Miss Jones protested loudly. Following a confusing altercation, she was forcibly removed, taken to the office of Dr. Lee K. Buchanan, chief of the Department's health division, and locked in. A short time later, she was taken to the District of Columbia General Hospital and confined in a mental ward.

The on-the-record version of what happened when Miss Jones and Freeman's staff confronted each other is unclear. What is clear is the principle that was trampled. It came to light with the words of a U. S. Senator.

Senator John J. Williams charged on the Senate floor, on May 17, 1962, that the Agriculture Department had "railroaded" Miss Jones to a mental ward. The Senator declared that the Department's medical chief had "arbitrarily" ordered her hospitalized, without consulting her personal physician or members of her family.[4]

"Never have I seen . . . the rights of an individual . . . so seriously violated," Senator Williams told the Senate. "She was placed in a mental institution on April 25. But there is no record anywhere . . . [that] any doctor signed the proper commitment papers until two days later. . . . I venture to say that if some of the rest of us had been confined in such a cell, sleeping, as she did, on a mattress on the floor, we would not be quite normal."

Senator Williams stated that government regulations require that the family be notified before any person is committed to a mental institution, but this was not done in this case. He pointed out that not even Dr. Buchanan signed a statement to commit Miss Jones that day, but left the matter in the policeman's hands.

Senator Williams went on to point out the difference in the law regarding taking a person out of a private home and taking a person out of a government building. If Miss Jones had been in a private home, legal procedures would have required the sworn signatures of two citizens and two doctors to commit her to a mental institution.

"However, from a public building," the Senator said, "a person can be sent off to a mental institution . . . without the certification or examination of any doctor or anyone else except the police officer.

"Once that patient is committed to the institution, she has this 'mental observation' charge on her record and from that moment on it is up to her to prove her sanity."

Senator Williams said he had talked to Miss Jones' personal physician, and was told that there was nothing in her medical history to warrant her commitment to a mental institution. The Sena-

tor also pointed out that the record showed Miss Jones was taken
to the hospital and committed on the signature of a District of
Columbia police patrolman, who had seen her for only a few minutes. Senator Williams said he had questioned the policeman, who
told him he had been summoned to Agriculture to take Miss Jones
out of the doctor's office. Dr. Buchanan told the policeman, the
Senator related, that Miss Jones "had been hitting him over the
head with a shoe, and that he [the doctor] didn't know what to do
with her."

The police officer, questioned by Senator Williams, said the only
unusual action by Miss Jones was that she paced back and forth
and walked over to a window. He said she made no effort to get out
of the window. He said she showed no inclination to hit anyone
while he was there.

Senator Williams declared that Dr. Buchanan "had carried her
from her office" and told her that "she was going to be sent to a
psychiatric ward."

"So, in the struggle, she hit him with a shoe," Senator Williams
told the Senate. He added that if he had been in Miss Jones' place,
Dr. Buchanan "would be fortunate if it were only a shoe he was
hit with!"

Miss Jones was discharged from the hospital twelve days after
being committed (including five days in a locked cell). The reports
stated she was pronounced sane. However, another official report
later stated that she was ill and needed medical care.

Senator Williams attacked the Agriculture Department's claims
that the alleged illness was proof that it was proper to have had
her committed. "I say to you Senators," Williams declared, "if your
wife, your sister, or your daughter were put in a cell for 12 days,
I think you would find that she would be sick too. . . . That was a
horrible experience, and to further try to discredit . . . [Miss
Jones] now after what she has gone through is even more reprehensible."

Senator Williams said that Miss Jones was "disturbed" by the
fact that Hales had been locked out of his office. Before the inci-

dent with the files, he said, "there was not a single blemish on her record," and "she had a very high efficiency rating."

"There was no trouble prior to the rumbling of the Estes case," Senator Williams asserted. "Certainly she got nervous. I venture to say that the loyal secretary of any employer would likewise have felt nervous and disturbed when her files were being ransacked. Remember that at this point she could well be the credible witness as to what was in those files."

The Delaware Republican viewed the actions of the Agriculture Department to commit the secretary of Billie Sol Estes' accuser as part of an overall effort to cover up the record in the case. But, he declared, the treatment accorded Miss Jones was even more disturbing than favoritism and fraud.

"The loss of dollars can be replaced," the Senator said. "But we can never repay [Miss Jones] for the suffering she has had to endure.

"We have heard a great deal about what a great crime it is if someone is denied the right to vote. . . . But there are rights that are more precious even than the right to vote. I think it is about time that some of those who expressed such great interest in civil rights and the dignity of the individual should begin to express some concern about what is happening right here in the Nation's capital."

Hales, too, was disturbed at what he considered the brutal treatment of his former secretary. But even before Miss Jones was released from the hospital, he had new problems of his own. It had become apparent to Hales that he was not going to get a chance to tell his story directly to Secretary Freeman. In the meantime, Robert E. Baskin, a Washington reporter for the Dallas *Morning News,* had been in touch with him. Hales told Baskin he had information that he believed proved "favoritism" on the part of Agriculture officials toward Billie Sol.

Baskin printed the story on May 4th—one day after Secretary Freeman finally held a press conference.[5] That was two weeks after Hales had tried to see him, and more than a week after Mary Jones was carted off to the hospital. Freeman had proclaimed:

"There has not yet been evidence of one bit of favoritism and special privilege to Billie Sol Estes."

As a matter of fact, Freeman had told the press, Billie Sol, "rather than getting favors . . . might well complain he had been dealt with very harshly here." A "marketing fee" had been imposed upon him, while he was on the Advisory Committee, for "over-planting" cotton.[6]

A reporter promptly asked: "Mr. Secretary, why did you appoint Mr. Estes to the Cotton Advisory Committee after he had been fined for overplanting on his cotton allotment?"

"Actually, if I remember the sequence of things right, he was appointed to the committee before his being fined," Freeman answered.

Baskin's story brought out the fact that Hales had been barred from his office and shifted to another job after he had tried to tell the Secretary of Agriculture about Billie Sol. He reported that it had been Hales who recommended strict action against Estes in connection with the illegal transfers. He further named Murphy, Godfrey and Jacobs as the officials who took part in the decisions that circumvented the stiff criminal and civil actions that Hales proposed.

Agriculture officials immediately arranged another press conference to answer the Baskin story. Hales was summoned to it. So were Murphy, Godfrey, Hughes and other officials.

Answering questions from reporters, Hughes, the Secretary's aide, admitted that Hales had tried to see Freeman. He acknowledged that it was he who had decided it would be "better" for Hales to talk with the F.B.I. Hughes admitted that Hales had been barred from his office and his files, but said this was simply because Hales suddenly had been transferred to another job.

For the rest of the conference, the Department officials concentrated on discrediting Hales' story.

But Hales refused to be cowed by the open antagonism displayed by his superiors—the men who could make or break his career. While those superiors listened, Hales repeated his charges for the benefit of the assembled newspapermen. Then he made a detailed explanation that led, among other things, to the story of the strange death of Henry Marshall, a Department of Agriculture representative in Pecos. To this day, the cause of Marshall's death has not been clearly established, and specifically whether it was suicide or murder.

On November 14, 1961, Hales related, he had attended a meeting in the office of Horace Godfrey. "At the time of the meeting," he said, "the individuals present . . . expressed the opinion that Billie Sol Estes' cotton-pool agreements were illegal and that penalties should be assessed on his 1961 production allotment. Godfrey actively objected to it on the grounds that the only witness who could conclusively state that Estes did not receive [proper] approval from the Texas ASCS office was now dead—that's Henry Marshall."

Hales added that Godfrey had said the penalty against Estes in connection with the 1961 crop should not be assessed because of a technicality in the regulations, that Godfrey then declared he "knew Mr. Estes," that he had worked with him on the Advisory Committee, and that he considered him "a very fine man" who "would not intentionally do anything wrong."

When Hales told the press conference that Godfrey had described Billie Sol as "a very fine man," Godfrey lost his temper.

"When you get through," Godfrey flared, "I want to correct the whole damn thing!" He later denied he had even met Estes.

Hales read from a summary report of the meeting at which he and others present advised Godfrey that another government witness had been present at a key meeting between the late Henry Marshall and an attorney for Estes. This man was available to testify to support the government position.

"This witness was Taylor Allen, the Southwest Area Director in charge of the administration of this [cotton allotment] program in the Southwestern States, including Texas," Hales told the press conference. A signed statement from Taylor Allen was among government records.

"With the exception of Godfrey," Hales said, "all of the individuals present at this meeting agreed that Allen's signed statement

was sufficient evidence to cause cancellation of Estes' cotton allotment." Godfrey terminated the [November 14th] meeting by
advising those present not to take any further action until he met
with Under-Secretary Charles Murphy and Emery E. Jacobs.

Hales told the press conference that he contacted the cotton
division and the general counsel's office a few days after this meeting.

"I was advised by these individuals that Godfrey, Jacobs and
the Under Secretary, Mr. Murphy, had made the determination not
to cancel the 1961 cotton allotment of Estes, and that further action was not possible with respect to his 1962 allotment until further meetings had been held."

Hales had charged that the cotton-allotment transfers by Estes
violated the law, and were recognized by the majority of the top
officials as violations of the law in November, 1961—a month
before Estes was made a member of a reshuffled and formalized
National Cotton Advisory Committee.

Even after the press conference, Godfrey and the Agriculture
Department press office continued to claim that no favoritism had
been shown to Estes. The Department's press agents explained
that the cotton-allotment matter was "still pending." Since there
had been no final decision, there could be no "favoritism," they
reasoned. However, four months earlier, on January 8th, Under-
Secretary Murphy had withdrawn an order that would have canceled Billie Sol's fraudulently obtained cotton allotments, and
Red Jacobs had sought approval for those transfers.

It soon became plain to reporters who were following the Estes
scandal that Agriculture Department officials were conducting a
determined whispering campaign against Hales. Newsmen heard
that he was "disgruntled" because he hadn't received a promotion; that he was "unstable"—and worse. However, Hales made a
sound presentation at the press conference—and the records seemed
to corroborate much of his story.

Public criticism of the Agriculture Department continued to
mount. Then the first evidence came to light that Estes had given
the $1,000 to Assistant Secretary of Labor Jerry Holleman. Holle-

man admitted accepting it to supplement his $20,000 salary as a sub-cabinet officer. On May 7, 1962, Freeman held another press conference. He still insisted that there was "no evidence" of favoritism for Estes, and again claimed the whole Estes investigation was being "ballooned" out of proportion by Republican critics and the press.

"All that appears so far is that three people may have received favors from Estes," Freeman said. "There is no indication that any of the three made any decision under the influence of these gifts."

Under-Secretary Murphy appeared with Freeman at the conference. He told reporters that a group of prominent Texans, including Senator Ralph W. Yarborough, the Democratic Senator from Texas, had recommended Billie Sol for the advisory post. Lyndon B. Johnson had made no such recommendation, Murphy explained for his own political mentor.

Public pressure persisted, and two days later, on May 9th, the Agriculture Department announced it had imposed penalties of $554,162 against Billie Sol Estes for violating the federal cotton-planting regulations.[7] His scheme for leasing and then buying back his own Texas farmland was recognized as a device for trafficking illegally in cotton allotments.

Although it had taken a long time, Secretary Freeman finally had come around to the view that an outraged employee, N. Battle Hales, had wanted to give him six months earlier. It had taken a national scandal of administration-shaking proportions to make the Department move to recover the government's money. And were any apologies made to the "railroaded" Mary K. Jones, or to N. Battle Hales? None.

CHAPTER 9

The Setting Sun

While the Agriculture Department was doing its best to discredit N. Battle Hales, who had touched off the investigation of Billie Sol Estes' fraudulent cotton allotments, Hales was getting a more favorable hearing from Chairman John L. McClellan, of the Senate Permanent Subcommittee on Investigations.

The committee's counsel, Donald O'Donnell, and his assistant, Paul E. Kamerick, had found many things wrong with the functioning of the cotton-allotment program in Agriculture. "It is very difficult," Kamerick told the subcommittee at the opening session of its hearings on June 27, 1962, "to attribute this entirely to organizational breakdown. It is difficult not to suspect bad faith."[1]

Secretary Freeman continued his periodic denials that Billie Sol Estes had been the recipient of any "favoritism," and President Kennedy reiterated that he had the "greatest confidence" in Freeman's "integrity." Freeman's behavior in the Estes case did the administration no good, however. For long periods he was unavailable for questioning by reporters. When he did appear, it was as a belligerent apologist for the Department's policies. Even when he fired Red Jacobs, the effect was watered down by the Secretary's obvious reluctance to do it. Firing Jacobs, Freeman said, "was like cutting off my right arm."

In all, only five heads had rolled as a result of the admitted "errors" and "mistakes," and the alleged maladministration and possible corruption. Three others forced to resign in addition to Jacobs were Assistant Secretary of Agriculture James Ralph; his administrative aide, William E. Morris; and, in the Labor Department, Assistant Secretary Jerry Holleman, who had admitted taking money from Estes. Also, the Agriculture Department "suspended" William P. Mattox, a member of the Stabilization and Conservation Service committee in Reeves County, Texas. Mattox, who had been involved in the approval of cotton-allotment transfers to Estes, allegedly had accepted plane fare and hotel accommodations from Billie Sol.[2]

Under-Secretary Charles Murphy and A.S.C.S. Administrator Horace Godfrey, who were deeply involved in the questionable decisions affecting Billie Sol Estes, remained firmly entrenched in the administration. At a White House press conference on May 17, 1962, a reporter asked: "Mr. President, with the word 'scandal' again in the wind in Washington, would you care to comment on the Billie Sol Estes affair and tell us if you believe that Secretary Freeman has handled the case properly?"

"Well, as you know, the Billie Sol Estes case came to public attention when the United States Government indicted him on April 5," President Kennedy said.

"We requested bail of $500,000 which was not granted, and it was [cut] down to $100,000 and since that time we have been conducting a very thorough investigation with nearly 75 members of the FBI involved. . . . These affairs are most complicated. . . . Estes dealt through almost 23 companies.

"I can assure you that if members of the Executive Branch are involved, any improprieties shown, they will be immediately taken action against and immediately disciplined appropriately."

Then the President launched into a defense of Freeman that dwelt at some length on the early political and military career of the ex-Minnesota governor. "I have the greatest confidence in the integrity of Secretary Freeman," he said. "I point out again that the matter of Billie Sol Estes came to public attention in the way that it has because the United States Government, this administration, indicted him."

A reporter observed that "it seems uncontradicted that Mr. Estes was around town, spreading quite a little money around, trying to be helpful." Did the President know of any evidence that these expenditures had led to Billie Sol's appointment to the Advisory Committee, or to favored treatment for him in the cotton-allotment dealings, or in government grain storage?

"These are all matters being investigated," the President replied. "I think Secretary Freeman has already suggested that he has not been able to determine such favoritism, but I believe that we should wait until the investigations are completed. I am not informed about all the details of all transactions."

Then the usually articulate Mr. Kennedy went on: "All I know is that as of today, it does not appear that Mr. Estes was given, as Secretary Freeman has said, but I don't take anything for granted in this matter. This is why we have 76 [sic] FBI agents working on it. As I have said, the Department of Agriculture has assigned a penalty against him of nearly $600,000. . . . I am sorry our bail was not accepted of a half million dollars. This Government is staying right on Mr. Estes' tail."

There was little doubt that the Kennedy administration finally was "staying right on Mr. Estes' tail." However, what the McClellan subcommittee wanted to find out was why it hadn't been on his tail a year earlier, before the Estes case had become a nationally known scandal. And how had Billie Sol been able to expand his grain-storage business to the point where he was getting more than $5 million a year from the federal government?

At another press conference, a week later, President Kennedy admitted there had been "improprieties," but said: "There is no evidence that the Billie Sol Estes fraud has cost the United States Government any money."

The President could truthfully deny knowledge of government losses at that time. The fact, as later established by the McClellan subcommittee, is that he was unaware of many of the details in the Estes case. Much of the information actually was not given by Murphy to the White House, to the Justice Department, or even to Secretary Freeman himself until just before the Senate subcommittee opened its investigations.

Once they got this information, officials of the Kennedy administration realized they had a serious political problem on their
hands. The Republicans, too, tumbled to the fact that they had a
real issue to use against the Kennedy administration.

Now, behind the scenes in the investigation, political infighting
broke out. On June 22nd, two Republican members of the Mc-
Clellan subcommittee held a press conference to expose what they
said were efforts to "intimidate" them.

Senator Carl Curtis, of Nebraska, and Senator Karl Mundt, of
South Dakota, disclosed that they had obtained four affidavits showing that the Agriculture Department was making a survey of all of
their correspondence with the Department since 1953. Senator
Mundt named Thomas Hughes, Secretary Freeman's executive
assistant, as the one who had initiated this "unusual project."

The two Senators charged: "This raises the serious question as
to what the Secretary of Agriculture has to hide and why such tactics of desperation are resorted to in an effort to impede or intimidate the complete investigation."

Mundt said Freeman was a "politician" who was involved
with some White House figures in the alleged "intimidation" effort.
He said that he had been "informed" that excerpts from the correspondence of the two Republican Senators were to be released to
newsmen who were close to the White House, so that it "might be
twisted or distorted to create implications not substantiated by the
facts."

Mundt read an affidavit from Hughes in which Freeman's top
administrative aide admitted that he had initiated the correspondence check, but denied that it was for any purpose except to
obtain the views of the two Republican Senators on some of the
problems involved in the Estes grain-storage problems.

Secretary Freeman acknowledged that he knew of the survey,
but said he had discussed it only casually with Hughes. "I am surprised at the violent reaction of Mundt and Curtis to the department's review of their correspondence," Secretary Freeman
commented blandly. "There is not, and has never been, any intention to make public any material in the file, but rather to review

matters of concern to the senators by examining inquiries they have directed to the department."

But Senator Mundt declared that he regarded it as a "reprehensible act" and an effort at "blackmail." He added: "This attempt to thwart the investigation will be unsuccessful."

Shortly afterward, the Agriculture Department's correspondence check on the two Republican Senators was halted.

At this stage of the Estes investigation, this correspondent wrote a news story revealing that Thomas H. Miller, a cotton-allotment expert in the Agriculture Department, had given the McClellan subcommittee an affidavit admitting he had written a slanted report favorable to Estes. He said he had done it under specific directions from Emery Jacobs. He also stated that Red Jacobs had told him Under-Secretary of Agriculture Murphy wanted the report to be written in a manner favorable to Estes. Prior to writing this report, Miller stated, he had opposed action favorable to Estes. But he said he felt compelled to favor Estes because that was what Jacobs said his superiors wanted.

Simultaneous with these disclosures, a House Government Operations Subcommittee, headed by Representative L. H. Fountain (Democrat, North Carolina), specifically investigating the fertilizer-tank frauds, heard from Frank Cain, the Dallas lawyer who had investigated Billie Sol's affairs on behalf of a finance company.

Cain told the House investigators that Billie Sol had bragged of his political influence with both Democrats and Republicans. Cain said Estes told him that as long as he had the government grain contracts, he eventually could pay off the fraudulent mortgages. But he quoted Estes as saying he needed about $100,000 to $200,000 a year "for payoffs" to keep his grain and cotton businesses going.[3]

The payoff reference was never pursued or substantiated. (The $40,000 that Estes had withdrawn from his bank account just before going to Washington for the Kennedy anniversary in January, 1962, had been revealed earlier.) In this same conversation, Cain said Estes told him he was having some trouble because the "cotton allotments were tied up," but that he would "get it untied." Cain said that Estes boasted he had friends in high places in the Agriculture Department.

At the opening of the McClellan-subcommittee hearings, Assistant Counsel Kamerick charged that the Agriculture Department had been subject, at the least, to incredibly poor management in the handling of the Estes cotton allotments.

"We were handicapped by the failure of employees to make and retain minutes or any other written record of significant meetings or events," Kamerick said in his opening statement.

"Almost all of the meetings and conferences involved in the Estes allotment case were recorded only in the memory of those who attended. Thus, it is now impossible to produce records that should have been made but were not. It is inevitable that the department itself must be handicapped by these and other deficiencies. At the outset, some difficulty was experienced in locating documents believed to be germane to this investigation."

The subcommittee lawyer stated flatly that the investigation showed that "Under Secretary Murphy overrode an adverse recommendation by the review and adjudication division of personnel and directed the appointment of Billie Sol Estes to the . . . Cotton Advisory Committee."

Details were disclosed as to how one of Freeman's administrative assistants issued orders to "clean up" a derogatory report that was standing in the way of naming Billie Sol to the Advisory Committee. When John E. Francis, head of the review and adjudication division, declined to change the report or his recommendation, Estes' appointment was made by Murphy anyway.

Secretary Freeman appeared before the McClellan subcommittee to explain the occurrences that had put his job and his reputation in jeopardy. He took the offensive by admitting that Murphy was responsible for the Estes appointment, and that it had been a "mistake."[4] He admitted the appointment was made in the face of derogatory reports. But he contended that Murphy had acted "in good faith."

The Secretary said Murphy did not consult him on the appointment, and had not talked with him prior to the controversial decision in January, 1962, to rescind an earlier order that would have canceled Estes' illegal cotton allotments.

Although Freeman placed the responsibility for both decisions on Murphy, he then excused him by saying they were simple mistakes that looked worse by hindsight than they would have looked at the time. He emphasized that in 1961 and early 1962, Estes was very well thought of in his community and by many persons in the Agriculture Department. When it was pointed out that his own personnel office, in the fall of 1961, thought it was a bad appointment, Freeman still maintained that it was simply "a mistake" and "not favoritism."

Although Chairman McClellan was an aggressive interrogator, some Democrats on the committee assumed a neutral stance. As the hearings progressed, Senator Sam Ervin, of North Carolina, and Senator Edmund S. Muskie, of Maine, both Democrats, became outspoken champions of the thesis that no special treatment was given Billie Sol.

While the persistent defense efforts of Senators Ervin and Muskie helped Freeman over his trouble, it appeared that the Kennedy administration might be forced to sacrifice Under-Secretary Murphy. Freeman had placed the responsibility for the two most controversial Estes decisions on Murphy. The Under-Secretary was known as a "Johnson man," and it was not immediately clear how loyal President Kennedy and Attorney General Kennedy felt toward him.

Murphy was on the spot, and he knew it. Under questioning by Chairman McClellan, Murphy admitted that the investigative reports "on their face" contained sufficient information to indicate that Estes' acts were illegal. He pictured himself as harassed by hundreds of "important problems," too busy to give full attention to every detail. He insisted there had been no political favoritism involved in the dealings with Estes, and said he only had made "an effort to grant Estes the fairness and justice every American has a right to expect in dealing with the government."

McClellan pointed out that the F.B.I. reports gave strong indication that Estes was involved in fraudulent transactions in the mortgaging of storage tanks for liquid fertilizer. Murphy conceded that a more diligent investigation by the Agriculture Department might have unveiled this fraud earlier.

Referring to a 140-page report on the cotton allotments, McClellan reminded Murphy that he had access to all of this information at the time that he had talked with Estes on January 6, 1962. McClellan pointed out that the unusual size and dimensions of the acreage transferred, the lack of water, the lack of proper descriptions—all these should have called attention to the fact that Estes was not engaging in bona-fide sale of land necessary for a legal transfer of cotton allotment. "I agree that I should have known," Murphy said meekly. He said he had not examined the details of the transactions.

The investigation took a bizarre turn when Chairman McClellan began questioning Murphy about Henry Marshall. Marshall, the Agriculture Department's man-on-the-scene in Pecos, was reported in 1961 to be moving aggressively to cancel the illegal transfers of cotton allotments to Billie Sol Estes. The tall, fifty-one-year-old cotton-program expert had made a record indicating he would not be budged. On June 3, 1961, Marshall was found dead in a grassy lane on his ranch near Franklin, Texas. His death was ascribed by local officials to "suicide" without benefit of an autopsy.

Senator John Williams, prodding the federal government about the Estes case, called the Senate's attention to the mysterious death. On May 7, 1962, he told his colleagues it seemed strange to him that Marshall should shoot himself in the midst of his secret investigation of Billie Sol's affairs. It was more than strange, he went on, that Marshall, a Texan, should shoot himself five times with a bolt-action rifle. A bolt-action rifle requires someone to pull the bolt.[5]

At about the time Williams was telling the Senate of the strange end of Henry Marshall, Secretary Freeman was explaining at a press conference that, since "the key figure [Marshall] is now dead," further investigation of the cotton-allotment transfer was difficult. He did not mention the fact that Taylor Allen, Marshall's superior, had written a report stating that Marshall had opposed the transfer plan proposed by Billie Sol and his lawyers, and that Allen was still around and could be a witness.

Under questioning by McClellan, Murphy told the subcommittee that he and his subordinates accepted the word of Estes and his attorney that the late Mr. Marshall had given them verbal approval for transfers of the cotton allotments. Murphy contended that since Marshall was dead, he did not see any way of checking whether Estes and his attorney were telling the truth.

This turned out to be another instance of Murphy's not looking into the details thoroughly. Taylor Allen, Marshall's superior, testified before the McClellan subcommittee later that Marshall had not approved the allotment deal. Furthermore, Allen told the subcommittee, he had reported the fact of the dead man's disapproval in a report that was in Murphy's possession.

Now that the McClellan subcommittee turned the spotlight on the "suicide" who had shot himself five times, the Texas state police entered the case, and obtained court approval to exhume the body. The police found that, in addition to the five bullet holes, Marshall's lungs—a year after burial—contained fifteen per cent carbon monoxide. They reasoned that Marshall must have inhaled at least twice that much carbon monoxide before he died.

Homer Garrison, Jr., director of the Texas Department of Public Safety, wrote Senator McClellan that his department was continuing the investigation "based on the theory that he [Marshall] was murdered."

Suicide would have been almost impossible, Garrison informed McClellan: "It would have been necessary for Mr. Marshall to have had sufficient control of his equilibrium to have fired five bullets into the front of his left abdomen with a .22-caliber bolt-action rifle, taking it down each time and ejecting the shell.

"The five bullets passing through his body traveled at substantially the same angle, giving further indication that he would have had to have good control of his faculties. From the direction of travel of the bullets, Mr. Marshall would have had to hold the butt of the gun in an upward position, causing the bullets to range downward from the entrance wounds, which would have been even more difficult."

The report also stated: "Investigation revealed that it was difficult for Mr. Marshall to straighten out his right arm, due to prior injury; therefore, it would have been necessary for him to pull the trigger with his left hand."[6]

Garrison also made reference to a "serious brain injury and cut over his [Marshall's] left eye, causing his eye to protrude." There was other evidence, he said, that some severe struggle had taken place near the pickup truck where his body was discovered.

Moreover, no blood was found at the spot where Marshall's body actually was discovered, Director Garrison pointed out. Blood was found a few feet away, where there were signs that a struggle had taken place.

The Texas police official's report was placed in the subcommittee's record of the Estes inquiry. Chairman McClellan decided, however, not to make a full-scale investigation into the mysterious death. The circumstantial nature of the evidence and the nebulous connection with the Estes case prompted this comment in the Senate committee's final report: "The subcommittee has grave reservations, shared by others, about the possibility of suicide under these highly unusual circumstances. However, no testimony was heard by the subcommittee which indicates any connection between his death and his decision with respect to cotton allotments except Mr. Wilson C. Tucker testified that Estes stated to him that this pool allotment matter had caused the death of one person and then asked him if he knew Henry Marshall."[7]

N. Battle Hales had his chance to tell the McClellan subcommittee what he knew about the way Estes was treated at the Agriculture Department in Washington. The career civil servant, whose career was pretty well wrecked because he talked out of turn, testified that "Billie Sol Estes received extremely favored treatment from the Department of Agriculture in a manner unprecedented in my 21 years in this department."[8]

Hales declared that Estes had been in violation of the criminal law on fraud, which carries a penalty of up to $10,000 and a five-year prison term.

"Last November I could not understand why this case was not referred for criminal prosecution," Hales told the McClellan subcommittee. "Now I understand too well."

Even after this testimony, Murphy continued to defend the Department's failure to initiate criminal action. He also defended the Department's slowness in demanding the $554,000 in penalties from Estes. Time after time, Murphy said that he simply was trying to give Estes "due process of law."

Democratic Senators Ervin and Muskie stoutly defended Murphy and the Agriculture Department. But Republican Senators Mundt and Curtis charged that Estes was not given the same treatment that average citizens might have expected, in view of the F.B.I.'s adverse report on the tricky cotton dealings.

Chairman McClellan avoided stating a conclusion on the motives of Murphy and others in the Estes matter. He declared that there were "mistakes" made by the Department of Agriculture in its appointment of Estes to the advisory committee, and in its handling of the cotton allotments.

Later, on the "Meet the Press" television show, McClellan said there "were plenty of red flags" to warn the Department of Agriculture about Estes. He declared that while "wrong decisions" had been made by Murphy and others, the evidence was "not conclusive as to the motivation of Murphy."

The Kennedy administration now took the line that the Billie Sol Estes mess was something it inherited from the Eisenhower administration.

And Billie Sol himself became the target of a New Frontier crusade, as Secretary Freeman tried to demolish the rising Republican claim that Estes was Freeman's creature.

The government ordered the removal of $3 million worth of government grain from storage facilities owned by Estes and his associates, and indicated that all grain would be removed from the Estes-connected facilities over the course of about eighteen months.

In El Paso, a federal grand jury indicted Estes and three associates on further charges of mail fraud and illegal transportation of fraudulent securities, in connection with the mortgages on fertilizer tanks. A federal grand jury in Dallas indicted Estes on charges of misrepresenting his financial position to the Commodity Credit Corporation, by presenting a false financial statement in connection with a government storage agreement. Other state and federal indictments followed.

Estes was forced into bankruptcy court, where it was initially claimed his assets were about $20 million, but that he owed more than $35 million. He pleaded the Fifth Amendment on a number of questions dealing with his financial position. A federal referee-in-bankruptcy ordered all his assets sold to the highest bidder for $8 million.

On November 7, 1962, Billie Sol Estes was convicted of fraud by a jury in the state court in Tyler, Texas. He was sentenced to eight years in prison on a charge of swindling T. J. Wilson, a Pecos farmer, in connection with a mortgage on nonexistent fertilizer-storage tanks. Five days after the conviction, he filed a pauper's oath in federal court.

This was but the first of several convictions. On March 28, 1963, Estes was convicted by a federal jury in El Paso of mail fraud and conspiracy in the sale of $24 million in mortgages on nonexistent fertilizer tanks. Two weeks later he was sentenced to fifteen years in prison.[9] On June 7, 1965, the United States Supreme Court reversed the Texas state court conviction of Billie Sol Estes on a swindling charge. By a 5 to 4 decision, the Supreme Court held that the state court had erred in permitting the televising of the trial which had the effect of denying Estes the due process guaranteed by the Fourteenth Amendment to the Constitution. Earlier, on January 18, 1965, the Supreme Court had declined to review the federal court conviction of Estes on conspiracy and mail fraud charges. He was arrested then and started serving his 15-year federal sentence.

It was anticlimactic when Estes finally appeared before the McClellan subcommittee in September, 1963, and pleaded the Fifth Amendment on a broad range of questions about his dealings with the Agriculture Department and high officials of the Kennedy administration. He said that it might tend to incriminate him if he gave a truthful answer to the questions asked by Chairman McClellan and other members of the subcommittee.

The Kennedy administration continued to deny all wrongdoing, and several Democratic members of the McClellan subcommittee aligned themselves with the opposition to any harsh criticism of Freeman or Murphy.

The House Government Operations subcommittee pictured Billie Sol Estes as a "successful swindler" who made misrepresentation to the government and private financial houses to build his grain-storage empire. The committee found no evidence proving bribery or corruption in connection with the assignment of government grain to Estes warehouses. It did report many instances where Agriculture Department personnel "displayed a conspicuous lack of alertness or exercised poor judgment."

The many government investigations of Estes, going back to 1953, were conducted by various agencies "with an almost total absence of effective coordination or communication," which made it possible for Estes to get by with his multimillion-dollar deception.

Two Democratic members of the McClellan subcommittee—Senator Sam Ervin, from Murphy's home state of North Carolina, and Senator Edmund Muskie, of Maine—gave outright praise to Murphy for his handling of the Estes case. They justified Murphy's decision to name Estes to the National Cotton Advisory Committee with the argument that, at the time, Estes had "an untarnished reputation as a successful businessman." Senators Ervin and Muskie justified Murphy's lengthy delays in handling the Estes cotton-allotment problem with the argument that he was simply giving Estes "due process" of law:

"We commend the Under Secretary for his fidelity to one of

the basic American principles; namely, no man ought to be condemned until he is heard."

Chairman John L. McClellan believed Estes had more than an adequate hearing. He stated that it was not legal to sell cotton allotments, and that "the evidence and facts developed in the hearings clearly established beyond any doubt that the land sales of Estes had no purpose whatsoever other than to transfer cotton allotments to Billie Sol Estes in consideration for a sum of money."

He stated that the Washington office of the Agriculture Department was aware of the sale of allotments, and "failed and neglected or was unable to secure adequate compliance with its instructions and more than 3,000 acres of such transfers were approved."

McClellan found that Estes was "appointed as a member of the National Cotton Stabilization Advisory Committee by Under Secretary Charles S. Murphy in disregard of adverse recommendations made by John E. Francis, Chief of the Review and Adjudication Division, the departmental official who had the duty and responsibility to make such a recommendation."

While Chairman McClellan criticized Murphy, he "commended" Secretary Freeman for "prompt action he took in canceling those allotments" when the facts were finally called to his attention in April, 1962.

Two Republican committee members—Senators Karl Mundt, of South Dakota, and Carl Curtis, of Nebraska—declared that Estes "received favoritism on the county level, State level, and in the U. S. Department of Agriculture, Washington, D.C." They expressed the view that N. Battle Hales was a much maligned witness, and called attention to efforts to discredit Hales because he had given testimony of the favoritism extended to Estes.

The Agriculture Department kept N. Battle Hales in the doghouse. In March, 1964, the Department blocked Hales from receiving what should have been "an automatic in-grade" promotion. The Republicans had something to say about that.

"This shabby treatment of Mr. Hales . . . now compounds the allegation of favoritism," said Senator Jack Miller, of Iowa. "It lends credence to suspicion that favoritism was indeed extended, and, worst of all, that any civil service employee who cooperates in disclosing this fact does so under threat of retaliation by those of his superiors who are worried over what the evidence would disclose."

Representative H. R. Gross, also from the farm belt, told the House: "It is becoming increasingly apparent that when Federal employees take a stand in behalf of decent government, and this stand is counter to the position of their appointed political bosses, they are made the object of punishment."

There was a little postscript to the whole shabby episode. While Hales was being denied his in-grade promotion, Horace Godfrey, one of those who had been most vociferous in seeking to discredit Hales, was given a Distinguished Service Award for his administration of the Agricultural Stabilization and Conservation Service.

In a House speech, Representative Ancher Nelsen, the Minnesota Republican, said that "it seems strange that an award would be made to a man who is in charge of this agency where an investigation revealed poor organization and where obviously a coverup was attempted in the entire Billie Sol Estes case."

Senator John Williams also criticized the Johnson administration for honoring "Mr. Godfrey, the man who was partly responsible for the coverup in the Estes case."

It was futile to complain. Agriculture Secretary Freeman was not to be detoured from the politician's course of rewarding his friendly protector and punishing the subordinate who, as Senator Williams explained, "committed the unforgivable sin of giving Congress some information about skullduggery in his Department."

CHAPTER 10

The Department of (Self-) Defense

PART I: THE X-22

In the fall of 1962, suspicions began to arise in Washington that Robert S. McNamara and certain of his associates might be costing the U.S. taxpayers a lot of money by unwise political decisions.

McNamara had come in as Secretary of Defense with the late President Kennedy, but there were few around him who could be characterized as "Kennedy men." The roster of McNamara's band was a curious assortment. There was the corps of bright young men—human computing machines, by legend, as McNamara himself was said to be, and so-called Whiz Kids, which was what the Defense boss had been called during his days as the boy wonder and, eventually, as the president of the Ford Motor Company. There were the suave but tough-minded Texas and New York lawyers, bankers, and ex-lobbyists. Among the latter were men close to Lyndon Johnson. They were well versed, in their own right, in both political savvy and the methodology of how to succeed in (public) business by really trying.

In this and the next few chapters, the activities of McNamara and some of the principal members of his group—namely, Deputy Secretary of Defense Roswell L. Gilpatric, Secretary of the Navy Fred Korth, Assistant Secretary of Defense for Public Affairs Arthur Sylvester—will be examined.

Throughout 1961 and most of 1962, there was wide public acceptance of Secretary McNamara's claim that he was saving millions, perhaps even billions, of dollars through advanced "cost-effectiveness" studies. The Defense Department budget had sky-rocketed from $42 billion to $52 billion a year, but McNamara's "anticipated savings" won him the reputation of being a sort of fiscal miracle man—or machine.

If McNamara could force the Pentagon brass to "save" money, the public and most members of Congress seemed inclined to put up with a few authoritarian tendencies. The confidence continued in the face of periodic complaints from high-ranking military officers that the McNamara policies would harm our future defense capabilities.

Then came persistent reports that McNamara's team might waste millions of dollars on a decision to buy for the United States Navy what was described by Navy men as the "second-best" experimental plane for vertical takeoff or landing. The plane, referred to as the VTOL—meaning vertical takeoff and landing—was also designated as the X-22. It was designed to take off and land like a helicopter but to fly at the speed of a normal plane.[1]

Initial reports reaching the Preparedness Subcommittee of the Senate Armed Services Committee indicated that McNamara was buying the "second-best" plane for a higher price than he would have had to pay for another plane that had been evaluated as technically superior. It seemed incredible to the investigators that a man of McNamara's reputation would make such a decision. They proceeded to check the reports.

Top Navy officers had strongly recommended awarding the contract to the Douglas Aircraft Corporation, of Long Beach, California, on the basis of a "superior technical proposal" as well as a lower price. Deputy Defense Secretary Gilpatric had overruled the recommendations and given the contract to the Bell Aerosystems Development Company, of Buffalo, New York, a subsidiary of the Bell Aerospace Corporation.[2]

Chairman John Stennis and others on his subcommittee were concerned about this decision. Why would Gilpatric overrule the Navy's top specialists to buy what appeared to be the second-best plane from Bell for a price that was $350,000 more than the Douglas bid of $14,610,000?

The initial X-22 contract was small, as Pentagon contracts go, but the principle involved was not. Defense officials are obligated to get the best weapons and machines for the best price. If the work of technical experts was to be disregarded by political appointees, then why hire them? If contracts were to be awarded arbitrarily, then all the talk of competitive bidding was window dressing. Stennis, therefore, assigned Chief Counsel James Kendall and Assistant Counsel Ben J. Gilleas to the job of making a preliminary report on the X-22 program.

There was always the possibility that the initial information reaching the committee might be wrong. There was always the chance that, on closer study, the Navy might conclude that its initial recommendation for Douglas was in error. Chairman Stennis and his staff did not challenge Gilpatric's legal authority to override the technical experts. However, if the reports were true, there certainly was reason to question the wisdom of the decision.

Lawyers Kendall and Gilleas interviewed many Navy officials, including Admiral George W. Anderson, then the Chief of Naval Operations, and Vice Admiral Robert Pirie, former Deputy Chief of Naval Operations for Air. Six months had passed since Gilpatric had decided for Bell, but the Navy chiefs still preferred the Douglas plane.

The Admirals told the investigators that they believed the contract should have been awarded to Douglas, and that they could not understand Gilpatric's decision. Several expressed the view that great damage was done to the military procurement system when the work of experts was disregarded in what appeared to be an arbitrary decision. The records showed that seventy-five of these experts, after months of study, had found Douglas a "clear choice."

The subcommittee lawyers were told that the recommendations for Douglas had been based on these facts:

1. Douglas had submitted a technical proposal that had no un-

acceptable items requiring correction. In addition, Douglas's proposal showed higher engineering competence and offered a lower cost.

2. Bell's design had four areas (vision, escape, transmission and fuel system) that were unacceptable and required correction. On the other side, Bell was given a plus for greater experience in vertical-takeoff-plane construction. Bell also was located in a more depressed labor area.

The investigators learned that Navy technicians had prepared numerous charts for use in briefing civilian officials. The briefings were given to a number of highly placed men, including Admiral Anderson; Navy Secretary Korth; Dr. Harold Brown, Director of Defense Research and Engineering; Dr. James H. Wakelin, Assistant Secretary of Navy for Research and Development; and Dr. Jerome Wiesner, the President's scientific adviser. The technical experts had ended all briefings with what investigators called "a clear and definite recommendation that Douglas had the superior proposal and should receive the contract."

Counsels Kendall and Gilleas were surprised, therefore, to find that the briefing had not been given to Deputy Secretary Gilpatric, the man who made the ultimate decision. The investigators were even more concerned when they found that the only information available to Gilpatric at the time he made the award was obtained in a twenty- to thirty-minute meeting with Dr. Brown, Dr. Wakelin and Dr. Wiesner. As they dug deeper into the circumstances, they were amazed to learn that Gilpatric was unaware of many "material, pertinent and important facts."[3]

They found he did not know, for instance, "that 75 Navy technicians had spent some 4,000 man-hours evaluating the design and had concluded that Douglas was a 'clear choice.'" He did not know that "Bell's design had four unacceptable areas, while Douglas had none."

When the Deputy Defense Secretary made his decision, he was not aware of "the fact that Douglas' quoted price was $350,000 cheaper than Bell's, and that the Navy estimated Douglas' costs to be $780,000 lower." Nor did Gilpatric know that "it cost the government $442,000 to correct the deficiencies in the Bell design—a cost which would not have been incurred had Douglas' [design] been accepted."

Gilpatric was unaware of a memorandum written by Vice Admiral Paul D. Stroop on June 7, 1962, nine days before the contract award, recommending Douglas. Stroop was Chief of the Bureau of Naval Weapons. Gilpatric also did not know that "Douglas had expended some $3.8 million of its own funds on VTOL research, and, in addition, had acquired the VTOL designs, rights and some key personnel of Doak Aircraft Company."

The subcommittee investigators further declared Gilpatric did not know that "the Navy evaluators had concluded that the Douglas proposal showed 'higher engineering competence' in addition to its technical superiority."

The controlling factor in Gilpatric's decision, the investigators found, appeared to have been his own opinion that Bell had superior experience and past performance.[4] But they noted that the Navy evaluators apparently thought otherwise.

The question of comparative cost was not considered by Gilpatric. He did not know until after his decision that Douglas was cheaper both in its proposal and in the Navy's own evaluation of the bids.

The investigators declared the X-22 inquiry "significant and noteworthy," since it was the first known instance, as of that date, "when a unanimous service source selection recommendation was overruled by the Office of the Secretary of Defense."

As the subcommittee investigators inquired further, they were told by Defense Department officials that Navy Secretary Korth had disqualified himself from taking part in the decision. Korth, named to his post in December, 1961, had been a member of the board of directors of the Bell Aerospace Corporation.[5] He also had been president of the Continental National Bank, of Fort Worth, Texas, which had dealings with Bell.

Assistant Secretary Wakelin told the investigators that Korth had turned the X-22 contract over to him to avoid any appearance of a conflict of interest because of his past close association with Bell. Thus, the investigators were surprised to discover later that Gilpatric had consulted Korth about a key issue—the management capability of Bell.

It struck Kendall and Gilleas as inconsistent that Korth would disqualify himself to avoid any conflict of interest, but at the same time would consult with Gilpatric on such an important factor. Thus, with the help of subcommittee staff members Samuel R. Shaw, D. F. McGillicuddy, and Stuart French, they immediately launched an extensive study of every aspect of the contract award.

Chairman Stennis (Democrat, Mississippi) opened public hearings on June 12, 1963. In his opening statement, the stentorian-voiced chairman said: "Preliminary information indicates that at least $800,000, and possibly $1.5 million, could have been saved by awarding the contract to Douglas.

"We are interested in learning whether there are valid and compelling reasons for overturning the findings of technical evaluators," Chairman Stennis went on. "We also want to know what the ground rules are for the award of research and development contracts and whether there has been or is to be a change in them. If there is to be a departure from the concept that contracts of this type are to be awarded under the usual competitive process . . . then both the Congress and the affected industries should be informed."

The Navy's top experts appeared with charts and figures to give the Senators the same briefing that had been given to Pentagon officials prior to the award.

The Chief of Naval Operations, Admiral Anderson, was in Europe, but he sent a strong statement protesting the X-22 procedure.[6] Declaring that the reversal of recommendations for the Douglas plane "had come as a complete surprise," Anderson said: "We have had no reversals of our decisions in the past that I know of, except for this program and the TFX, which was . . . an Air Force-assigned procurement responsibility. . . ."

Clearly unintimidated by the political status of those who had overruled the Navy, the Admiral went on:

"The philosophy of reversal without adequate and thorough consultation is dangerous. It is my personal conviction that the reversal of source selection recommendations . . . is improper on two bases. First, the professional advice of military and civilian experts charged with the technical evaluation of design proposals should not be overturned except for the most compelling and persuasive reasons. Second, such reversals can only be detrimental to the competitive spirit of American industry."

The Admiral added that if the established rules of fair competition were going to be overthrown, industry was entitled to a warning on the nature of the new "ground rules."

A long list of Navy Department experts gave testimony favorable to the Douglas version of the X-22. One was Vice Admiral Stroop, who read his official memorandum stating:

". . . The Douglas design is considered superior to the Bell design.

". . . It is the opinion of the Chief of the Bureau of Naval Weapons that Douglas should be . . . awarded the contract for the VTOL aircraft if we proceed with the flight vehicle program as presently planned."

He told the Senators: "I do not know anybody in the Navy who recommended Bell."[7]

But if everyone in the Navy was clear about how the Navy felt, Roswell Gilpatric was not.

The Deputy Secretary of Defense, testifying that he had never seen or heard of Stroop's memorandum, said he had had only the brief meeting with Brown, Wakelin and Wiesner. Dr. Wakelin and Dr. Brown both mentioned that Douglas had a "superior design," but Gilpatric testified that no one mentioned Admiral Stroop's strong recommendation for Douglas.

"I did not overrule the source recommendation [for Douglas] because none was made to me," Gilpatric testified. The Senate subcommittee later was to conclude that Gilpatric's denial was "a matter of semantics."

Gilpatric insisted that all factors were given adequate consideration. Yet he admitted he did not know of the numerous factors that led the Navy experts to decide overwhelmingly in favor of the Douglas plane.

Then Gilpatric, a former New York lawyer, proceeded to explain that, in his judgment, there was a better chance of success for the high-risk project if Bell received the contract. But outside of the conversation he had with the scientists, who told him Douglas had the "superior design," he had not asked anyone's advice in judging the merits of the two companies—except Fred Korth's.

"I knew the Douglas people better," Gilpatric explained. "But I did want to check up before I made the decision to be sure the management of Bell . . . was still of the high caliber its past performance indicated. So I called Secretary Korth. And you know, because he was a director of Bell, and because his bank in Fort Worth, the bank of which he was president, was the bank of the Bell Company, he felt, even though there was no, as he understood it, legal or ethical reason for him disqualifying himself, he felt he should stand out of this matter, which he did.

"I did not ask him for a view as between the two which should be chosen. But I did ask him to give me his judgment, based on his close association with the Bell Company, as to the caliber and quality of the management. That was the only check I made, outside of my own knowledge—and the discussions I had had with Dr. Brown."

The subcommittee took up the question of how Gilpatric thought the former Bell director and Bell banker could give him an objective opinion about the company's management.

"As I understand it," subcommittee counsel Kendall said, "Secretary Korth entirely disassociated himself from the award because of his previous connection with Bell in the banking business, and as a member of the Bell board of directors. . . . Then why do you go back to Secretary Korth to ask information about Bell's management?"

"Well," Gilpatric said, "I approached him in a different capacity than in a capacity as Secretary of Navy. I asked him for a personal opinion on a matter with which he had knowledge and experience. I did not ask him to help advise me in making a decision. I asked him to give me a judgment on certain facts. And I felt that I could rely on his judgment as being objective, since I had to make the decision and he did not."

"And he gave the Bell management a higher rating, is that correct?" Kendall asked.

"He told me that I could have confidence in the present management as contrasted with the competence of the previous management," Gilpatric answered.

"Mr. Secretary," Kendall asked, "can you tell us why, in view of the fact that you were the person who was going to make the ultimate decision, you did not receive the technical briefing that Dr. Wiesner, Dr. Wakelin, Dr. Brown, and all the responsible officials of the Department of the Navy, from Secretary Korth on down did receive?"

"I do not believe it is necessary in the role that I played in this for me to listen to a long exposition of the technical factors, when I accept the judgment of the experts," Gilpatric replied.

"You did not think those facts would help you?" Kendall asked incredulously.

"No," said Gilpatric. Then he added a rather confusing explanation: "I considered myself adequately informed, and I considered there was adequate consultation with the experts in view of the fact that there was no decision . . . left to me in the technical field. I am not an expert. And I do not know whether it would have helped me very much to have listened to a technical explanation."

In its subsequent report, the subcommittee concluded that "Secretary Gilpatric's decision was obviously inconsistent with procurement practices and procedures established over the years."

"The source selection people recommended Douglas as a clear choice," the subcommittee stated. "The award went to Bell. Thus the source recommendation was overruled. Secretary Gilpatric made the decision. The fact that he did not know of the recommendation does not alter the fact that the source recommendation was overruled."

The subcommittee also noted that Gilpatric testified he knew nothing of the lower bid by Douglas, and that Dr. Brown had ignored the lower bid. "If price estimates are to be disregarded altogether, then there is little reason to require that detailed cost information is to be furnished," the report stated.

"The subcommittee believes that a difference in price of at least several hundred thousand dollars is material and should have been considered. A minimum of $350,000 and possibly $1 million of the taxpayers' money could have been saved by an award to Douglas. We see no basis for ignoring this factor. So to do violates applicable regulations."

The fact that Bell's plant was located in a depressed area, the subcommittee said, "was not a pertinent or relevant consideration."

In defending the Bell award, Dr. Brown had argued that cost estimates are unreliable. But the subcommittee noted in its report that Douglas had concluded a previous defense contract for $639,-369,000 when "the original estimates had been $653,058,000."

"This represented a remarkably low error of 2.1 per cent"—and on the side of the government, at that, the subcommittee said. "This is a rather enviable record and one that would appear to lend credibility to their [Douglas'] proposals on the X-22."

The subcommittee found that there were no "clear, compelling, convincing and persuasive reasons for upsetting the recommendation for Douglas.

"It is equally clear . . . that Secretary Gilpatric acted hastily and prematurely and at a time when he was not in possession of all material, pertinent, and important information and facts at the time he made the decision," the report said. "The information which he had was given by Dr. Brown and Dr. Wakelin and was hastily supplied and was inadequate and superficial. . . . We conclude . . . that in the instant case there was reversal of the source selection recommendation without full, thorough and adequate consultation and without knowledge by the decision-maker of facts which would have justified an opposite conclusion. Reversals under such circumstances threaten and jeopardize the integrity of the source selection systems."

The subcommittee criticized both Gilpatric and Korth, stating: "The clear fact is that it would have been far better for Secretary Gilpatric to have refrained from consulting Mr. Korth about this matter. It would also have been wiser if Secretary Korth had declined to express an opinion or judgment. His statement that Secretary Gilpatric 'could have confidence in present management as contrasted with the competence of previous management' obviously carried considerable weight. If this had not been an important point Secretary Gilpatric would not have inquired about it."

The report was signed by six of the seven members of the Preparedness subcommittee. They were: Senators Stennis, Jackson, Thurmond (Democrats), and Senators Leverett Saltonstall, Margaret Chase Smith, and Barry Goldwater (Republicans).

Only Senator Stuart Symington, the Missouri Democrat, defended Gilpatric's decision. Symington, Gilpatric's long-time personal friend, wrote a minority report stating flatly: "There was nothing improper in Mr. Gilpatric's asking Mr. Korth for information about Bell's management. . . . To give to this conversation between Mr. Gilpatric and Mr. Korth the significance suggested in the . . . report is neither warranted nor fair."

But Symington stood alone against the six other Senators on this interpretation of the evidence.

The troubles of McNamara's band were just beginning. The X-22 probe was only a curtain-raiser for the investigation of a multibillion-dollar warplane program, which was getting under way about this time. The new case was a shocker with political overtones that would do serious damage to the public images of McNamara, Gilpatric, Korth & Co.—and to the public image of a man who was to fall heir to the White House.

CHAPTER 11

The Department of (Self-) Defense

PART II: TFX – BILLIONS FOR TEXAS

The TFX-warplane (tactical fighter experimental) contract was a much-coveted multibillion-dollar prize. The program would include more than 1,700 planes for the Navy and the Air Force. Government spending, it was estimated, would exceed $6.5 billion—the largest contract for military planes in the nation's history.[1]

The competition was intense. Such a contract could mean prosperity for an entire state.

Early in 1962, the rivalry for the TFX contract narrowed down to two major firms. The Boeing Company, with headquarters in Seattle, Washington, proposed to build the plane at its plant in Wichita, Kansas. The General Dynamics Corporation's Convair Division, in Fort Worth, Texas, cooperating with the Grumman Engineering Company, of Bethpage, New York, planned to build the Air Force version in Texas and the Navy version in New York.

Inevitably, political figures from the states of Washington, Kansas, Texas, and New York became interested in the TFX award. Senator Henry M. (Scoop) Jackson was one who followed the progress of the contract from the beginning. He had a triple interest: he was a Senator (Democrat) from the State of Washington, he was a member of the Senate Armed Services Committee (military), and he was a member of both the Senate Government Operations Committee and its important Permanent Subcommittee on Investigations (waste).

Despite the big stakes involved, Jackson avoided contact with Defense Secretary McNamara and other top decision-makers. He knew and respected McNamara, and felt the contract would be awarded to the company producing the best plane for the lowest price. He also had confidence in the ability of the Boeing firm to compete effectively. The firm had good management, skilled technical personnel, and an outstanding record for efficient production.

Senator Jackson, an original Kennedy supporter, had good personal and political relations with the President. However, the Washington Democrat had practical reasons for wanting to avoid a political tug-of-war over the TFX contract. From a political standpoint, the Texas-New York combination that backed General Dynamics and Grumman had a distinct advantage. The 24 Texas electoral votes and the 45 New York electoral votes had gone to Kennedy in 1960, while Washington's nine electoral votes and the eight Kansas votes had gone to the Republican candidate, Richard M. Nixon.

In the late summer of 1962, Senator Jackson heard disturbing rumors of Texas political pressure on the TFX contract. He called Deputy Defense Secretary Roswell Gilpatric, and told him of the talk that General Dynamics had the contract in the bag. Nothing to it, Gilpatric said; the decision would be made "strictly on the merits."

On October 24, 1962, a story in the Fort Worth *Press,* under the by-line of its Washington correspondent, Seth Kantor, stated: "General Dynamics of Fort Worth will get the multibillion-dollar defense contract to build the supersonic TFX Air Force and Navy fighter plane, the *Press* learned today from top Government sources."

Kantor wrote that he got the story from two "very high echelon people" in the Kennedy administration. "Unofficial estimates are that the contract will pump up to $6 billion in federal contract money primarily in Fort Worth between the start of 1963 and 1970," he reported.[2]

Again Senator Jackson called Gilpatric to ask if this were true. And again Gilpatric assured the Senator that no decision had been made. He confided that competition was "extremely close."

Senator Jackson accepted Gilpatric's statement. He did not wish to call President Kennedy or McNamara. He hoped the news stories and rumors were not true. He still believed that McNamara would seek the best plane for the lowest cost, even if politically potent Texans were trying to lasso the contract for the home-state firm.

On November 24, 1962, the Pentagon announced that the TFX contract would be awarded to General Dynamics. Boeing had lost, and Senator Jackson was disappointed, for Boeing had been working on the TFX movable-wing concept for months before the competition opened. But he was philosophical about it, and took the attitude that "you can't win 'em all." Besides, the loss wouldn't put the big Washington concern out of business. Senator Jackson reasoned that General Dynamics must have come up with a plane that was regarded as better for Air Force and Navy needs.

A few days after the award, Senator Jackson was disturbed to hear that four separate evaluation studies by the services—an unprecedented number for a single plane—had all said that, between the Boeing and the General Dynamics planes, the Boeing version promised "superior performance." Also, Senator Jackson was informed that Boeing's bid was "substantially lower" than its competitor's.

Scoop Jackson could not believe the reports were accurate. It just didn't make sense that Secretary McNamara, supposedly a hardheaded businessman, would take the second-best plane, and pay more for it.

The reports indicated that Boeing's bid was $100 million lower on an initial development contract. On the total $6.5 billion procurement, the cost difference might run as high as $400 million.

It was hard to believe that any responsible official would waste nearly half a billion dollars, regardless of the political pressures involved.

Jackson concluded that an immediate check was necessary on the validity of the reports. If they were true, he intended to ask for a Senate investigation. If they were not true, he would drop it. He tried to call McNamara or Gilpatric on December 1st, but they were at the Army-Navy football game.

Next day, Jackson got his call through to Gilpatric. The pleasant-voiced New Yorker again assured Jackson that the competition between Boeing and General Dynamics had been "very close," and that the decision for General Dynamics had been arrived at by a narrow margin.

But this time Jackson, ordinarily a mild-mannered man, was not so easily soothed. What about those reports, he asked the Deputy Defense Secretary, that the Pentagon Source Selection Board had unanimously recommended Boeing on the basis of price and performance? Gilpatric conceded that Jackson's information was correct. But, he explained, the competition was so close that it really had been immaterial which firm was finally selected.

Without anger, Jackson notified Gilpatric that he intended to ask Senator John L. McClellan, chairman of both the Government Operations Committee and its Permanent Subcommittee on Investigations, to direct the professional staff of the investigating subcommittee to start looking into the TFX matter.

The McClellan-subcommittee investigators went to work immediately. They questioned witnesses, and examined basic documents. Senator Jackson's basic complaint seemed valid. The material gleaned from their work established that:

1. The four service evaluations *did* favor Boeing.

2. The Boeing price *was* $100 million lower on the first phase of the contract, and it might be $416 million lower on the total job.

3. The Pentagon Source Selection Board, composed of top generals and admirals, was unanimous in its finding that the Boeing plane would be cheaper and better.

4. The only document at the Pentagon that supported the General Dynamics plane was a five-page memorandum of justification, dated November 21, 1962. [See Appendix A for full text.] It was signed by McNamara; Eugene Zuckert, Secretary of the Air Force; and Fred Korth, Secretary of the Navy. (Gilpatric also agreed with the award, but his signature was not necessary because his boss, McNamara, had signed.) And this document, the investigators reported, appeared to be loaded with errors.

In fact, the investigating-subcommittee staff members were jolted by the inaccuracies in the memorandum. It claimed certain patently inflated performance ratings for the General Dynamics plane that did not square with the military evaluations. More surprisingly, the arithmetic was erroneous. Thomas Nunnally, a veteran accountant for the McClellan committee, found separate mistakes of $32 million and $22 million in the document signed by McNamara, Zuckert, and Korth. [See Appendix B for McClellan Statement.]

In addition to these factual errors, the memorandum contained other statements that were highly questionable when viewed against the comments of technical experts.

McNamara and his civilian secretaries opposed the Boeing plan to use a modern "thrust reverser" braking device in the TFX. They found it a "risky" development that made the plane less acceptable than the General Dynamics plane, with its conventional dive brake. But the military engineers considered the thrust reverser a non-risky and highly desirable feature of the Boeing plane.

McClellan's investigators suggested that McNamara believed he knew better than the engineers and metallurgists about the advisability of titanium for the wing structure of the Boeing plane. McNamara contended that the use of titanium in the Boeing plane was risky and might interfere with Boeing's ability to meet the specified delivery dates.

The engineers and metallurgists told the McClellan-subcommittee investigators that Boeing's use of titanium in the wing structure was a "conventional use" of the metal. It made the plane lighter, as the Navy had requested for use on carriers, and it entailed no unusual risk in the way Boeing was using it, the metallurgists said.

The evidence against McNamara was strong, but the investigators were still reluctant to judge him wrong. Even after several weeks of disillusioning investigation, they were still a little mesmerized by the flood of stories and articles that pictured McNamara as one of the greatest military minds since Alexander the Great. They kept thinking the former Whiz Kid might still prove he was right in awarding the contract to General Dynamics.

However, they wanted to know how McNamara was going to explain all the inaccuracies and conflicts, the substitution of his judgment for that of engineers and metallurgists on technical matters in their fields, the glaring mistakes in figures. And how was he going to explain overriding such august military figures as General Curtis E. LeMay, the Air Force Chief of Staff, and Admiral Anderson, the Chief of Naval Operations, who said flatly that the Defense Secretary had made a "wrong decision"?

In December, General Counsel Jerome S. Adlerman and Assistant Counsel Robert E. Dunne went to Seattle to brief Senator Jackson on the results of the preliminary investigation. Jackson was shocked to learn of the major errors in a memorandum to justify a multibillion-dollar contract. Now he was firmly convinced that a full public hearing was necessary. So was Chairman McClellan.

While the McClellan investigators quietly pushed their investigation of the TFX contract, there were loud hosannas and hand-clapping deep in the heart of Texas. In his column "The Home Towner," in the Fort Worth *Press,* Walter R. Humphrey hailed the contract as one of the major events in Fort Worth's history.

"The news, of course, was the biggest we'd had around here in a long time," Humphrey wrote. "I want to pause to pay tribute to our Washington reporter, Seth Kantor, for his fine work on this TFX story. He got the official word—in confidence as to source—one month ago. We printed the story October 24 that the deal had been wrapped up. I talked to Seth on the phone that day and knew he was correct—and safe. Trusting him and his source, we went ahead and printed the story. Some folks said we were out on a limb, but I think the people on the inside knew that we weren't."[3]

A few days later, on December 12th, there was more celebrating in Fort Worth. Vice-President Lyndon B. Johnson was in town to join in the festivities at the General Dynamics plant. More than three hundred union members crowded the union hall near the entrance to the General Dynamics plant to cheer the Vice-President, and wildly waved signs crediting Johnson with delivering the TFX contract to Texas.[4]

"LBJ SAVED THE DAY," one of the signs read. "WE ARE HERE TO STAY, THANKS TO LBJ."

"WE HAVE GOT JOBS, THANKS TO LBJ," another stated.

Congressman James Wright, the Texas Democrat representing the Fort Worth district, introduced Vice-President Johnson as "the greatest Texan of them all." Wright was quoted by the Fort Worth *Star Telegram* as saying the TFX decision was made on merit, but adding: "You have to have friends and they have to stick with you through thick and thin even if you do have merit on your side."

Lyndon Johnson was in good form. He had the air of a man who was letting good friends in on something confidential. Speaking slowly, in his best "mission accomplished" style, with plenty of knowing pauses to give people time to applaud, he told the Fort Worth crowd: "The Twentieth Century is one of the most exciting, challenging times in the history of the world. . . .

"Texas is going to have a little hunk of the century," Johnson added. The crowd, already basking in the satisfaction of having been delivered a whopping chunk of the Defense Department budget, went wild.

In New York, officials of the General Dynamics Corporation named a new member to the board of directors—Maurice T. (Tex) Moore, of the law firm of Cravath, Swaine & Moore. That was Deputy Defense Secretary Gilpatric's old firm.

Gilpatric had served as lawyer for General Dynamics from 1958 until January, 1961, when he dropped his partnership in the firm and turned over the General Dynamics business to Moore. Then Gilpatric became the No. 2 man in the Defense Department, and participated in the TFX decision to award the TFX contract to General Dynamics. It was his contention that he dropped his interest in his old law firm so there could be no conflict of interest to interfere with his objectivity in a decision involving his former client.

On December 22nd, Chairman McClellan wrote McNamara asking that the formal signing of the TFX contract be held up pending a full investigation. McNamara was out of the country. Acting for him, Gilpatric answered McClellan's letter, turning down the request.

"I consider it to be in the national interest for the program to proceed without further delay," Gilpatric wrote.

Even before McClellan received the reply from Gilpatric, the contract was signed. As a matter of fact, it was signed within a few hours after the Defense Department received McClellan's request for its delay.

John McClellan, a slow-moving, deliberate man who takes his Senatorial duties seriously, did a slow burn over what he considered a high-handed rejection of a reasonable request. The Congress had an obligation to investigate, in order to determine if the money it was appropriating was being spent to buy the best weapons at the best price. Why, the Arkansas Democrat wondered, was Gilpatric in such a hurry to have the Defense Department sign the contract with the firm Gilpatric formerly represented?

But even as McClellan was making preparations to go deeper into the TFX decision, he did not expect prolonged hearings. Undoubtedly there were some mistakes, but the TFX contract could not be as bad as preliminary reports hinted. It was difficult to believe that a man with McNamara's background could be so wrong.

McNamara's reputation, aided by an efficient publicity machine, was almost supernal around Washington. Even the tough-minded Senator McClellan and his experienced staff, who had dealt in the past with many exalted and less exalted figures in labor, business, and government, had no wish for a head-on clash with McNamara. They expected the dazzling Defense Secretary at any moment to pull out some clever and logical explanation that would make everything seem all right.

In two years, McNamara had established himself as the strong man of the Kennedy administration. He had come to government with substantial credentials. The forty-six-year-old former Ford Motor Company executive was a Phi Beta Kappa graduate of the University of California, and had received a Master's degree in business administration at Harvard in 1939. He was an assistant professor of business administration at Harvard from 1940 through 1943, and from 1943 to 1946 was a lieutenant colonel in an Air Force group that specialized in the study of military organization.

In 1946, he was one of the small group of bright young men who went to work for the Ford company. Three years later, McNamara was controller of Ford. In 1953, he became assistant general manager of the Ford division, and in 1955 he was named vice-president and general manager of the Ford division. Though the ill-fated Edsel blemished many a Ford executive reputation in that period, McNamara managed to win praise from some writers for his decision to take a $250 million loss and end the Edsel before it was even more costly.

McNamara had just been named president of the Ford Motor Company, in November, 1960, when he was suggested to the newly elected President, John Kennedy, as the genius needed to bring organization and real unification to the Defense Department.

He knew how to flatter the key figures in Congress. McNamara missed none of the important personages. He paid special court to such figures as Senator Richard Russell, the Georgia Democrat who headed the Senate Armed Services Committee; Representative Carl Vinson, another Georgia Democrat, who headed the House Armed Services Committee; and Representative George H. Mahon, a Texas Democrat, chairman of the House Appropriations Subcommittee dealing with the Defense Department budget.

In the executive branch, McNamara had an equally keen sense for understanding the centers of power. His ardent attention was directed at President Kennedy, Attorney General Robert F. Kennedy, and Vice-President Johnson.

From the outset, McNamara's Defense Department was well

supplied with Johnson men. Cyrus R. Vance, a long-time Johnson protégé, was general counsel for the Department, later Secretary of the Army, and finally Deputy Defense Secretary. John B. Connally, Jr., lawyer for the oil millionaire Sid Richardson, and one of Johnson's closest political allies, was named Secretary of the Navy. When Connally resigned to run for Governor of Texas, he was replaced by Fred Korth, of Fort Worth, an original Johnson-for-President booster in 1960. Solis Horwitz, another Johnson man, was director of organizational and management planning in the Defense Department general counsel's office. The Assistant Secretary of the Navy was Kenneth E. BeLieu, who had been staff director of Johnson's Senate Preparedness Subcommittee a few years earlier.

Chairman McClellan and Chief Counsel Adlerman knew the TFX probe was not going to be easy. There were obvious political reasons why President Kennedy would not want anyone to challenge the award of the multibillion-dollar contract to the Texas-based General Dynamics Corporation. Also, President Kennedy apparently had total faith in McNamara, and it was unlikely he would upset a McNamara decision unless it involved some major political hazard.

Neither McClellan nor Adlerman wished to embarrass the Kennedy administration if it could be avoided. President Kennedy had been a member of McClellan's labor-racket investigating committee from 1957 through 1960, and Bobby Kennedy had been its chief counsel when Adlerman was assistant counsel. Both McClellan and Adlerman considered themselves friends of the Kennedys.

Chairman McClellan preferred to give the Kennedy administration every opportunity to reverse what appeared to be a wrong decision. He received no encouragement. Former friends in the administration used curt answers and sharp comment to let McClellan and Adlerman know that McNamara's decision would not be changed or substantially modified.

McNamara was wearing double armor. Not only was the Democratic President backing him, but McNamara was a Republican and that *rara avis,* a bureaucrat in politics who talked like a businessman, a man who'd met a payroll. He was the apostle of efficiency and economy in government, and his image was so souped up that some Republicans were openly talking about using him *against* John Kennedy as the G.O.P. Presidential nominee in 1964. Naturally, the Republicans in Congress were going to think twice before they'd carve up a man who might be their candidate.

Meanwhile, the President leaned on McNamara more and more each month. He used McNamara for all sorts of "selling chores" —foreign aid, domestic programs, and so on. When the Cuban crisis came up in October, 1962, it was McNamara rather than Secretary of State Rusk who went on TV to explain the situation to the American people. Some sources unenamored of McNamara remember that McNamara *first* told the people there was no evidence that Cuba was being used as a base for subversive activities in Latin America, and that other high officials had to set the record straight in a few days. But no matter—Bob McNamara stood ace-high with President Kennedy.

Some of McNamara's decisions infuriated many members of the Congress. He killed off the RS-70 reconnaissance bomber over the recommendations of Air Force Chief LeMay. He abandoned the Skybolt missile over the objections of many Pentagon officials as well as the British. And when McNamara decided to offer to sell Polaris missiles to the British, he didn't even bother to inform his own Joint Chiefs of Staff until the deal was settled.

But in every instance McNamara seemed to emerge from controversy stronger than ever. If military officials disagreed, then McNamara was billed as putting the incompetent brass in their place. If McNamara trampled over the views of Congressmen, he was credited with being a man of lofty principle intent on minimizing the influence of those incompetent politicians on Capitol Hill. Although the Defense Department budget had soared from $42 billion to $52 billion, McNamara was painted as a true economizer whose savings would not be apparent in the budget until three to five years later.

Even when McNamara awarded the TFX contract to General Dynamics—a sprawling giant that epitomizes military-industrial bigness—he was pictured by many as striking a salutary blow at the military-industrial complex, largely because he upset a decision by high-ranking military men.

While the McClellan investigators were compiling figures showing that the General Dynamics TFX award could waste $415 million in tax money, McNamara was boasting that the contract would "save" the American taxpayers approximately a billion dollars.

And in a defensive press briefing at the Pentagon, McNamara's chief publicity general, Arthur Sylvester, Assistant Secretary of Defense for Public Affairs, undertook to lay down the law to his former colleagues of the press about the TFX contract. McClellan and his investigators, Sylvester insisted, just weren't qualified to question McNamara's judgment on such a complicated matter. McNamara's press man belittled the Source Selection Board's unanimous recommendation for Boeing, and declared the records showed that both the Boeing and the General Dynamics planes "were acceptable."

Stating that there was no substantial difference between the performance ratings of the Boeing and the General Dynamics planes, Sylvester went on to say that McClellan's investigators were wrong in saying the Boeing plane would cost less money. He explained that McNamara himself had concluded that the Boeing costs "were not realistic," and had therefore disregarded them.

The most important reason for the award, Sylvester said, was that General Dynamics offered 85 per cent "commonality" of parts in the Air Force and Navy versions. This compared with only 60 per cent "commonality" in the two versions of the Boeing plane.

The term "commonality" was a new one. Reporters pressed Sylvester for an explanation, and he obliged. It was Pentagon gobbledygook for parts that were interchangeable. Since allegedly only 60 per cent of the parts in Boeing's TFX had "commonality," to choose Boeing, the press man reasoned, would have amounted to building two planes—one for the Air Force, the other for the Navy.

McNamara contended that Boeing had disregarded his instructions to make the Air Force and Navy versions as much alike as possible, Sylvester explained. So Boeing lacked "commonality," while General Dynamics had it, and it was this "commonality" that would result in the saving of McNamara's vaunted billion dollars.

Later, after the hearings began, Air Force and Navy engineers with recognized high technical competence in the fields McNamara and Sylvester were talking about were to take total issue with the McNamara-Sylvester "commonality" doctrine. One of them went so far as to call the Defense Secretary's claims "poppycock."

The McNamara-Sylvester refutations, and their reiterations that Boeing had submitted plans for an infinitely superior plane for less money, will be taken up in succeeding chapters. But in late February, 1963, just before the opening of the hearings, Arthur Sylvester was telling the press: "There is no controversy about it now. Secretary McNamara has made the decision as the civilian authority in the Pentagon, and that is it."

CHAPTER 12

The Department of (Self-) Defense

PART III: I.B.M. — "I, Bob McNamara"

One of the biggest problems in Congressional investigations is persuading a subordinate official to come in and give truthful, though damaging, testimony about his boss. The TFX-warplane hearings, which began on February 26, 1963, were no exception. Men of high rank—military and civilian—were asked to testify in opposition to an important decision by Defense Secretary McNamara, a man with a marked distaste for dissenters.

Some high-ranking military men and civilian experts remained firm in their position, but others vacillated and tried to compromise. A few said they were fearful for the future of their careers if they maintained a strong position against McNamara's decision. Fortunately, most of the key witnesses had made written records of their views on the $6.5 billion airplane program, for there was much nervousness as the hearing date approached.

The TFX hearings caught the public's attention almost immediately. McNamara, accustomed to the adulation of the press, suddenly found himself battered by front-page headlines.

It was necessary to conduct the hearings behind closed doors because of the classified data involved in the TFX performance ratings. The testimony was scrutinized by Pentagon and committee personnel, all classified figures were removed, and a "security-cleared" transcript was made available to the press. This process removed some of the drama that took place, but the cold facts were forceful enough to jolt the public.

There was, first off, shock at the testimony that McNamara's decision to award the contract to General Dynamics might result in a waste of $100 million to $415 million for a second-best plane.

Republicans were referring to the plane caustically as the "LBJ" because it appeared to have been awarded arbitrarily to Texas. Senator Clifford Case (Republican, New Jersey) warned in a Senate speech against the possibility of political influence in the awarding of multibillion-dollar defense contracts.[1]

Case said it was time for Congress to make certain that the "national interest is the sole criterion in awarding government contracts."

"The scale of space and defense commitments calls for unusual measures to safeguard the integrity of the contract award system, to make sure that awards are made on the basis of merit—and that politics, influence or any other extraneous interest are ruled out," Case said.

The New Jersey Republican said that the TFX award, and statements by high officials, including President Kennedy, "raise doubts as to whether what actually goes on . . . conforms with official policy" of awarding contracts on merit. He pointed specifically to a major scientific contract, the so-called Mohole Project, to drill a hole in the bottom of the sea.

Senator Case said that the five-year Mohole contract had been awarded to Brown & Root, Inc., of Houston, Texas, under questionable circumstances. The contract was let to the politically connected Texas firm "despite the fact that one National Science Foundation panel rated this firm third best in a field of three."

"Initial progress reports on this project indicate an eventual cost of $70 to $85 million—almost double the original ($43,600,-000) estimates—and the contractors are behind schedule," the Senator declared.

The fact that Brown & Root was owned by some of Vice-President Lyndon Johnson's strongest political supporters was well known to most of the Senators who heard Case attack the contract award.

As the hearings before the McClellan subcommittee began, further attention was focused on the TFX award by Hanson W. Baldwin, military writer for the *New York Times*. Baldwin, an Annapolis graduate and the dean of newspaper military analysts, wrote a scathing article[2] attacking "McNamara's monarchy" at the Pentagon.

"Objections or dissent, even to Congress, are discouraged, muted or, when possible, stifled," Mr. Baldwin wrote. "Mr. McNamara has pressured the Joint Chiefs of Staff to sign written statements testifying to Congress that the Administration's defense budget is adequate. He has censored, deleted and altered statements to Congress by the chiefs of the services and their secretaries. He has downgraded, ignored, bypassed or overruled the advice of the Joint Chiefs of Staff. General Maxwell D. Taylor, the Chairman of the Joint Chiefs, is a known advocate of the abolition of the Joint Chiefs of Staff system. He favors a single voice.

"Mr. McNamara has not yet succeeded in forcing all the services to speak, officially or unofficially, with one public voice. But he has come much closer to it than anyone before him, and he is still trying. And the progress he has made carries its own political dangers."

Mr. Baldwin wrote of the threat of the concentration of politico-military power in one department, and explained:

"It places more and more power over the military-industrial complex in the hands of a few men in the executive branch of government. The dollar volumes of military contracts amounts to more than $20 billion annually, with billions more in backlog orders outstanding. The individual services no longer have the final power to contract. The rewarding or cancelation of contracts —which may make or break companies and affect thousands of workers—is now ultimately controlled by a very few men in the top echelons of the Defense Department."

Against this background of an aroused public, the McClellan subcommittee heard testimony that inaccurate and misleading figures were used to justify the award of the TFX contract. Air Secretary Eugene Zuckert was identified as primarily responsible for preparing the five-page memorandum of justification with an erroneous and highly inflated performance rating listed for General Dynamics.

"An explanation is very much needed," Chairman McClellan intoned.

In the House, Representative H. R. Gross (Republican, Iowa) quipped: "Mr. Zuckert's letter of justification appears to create a situation in which he has tried to justify the purchase of a Ford by giving detailed quotations on all of the advantages of the Cadillac."

Zuckert admitted using erroneous performance-rating figures. He explained lamely that it was due to "some slip-up" during preparation of the memorandum.

Next day, the Senators heard testimony that it would cost at least an additional $400 million to put the modern "thrust reverser" braking devices, which both the Air Force and the Navy wanted, into the General Dynamics plane. The rejected Boeing plane had had this feature included, and under a lower bid.

The rash of critical stories concerned President Kennedy, who was sensitive to charges of political influence on defense contracts. The White House wanted the hearings ended quickly.

McNamara was informed of the President's concern over the harmful impact of the TFX hearings, and, shortly after, a new and disruptive phase of the investigation began. The McClellan subcommittee's work was harried by attacks from the Pentagon snipers—often firing from under cover ("a Pentagon source"). Sylvester told reporters: "You will hardly get a judicial rendering by a committee in which there are various senators with state self-interest in where the contract goes. So far there is only one senator I have seen on the committee, Senator [Edmund S.] Muskie [Democrat, Maine], who hasn't got an interest in it."

To put it in bald language, Sylvester was charging that every member of the McClellan subcommittee, including the chairman, with the sole exception of Muskie of Maine, had an ulterior motive, involving his own state, in the TFX contract.

The Senators were furious. McClellan and Senator Karl Mundt (Republican, South Dakota) knew they represented states without even a remote interest in any aspect of the TFX contract. The others felt it was unjust to accuse them of acting in the interest of their states alone, instead of for the public good. The real issue, they felt, was not *where* the contract went but what the government got for its money. And by now the evidence indicated that Secretary McNamara was buying the second-best plane at a higher price than the best plane.

So Sylvester was called before the subcommittee to explain his charges. His performance was hardly instructive.

First, Sylvester admitted that the press had quoted him accurately, and then that he had no evidence that McClellan and Mundt had any "state self-interest" in the TFX award.

But Sylvester had also told reporters: "I have read the testimony. It sounds to me as if I were reading the counsel for Boeing."

Now, facing the Senators, Sylvester admitted he had not read the whole record, but had only gained "impressions" of "distortion" from having read parts of the TFX transcript.

There is only one way to describe Sylvester's performance under Senatorial fire—he squirmed. He talked discursively about the irresponsibility of the press, how reporters took statements out of context, and how they attributed motives and intentions to him that weren't really what he had in mind at all.

"How can you complain about . . . former colleagues in the press," Senator Jackson said witheringly, ". . . when you have admitted before this committee that the statement that you made to the press was not correct?"

The Washingon Senator and McNamara's press man had further exchanges.[3] Then there was a heated outbreak when Sylvester remarked that, in this instance, "a contract has been let, and an effort is being made by the disgruntled loser to knock the contract down."

"Now wait a minute," Jackson flared. "Just get something clear, sir. The Boeing company never asked for this hearing. Do you understand that? I asked for it. They did not ask me."

"I made no suggestion," Sylvester started to reply.

"You are just making one," Jackson snapped. "Will you explain what effort is being made by the 'disgruntled loser'?"

"I will simply have to refer you to my impression," Sylvester hedged.

"I think," Jackson finally told him, "this all brings out something, that you are a little careless with words. This is where you get in trouble, Mr. Sylvester."

Sylvester offered the view that the McClellan subcommittee had given a fragmentary and distorted picture of the TFX contract, and that its procedures were wrong.

Challenged by Senator Curtis to identify the distortions, Sylvester said it included failure to point out that "the Boeing plane relies upon procedures and materials that, so far, are apparently not proved."

This, apparently, was a reference to the "thrust reversers" and to the use of titanium as a lightweight material. McClellan's investigators already had been told by Pentagon technical experts that neither development was anything radical or risky—that, in fact, both had been used in plane construction for several years.

Sylvester then complained that it would have been "fairer" if Secretary McNamara and Deputy Defense Secretary Gilpatric had been called as the first witnesses to put the testimony in its proper framework.

Patiently, Chairman McClellan pointed out to the press secretary, who should have known it, that McNamara had been invited to appear as the first witness but had rejected the opportunity. So it was "an accommodation" to McNamara and Gilpatric that their testimony was deferred, McClellan said.

In the end, Sylvester admitted that he had been in error on his statements about the committee members. He apologized, and they assumed that the Pentagon snipers, exposed and chastened, would now refrain from further irresponsible attacks on the McClellan subcommittee.

During the very week in which McNamara's spokesman was apologizing, another Pentagon attack was taking shape.

On March 12th, McNamara wrote McClellan that the investigations had "needlessly undermined public confidence in the integrity and judgment of the highest officials in the Defense Department." In the face of much evidence to the contrary, the Defense Secretary again said the award was "not only proper but definitely served the public interest." "Fragmentary release" of portions of the TFX testimony had created "wrong impressions," the Defense Secretary claimed. He asked permission to file a detailed statement to set the record straight.

McClellan said he would accept a statement from McNamara at any time, and again pointed out that McNamara could have been the first witness, had he so desired.

The statement McNamara presented on March 12th repeated previously stated facts. It contained nothing that was new to McClellan and his investigators, and little that was new to the press. McNamara again stressed the "commonality" of component parts of the General Dynamics plane. Again he implied that the award to General Dynamics would save the taxpayers $1 billion.

"If I had approved what was essentially two different airplanes [in the Boeing design], the prospect of saving $1 billion would have evaporated," McNamara declared.

He admitted that "in the operational area, the Boeing proposal received the higher score, but the report stressed that either design was considered acceptable from the user's viewpoint." He stubbornly refused to concede that the Air Force and the Navy had expressed a strong preference for the Boeing plane.

McNamara reiterated his belief that General Dynamics had demonstrated awareness of "cost realism" and that this "demonstrably credible understanding of cost" was a vital issue.

The McClellan investigators could not understand how McNamara could conclude that General Dynamics had exhibited more "realism" on costs than Boeing. The investigators knew that Boeing's past performance record was superior to that of General Dynamics. Also, the only cost studies the investigators had been able to find at the Pentagon did not warrant a finding that General

Dynamics was more efficient in production or more realistic about costs.

Yet somehow—without explaining why (to the committee's satisfaction)—McNamara had concluded: "It appeared to me that Boeing simply did not appreciate the complexities of developing the TFX. This is understandable because Boeing's past experience in aircraft development and production has been with bombers and transport aircraft—experience which is largely inapplicable to TFX estimating."

McNamara's statement, however much the subcommittee disagreed with it, at least was an out-in-the-open expression of his views. Guerrilla warfare continued in other quarters. Two days after Sylvester had testified, giving the subcommittee the impression that there would be no more underhanded sniping from the Pentagon, Deputy Defense Secretary Gilpatric met with a group of reporters for a "background" press conference.

The ground rules were explained to the newsmen. Gilpatric was not to be quoted by name. Nothing was to be written that would in any way identify him. But the reporters were free to use the "information" he disseminated "without attribution" to explain the Pentagon's position on the TFX contract, and to inform the public that the McClellan subcommittee was not playing fair. Gilpatric even set a "release date." The stories from the Thursday meeting were not to be used until Sunday morning, March 17th, three days later.

On Sunday McClellan and Jackson were hit with the Pentagon-inspired stories accusing them of "misleading" the Pentagon, of playing "politics" and of using generally "foul" tactics in the TFX inquiry. It was an unusual situation, in which the press permitted itself to be used for a broad-scale anonymous attack.

Unidentified Pentagon officials were quoted as saying that McClellan and Jackson had doublecrossed them, having given McNamara and Gilpatric assurance that the probe would be short and routine. It was stated that McNamara and Gilpatric were told the TFX inquiry was staged "simply to help Senator Jackson get off the hook with his constituents" at the Boeing company in Seattle.

As an example, the Washington *Post* story declared: "Because of what Jackson and McClellan told them, Pentagon officials said, they gave the subcommittee full cooperation in providing documents and let lower-ranking officials who handled the TFX contract testify before McNamara did."

Senator Jackson struck back. He said the anonymous Pentagon version was "just plain absurd." He explained that he had called Gilpatric initially about "rather serious allegations" in connection with the TFX award.

Senator McClellan declared: "Unidentified sources at the Pentagon are not in charge of this committee. Some of these statements apparently have about as much foundation as those emanating from a previous 'high source' at the Pentagon who proved to be Mr. Arthur Sylvester."

Now the Pentagon sniping became an almost unbelievably shabby affair.

On the next day—March 18th—Senator McClellan called Gilpatric. He asked him point-blank if he knew the source of the planted stories. At this time, McClellan did not know that Gilpatric himself was the source. He called Gilpatric because the Deputy Defense Secretary was the liaison man on TFX matters.

Gilpatric said he had no knowledge of the source of the series of Sunday stories, but that he would look into it. Too many people knew differently, however, and before the day was over, McClellan and Jackson had information indicating that Gilpatric had been the spokesman.

McClellan found this incredible. He asked Gilpatric to come to his office.

Confronted in person by McClellan, Gilpatric admitted he had held the off-the-record "background" conference with the reporters who had written the series of stories. Then why had he tried to mislead the Senator? He hadn't, he replied. He had "misunderstood" McClellan's questions. Gilpatric said he did not *know* that he was the source of the anonymous attack on McClellan and Jackson, but said he now *believed* he was probably a source.

Gilpatric appeared for questioning by the subcommittee on March 23rd, and McClellan met the issue of the anonymous attacks head on.[4]

"Did I not seek to find out at the [first] conference the source or identity of whoever was responsible for the statements in these articles?" McClellan asked Gilpatric.

"My recollection . . . was that you asked me who made these statements that appeared in some of the headlines and I told you that I did not know," Gilpatric answered.

"Not only the headlines but the articles," McClellan snapped. "I did not confine it to the headlines."

"My impression was that you were trying to find out who put out these stories," Gilpatric answered.

"Didn't you tell me that you didn't put out any such stories?" McClellan demanded.

"I told you that I had not put out the stories that were reflected in the headlines such as 'The Pentagon Cries Foul,' that we were misled," Gilpatric answered.

"Did I not ask you then who put out these stories?" McClellan persisted.

"And I told you I didn't know," Gilpatric admitted.

"Did you know at the time I talked with you . . . that these stories came out of the conference you held?" McClellan asked.

"I was not apprised of the fact that all of them came out of it, because some of them did not correspond to what I said," Gilpatric replied.[5]

Pointing out that most of the stories were quite similar in their content, Senator McClellan asked Gilpatric if he was blaming all the reporters for misquoting him.

"Oh, no," Gilpatric replied.

"For misrepresenting this thing and false reporting?" McClellan continued.

"No, Mr. Chairman," Gilpatric said. "I am suggesting that what I said was apparently open to misinterpretation."

Even while Gilpatric was attempting to smooth over this incident, still another Pentagon effort was being launched to discredit the McClellan subcommittee staff. A story had been leaked to Richard Fryklund, of the Washington *Evening Star,* charging that three men on McClellan's staff had engaged in abusive questioning of Pentagon witnesses. Fryklund, then a favorite press conduit for the McNamara regime, had obtained a copy of a memorandum in which a Pentagon officer charged McClellan's investigators had questioned him and other officers far into the evening and had made unreasonable demands that they produce records within a short period of time.

Sylvester, unchastened from his first encounter with the committee, helped to dramatize the story by commenting:

"The conduct it [the memorandum] ascribes to the McClellan committee investigators is outside of anything I have ever heard of in 17 years of reporting senatorial committee investigations."

Air Force Secretary Zuckert also jumped into the fray, and characterized the interrogation of the Pentagon witnesses as "severe by any standards." He added: "I don't think that in a fact-finding investigation of this sort people should be subjected to this sort of treatment."*

The Pentagon-inspired stories that three of McClellan's staff members had abused Defense Department witnesses was similar to the charge leveled against Senator Joseph McCarthy nine years earlier. McClellan prided himself on fair play, and a careful avoidance of the abusive treatment of witnesses that had marked the McCarthy era. The men under attack were General Counsel Adlerman, a quiet and gentle sixty-two-year-old lawyer, and Thomas Nunnally, an accountant who rarely raises his voice except to ask a factual question. Assistant Counsel Robert E. Dunne also was accused of questionable tactics, but not to the specific degree that Adlerman and Nunnally were.

Now the wrath of John McClellan was mighty to behold. He

*The counteroffensive seemed to be a repetition of tactics the Pentagon had employed successfully earlier in the year against the Senate Preparedness Subcommittee, which also was conducting an investigation into Pentagon activities. By attacking the staff of the Preparedness Subcommittee, the Pentagon had created confusion and discredited the investigation.

seemed to resent the attack on his staff more than he did the previous attack on himself. He took the floor in the Senate and expressed confidence in his staff members. He referred to Adlerman, Nunnally, and Dunne as "humble men," doing their job in a proper way. He served notice that he would call to account those who tried to "delay and obstruct" the progress of the TFX inquiry.

Emotions ran high. The Pentagon's crude and persistent attacks, instead of scaring off the McClellan committee, had intensified the investigation. The Kennedy administration, sensing that the TFX affair had become political poison, was worried.

Robert McNamara appeared before the McClellan subcommittee on the day the Fryklund story appeared. He was questioned about the leaking of the memorandum.

McNamara denied that he had instigated the leaking of the memo or had any knowledge of the attacks on the McClellan subcommittee. He went on to say that after listening to Gilpatric's testimony earlier that morning, he thought there was agreement that there would be no more attacks. Then, during the lunch hour, he was as surprised as anyone, McNamara said, to see the newspaper story, emanating from the Pentagon sources, criticizing the subcommittee staff members for "abusive" treatment of witnesses.

On the one hand, McNamara denied having anything to do with this new attack, but he then proceeded to give it support by stressing the seriousness of the Air Force memorandum criticizing McClellan's staff.

McNamara told McClellan that he had taken "no action to report . . . [the memorandum] to the press, or in any other way to benefit from the criticism implicit" in it.

"I cite this only as an indication of the fact that I have had ammunition in my possession since approximately the 14th [of March] that reflected very adversely on the process of the investigation, and I hid it," McNamara said. "I instructed the individual who gave it to me to put a copy of this in his safe, which he did."

"Can you explain why," McClellan asked, "if you lock it [the memorandum] up, someone else gets it and puts it out to the press?"

"Mr. Chairman, two years ago . . . I would have thought it impossible for such a situation to develop," McNamara said. "This has happened to me 15 or 20 times in the last 26 months. I became so upset about the situation that on several occasions I have discussed it with the Attorney General and J. Edgar Hoover. . . . We are making strenuous efforts to, as Mr. Gilpatric referred to it this morning, manage the leaks. We believe we are making some progress."

"You don't approve of the statement being released?" McClellan asked.

"I do not," McNamara answered. But then he added: "I don't wish by that, however, to indicate that I doubt the truth of the statement."

"You are saying it is true, the statement?" McClellan asked.

"No, sir," McNamara equivocated. "I just don't wish to indicate that I doubt the truth."

"You have made some serious charges there against a staff which I think is a credit to any committee and to the Congress, and I don't intend to just let these charges go out against the staff and not have them answered," McClellan said.

"I have not made any charges against the staff," McNamara said.

By now McClellan was thoroughly angry.

"You said you have a statement prepared by somebody under your direction and supervision, upon which this article is based," the chairman said. "You said you locked it up, but it is out now and the charges are out."

"I didn't say that this [memorandum] had been prepared under my direction and supervision," McNamara said. "I stated it had been prepared by an officer of the Air Force."

"The import of it [the memorandum] would be to try to discredit the committee, that it is using Gestapo tactics," McClellan said. "That is why these hearings are not being expedited more than they are. We are having to spend our time getting folks in here from the Pentagon to correct statements that they have given to the press that are erroneous and inaccurate, which are a reflection upon the committee. Is Mr. Sylvester under your direction and supervision?"

"He is indeed, sir," McNamara answered.

"Do you condone the statement he issued?" McClellan asked.

"I believe Mr. Gilpatric mentioned this morning that I was the individual who asked Mr. Sylvester to write the letter to the committee . . . which the press, I think, quite properly, interpreted as an apology for possible misinterpretation of his remarks," McNamara answered. He went on to say that he did not "condone" the Sylvester statement, and, as if in proof of that statement, he added: "I have sat on a highly explosive document for over a week, knowing that it was critical of the committee. I haven't in any way objected to the committee's tactics."

"Did I ever hear . . . criticism at all of the staff from you or anybody representing you?" McClellan asked.

"Certainly not," McNamara answered. "At no time have I criticized the staff."

McClellan said he had received a letter from Gilpatric, commending "the courteous and professional manner in which your staff has conducted the investigation."

The chairman said he would not tolerate abuse of government personnel by the committee staff, and added: "I believe in asking hard, tough questions. . . . I think that is the only way, sometimes, you get information."

At this point, the Senator and the Secretary seemed to have a meeting of minds. Then McClellan asked: "How do you expect us to operate and expedite this [hearing] if we are going to be confronted every day with some kind of accusation?" McNamara promptly took the offensive again.

"I am told," he said, "that the facts outlined in the memorandum reported in the newspaper are correct. I became disturbed myself on Saturday afternoon. . . . I asked the medical officer to examine one of the individuals referred to in the memorandum . . . I have the medical report with me if you care to have it."

"You are not blaming this committee for somebody getting ill, are you?" McClellan demanded.[6]

"No, sir, I am not," McNamara said.

McClellan explained that it is standard procedure for the sub-committee investigators to take a witness's physical condition into account whenever it questions a person known to have a heart condition. However, he said there were no indications that any of the Pentagon witnesses in the TFX investigation had heart conditions or needed special consideration. The Senator then made public a transcript of the questioning involved in the controversy. He said he saw no indication in the transcript of any unduly severe interrogation.

Turning aside from the issue of how witnesses had been treated, McNamara said he wanted to see the hearings terminated quickly. In his opinion, he said, there were only three grounds on which his decision might be challenged: "That I yielded to political influence . . . that I yielded to self-interest . . . or . . . that through ignorance, stupidity, or poor judgment I made the wrong decision.

"To the best of my knowledge, no one has submitted any evidence whatsoever indicating that I was influenced in the slightest degree by political matters," McNamara said. "Specifically, the Vice President [Johnson] never discussed the matter with me, nor did Governor Connally of Texas, nor to the best of my knowledge did any other political figure in the country discuss the matter with me. They have all learned long since that I pay no attention whatsoever to any such pressure."

He submitted an inventory of his personal property to demonstrate he had no personal self-interest in TFX, and concluded: "I think we are left with ignorance, stupidity or poor judgment. Those are the issues and in my opinion the only issues involved."

The Defense Secretary did not feel it necessary to outline why he would not be guilty of either ignorance or poor judgment. He asked the subcommittee to ring down the curtain on the hearings quickly, saying: "I think there is going to be tremendous harm done to many individuals as a result of this hearing."[7]

"I doubt that more harm will come from clearing it up if that is what we can do," McClellan said dryly. "I doubt if more harm will come from doing that than we would if we abandon this now and leave all of these things up in the air."

"I know that that is your desire and intention," McNamara replied. "I hope that that is the result. I don't believe it will be."

At this point, Robert McNamara gave way to his emotions. According to Chairman McClellan, other committee members, and staff members, tears came to the Defense Secretary's eyes and his voice broke:

"Last night when I got home at midnight, after preparing for today's hearing, my wife told me that my own 12-year-old son had asked how long it would take for his father to prove his honesty."

When the Defense Secretary regained control, McClellan asked, "Well, don't you think that is true with all of us in public?"

"I call it harm and not good," the Defense Secretary insisted.

"I feel strongly about it, too," McClellan said. "I have been charged with about everything, and I have the same sentiment and feeling as you. But I have a duty to perform, and I don't think that I ought to shirk my duty."

"I don't believe that you should," McNamara said, "but I don't believe any good is going to come of it."

"Mr. Secretary," Senator Jackson interrupted. "Some of us . . . have been subjected to some rather serious charges from anonymous sources. . . . Mr. Secretary, I had to try to answer questions over a whole weekend and I didn't know who my accuser was. . . . You have told me personally you don't like those tactics."[8]

"I don't condone [them]," McNamara said. "I think you have been harmed. I don't see how any good to you or good to me or good to the nation can come out of this hearing. I don't believe it is the intention of this committee to do anything but act in the national interest, and therefore my sole guiding principle at the present time is to cooperate in every possible way with the committee."

To Chairman McClellan, a temporarily chastened McNamara added: "You can pick up the telephone at any hour of the day or night. You know that I have never yet failed to give you the truthful answer to whatever question you posed."⁹

McClellan hoped that with this exchange, the warfare between the Department of Defense and his subcommittee was at an end. He thought he had McNamara's promise that, in the interests of winding up the controversial hearings expeditiously, cooperation and truthful answers from the Pentagon from now on would be the rule. However, in the months ahead, John McClellan was to have many occasions to think back wryly on the day of the emotional scene before the subcommittee, when Robert McNamara, he thought, took the pledge.

CHAPTER 13

The Department of (Self-) Defense

PART IV: McNamara's "Rough Judgment"

By late March, 1963, the TFX-warplane contract had become a flaming headache for the Kennedy administration. The President had the difficult task of trying to defend his Defense Secretary without irremediably alienating the influential Democratic senator from Arkansas, John McClellan. It was recognized now that McNamara's subordinates had been inept in their attempts to discredit McClellan and his investigators.

At his press conference on March 21st, President Kennedy was asked:

"Mr. President, the TFX contract is causing a lot of controversy on Capitol Hill. Senator Symington told the Senate today that the investigation was affecting military morale and ought to be wound up quickly. How do you feel about it?"

"I see nothing wrong with the Congress looking at these matters," President Kennedy replied. "Mr. McNamara chose the [General Dynamics] plane . . . because he thought it would save the government hundreds of millions of dollars. . . . I think the Secretary did the right thing . . . I think this investigation will bring that out and I have no objection to anyone looking at the contract as long as they feel that a useful function is served."

"Do you think the hearing that has been held has been fair and objective?" the President was asked.

"I am confident that we all know a lot more about the TFX

than we did before and that is a good thing," the President temporized. ". . . My judgment is that the more this hearing goes on, the more convinced people are finally that Secretary McNamara is a very effective Secretary of Defense and that we are lucky to have him."

The next questioner referred to Senator Clifford Case's criticism a few days earlier of Democrats who campaigned for office on the promise that, if elected, they could bring more government defense contracts to their area. Senator Case was speaking of the President's younger brother, Edward Kennedy, who in his 1962 campaign for a United States Senate seat had promised to do more for Massachusetts.

"Do you feel that this . . . builds confidence that these big defense contracts are being let fairly?" President Kennedy was asked.

"I think the contracts are being let fairly," the President replied. "Of course, there is great competition and it is no wonder because thousands of . . . jobs are involved. . . . The fact of the matter is that we have a Secretary of Defense who is making very honest judgments in these matters."

"Mr. President, in regard to the TFX contract, would you describe your personal role?" Kennedy was asked. "Specifically, did you make any suggestion as to who should get the contract?"

"No, I did not," President Kennedy replied. "This was completely the Defense Department."

Another reporter tried to draw out the President on the political feuding. He asked if the President agreed with certain Pentagon officials that members of the McClellan subcommittee who were up for election next year were politically motivated in attacking the General Dynamics award. The President replied that he had confidence both in McNamara and in the members of the Senate group.

Actually, President Kennedy was seriously concerned over the feuding. On March 26th, the President's brother and No. 1 troubleshooter, Attorney General Kennedy, went to talk with Senator

McClellan on a peacemaking mission. It was understood to have the President's approval.

Robert Kennedy had worked for McClellan as counsel to the same subcommittee, and he knew it would be futile to ask the tough-minded Arkansas Senator to rush the hearings to an end. What the White House wanted was to eliminate some of the bitterness. Few persons knew better than Bob Kennedy how hard a man McClellan was to deal with once his integrity was challenged —and McNamara's group had done just that.

When the hearings had started, only a few weeks earlier, Robert McNamara had seemed invulnerable. His reputation was tremendous, even though a few detractors insisted that I.B.M. stood for "I, Bob McNamara."

McClellan's staff had done its research thoroughly, and at the hearings a mass of devastating testimony from senior Air Force and Navy officers accumulated. McNamara's reputation was challenged.

Admiral Frederick L. Ashworth, senior naval representative on the Source Selection Board, testified that "Secretary McNamara compromised the requirements" by insisting on one plane for the Air Force and the Navy. Then McNamara had injected an additional compromise by awarding the contract to General Dynamics, the Admiral said.

The Navy had voted for Boeing on the basis of performance and price, Admiral Ashworth stated. These reasons were given by the Admiral as the basis for the Navy's decision for Boeing: lower gross weight; better subsonic flight characteristics vital to a carrier operation; better performance rating on Navy combat missions; and a substantially lower price. It was also recognized by the Navy that the Boeing plane had significant operational advantages for the Air Force, the Admiral said.

"It would be an economic catastrophe if we end up producing an aircraft for either the Navy or the Air Force that would not do the job," Admiral Ashworth declared.

Major General Robert G. Ruegg, chairman of the Source Selection Board, said the board had considered the "commonality" factor.[1] McNamara had said the fact that the General Dynamics plane had more parts which could be used in both the Navy and the Air Force versions was a vital reason for his decision.

The Source Selection Board chairman disposed of the "commonality" argument with an explanation of the technical points involved. "It was conceded that General Dynamics had more identical parts," he said. But this "commonality" was achieved at the cost of 1,450 pounds weight added to the already overweight Navy plane, which, incidentally, would make it far heavier than the Navy desired for aircraft-carrier operations. In other words, because of "commonality," the Navy was going to get an overweight plane that it really didn't want.

Then General Ruegg went on to explain that the particular parts which had "commonality" in the General Dynamics version were "parts that we do not normally stock and buy as spares."[2]

"In other words, those were parts that are seldom replaced, because if they got broken, the plane was destroyed, is that right?" McClellan asked.

"Generally, that is right," Ruegg replied.

"You think you would be getting more for your money if you got the Boeing plane, I mean in weaponry and meeting the requirements?" McClellan asked.

"Yes, sir, I think my statements [on that] are plain enough," the Source Selection Board chairman said.

General William F. McKee, the Air Force Vice Chief of Staff, testified: "It is my view that the operational factors [favoring Boeing] should be the overriding consideration."

The Air Force gave Boeing a "clear and substantial" recommendation over the General Dynamics plane, he said.

General McKee said the Boeing "thrust reverser" braking device had special merit because it "provides far better deceleration, whether it is for air-to-air maneuvering, diving or landing roll."[3]

General Walter C. Sweeney, Commander of the Tactical Air Command (T.A.C.), testified he recommended the Boeing TFX because of "superiority in all major aspects of operational capability."

"The Boeing plane is a much better aircraft . . . far superior for the T.A.C. role," General Sweeney testified.[4]

George Spangenberg, the Navy's top civilian aeronautical engineer, was another witness who contradicted the Defense Secretary on the "commonality" argument. It was Spangenberg, an engineer for twenty-five years and holder of the Defense Department's Distinguished Service Medal, who earlier had told the subcommittee investigators that the weight of the General Dynamics TFX was a serious problem. Even on the fourth evaluation, it was far in excess of what the Navy considered acceptable for carrier use. Now, addressing himself to McNamara's "commonality" factor, Spangenberg said:

"It's all poppycock. We think that Boeing gave us a better proposal at a better price. You certainly don't want to pay more money to get an inferior product just because it meets some word —commonality—better."[5]

General Curtis E. LeMay, the Air Force Chief of Staff, testified that he was not consulted prior to McNamara's decision to overrule the Source Selection Board.

"I thought we had such a clear cut and unanimous opinion all up and down the line that I was completely surprised at the decision," the blunt-speaking Air Force chief declared.[6]

"Did any group, any authority at any level from you on down to the evaluation group ever recommend the General Dynamics plane?" McClellan asked.

"No, sir," LeMay answered. He added, in response to another question, that in all his experience he could not recall a single instance where a service selection board had been overruled by a civilian secretary.

"Would you have expected . . . that you would have been consulted and the matter would be discussed with you?" McClellan pressed.

"Yes, sir," LeMay replied. "I was surprised that the decision was made without consultation."

More than 200 experts had spent 275,000 man-hours and nearly a year appraising the Boeing and General Dynamics designs, General LeMay said, adding: "The Boeing team had a much better knowledge of what was required in this sort of an airplane."

The crusty airman summed up by asserting that McNamara had made a "wrong" decision in awarding the contract to General Dynamics.[7]

Admiral George W. Anderson, then the Chief of Naval Operations, warned that McNamara's decision could mean that the United States would lose "the edge" to Russia on air power.[8]

The Boeing plane had superiority over the General Dynamics plane where it counted, Admiral Anderson told the subcommittee. Though aware of Boeing's lower bid, Anderson did not stress price. He told the subcommittee that the U.S. military services must obtain the best possible performance from new weapons if we are to keep the lead over the Communists.

Anderson said the Russians had demonstrated a capability for developing superior aircraft. He cited the MIG-15 as being superior to all but one U.S. plane—the Navy-developed F-4H Phantom. He reminded the subcommittee that the Japanese Zero had some superiority in maneuverability at the start of World War II, and that it would be impossible to calculate how much this had cost in lost pilots, planes, and ships in the early months of the war.

The Admiral related that in the Cuban crisis of the preceding October, it had been necessary for the United States to bring Phantom fighters from all parts of the country to the southeastern area to provide protection against any possible aggression by Cuban-based MIGs.

"We put our best one [plane] there," Admiral Anderson said. "In the military profession as in every other, an edge of advantage is of greatest importance. . . . If a potential enemy either believes or knows his prospective adversary possesses such an edge, he thinks twice before committing himself to armed conflict. If other considerations compel him to act, this edge can make the all-important difference between being able to defeat the aggressor . . . or lacking the edge, losing quickly."

Admiral Anderson then put forth the crushing argument: Selection of the General Dynamics plan, he said, could mean that *the Navy would end up with a plane so heavy it will not be able to operate from the majority of the aircraft carriers.*[9]

"Now we will have an aircraft 13,500 pounds heavier than our original specifications and 8,500 over the revised Navy requirement," the Chief of Naval Operations said.

"Did you have anything to suggest to you . . . that the unanimous verdict and recommendation, all the way up from the military, would be doubted or rejected?" McClellan asked Anderson.

"No, sir, I did not, and it came as quite a surprise to me that the recommendation was reversed," Admiral Anderson said.[10]

There were more damaging contradictions of McNamara's stand yet to come. At this point, however, it is necessary to recount another diversionary action staged by the aggressive Defense Secretary at this time—in mid-April, 1963.

The Secretary went before the annual meeting of the American Society of Newspaper Editors (A.S.N.E.) in Washington on April 20, 1964, to explain his case. Totally ignoring what his military chiefs had testified under oath, McNamara said:

"After extended discussions and great controversy, both civilian and military leaders now agree such a program will meet the military requirements."

"It [the TFX award] will yield a saving of approximately $1 billion," McNamara told the editors.

"The choice of a contractor for such an aircraft was a subsidiary decision," McNamara continued. "Both contractors presented acceptable designs, each capable of meeting the military requirements, and with little to choose between them on the basis of performance."[11]

This certainly seemed a deceptive speech in the light of testimony and records that the Boeing plane had a significant edge on performance. Again McNamara was tossing around the $1 billion savings figure, indicating that his decision would result in great economy to the taxpayers. Many reporters and editors, still influenced by articles about McNamara's alleged genius for economy, accepted and parroted the statement that the TFX award to General Dynamics would save the nation's taxpayers $1 billion.

This speech to the editors, while it helped McNamara on the publicity front, did him harm on Capitol Hill. Chairman McClellan became more determined than ever to probe McNamara's claim of a billion-dollar saving. He sent his investigators to the Pentagon to reexamine all available cost studies. Meanwhile, the subcommittee already had obtained new evidence that made all bases for McNamara's decision—including the alleged billion-dollar savings —look weak.

Accountant Nunnally had come up with strong proof that the only cost studies available to McNamara had some rather substantial errors—errors of the magnitude of $290 million and $340 million. If McNamara had relied on those cost figures, his decision could not have been the correct one.

Evidence also came to the attention of McClellan's investigators that McNamara was trying feverishly to construct a new paper record in April, 1963, to prove that his decision of six months earlier was correct. The subcommittee already had taken testimony showing efforts by the political secretaries at the Pentagon to pressure some career military men into changing their position and supporting McNamara.

Air Force Colonel John L. Gregory, co-chairman of the operations division of the TFX evaluation team, made a revealing admission. He testified that certain aides in the office of Air Force Secretary Zuckert had persuaded him in February, 1963, to sign a statement changing his position on the TFX award.

Colonel Gregory initially had favored Boeing. But in February, 1963, he said he "reluctantly" signed a statement on the TFX's weapon-carrying capability that was more favorable to General Dynamics. He said he was told the matter was of "extreme interest to the [Air Force] Secretary."

Colonel Gregory said he was surprised when he was later informed that his statement was being interpreted to mean he supported the awarding of the contract to General Dynamics.

Colonel Gregory told the McClellan subcommittee he regretted having signed the inaccurate documents, as requested by representatives of Zuckert's office. It was "an improvident decision," he said.[12]

Republican Senator Mundt said it amounted to "manufacturing documents that won't stand the scrutiny of the committee."

Chairman McClellan asked: "Where were these documents when the [TFX] decision was made last December?"

While freshly contrived documents and statistics were flowing from the Pentagon, the McClellan subcommittee hit a snag in attempting to obtain one bona fide document that it really wanted. This was a file memorandum, dated March 1, 1963, from Albert W. Blackburn, the key TFX technician in McNamara's own office.[13]

Many persons considered Blackburn to be "Mr. TFX." He was a Naval Academy graduate, an aerodynamics engineer, and a test pilot. His military combat record was impressive; he held a master's degree in aeronautical engineering from the Massachusetts Institute of Technology, and he had had considerable experience with the North American Aviation Company, a manufacturer of airplanes. In 1959, he became a special assistant in the Office of the Director of Defense Research and Engineering, in the Office of the Secretary of Defense.

For the past two years, Blackburn had been assigned the job of keeping up with the day-by-day developments in the TFX program. He was probably the man best informed on the TFX in America. He was the man from whom McNamara's office—which meant McNamara himself—obtained information.

It was Blackburn who had prepared an earlier memorandum, signed by McNamara on September 1, 1961, which officially initiated the TFX program. At that time, Blackburn estimated that a billion dollars might be saved through construction of one plane for both the Navy and the Air Force. Nothing in his memo, however, indicated that the savings would come through awarding the contract to any single firm.

No one was more surprised than Mr. TFX when the Defense Secretary awarded the contract to General Dynamics. In his memorandum of March 1, 1963, which the McClellan subcommittee finally obtained from Secretary McNamara in May, 1963, Blackburn wrote:

"There is no real, supportable case to be made for his [McNamara's] choice of . . . [General Dynamics] on the grounds of operations, technical management, or cost considerations."

Blackburn concluded:

"The secretary [McNamara] chose to make a decision on the basis of information different from that evaluated under the established ground rules."

When Blackburn appeared before the subcommittee as a witness in May, 1963, he testified that lawyers in McNamara's office asked him for historical and technical background for use in building McNamara's case. In response, he prepared the March 1st memorandum, which struck at the heart of every argument that McNamara had put forward. [See Appendix C for full text.]

The memorandum stated that Boeing had been ahead at every stage in an unprecedented four evaluations. Blackburn detailed the skill and ingenuity exhibited by Boeing, and commented on examples of difficulties General Dynamics was having.

"At this point in time, there was no doubt in anyone's mind as to the relative competence of the two competing companies," Blackburn noted.

He stated that although Boeing won the third evaluation, Secretary McNamara "made it known he would not permit the continuation of the program with a single contractor and elected to continue . . . giving each contractor an additional $2.5 million to further refine their design proposals and validate their data."

"During the 90 days following the three submissions by the contractors, two very different types of activity were taking place at Fort Worth [General Dynamics] and Seattle [Boeing],"

Blackburn related. "The General Dynamics engineers were desperately seeking to evolve a satisfactory configuration, whereas the Boeing engineers were carrying their design into detailed wind-tunnel analysis for both subsonic and supersonic performance. . . ."

Even when the competition ended with the fourth design, General Dynamics was still far behind, Blackburn said. He explained: "The General Dynamics engineers were still in the early stages of their configuration evolution . . . whereas the Boeing designers . . . were clearly much further down the line in coming to terms with the total design problem.

"When the announcement was made that General Dynamics would be given the development program, it was clear to all those involved that this decision could be justified only on the basis of a broad, high-level policy of the administration, and could not in any way be associated with the merits of the two proposals on either an operational, technical, management, or cost basis."

Blackburn praised "the depth of technical development of the Boeing design . . . its imaginative innovations such as thrust reversers" and other factors in Boeing's favor. He compared it with the "notoriously poor management exercised by General Dynamics" in its jet-transport program, which resulted in a $400 million loss to the company.

It was obvious why the McClellan subcommittee had had a difficult time obtaining the damaging memorandum from McNamara. Chairman McClellan actually had obtained a copy of the memorandum from a confidential Pentagon source prior to the time McNamara yielded it, and from that point McNamara's effort to hide it could not succeed.

When Blackburn testified, McClellan brought out that Blackburn had not given the memorandum a security classification, but that it was later stamped "Secret," and efforts were made to hide it from the investigators. McClellan's investigators also were told it was a confidential "executive department" paper that they need not produce for Congress.

Blackburn's testimony revealed yet another McNamara stratagem to support his ruling for General Dynamics. He used a military device popular in working out theoretical problems—the organization of "teams" to develop a case for each side. A "blue team" was to present the case for General Dynamics, while a "red team" was to present the Boeing case. But, Blackburn insisted, the whole arrangement was loaded in favor of the General Dynamics side.

Blackburn explained that he was a member of the "red team," which was restricted to the use of available data in making the Boeing case. The "blue team" had access to newly created data and a larger staff at work on still more facts and studies designed to prove that McNamara was right in giving the contract to General Dynamics.

"From my professional background, I immediately became struck with the firm opinion that the work being undertaken in defense of the Secretary's position was not being done objectively," Blackburn testified.

When the one-sided "team" contest was over, the suggestion was made—through Solis Horwitz,* a Johnson man in the Secretary's office—that the technical professionals on the "red team" now concur with the "blue team's" decision. Horwitz had headed the "blue team." The "red team" professionals—including Blackburn—refused.

Blackburn said that he and other aerodynamics engineers found it "professionally repugnant" to be told to change their professional judgment.

"I personally went to Dr. [Harold] Brown [Director of Research and Engineering] on two occasions . . . to urge him that it would not be in the best interests of the country to do this," Blackburn said. "My impression from these conversations was that the secretary intended to go ahead with releases of such after-the-fact data."

---

*Horwitz was Director of Organizational and Management Planning in the office of Defense Department General Counsel Cyrus Vance. In the Johnson Administration, Horwitz became Assistant Secretary of Defense for administration; Vance also moved up and became Deputy Secretary of Defense.

Following this incident, the TFX expert told the subcommittee, he reached the conclusion that he "could no longer, in my conscience, remain associated with the Office of the Secretary of Defense." Accordingly, he gave notice to his immediate superior that he was quitting.

Blackburn further said he did "much soul-searching prior to making a decision to testify against McNamara." He said he had examined the directives on standards of conduct for the Defense Department, and concluded he should testify in a frank manner as the directive stated, putting "loyalty to the highest moral principles and to country above loyalty to persons, party or Government department."

Blackburn testified that the $1 billion saving McNamara had estimated was only a "rough ball park figure," and that it applied to possible savings if one plane were used for both the Navy and the Air Force. The $1 billion figure could not be properly claimed by McNamara once he had selected the higher-priced General Dynamics plane, Blackburn said.

Even before Blackburn testified, McClellan had initiated other examinations of the validity of McNamara's claim of a billion-dollar saving, as well as other cost estimates used by the Secretary.

If McNamara had used the Air Force cost figures with the mammoth errors—$290 million and $340 million—he could not have been right. McClellan wrote to Comptroller General Joseph Campbell, of the General Accounting Office, on April 2, 1963, asking for "an independent review of the cost standards prepared by the Air Force and used by the Department of Defense in making its decision on the award of the contract." McClellan urged that the G.A.O. probe make "careful distinction" between figures available prior to the TFX award to General Dynamics and the after-the-fact studies.

A copy of McClellan's letter went to McNamara, and the Defense Secretary replied immediately. He said he did not use the Air Force cost studies because they were "so unreliable . . . they could not be used as a foundation for source selection."

Then what figures did McNamara use? McClellan again wrote

to Campbell: "Since the Secretary states that Air Force cost estimates were not used, I would like you to review the cost estimates and related cost data actually used by the Secretary in reaching his decision to award the TFX contract to General Dynamics. . . . Advise the subcommittee as to whether such cost estimates and data are reasonably supported."

Now the truth finally came out. On April 26th, Campbell replied to McClellan: "We have found no independent or additional cost estimates covering the TFX program as a whole, and the Secretaries advise us that none exist. . . . Both Secretary McNamara and Secretary Zuckert have stated to us that the conclusions reached by them were on the basis of their judgment, rather than on independent [cost] studies."

Since there were no cost figures available, further review "would serve no useful purpose," Cambell advised McClellan.[14]

The report seemed incredible to McClellan. McNamara, the man who boasted of deep cost documentation for every decision, had no cost studies to support him on a multibillion-dollar program.

In the hearing that followed, Comptroller General Campbell testified: "We were advised by both Secretaries that there were no independent [cost] studies."

"You can't make an audit without figures or records or something upon which to base the audit, can you?" McClellan asked.

"That is correct," Campbell said.

"The General Accounting Office is unable to make an audit [or] to find records . . . or to substantiate the judgment and decision made by the Secretary of Defense in this case?" McClellan asked.

"Not with respect to the costs," Campbell answered.

William A. Newman, Director of the Defense Accounting and Auditing Division of G.A.O., testified of the meeting with McNamara: "We requested any information that was prepared at his level concerning the cost estimates. . . . When it came time to examine the records . . . he stated that he had the figures in his head, indicating he did not have them on paper."[15]

"Can you audit figures in somebody's head?" McClellan asked. "No, sir," Newman replied.

After this lack of documentation had been developed, McClellan asked Comptroller General Campbell what he would expect to find in making an audit of this sort. The Comptroller General replied that he "would expect the fullest kind of documentation" because of the "enormous expenditures" involved and the need for supporting documents for later audits.

Not visibly troubled by exposure of his lack of documentation, McNamara issued a statement. He said that the proof of major errors in the Air Force cost figures only "strengthens my own conclusion . . . that the Air Force cost estimates were so unreliable . . . they could not be used." He added that in his view the contractors' cost figures "were equally unusable." Yet, without any independent cost studies, McNamara had ruled that Boeing was less realistic than General Dynamics, and he had tossed out Boeing's low bid.

This brought return fire promptly from Boeing's president, William M. Allen. He testified that his firm had depth cost studies available to back the TFX bid. Allen and his top specialists ridiculed the Defense Secretary's use of "a rough estimate" on cost realism.

"It has been stated that our cost estimates were unrealistic, demonstrating that we did not appreciate the complexities of developing the TFX," Allen said, paraphrasing McNamara. "According to the testimony, the government has contracted [with General Dynamics] for a 23-airplane test program at an adjusted contract ceiling price of approximately $630,000,000. Our contract ceiling price . . . similarly adjusted for 23 airplanes, would be approximately $482,000,000, or $148,000,000 less than our competitor. . . . Yet, we were definitely downgraded by reason of our lower price. In fact, our low price is one of the principal reasons given for awarding the contract to our competitor."

He declared that his company had based its bid on careful calculations, not on a "rough judgment," and could support the figures. Those figures were never challenged by the Defense Department, Allen said. He asserted that his company was fully prepared to carry out its commitment at the quoted price, which would mean a $148 million saving for the government on the test program alone.

Allen told the subcommittee it was "discouraging and disillusioning" to be judged to have the superior plane and the lowest price and to still lose the contract. It was particularly bitter to lose on the basis of rough estimates and, as Senator McClellan put it, "the arbitrary judgment" of Defense Secretary McNamara.

McNamara had disclaimed any political motive in giving the contract to the Texas-New York combine, but the big question remained: Why would McNamara make an award of a multibillion-dollar contract on the basis of what appeared to be an arbitrary estimate and with no independent cost studies? For the answer—or answers—Senator McClellan and his subcommittee turned their scrutiny to two of McNamara's principal advisers—Roswell Gilpatric and Fred Korth.

For my own part I sought an interview with McNamara to see if he had any explanations that had not come out in the hearings. Having held him in high regard during the first two years of the Kennedy administration, I was unwilling to accept the devastating picture painted by the hearings. McNamara was a busy man with a big job, and it was possible that he was unaware of all the facts, had been misled by subordinates, or felt compelled to bend to great political pressure.

I had conscientiously followed the investigation, challenging and looking for loopholes in the McClellan-subcommittee record. It was a record of hard evidence from experts—metallurgists, aerodynamics engineers, accountants, and military men. The testimony they gave had been met only by vague claims from the Pentagon that seemed to contain more hope than substance. There were assurances that General Dynamics would undoubtedly come up with a plane substantially as good as the one Boeing proposed. There was a vague claim that by the time the contract was completed, the General Dynamics plane would probably cost no more than the Boeing plane. On the record the Pentagon position looked weak. But, I told myself, it was possible I had overlooked some factor that would change or at least modify the picture.

When I entered McNamara's office in the late afternoon of Wednesday, June 26, 1963, I was bent on penetrating the vagueness—to get at facts. I wanted to ask direct questions to determine if there had been any political pressure. I wanted to find out just how much the Secretary of Defense knew of the past connections and business dealings Gilpatric and Korth had had with General Dynamics.

The Defense Secretary was all salesman from the time we shook hands at the corner of his big desk.

"I know you are an intelligent man, Mr. Mollenhoff," he said after some small talk. "I know you can see what we are trying to do."

He discussed the need for civilian control over a wasteful military organization, and of the great improvements he had made over the Eisenhower administration in terms of defense posture. It was a persuasive monologue, punctuated periodically by flattering references to my intelligence. The Secretary took pains to include me in that select category of men capable of understanding what he was trying to do with the Defense Department.

When McNamara moved into the TFX contract, he emphasized that the Air Force and the Navy had opposed the idea of developing one plane for both services, as he originally suggested.

I said I was aware of the initial dispute on this point, but understood that this was not an issue in the evaluations that resulted in "unanimous recommendations for Boeing."

He challenged my use of "unanimous" and said there were some lower-ranking officers in the Navy and the Air Force who did not favor the Boeing plane. He did not remember the names, but said he had noted them in some of the reports.

I explained that I was not contending that everyone in the Air Force and the Navy had recommended Boeing, but that there was a "unanimous recommendation" for Boeing by the properly authorized committee—the top-level Pentagon Source Selection

Board. It was composed of the highest-ranking, and presumably the most experienced, Navy and Air Force officers.

"Isn't it true that there were four evaluations that favored Boeing?" I asked.

McNamara admitted this, but scoffed at the weight the McClellan subcommittee gave to the evaluations. He said he knew that some officers who had worked on the evaluation reports did not agree with those who concluded that Boeing had a "superior" performance rating.

I told Secretary McNamara that it was always conceivable he was right, but that it seemed to me the burden was on him to produce substantial proof if he overruled a board of highly qualified admirals and generals.

He said he felt he had presented a strong case, but I called attention to the fact that the five-page "memorandum of justification" had a number of substantial errors. One of those errors was inflating the entire performance rating of the General Dynamics version of the TFX. The memorandum erroneously credited General Dynamics with a performance rating essentially the same as the higher-rated Boeing plane. I pointed out that his Department had tried to excuse this as "a little slip-up."

McNamara declared it was an "immaterial" error in the memorandum of justification, and had not influenced his decision. He said that regardless of what appeared in the official memorandum, he had understood the proper figures when he made his decision.

When I referred to errors of $32 million and $29 million in the memorandum of justification, he quarreled with the term "errors." He characterized these as "immaterial variances," which, he said, would make no difference in his decision on a multibillion-dollar contract.

I recalled Comptroller General Campbell's criticism that he had no "independent cost studies" available when he tossed out the Boeing low bid on the ground that the firm had not engaged in "cost realism."

"How will you justify discarding the low bid on the basis of a rough judgment and without cost studies?" I asked.

"I'm a $500,000 a year executive," McNamara snapped back. "I was the second-highest-paid accountant in the United States. I was paid for my judgment on contracts involving millions of dollars."

"But, Mr. Secretary," I said, "assuming that you can make these judgments on multibillion-dollar contracts, do you feel it is good government operations when there are no documented cost studies to justify throwing out the low bids?"

"I know what I'm doing," he snapped, a little angry now. "I was the second-highest-paid accountant in the United States."

He insisted that there had been no political pressure on the TFX decision, and no discussions with Vice-President Johnson. He said that President Kennedy and Johnson "know me better than to try to use political pressure."

It was difficult to believe there had been no political pressure on a $6.5 billion contract, but I moved on to other questions about Gilpatric and Korth. Did he know the details of Gilpatric's role as a lawyer for General Dynamics just prior to coming into government, the role of Gilpatric's law firm in continuing to represent General Dynamics, and the amount of money Gilpatric had received from the law firm since becoming Deputy Defense Secretary?

McNamara said he knew all about it, and saw nothing wrong with Gilpatric, a former lawyer for General Dynamics, taking a full part in the TFX contract decision.

He said he felt that "a close personal friendship" between Gilpatric and William Allen, president of Boeing, more than counterbalanced the fact that Gilpatric had been a lawyer for General Dynamics for three years.

I asked him if the conflict-of-interest laws and rules were not aimed at men with possibly compromising financial and business ties. Didn't he see some problem in a man's being a lawyer for a firm and then being totally objective in a decision on a contract which involved that firm?

"Personal friendships can be a lot more important than business ties on these matters." McNamara brushed off the possibility of any conflict of interest.

McNamara also maintained he saw nothing wrong with Korth taking part in both the TFX and the X-22 decisions. He declared that Korth had severed his ties with his bank in Fort Worth and with Bell Aerospace, and he saw no reason why Korth should disqualify himself from either the TFX or the X-22 decisions.

McNamara's attitude on "conflicts of interest" was amazing. Certainly, I could understand that he might have faith in two such close associates as Gilpatric and Korth. I could see how he would accept on face value the claim that Korth had severed his ties with his bank, and that Gilpatric had resigned from his law firm. However, the Kennedy administration had issued rather broad orders on "conflicts of interest," which warned government officials that avoiding law violations was not enough. President Kennedy had declared that officials in his administration must avoid any activity that might give the appearance that objectivity might be lacking.

When I left that eighty-minute conference, I was saddened by what seemed to me a total lack of sensitivity on "conflicts of interest." The United States Supreme Court had ruled in the Dixon-Yates case (*United States* v. *Mississippi Valley Generating Co., etc.,* January 9, 1961) that the law is designed to prevent "federal agents who have interests adverse to those of the Government from advancing their own interests at the expense of the public welfare."

The Court said further: "The statute is thus directed not only at dishonor, but also at conduct that tempts dishonor. This broad proscription embodies a recognition of the fact that an impairment of impartial judgment can occur in even the most well-meaning men when their personal economic interests are affected by the business they transact on behalf of the Government."

Gilpatric and Korth might be "most well-meaning men," but it seemed to me that there was certainly a temptation for them to favor General Dynamics because of past ties. Perhaps I was depressed because I had expected much more from the Kennedy administration. Certainly I had expected the strictest standards from McNamara. On the admitted facts, it seemed to me that President Kennedy and Secretary McNamara had permitted their actions to fall far below the standards they had set for themselves. Since McNamara told me he knew all the facts then in the record, I could no longer excuse him on the ground that he did not realize the details of past relationships and errors.

CHAPTER 14

A Generally Dynamic Lawyer — Roz Gilpatric

Roswell Leavitt Gilpatric, facile, polished, and suave, is in many ways typical of a new breed of political lawyers. They are men who successfully combine a highly lucrative law business with a career of what they regard as public service, shuttling back and forth between jobs in government and jobs in industry. Gilpatric, a 57-year-old New Yorker, graduated as a Phi Beta Kappa from Yale College in 1928, and finished Yale Law School in 1931. He became a partner in the eminent New York City law firm of Cravath, de Gersdorff, Swaine & Wood, now Cravath, Swaine & Moore. He was a Sterling Lecturer at the Yale Law School, was an active clubman, and traveled in powerful political and social sets.

Gilpatric was known in the law—and in politics—as a persuader, rather than a thunderer. He left his law firm briefly to serve, from 1951 to 1953, as Under-Secretary of the Air Force. He returned to the law firm in 1953, and was active in Democratic politics.

Roswell Gilpatric found that his Washington contacts served him well. In 1958, Frank Pace, former Secretary of the Army in the Truman administration, asked Gilpatric to handle some extensive legal work for the General Dynamics Corporation, which Pace then headed. The firm was in trouble because of a loss by its Convair airplane division that eventually came to more than $400 million. Gilpatric successfully worked out a merger of General Dynamics with a Chicago firm, Material Services, Inc., which was headed by Colonel Henry Crown, a rich and prominent Illinois Democrat.[1]

When Gilpatric entered the Defense Department as Deputy Defense Secretary, in January, 1961, he was regarded as the perfect fellow to serve as Defense Secretary McNamara's No. 2 man. He was smooth and knowledgeable in the ways of dealing with big defense-contract problems. They were the "Bob and Roz" team, and they quickly acquired a public image as one of the brightest combinations of the Kennedy administration.

At the time his nomination was being considered by the Senate Armed Services Committee, Gilpatric frankly said his law firm would continue to pay him "sums of money that will represent my interest in work that was done before I left the firm." They were "not large sums of money," he assured the committee.[2]

No one asked for details on either the money or the defense contractors who were his clients. Gilpatric had all the proper credentials of school, service, law firm, wealth, and social contacts. He and his wife gave wonderful parties. To many, perhaps, it would have seemed crude to press such a gentleman for details on finances. Thus certain facts remained unknown to the public until 1963.

In the first weeks of the TFX-contract hearings, investigators were told that two of the top political appointees who had worked on the contract had been close to General Dynamics. The men were identified as Gilpatric and Navy Secretary Fred Korth. Gilpatric had served as a lawyer for General Dynamics, and Korth had been president of a Fort Worth bank that had done considerable business with General Dynamics. There were no charges of wrongdoing—only suggestions that it might have been difficult for the two men to be objective.

Chairman McClellan delayed inquiry into the Gilpatric-Korth-General Dynamics relationship. First, he wanted to establish clearly that Gilpatric and Korth had taken a real part in the decision to give General Dynamics the contract. Then he wanted to make sure it really was a "wrong decision."

From the time some reporters first started to inquire about

Gilpatric's role in General Dynamics, the Pentagon press office
became extremely sensitive to such queries. Press officials said
they had no information on the subject, and Gilpatric was unavailable for questioning by reporters suspected of being unsympa-
thetic to Secretary McNamara's position. When the McClellan
subcommittee started a quiet inquiry about Gilpatric, one properly
sympathetic columnist wrote a friendly article explaining why he
was certain no "conflict of interest" existed. It was the first of
many defenses made by friends of Gilpatric.

Senator Stuart Symington, the Missouri Democrat, took the
Senate floor to defend his old friend. Symington had been Secretary
of the Air Force during the Truman administration, when Roz
Gilpatric was Under-Secretary. He said he was certain Gilpatric
never would let his decision on the TFX be influenced by a prior
relationship as lawyer for General Dynamics.

The way Senator Symington explained it, another factor made
any possible "conflict of interest" unlikely. Gilpatric had done
legal work for the Boeing firm, as well as for General Dynamics.
Since Gilpatric had worked for both plane companies, there could
be no question about his impartiality, Symington implied.

Even before Stuart Symington came to his defense, Gilpatric
volunteered to tell the McClellan subcommittee of his General
Dynamics legal connection.

"I stand ready at any time to answer any questions of this committee or any other committee of the Congress," Gilpatric told the
subcommittee on March 21, 1962. "When I appeared before the
Armed Services committee on January 17, 1961, I stated that I
would sever my connections with that law firm [Cravath, Swaine
& Moore] which I did. . . . I also stated that I would have no
financial interest or any other interest in the firm during my period
in public office, but I indicated that that law firm, like many other
large firms from which men have come into government in the
past several decades . . . had relations with many . . . businesses
which do business with the Defense Department. They will continue to do so. . . .

"Now after I left the Air Force in 1953 . . . I made it a matter of my personal policy never to represent any client in any dealings with the Defense Department.

"I did do certain work for Boeing, and for General Dynamics, but I had no direct dealings with the Defense Department," Gilpatric read from a prepared statement. Some McClellan-subcommittee members said it gave them the impression that Gilpatric had served Boeing and General Dynamics in much the same way.

Chairman McClellan asked Gilpatric if his testimony could be taken as a "full statement regarding any possible conflicts of interest that you might be charged with having." The witness replied that it was. McClellan asked the question again, as if to give him a chance to amplify or modify his testimony. Gilpatric said: "Well, I have a written statement of my connection that I would like to . . . make a part of the record because it is longer than the one that I gave."

The statement was accepted, and, after glancing at it, Senator Carl Curtis (Republican, Nebraska) immediately asked who wrote it. "I see it is written in the third person," Curtis observed.

"Well," said Gilpatric, "I wrote it."

Gilpatric's prepared statement—the source of much later controversy—said:

"He [Gilpatric] did . . . serve as an adviser on other matters on a few occasions for such concerns as Boeing and Convair (General Dynamics). Thus during 1957 and 1958 Mr. Gilpatric was asked by the Boeing Company to assist it in preparing its case against the Renegotiation Board in the U. S. Court of Claims, and in 1958, he appeared as a witness for Boeing in the proceeding, testifying as to Boeing's performance in the production of B-47 bombers on the basis of Mr. Gilpatric's knowledge of that program while with the Air Force in 1951–53.

"Mr. Gilpatric also served as legal adviser to General Dynamics Corp. during 1959 and 1960 in connection with its acquisition of the business of Material Service Corporation, a concern controlled by Colonel Henry Crown, of Chicago, and members of his family."[3]

The sequence in the statement gave the impression to some that

Gilpatric had been legal adviser for Boeing and "also served" as General Dynamics' lawyer.

"As I hurriedly read that statement," Senator Curtis asked, "the employment of that [law] firm [Cravath, Swaine & Moore] by Boeing was in 1957 and 1958; is that correct?"

Gilpatric answered that it was he, not the firm, who was employed. "I was asked by the Boeing Company to assist in the particular matter which I did, during 1957 and 1958," he said.

"As an attorney or as a witness?" Curtis asked.

"I was asked to assist them in preparing the case, and then to appear as a witness," Gilpatric answered.

"You were both attorney and witness?" Curtis pressed, seeking a clear answer as to whether Gilpatric actually was a lawyer for Boeing.

"They had their regular counsel out in Seattle, and I was just asked to help prepare a particular part of the case, and testify on that," Gilpatric answered.

"Now were you preparing as counsel for them or as witness for them?" Curtis asked.

"I was preparing primarily as a witness, but I also supplied them with certain facts because of my knowledge of their performance of a very important contract," Gilpatric answered. Again his response avoided the direct issue of whether he had been a lawyer for Boeing.

". . . Then Boeing has not retained the firm?" Curtis asked.

"No," Gilpatric said, finally giving a direct answer.

"It wasn't [Boeing's counsel] then and it hasn't been since?" Curtis pressed.

"The firm is not counsel for Boeing, and never has been," Gilpatric answered.

"Is the firm at this time counsel for General Dynamics?" Curtis asked.

"It is acting for it [General Dynamics] in certain matters," Gilpatric answered.

"So the first representation . . . of General Dynamics began when you handled the matter beginning in 1959?" Curtis asked.

"That is correct," Gilpatric answered. "I was special counsel on a particular matter."

Senator Curtis went on to ask if it was not true that Gilpatric's firm was not the general counsel for General Dynamics "even at the present time." Gilpatric said this was his understanding, but that he wasn't in the firm at the time and did not know what the arrangements were. The fact, as developed later by the McClellan subcommittee, was that Cravath, Swaine & Moore had been general counsel for General Dynamics since December, 1962—only a few weeks after the TFX contract was awarded to the firm with the Texas factory.

The McClellan investigators had not yet conducted a field investigation, so Senator Curtis had no further questions at that time.

Under questioning by Senator Sam Ervin (Democrat, North Carolina), Gilpatric acknowledged that "I did participate, I did assist [and] consult" in the TFX decision.

"But my former connection with the firm, my former friendship with Frank Pace, and I am just as good a friend of Bill Allen [president of Boeing] . . . would never influence my judgment [in] upholding my oath of office in this position," Gilpatric insisted.

Senator Ervin said: "I have noticed a number of insinuations in the press that the General Dynamics was selected because it happens to have its principal place of business in Texas, and that the Vice President of the United States happens to be a resident of Texas. Are you convinced that the selection of General Dynamics to perform this contract was not influenced in any way by [these] fact(s) . . . ?"

"It had no effect, Mr. Senator, on that decision," answered Gilpatric. "The Vice President never spoke to me or, to my knowledge, to Secretary McNamara, about this matter."[4]

That was the same day that Senator Symington, on the Senate floor, made much of the fact that Gilpatric "has done legal work for both these corporations [Boeing and General Dynamics]."

But this claim was to be flatly contradicted by William Allen, president of Boeing, who testified under oath before the McClellan subcommittee. When Allen took the witness chair, Senator Curtis, observing that Gilpatric's testimony left "the impression that he had acted as counsel for Boeing," said:

"I seriously question the truthful import of Mr. Gilpatric's statement, and so I am going to ask you some questions.

"Has Mr. Gilpatric ever been retained as an attorney for Boeing?"

Allen answered unequivocally: "No, sir."

He went on to explain that Gilpatric had served as a witness for the Boeing firm in connection with one lawsuit. "A subpoena was issued," Allen said. "He came out and testified and we paid his expenses for the trip."

"Did you pay him anything for his time in preparing his testimony?" Curtis asked.

"No, sir," Allen answered. "We paid his expenses, his travel expenses on the trip."

"Did you, in that connection, pay him any attorney fee, give him any retainer, at all as a lawyer?" Curtis asked.

"No, sir."

"I am glad to have that cleared up because in these two instances on one day, he [Gilpatric] clearly conveyed to this committee that he had acted as your lawyer," Curtis said.[5]

On May 7th, Gilpatric held a press conference on other matters, but there were questions about the TFX. Gilpatric said he would answer no questions relative to the money he had received from Cravath, Swaine & Moore since becoming Deputy Defense Secretary.

He was asked if it had not been true that he once had a private office in the General Dynamics headquarters. Gilpatric answered that he was permitted to use the "empty room" office of a deceased official for a period of time. He never regarded it as his office, however, nor his relationship with General Dynamics as that close, Gilpatric said.

Gilpatric was asked if top Defense Department officials ever had suggested to him that he should disqualify himself from participating in the TFX award. Assistant Defense Secretary Sylvester, the press secretary, jumped to his feet and moved in front of Gilpatric as if to prevent him physically from answering. While reporters stared, and one or two laughed at the spectacle, Sylvester and Gilpatric huddled briefly. Then Gilpatric announced he would answer no more questions on the subject of the TFX or his financial dealings with his former law firm.

Two days later, General Dynamics officials testified that they had paid or had been billed for more than $300,000 from 1959 through the first three months of 1963 by the Cravath law firm.[6]

Roger Harris, vice-president of and chief counsel for General Dynamics, said that the firm paid $269,500 to the law firm of Cravath, Swaine & Moore up to the end of 1962, and had been billed for another $31,500 in fees for the first three months of 1963. Harris testified that Gilpatric had handled the bulk of the General Dynamics work for the Cravath, Swaine & Moore law firm until he joined the Defense Department. It had been Gilpatric's acquaintanceship with the then General Dynamics president, Frank Pace, that had resulted in the business coming to the law firm, the witness said.

Then Harris gave testimony revealing that Deputy Defense Secretary Gilpatric had reason to be aware of the relationship between his old law firm and General Dynamics.

"In January, 1961, Mr. Gilpatric arranged with us and his firm that Mr. M. T. Moore take over the account," Harris testified. Moore was the senior partner of Cravath, Swaine & Moore, he explained.

Moore became a director of General Dynamics on December 20, 1962, said Roger Lewis, president of General Dynamics.

"That is a couple of weeks after this contract was awarded?" Senator Curtis asked.

"A month after," Lewis replied.

Even in the face of this testimony on the substantial connections between General Dynamics and his former law firm, Gilpatric refused to tell the press how much he received from his law firm after becoming Deputy Defense Secretary.

Now criticism began to mount on the Hill. Some Congressmen

expressed indignation over the fact that Gilpatric, the No. 2 man in the Defense Department, took part in a multibillion-dollar award to a company he had formerly represented—a company that his old law firm, which was paying him "sums of money," still represented.

On May 13, 1963, Representative H. R. Gross, a rough-tongued Republican from Iowa, told the House the TFX award "smacks of conflict of interest and has overtones of political reward."

Gross reviewed the evidence on Gilpatric's role as a lawyer for General Dynamics. "In the light of the foregoing, the only way that Gilpatric could clear his skirts of interest and prejudice in favor of General Dynamics, his erstwhile client, would have been to publicly divorce himself of any activity in connection with the contract or resign as Deputy Defense Secretary," Gross said.

The Iowa Congressman pointed out that Gilpatric, instead of disqualifying himself, had taken an active role in writing letters, conducting conferences, and negotiating the $6.5 billion contract.

Senator Wayne Morse, the Oregon Democrat, said he was "shocked" that high Defense Department officials would take any part in the handling of contracts involving former law clients or business associates.

Senator John J. Williams, the Delaware Republican, said there appeared to be a "lack of sensitivity" to the problem of conflicts of interest. He declared that it is not enough to have the assurance of the official that he is objective, but that high Defense Department officials should be required to avoid any decisions where there could be reasonable grounds for challenging their objectivity.

Senator Williams asked Attorney General Robert F. Kennedy for his view on Gilpatric's role in the TFX contract. Williams reviewed Gilpatric's role as lawyer for General Dynamics, the fact that M. T. Moore became a director of General Dynamics, the sum of $300,000 in legal fees, and the fact that Gilpatric recently had indicated he would leave the government and return to Cravath, Swaine & Moore within a few months.

"Deputy Secretary of Defense Gilpatric took an active role in the contract discussions, wrote letters in connection with bidding

procedures, and recommended that the award be given to General Dynamics," Williams wrote. "Do the facts as established by the McClellan subcommittee record constitute a conflict of interest that is against public policy as outlined by the Presidential memorandum of July 15, 1962?

"This directive states that 'even though a technical conflict of interest as set forth in the statutes . . . may not exist, it is desirable to avoid the appearance of such conflict from a public confidence point of view.'"

The Delaware Senator also asked if the Justice Department believed that Gilpatric's acts constituted a violation of the criminal law on conflicts of interest.

Norbert A. Schlei, Assistant Attorney General in the Office of Legal Counsel, replied for Attorney General Kennedy. Without consulting the McClellan-subcommittee staff for further information, the Assistant Attorney General told Williams that he found nothing wrong with Gilpatric's role in the TFX contract.

"The question presented with respect to Mr. Gilpatric is whether at any time during his work on the TFX contract he was 'directly or indirectly interested in the pecuniary profits or contracts' of General Dynamics through his former law firm," Schlei wrote. "As noted in your letter, it appears that General Dynamics remained a client of Mr. Gilpatric's former firm after he resigned to accept his present position and that Mr. Gilpatric has indicated an intention to return to the firm upon ending his service in the Department of Defense.

"However, nothing has come to our attention indicating that either Mr. Gilpatric or the firm has ever been committed to his return or that they engaged in negotiations to that end.

"Moreover, so far as we are aware, Mr. Gilpatric's former firm neither performed nor expected to perform any services for General Dynamics in relation to the TFX contract either before or after it was awarded. . . ."

Attorney General Kennedy's aide continued:

"In the instant situation, Mr. Gilpatric was not a member of his former law partnership or sharing in its profits, and there was no apparent prospect that the firm would perform any services for General Dynamics in connection with the contract. We, therefore, are of the opinion that Mr. Gilpatric's work on the TFX contract did not contravene section 434."

Even before the letter had been received by Senator Williams, the McClellan subcommittee investigators had obtained information that Gilpatric was receiving approximately $21,000 a year from the Cravath, Swaine & Moore law firm while serving as Deputy Secretary of Defense. Gilpatric contended the money was from law business he had delivered before he resigned to join the Defense Department.

There were letters in the law firm's files and in the files of an insurance firm stating that Gilpatric and his secretary, Anne Hatfield, were on "leaves of absence" from the law firm.[7] One part of a letter, in connection with continuation of group insurance coverage for Gilpatric and Miss Hatfield, stated: "We are agreeable to continuation of the insurance of . . . Gilpatric and that of his secretary, Anne Hatfield, during their leaves of absence to serve in the Defense Department . . . for a period of two years.

"If either Mr. Gilpatric or Miss Hatfield should leave the Defense Department and not return to the service of Cravath, Swaine & Moore, their insurance will, of course, be cancelled. Furthermore, if their leaves should continue beyond two years that matter of further continuation should be referred to us."

A survey of the records of the General Dynamics Corporation disclosed that Gilpatric had attended eighteen board meetings of General Dynamics between November 25, 1958, and November 30, 1960. While he had stated in his first appearance that in representing General Dynamics he "had no direct dealing with the Defense Department," there were memorandums that disclosed he had conferences with Defense Department officials on matters involving disputes of as much as $12 million.

The records of General Dynamics and of the law firm also disclosed that Gilpatric had been active in making suggestions of high-level personnel for General Dynamics, and in writing memos for General Dynamics' president, Frank Pace, on the overall outlook for contracts. These matters included the problems that faced the General Dynamics-Convair plant in Fort Worth, Texas.

Gilpatric was recalled by the McClellan subcommittee to explain the insurance matter. He claimed that a "clerical error" accounted for the statement that he was only on a "leave of absence" from his law firm for two years. He conceded that he had initially discussed a two-year tour of duty with his partners and with Defense Secretary McNamara, but he insisted that this was not a firm commitment to return to the law firm.

Gilpatric further insisted he had "retired" from the law firm in January, 1961, and merely retained a right to rejoin the firm. There was no letter or other document concerning the retirement. He insisted, though, that the McClellan subcommittee should accept his description of his status, backed by the oral statement of his law partners, and disregard the evidence of the group-insurance-company's letters.

Gilpatric acknowledged that he attended many General Dynamics board meetings, made recommendations on personnel policies, and held conferences with Defense Department officials. However, he maintained it was not untruthful or misleading for him to have informed the subcommittee that he "had no direct dealings with the Defense Department." Presented at the hearing next was a Defense Department statement, which Gilpatric had approved, reading: "Mr. Gilpatric followed the policy of never representing any member of the defense industry in dealing with the Defense establishment."

Although he held conferences with Defense officials on multi-million-dollar matters for General Dynamics, Gilpatric insisted that that was not "representing" General Dynamics.

The questioning now grew sharp.

"You were down there [to the Defense Department] with Mr. Pace and talking to General McKee, and you had already talked to Mr. Pace, hadn't you?" McClellan asked.[8]

"I accompanied him [Pace] on that meeting and I advised him during that meeting," Gilpatric answered.

"Why would you accompany him if you were not representing him?" Chairman McClellan asked.

"I was representing him, but I was not handling the dispute. That is the distinction," Gilpatric answered.

"You either represented them or you didn't," McClellan said. "Did you or didn't you?"

"I think the facts speak for themselves," Gilpatric replied.[9]

"I know they do," McClellan answered, emphasizing the words. "I don't think any lawyer or anyone could possibly construe it otherwise. You get a fee for it, and you take your client or a representative of your client and you go to the Defense Department and you talk to them about a matter in which your client is interested, a serious matter according to your testimony, and then you say that you are not representing them. . . . I don't understand that kind of professional services, if it isn't representation."

From the files of the General Dynamics Corporation, the McClellan subcommittee produced a memorandum showing that Gilpatric was keenly aware of political factors that become involved in the decision-making process on major defense contracts.

The memorandum, written August 3, 1960—only a few months before Gilpatric became Deputy Secretary of Defense—emphasized the importance of the election of either Richard M. Nixon or Lyndon B. Johnson to high political office in the 1960 campaign. In an analysis of the future prospects of General Dynamics plants in Fort Worth and San Diego, Gilpatric advised:

"If the foregoing assumptions turn out to be valid, Convair must face up to a choice between San Diego or Fort Worth as the point of concentration for future weapons systems production. While political considerations may play a part (Nixon for California versus Johnson for Texas), objectively viewed the plant complex to be selected for continuance would appear to be San Diego. . . ."

Chairman McClellan read the paragraph on "political considerations," and asked Gilpatric what he had in mind.

"Well, my crystal ball was a little cloudy that day," Gilpatric replied.[10] "I apparently didn't predict the future very accurately, because what has actually happened was that both the San Diego plant in California, and the Fort Worth plant . . . have continued. No doubt a testimony to the wise administration of this administration."

"What were the political considerations that might play a part?" Senator Mundt asked.

"All I was referring to here was, if you tried to close a plant in Texas, you have pressures from Texas, and if you try to close a plant in California, you have pressures from California," Gilpatric answered. "That is all."

"You name two individuals here, Mr. Nixon and Mr. Johnson," Senator Curtis pointed out.

"I would suspect that at that time, any closing or opening of a plant in California would receive the attention of Vice President Nixon," Gilpatric said.

"How about Texas?" Curtis asked.

"I think that Senator Johnson always took care of the interests of Texas, when he was a Senator from Texas," Gilpatric replied.

Senator Curtis then presented a Fort Worth newspaper of December 12, 1962.[11] It told of the joyous celebration in Fort Worth, shortly after the TFX award, at which the then Vice-President Johnson was given credit for delivering the big contract to his home state. Gilpatric said he didn't know anything about the statements made giving Johnson credit for the TFX contract award, but he added:

"I do agree with one statement in it: namely, that Lyndon B. Johnson has enhanced the office of the Vice President of the United States."

Chairman McClellan asked Gilpatric if Secretary McNamara had been informed of the details "with respect to your representing General Dynamics."

"Yes; Mr. McNamara knew, early in 1961, of all my prior major associations," Gilpatric replied.

"In other words, there is nothing in the record now here that he didn't know about?" McClellan asked.

"Oh, he doesn't know all the details you brought out of my

going to particular board meetings," Gilpatric said. "I didn't take him through all my private life history as a lawyer. He knew the nature of my work . . . and specifically he knew the major accounts that I was handling, such as General Dynamics. He knew it long before there was any award in the TFX case."

"Mr. Secretary," Senator Mundt asked. "Let me ask you this question: Under the canons of judicial ethics, if you were on the judge's bench, would you feel that, with your background of association, you would be in a position to hear a case where General Dynamics was a part of the controversy?"[12]

"That is a hypothetical question I have never addressed myself to," Gilpatric replied. "All I know is I have addressed myself to the position which I find myself in here, and I have reached a conclusion that I should not, in this or other matters, disqualify myself because of a prior relationship with a firm in which I have no financial interest, and no future economic gain at stake."

"I don't think it is exactly a hypothetical question," Senator Mundt disagreed, "because, in a sense, you served as a judge, one of four judges, trying to decide a decision on the largest government contract ever issued to anybody in the history of the world.

"You served there as a judge to the extent that you advised the Secretary of Defense. . . . Under the code and canons of judicial ethics . . . do you think you should disqualify yourself or hear a case in which General Dynamics was a party?"

"I was not a judge in this case," Gilpatric insisted. "I have gone into it with the committee in full, and I was acting as a staff adviser to the Secretary. The Secretary made the decision, and he was the judge. I gave him the benefit of my advice and judgment."

Chairman McClellan took up the questioning. He asked:

"He [McNamara] makes the final decision, and he relied upon and consulted with his aides, and you were one of the top ones, to arrive at that decision. That is what it amounted to?"

"There is no question about it," Gilpatric answered.

McClellan then referred to a memorandum and a list of telephone calls, showing consultations between Gilpatric and his former law partner, Maurice T. Moore, in 1961 and 1962 about persons being considered as chief executive officer for General Dynamics.

"Do I understand from that, that you were called by a member of your previous law firm and . . . consulted about who should become the head of General Dynamics?" McClellan asked. "Is that right?"

"No, I was being asked for my personal knowledge of certain individuals who Mr. Moore knew that I was acquainted with," Gilpatric answered. "One of them was Mr. Roger Lewis . . . Mr. Moore . . . called me to ask me my opinion of Mr. Lewis [and] in the course of the conversation he told me why he was calling me; namely, that Mr. Lewis was one of a number of individuals who were under consideration by the executive committee of General Dynamics as a possibility for a new chief executive."[13]

(At an earlier stage of the hearing, Mr. Lewis had told the subcommittee that he became president of General Dynamics in February, 1962, and had been hired by the company's executive committee. Mr. Moore was counsel to this executive committee.)

McClellan asked Gilpatric:

"Is this [the] Mr. Moore who is now the senior member of the [law] firm?"

"That is right," Gilpatric answered. "He was then acting . . . as the counsel of the [General Dynamics] executive committee."

"He took over your work for General Dynamics as a member of the firm when you came to . . . [the Defense Department]?" McClellan asked.

"Yes," Gilpatric replied. "That is right."

Chairman McClellan said that he believed Gilpatric should have disqualified himself from any role in the TFX contract. He declared that the principles of "conflict of interest" as set out in the Dixon-Yates case by the Supreme Court and in the presidential directives would require that Gilpatric, a former lawyer for General Dynamics, take no part in the TFX decision.

Senator Mundt and Senator Curtis expressed similar views. Senator Jackson said Gilpatric should have disqualified himself in the interests of complete objectivity. But Jackson said he was even more concerned about the fact that Gilpatric had "misled" the sub-committee on matters relative to his relationship with Boeing.

Gilpatric had his defenders—Senator Sam Ervin, the North Carolina Democrat; Senator Edmund Muskie, the Maine Democrat; and Senator Jacob Javits, the New York Republican. They said they did not believe Gilpatric's actions constituted a violation of the "conflict of interest" law, and they further indicated they did not question the propriety of his role in the TFX decision.

There also was support from President Kennedy, who said publicly that he found nothing to criticize in Gilpatric's conduct. It was a source of disillusionment to many in Washington—and many critics said as much in print—that President Kennedy, the inspired author of many fine words on ethics in government, was a willing defender of the TFX decision and of all his political appointees.

As for Roswell Leavitt Gilpatric, he resigned from the government on January 9, 1964, and left Washington to return to his old law firm in New York City—a firm that still represented General Dynamics at a price of more than $100,000 a year.

The McClellan-committee hearings were terminated abruptly as a result of the assassination of President Kennedy only a few days after Gilpatric's testimony. That tragedy made it seem questionable to continue hearings that reflected unfavorably on an important and controversial decision by the Kennedy administration.

Despite widespread criticism of Gilpatric's role in the TFX contract and other matters, President Johnson announced in September, 1964, that he was naming Roz Gilpatric to a high-level Committee on Nuclear Proliferation, a Presidential task force being set up to study means of preventing the spread of nuclear weapons. There were also many published reports that the President was considering Gilpatric to succeed John McCone as Director of the Central Intelligence Agency.

It appeared that Gilpatric might well continue to move back and forth between high government posts and Cravath, Swaine & Moore. Criticism alone was futile when the critics lacked the voice in Congress to make the Congressional leadership or the President listen.

CHAPTER 15

Talent from Texas — Fred Korth

During the Kennedy administration, the Pentagon, bossed by Secretary McNamara and bulging with defense billions, was prime grazing pasture for Texans. The friends and political supporters of the then Vice-President, Lyndon Johnson, seemed to have an affinity for hanging their hats in the Pentagon offices where the power was. And for a long time Fort Worth, Texas, in particular, appeared to have a monopoly on the office of the Secretary of the Navy.

The first Navy Secretary under President Kennedy was John B. Connally, one of the major boosters of Johnson for President in 1960. (Connally, a Fort Worth lawyer, later became Governor of Texas and was riding in the open car with the President on the day Mr. Kennedy was assassinated.) Connally was initially unpopular with Kennedy's inner circle, the so-called Irish Mafia, because during the Kennedy-Johnson fight for the nomination he had made some biting remarks about Kennedy's health. Despite this, Connally was given the Navy job.

When John Connally resigned to seek the Democratic gubernatorial nomination in Texas, he was succeeded in January, 1962, by Fred Korth. Korth, a fifty-two-year-old lawyer and banker, had been Assistant Secretary of the Army in the last years of the Truman administration. Then he returned to Fort Worth, where he became president of the Continental Bank.

Korth was less suave than his colleague, Gilpatric, and more the backslapping type. It was, possibly, the stylistic difference between the University of Texas and Yale. He usually wore a slightly worried expression, which became more worried as his time in the Pentagon wore on.

The Secretary of the Navy had been active in Fort Worth business affairs, and many of his close friends were officials of the General Dynamics-Convair plant in Fort Worth.[1] General Dynamics was one of the best customers Korth's bank had.

In fact, in the late fall of 1962, Korth arranged a $400,000 loan to General Dynamics, which was part of a huge loan arrangement set up by the Chase Manhattan Bank of New York. In all, $200 million was needed to bail out General Dynamics after a major business loss, but even $400,000 was a substantial sum for Korth's bank, which had a loan limit of $600,000.[2]

When Korth went before the Senate Armed Services Committee on January 18, 1962, for a hearing on his confirmation, he had outlined his banking and other business interests. He said he would retain his stock interest in the Continental National Bank. Nothing was volunteered and nothing asked about the bank's dealings with defense industries. There was no mention of the bank's relationship with General Dynamics.

Korth resigned as president of the Continental National Bank, but retained more than $160,000 in stock.

"I am hopeful . . . that when my Government service is finished, that I may go back to Fort Worth and might also become associated again with the bank which I was formerly associated with," Korth told the Senate committee.[3]

There was only one slight hitch in the confirmation hearing. Senator Francis Case noted that Korth was treasurer (although inactive) of the Texas and Southwestern Cattle Raisers' Association. The South Dakota Republican said there was the possibility of Navy decisions that might affect the livestock industry. "I should insist," he said, "upon your resignation being accepted" as an official of the Cattle Raisers' Association.[4] Korth agreed to sever this relationship completely, and the Armed Services Committee was satisfied.

Once confirmed, Navy Secretary Korth went to work on the TFX-warplane contract as part of his regular duties. On the fourth evaluation of the two planes, General Dynamics' and their rival, Boeing's, all top Navy officers involved in the selection expressed preference for the Boeing version. Their report stated:

"The system Source Selection Board, with naval flag officer representation, unanimously recommends that Boeing be selected on the basis of: One, superiority in all major aspects of operational capacity. Two, lower quoted cost. Three, positive ground deceleration (thrust reverser) mechanism. Four, greater weapon selectivity and carry capability. Five, less risk of foreign object damage and military loss through degradation of engine performance."

Korth recommended that the $6.5 billion contract be awarded to General Dynamics.

Even in the early stages of the investigation, some members of the subcommittee questioned whether it was possible for a man from Fort Worth to be totally objective about a decision on a contract that could pour almost $5 billion into one of his home town's biggest industries. Korth became furious when Senator Karl Mundt, of South Dakota, referred to him as "Mr. Fort Worth."[5]

"I am a man of integrity," Korth declared. He said he resented any implications that he could not be objective, or that his interest in promoting his bank's welfare would come ahead of his "patriotism."

Korth testified he didn't know that the top Navy officers—Admiral George Anderson, Chief of Naval Operations; and Admiral Frederick Ashworth, a member of the Pentagon Source Selection Board—strongly preferred the Boeing plane.[6]

He said that both planes were "acceptable," and that there was no clear and definite preference on the part of either the Navy or the Air Force.

"There was no strong statement which might have been put

forth, that, by gosh, this [selection of Boeing] is the only way we can go," Korth testified.

Chairman McClellan and Senator Jackson cited written reports by the Navy, the Air Force, and the Source Selection Board. All gave clear preference for Boeing. They pointed out that these records were available to Korth at the time he made his decision. They said that Korth should not have expected strong oral pleadings for Boeing when the written recommendations for Boeing were unanimous, and when Korth did not indicate he was going to overrule the unanimous recommendation.

"Did any officer in uniform having the responsibility of making evaluation for the Navy recommend General Dynamics?" Jackson asked.

"No, sir," Korth answered. "But I certainly don't want the record to indicate thereby that there was unanimous opinion for Boeing among all of the uniformed personnel."

"That would indicate that some dissented. . . . Could you indicate who dissented?" Jackson said.

"No, sir," Korth replied. "I did not mean that, but some expressed no preference."

"But those who expressed a preference stated *what?*" Jackson asked.

"Those who expressed a preference did express a preference for Boeing," Korth said. "This is absolutely a correct statement."

Korth added that he favored the General Dynamics plane because he felt he might get delivery quicker. But he could give no specific facts to support his expectation of an early delivery.

"I have no concrete evidence," Korth said. "But I think it is general knowledge, that the more complex a weapon system is, the more developmental time needed . . . and certainly these things normally would lead to a delay in delivery."

"If it was a factor, Secretary Korth, why was it not included in the November 21 memo [a memorandum of justification] that you signed with Air Force Secretary Zuckert and [that was] concurred in by the Secretary of Defense?" Jackson asked.

"I cannot answer that," Korth replied.

Senator Mundt read from the written recommendations for Boeing and commented: "I just don't see how you could ignore that. This, to me, is a pretty clear cut recommendation from the highest authority with whom you necessarily consult in making up your mind."

Korth replied that he "didn't ignore it," but that he had put more weight on a letter in which Admiral Ashworth had used the phrase "Both designs now considered acceptable."

Senator Mundt countered by reading from a transcript in which Admiral Ashworth stated: "My recommendation was selection of Boeing as the contractor."

Chairman McClellan declared that Korth was taking one phrase out of context to contend that both designs were "considered acceptable." Time after time, Korth used that phrase, or quoted another phrase to the effect that there was "no clear-cut choice in the naval configuration between contractors." The committee chairman said Korth used that "one little peg" to try to justify the decision for General Dynamics, though the overall report from which it came stated: "There is clear and substantial advantage in the Boeing proposal over the General Dynamics proposal."

Senator McClellan declared that if McNamara had used "rough judgment" in making his decision, Korth had used "raw judgment." Under questioning, Korth admitted that he had not read the evaluation reports on the TFX warplane before upsetting the recommendations of the top admirals.

He defended his failure to read the evaluation reports by observing that he had been told that members of the top Pentagon Air Council had not read them.

"Everybody may have been negligent!" Chairman McClellan snapped. "I don't know." McClellan emphasized that he was not at that time pursuing the negligence of others, but was interested in what Korth as Navy Secretary had done in making a decision on a multibillion-dollar contract.

"Mr. Secretary, would you make a decision in a matter as vital as this, with as many planes as you are getting here, and spending as much money, and not actually read the evaluation reports upon which you are going to predicate a decision?" McClellan asked incredulously.

Korth replied that he had discussed it with Air Force Secretary Eugene Zuckert. McClellan snapped back that it appeared to him that Korth had a responsibility to read the reports himself if he intended to protect "the Navy interest," as he insisted he was doing. Records indicated that Korth was with Zuckert for thirty-seven minutes to discuss the $6.5 billion contract reports.

Senator Karl Mundt said that Korth had a "predisposition toward General Dynamics," remarked again that he was "Mr. Fort Worth," and suggested that the Navy Secretary had been "more of an advocate for General Dynamics."

Under questioning, Korth said that he did not examine the past performances of either Boeing or General Dynamics before deciding that Boeing's low bid could be disregarded because of a lack of "cost realism."

The McClellan subcommittee pursued this matter of "cost realism." It learned that, on labor costs alone, Boeing was one of the most efficient producers in the aircraft industry. Based on the standard "cost per man hour per pound of production," Boeing operated at less than 50 per cent of the industry average. The figures presented in the McClellan record showed that General Dynamics' operating costs were more than 300 per cent of the industry average. Thus, on labor costs alone, it would have been possible for Boeing to underbid General Dynamics by nearly $400 million on the $6.5 billion contract, according to the testimony of investigator-accountant Thomas Nunnally.[7]

In one of the most scathing attacks made upon any official during the eighty-eighth session of Congress, Representative H. R. Gross told the House that the Navy Secretary should be fired. Gross declared that Korth was involved in a "clear conflict of interest" and that "this is a real Texas-size raid on the U.S. Defense budget."[8]

Gross told his colleagues that Korth's background suggested "a shocking picture of the factors that went into the decision." When Korth became Navy Secretary, Gross related, he retained stock in the Fort Worth bank, which had a large amount of money tied up in the future of General Dynamics."

The Iowa Republican declared that the Korth-General Dynamics relationship "indicates a pattern of activity that compares with the RFC scandals and the activity of T. Lamar Caudle of the Truman era, or the Talbott case and Dixon-Yates case of the Eisenhower administration.

"Fred Korth should have recognized that he could not be objective, even if there was no conflict of interest law in existence," Gross said. "Korth should have disqualified himself from handling the contract. Instead, we now see the evidence of Korth's 16 conferences and five telephone calls from General Dynamics officials he characterizes as 'long-time friends.'"

Gross pointed out that while General Dynamics officials had a total of 21 conferences and telephone contacts with Korth on the TFX, there were only two visits from Boeing officials, and only one of these dealt with the TFX.

"It would appear that Korth and Gilpatric brought not only their experiences from the Truman administration, but also some of the loose ethical standards that characterized the era of 'influence-peddling' and government-by-crony," Gross said.

"If President Kennedy . . . and McNamara have any ethical sensitivity they should fire Korth immediately.

"It is possible that they did not know all the facts on the transactions between Korth's bank and General Dynamics until the admissions [by Korth] before the McClellan subcommittee," Gross added. "However, from this point on, there can be no excuse."

Senator Milward L. Simpson (Republican, Wyoming) took up the attack in the Senate. He said he was "shocked" by the "business and political cross-currents" which figured in the TFX decision. Simpson declared that Korth's "conflicts of interest" paralleled the conflicts in the Dixon-Yates case. He said it was possible that Korth did not reveal his involvement to President Kennedy, Defense Secretary McNamara, and Air Force Secretary Eugene Zuckert.

"If he [Korth] did not, he should have," Simpson declared. "If he did, then McNamara and Zuckert are equally culpable. These Secretaries owe the public answers to many questions stemming from his [Korth's] judgment."[9]

Despite the McClellan-subcommittee's findings, and his own past statements on the need for high standards in government, President Kennedy, on August 20, 1963, said he saw no conflict of interest in Korth's role. He said he was satisfied that McNamara, Gilpatric, and Korth all conducted themselves properly in the TFX matter.[10]

While President Kennedy was affirming his confidence in the political Secretaries, he was also weighing steps to punish those who dissented or gave evidence contrary to the McNamara position.

Admiral George Anderson, the most vigorous dissenter, was dropped as Chief of Naval Operations, on McNamara's recommendation. General Curtis LeMay, who dissented a few degrees less strongly and was a better-known public figure, was reappointed for only one additional year as Air Force Chief of Staff. (Customarily, they are appointed for two-year periods.)

The TFX squabble put Attorney General Kennedy at odds with Senators McClellan and Jackson, who had been helpful and friendly to him in the past. Chairman McClellan had named Robert Kennedy chief counsel of the Senate Permanent Investigating Subcommittee in 1955, and had given the young Massachusetts lawyer the opportunity to make a name for himself in the labor-racket hearings. Senator Jackson, a long-time friend of the Kennedys, had urged Chairman McClellan to give Bob Kennedy a chance as chief counsel.

But holding the McNamara line on the TFX warplane was more important to Bobby Kennedy than the old personal friendships.

As the Korth testimony was generating trouble, White House political operators were busy convincing the younger Democratic Senators of the subcommittee—Senator Edmund S. Muskie, of Maine; Senator Daniel Brewster, of Maryland; and Senator Thomas J. McIntyre, of New Hampshire—to back McNamara to the hilt. One Republican, Senator Jacob Javits, was in the Defense Secretary's corner. The Senator was from New York, not Texas, but the contract was of interest to his Long Island constituency. The Grumman Engineering Company, of Bethpage, Long Island, was going to build the Navy version of the TFX in association on the contract with General Dynamics.

Senator McClellan, Senator Jackson, and two Republicans— Senator Carl Curtis and Senator Karl Mundt—were in sharp opposition to McNamara.

The ninth member of the committee, who could break the four-four tie on a committee vote or report, was Senator Ervin. Sam Ervin had strong praise for McClellan's ability and fairness in conducting the TFX investigation, and he had been highly critical of the Pentagon for its sneak attacks on the chairman and the staff. However, White House political operators boasted that when the chips were down, they believed they could swing Ervin to the McNamara camp with practical arguments for party loyalty.

Chairman McClellan plowed ahead, developing a voluminous record and paying little attention to any political string-pulling to undercut his influence with his committee.

"We are making a good record and a complete record, and I believe that in the long run the facts will prevail," McClellan said. He was not overly concerned when the Justice Department wrote a letter to Senator John Williams stating that Korth was not involved in a violation of the "conflicts of interest" law. He said merely that he felt it was unwise for the Justice Department to be drawing conclusions one way or the other until all of the evidence had been examined.

Committee Counsel Adlerman had informed McClellan that the Justice Department letters on the Korth and Gilpatric cases had been written without consulting the McClellan staff to try to determine all the evidence available.

Even before the Justice Department letter was released to the public on September 26th, McClellan's investigators had found important new evidence indicating that Korth had kept a close tie with the Continental National Bank after becoming Navy Secretary. When the investigation started, Chairman McClellan had been reluctant to conduct broad probes of the government official's activities. However, by the late summer and early fall of 1963, McClellan had changed his mind. He was convinced a wrong decision had been reached. Now he wanted the details of Korth's connections with the Continental Bank and his associations with General Dynamics officials.

Telephone calls and letters to the McClellan subcommittee indicated that Korth had continued to keep in close contact with the bank's operations. A reputable citizen in the Dallas-Fort Worth area suggested to Senator Karl Mundt that investigators examine the record of a multimillion-dollar insurance-fraud suit in which Korth had been one of the defendants. Others suggested that an examination of the correspondence between Korth and the bank officials would be rewarding.

The bank's files revealed that Korth had continually corresponded with bank officials on bank business. He had issued invitations to some of the bank's "very best customers" for a pleasure ride on the Navy yacht *Sequoia,* and he had been active in promoting large deposits for the bank.

Korth had testified that his bank did "a modest business" with General Dynamics, but indicated he paid no attention to the details of the bank's loans to General Dynamics. "I do not know now, as I have testified before, nor have I kept abreast of, nor am I interested in, whether General Dynamics Corporation continued to maintain an account at that bank of which I was president, of which I am a stockholder, or whether they presently owe any indebtedness to that bank."

The correspondence between Korth and the bank disclosed that General Dynamics maintained a corporation fund of $100,000 to $500,000 in an interest-free account, and the correspondence between Korth and operating officials of the Continental National Bank showed that Korth, while serving as Navy Secretary, had received glowing letters of praise from officers of the bank for bringing them $20,000 and $30,000 accounts.

Some of the letters written by Korth to promote the bank's business were written on his official Navy stationery.

The correspondence disclosed further that Korth was kept posted on bank matters and that his associates at the bank wrote to him regarding their eagerness to see the TFX award go to General Dynamics.

McClellan concluded that high officials in the Kennedy administration did not know all the facts his investigators had accumulated about Korth's continued activities for the Continental National Bank. He called Attorney General Kennedy for a conference in mid-October and confronted him with the fact that Korth had been promoting bank business on Navy stationery. This was after the Justice Department had written the letter stating that Korth had no conflict of interest.

The youthful Attorney General could have only one reaction, for he had taken a strong position in a similar situation a few years earlier. As McClellan's chief counsel, Kennedy had uncovered the fact that the late Harold Talbott, Air Force Secretary in the Eisenhower administration, had been using Air Force stationery to promote his private public-relations business. Infuriated at this conflict of interest, Kennedy had played a leading role in bringing about the forced resignation of Talbott for a "conflict of interest."

It was Attorney General Kennedy's opinion now that Korth must resign. This put the Kennedy administration in an embarrassing position because of the President's insistence that no questionable activities had touched the TFX contract. President Kennedy informed McNamara that Korth had to go, and he let the Defense Secretary handle the timing and the explanations. On October 14, 1963, Korth resigned as Navy Secretary. The letter of resignation stated only that Korth was leaving government "so that I may return to private business and attend to my pressing business affairs."

The public did not know of Korth's letter-writing, and there were audacious efforts to hide the real reason for the resignation. At the Pentagon, off-the-record press briefings were arranged to give correspondents confidential background. Korth was leaving because of a dispute with Secretary McNamara over a decision not to proceed with a nuclear-powered carrier, reporters were told.

The Pentagon's confidential explanation was accepted for a few days, but in less than a week the skeleton was out of the closet. Reporters learned the details of Korth's activities on behalf of the bank. The camouflage was stripped away.

On October 31, 1963—the day Korth's resignation became final—Senator Simpson told the Senate: "It is erroneous to think Korth was felled by a runaway aircraft carrier." The Wyoming Republican declared that Korth's activity in the TFX case justified a demand for his resignation.

"I believe the extent of Mr. Korth's improprieties far exceed the 'indiscretions' that the newspapers have been discussing," Senator Simpson said. "The issue goes farther than a question that can be terminated simply by a resignation."

He pointed out that Korth had pictured himself as a "man of integrity" before the McClellan subcommittee, but that the court record on the million-dollar insurance-fraud case in Texas raised many serious questions about Korth's background.

"Mr. Korth was a defendant in a fraud action in State and Federal courts in Texas in 1961, shortly before becoming Secretary of Navy," Senator Simpson said. "The suit was settled without going to trial by a judgment [of nearly $1 million dollars] against the principals in the insurance company involved. Mr. Korth [was] . . . one of the principals . . . listed in the suit. . . .

"Frank Pace, president of General Dynamics Corporation, made the introduction [to B. F. Biggers, president of the insurance company] that eventually brought Mr. Korth a quarter of a million dollars in stock in the insurance company—stock for which he was required to make no investment whatsoever," Senator Simpson said.

Senator Simpson said that "disturbing as the insurance story" was, it somehow failed to reach the attention of the Senate at the time Korth was confirmed as Navy Secretary.

"We [of the Senate] must strongly condemn . . . his use of his official stationery to promote his Texas banking interests," Senator Simpson said. "Did we not in the case of Harold Talbott see a Secretary of the Air Force compelled to leave his Cabinet post because he used his official stationery to promote his private business interests?

"Mr. Korth has plaintively declared that his letters constituted 'less than a dozen' instances in which he violated his trust as a top government official. I submit . . . that his plea of relative innocence, his only action to clear the record, is not sufficient. One or more instances would have been enough to violate the administration's own guides to proper ethical conduct for federal officials and employees."

Early in the investigation, Senator Simpson commented critically on the Senate floor on the evidence of Korth's continued involvement with his Fort Worth bank, which had General Dynamics as one of its best customers.

Simpson, a Wyoming lawyer and a former governor of that state, pointed out that Korth had $160,000 in Continental National Bank stock, and said Korth had given his personal approval to the bank's $400,000 loan agreement with General Dynamics just prior to becoming Navy Secretary. Since General Dynamics was the key business in Korth's home community, the Navy Secretary "should have disqualified himself from any role in the TFX contract," Senator Simpson declared.

The Wyoming Senator ridiculed the Justice Department for accepting Korth's rationalization that the $400,000 loan from his bank to General Dynamics was "only two-tenths of 1 per cent of the total available under the agreement. . . .

"Further, the Justice Department makes the fascinating comment that the 'amount involved was less than one-half of 1 per cent of Continental Bank's deposits,'" Senator Simpson added.

The Wyoming Republican scoffed at the Justice Department's effort, in the legal opinion rendered in response to an inquiry from Delaware's Senator John Williams, to minimize the transactions between Korth's bank and General Dynamics:

"We are not concerned with minute fractions of percentages of insignificant comparisons, as the Justice Department apparently wishes us to believe," Simpson said.

"I suggest that if a masked man had entered the Continental National Bank, drawn a gun and absconded with no more than $1 of the bank's money—an amount of four-hundred-thousandths of the minuscule percentages the Justice Department has quoted—that man by his action would merit attention by the Justice Department."

He quoted the federal law on conflicts of interest and added: "We are dealing directly with conflicts of interest by the Secretary of the Navy. We are dealing with a man who, by his own declaration, is the past and future president of Continental National Bank."

He explained to the Senate that the bank loan to General Dynamics "was outstanding in January of 1962 when Korth became Secretary of Navy, and it was not paid out until April of 1963—months after Mr. Korth had played a major and decisive role in the TFX decision-making."

"Why did General Dynamics need the loan?" Simpson asked. "It had undergone the largest corporate loss of any business concern in American history.

"Why does General Dynamics now seem to have a glowing future? It is because Mr. Korth participated in the decision that gave General Dynamics a government contract that promises to total more than $10 billion—the largest contract in our history."

(The $10 billion figure was based on a later and higher estimate.)

"Is there any doubt whatsoever," Senator Simpson continued, "that Fred Korth was derelict in his duty in not disqualifying himself because of conflict of interest from participation of any kind in the TFX decision? Can there be any question that Mr. Korth's conduct was improper, injudicious and suspect?"*

---

*Commending Senator Simpson, Senator Wayne Morse, the outspoken Oregon Democrat, declared: "I have always been opposed to conflicts of interest, no matter whether the individual involved was a Republican or a Democrat.

"I was a leader," Morse continued, "in the opposition to Secretary of the Air Force Talbott some years ago, because I thought he was guilty of a conflict of interest. I think Mr. Korth is also. As to the question raised by the Senator from Wyoming concerning conflict of interest, I agree."[11]

President Kennedy still tried to defend the propriety of Korth's role in the TFX contract, but he indicated that he did question the ethics of Korth's letter-writing for his bank. The President seemed to be taking the position that it was wrong for Korth to write letters on Navy stationery promoting his bank, but it was all right for him to make a decision on a contract involving his bank's best customer.

President Kennedy minimized the $400,000 loan from Korth's bank to General Dynamics: "That bank," he told a press conference on October 31, 1963, "was one of a number of banks which participated in a line of credit, and it was relatively a small amount of money, as bank loans go.[12]

"So, I have no evidence that Mr. Korth acted improperly in the TFX matter. It has nothing to do with any opinion I may have about whether Mr. Korth might have written more letters and been busier than he should have been in one way or another.

"The fact of the matter is, I have no evidence that Mr. Korth benefited improperly during his term of office in the Navy . . . I have no evidence—and . . . as I understand it the press has not produced any, nor the McClellan committee—which would indicate that in any way he acted improperly in the TFX."

Arthur Krock wrote in the *New York Times* on November 3, 1963, "Mr. Kennedy's news conference comments furnish only another illustration that the stern ethical attitude of Presidential candidates is prone to undergo a softening process when they enter the White House."

The veteran *Times* columnist declared that, after Kennedy had obtained Korth's resignation, he then engaged in "condoning in words a breach of ethics" which he had pledged his administration to fight.

Krock called attention to the speech at Wittenberg College, October 17, 1960, in which Candidate Kennedy promised that, if elected, he would impose "a single comprehensive code on conflicts of interest . . . drawing a clearer line between propriety and impropriety . . . protecting the public against the unethical behavior. . . ." Candidate Kennedy had added: "The next President must set the moral tone, and I refer not only to his language. . . ."

"This was the part of the pledge which Mr. Kennedy failed to serve by excusing in words the official actions he had by deed certified as inexcusable," Krock wrote.

A carelessness in analysis of the Korth case, or a desire to show loyalty to his political Secretaries, had, to some observers, destroyed the image of ethical leadership that President Kennedy wanted to project. It was a heavy price for a down payment on Texas political support in 1964.

Meanwhile, McNamara, still affirming his political chastity, forged right ahead with plans to build the TFX at the Texas-based General Dynamics plant. The costs shot up even higher than the highest General Dynamics bid. There were dozens of developmental problems, and the TFX soared—that is, its weight soared—well above the maximum weight the Navy had set for carrier use. McClellan sought Defense Department records to document the rising costs and the development problems, and McNamara stalled or refused to produce what McClellan requested.

In the face of such evidence, McNamara still insisted that he had made a right decision, and attempted to clamp a tight secrecy lid on all information that might contradict him. He held the power as long as he held the office, and he had the backing of the Texan who was to fall heir to the White House before the plane was built.

Several big questions remained unanswered: Would the General Dynamics TFX warplane meet the requirements of the Air Force and Navy missions in the best way possible? Would the modifications necessary to bring it up to minimum performance boost the costs—already more than $400 million—above Boeing's proposals?

Even before the plane was through the research-and-development phase, the costs were reported by the McClellan subcommittee to be running 50 per cent above the General Dynamics proposals. In Congress it was being referred to as "the flying Edsel." Secretary McNamara and the Pentagon press office issued optimistic reports on the progress of the TFX project, but refused to keep the McClellan committee posted on the details of either cost or performance. It will be years before the McClellan subcommittee or the public will be able to add up the costs and analyze the performance. By that time, Defense Secretary Robert McNamara will probably be long gone, and the problems will belong to another Secretary and to the American taxpayer.

CHAPTER 16

"The Floating Edsel"

While the Senate Permanent Subcommittee on Investigations was still probing the TFX affair, Robert McNamara, the embattled Defense Secretary, was put on the defensive in still another matter involving his judgment. In December, 1963, the Congressional Joint Committee on Atomic Energy issued a caustic report charging that McNamara was committing the Navy to a "future of planned obsolescence" in rejecting nuclear power for the fleet's newest aircraft carrier.[1]

A few weeks earlier, McNamara had ordered the Navy to proceed with the building of a conventional carrier, the still unnamed CVA-67. But the Navy wanted the versatility and effectiveness of a nuclear-powered aircraft carrier.[2] Top Navy men argued that by reason of its endurance, speed, and lack of dependence on logistical support, a nuclear carrier would provide unequaled striking force anywhere in the world. The Joint Committee agreed. There would be "incalculable waste" of years of research in naval nuclear propulsion if a conventional carrier with a life expectancy of thirty years was chosen, the Joint Committee said.[3] It would be comparable to building Model T's in a Mustang age.

Some critics, harking back unkindly to a colossal failure when McNamara was an official of Ford Motor Company, quipped that he seemed set on building "a floating Edsel."

McNamara conceded the effectiveness of nuclear-powered carriers, but contended that such a choice would not strengthen us in relation to the Russians. "I say this because with the total force we have available we are, in our opinion, completely protected against Soviet military and political pressure and we don't need additional force."

Would our potential enemies discontinue their attempts to improve their capabilities over, under, and on the sea? The Joint Committee members did not believe so. They reasoned that it is foolhardy to rely on conventional power in a carrier which is supposed to remain in use until the twenty-first century. They believed construction of a conventionally powered carrier would "create an intolerable peril to our national security."

The committee charged that the Defense Secretary was misinformed as to the performance advantages and the cost of a nuclear-powered craft.

Testifying before the committee, McNamara gave cost figures indicating that nuclear warships would cost about two and a half times as much as conventional ships. The comparison was based on the costs of the first nuclear ships—the carrier Enterprise, the cruiser Long Beach, and the frigate Bainbridge.

Challenging McNamara, the report stated: "The fact is that on a comparable basis these nuclear-powered ships cost less than 50 per cent more than they would have cost had they been conventionally powered."

Precise figures were difficult to pry from McNamara, but finally he was pinned down to a price of $440.4 million for the nuclear-powered craft, as against $277.2 million for the conventional one.

The higher figure was padded with costs not included in the conventional carrier, the Joint Committee pointed out: "The Department of Defense overestimated the cost of nuclear propulsion for surface ships. . . . For example, it was claimed that a nuclear-propelled carrier would be capable of carrying an additional squadron of aircraft. The purchase and operating costs ($37,-400,000) of the additional aircraft squadron were charged to the nuclear-propelled ship and used as a cost argument against nuclear propulsion. This nearly tripled the extra cost attributed to the nuclear carrier over its lifetime. Obviously, the additional costs are not related to nuclear propulsion and can be eliminated by not supplying the additional squadron of aircraft." (Actually, Navy witnesses testified that they planned to provide both the conventional and nuclear-powered aircraft carriers with the same number of aircraft.)

"Also, in the construction of cost comparison, the initial reactor cores ($32,000,000) which provide fuel for at least 7 years, were charged against the cost of the nuclear carrier while no comparable fuel costs were attributed to the conventional carrier."

The Defense Department made certain cost-effectiveness comparisons to support its contention that nuclear propulsion in surface warships has no particularly significant advantages.

These comparisons contained a "fundamental weakness" that negated their validity, according to the Joint Committee on Atomic Energy. Said the committee:

"The comparisons cited [by McNamara] were based on the assumption that in wartime, logistic support forces will be able to operate unhampered and without losses as they do in peacetime. The defect in this analysis is immediately apparent." (The members of the Joint Committee emphasized that in wartime the lines of supply for fuel are important, and that there is no need for continually refueling a nuclear-powered ship, as is necessary with a conventional ship.)

"We must plan for a time of crisis. It is precisely in such situations that the superior mobility, maneuverability and reliability of nuclear warships will give the United States an unequaled striking force. It is fundamentally illogical and wasteful to fit our new first line warships with power plants that are perhaps, already, obsolete."

The committee insisted that if proper comparable costs were employed, the lifetime cost of the nuclear carrier, with all its aircraft, was only about 3 per cent more than the lifetime cost of the conventional carrier and aircraft.

"It is apparent that the increased cost of nuclear power is not significant in relation to its demonstrated military advantages," the Joint Committee declared.

When questioned as to why he did not buy the best and most

advanced aircraft carrier, McNamara replied: "We don't buy the best there is in terms of technology in one of our weapons systems.

"We would be fools," he went on. "No one does. . . . We would be foolish if we bought the best . . . in terms of speed and range and firepower, when we don't need it. . . . We should buy only what we need and what we need is usable effective combat power."

In direct disagreement with McNamara, the committee warned that "our first line of naval striking force (major warships) should be the best that our technology will allow and should, therefore, have nuclear propulsion, even if a somewhat higher cost is incurred to pay for the increase in military capability."

The Joint Committee cautioned:

"Our potential enemies may not use the same cost effective criteria and thus will oppose us with the best weapons technology can provide."

The Joint Committee related that efforts were made to determine the source of the advice McNamara used in deciding against nuclear propulsion in the new aircraft carrier. The Defense Secretary said he had talked with Navy Secretary Fred Korth (before his resignation); Admiral David McDonald, Chief of Naval Operations; Captain Vincent P. dePoix, former commanding officer of the U.S.S. *Enterprise;* Dr. Glenn T. Seaborg, Chairman of the Atomic Energy Commission; and Vice Admiral Hyman G. Rickover, manager, Naval Reactors, Division of Reactor Development.

"All of the above mentioned persons testified to the committee that they had recommended that the new aircraft carrier be equipped with nuclear propulsion," the Joint Committee stated.

McNamara "cited two authorities supporting his view," but the Joint Committee discredited both of these so-called experts.[4]

"The first was a flag officer from another service who had recommended that we not build any aircraft carrier," the report said. "When it was suggested that perhaps this officer, being of another service, was not fully qualified to speak on this matter, the secretary defended the officer as having broad military experience and judgment in other matters. The advice of this officer, however, was apparently rejected since the secretary stated that he personally thought we should build more aircraft carriers and that plans are being made to build a new aircraft carrier."

The Joint Committee noted parenthetically: "The Secretary of Defense did not indicate whether the . . . officer concerned had expressed any opinion on whether the new carrier should have nuclear or conventional propulsion, once it had been decided a carrier of some type would be built." This was hardly the support McNamara initially indicated it was.

The other authority cited by McNamara was a report by the Center for Naval Analyses. McNamara said that the Naval Analyses study indicated there was nothing "to show that the nuclear power forces are superior to conventional forces of equal cost."

The Joint Committee said that this report by the Center for Naval Analyses was rejected by the Navy as being based on "erroneous assumptions." The report, said the Navy, "clearly does not represent Navy views, opinion and findings on nuclear propulsion."

In short, the only analysis McNamara relied upon in questioning the value of nuclear-powered forces was regarded by the Navy as without substance. But there was still a more interesting note on McNamara's method of operation.

Under questioning, McNamara admitted he had not read this erroneous report before making the decision against the nuclear-powered carrier. Thus, he came across this so-called "authority" for his decision at some point after the decision, concluding then that it would help him explain his earlier actions.

The Joint Committee drove the point home: "In summary, the committee still does not know of any qualified technical person or group who recommended to the Defense Department that nuclear propulsion not be installed in the new aircraft carrier."[5]

Again it appeared to be McNamara's rough judgment against the technical experts and the military men. With all of the opinions and facts against him, Robert S. McNamara made the decision that the United States should not go ahead with a nuclear carrier. The McNamara decision, in McNamara's view, needed no competent studies to support it, it would appear. Nor did he think it needed any technical advice or military expertise. McNamara made his own decisions and his own declarations on whether his decisions were sound. His claims of possible savings were good enough for the White House and good enough to satisfy many magazine writers and editorial writers.

There were important voices raised against McNamara—those of Admiral George Anderson and Admiral Arleigh Burke, the Chief and the former Chief of Naval Operations; General Curtis LeMay, the Air Force Chief of Staff; dozens of influential Senators and Congressmen; and the entire membership of the Joint Committee on Atomic Energy. The eighteen members of this committee are hardly a partisan group. There were ten Democrats and eight Republicans. The chairman was Senator John O. Pastore, of Rhode Island, and the vice-chairman was Representative Chet Holifield, of California, both Democrats.

Concern was expressed over the carrier and other programs by men who believed McNamara's actions were weakening our military effectiveness and destroying the military procurement system. (As shown in preceding chapters, the opinions of technical experts and military experts also were overruled by McNamara in the procurement of the X-22 and TFX warplanes.)

Admiral Burke warned that McNamara's practices could result in the destruction of our military procurement system.[6] He called attention to a memorandum prepared by Dr. John H. Rubel, one of McNamara's top aides, which proposed an end to the "recommendations" by the Pentagon Source Selection Board. Dr. Rubel's plan, seemingly based on the theory that "If you can't lick 'em, abolish 'em," was said by him to have McNamara's blessing. Under the procedures in the Rubel memorandum, there simply would have been no recommendations. The Source Selection Board was to be replaced by a Source Evaluation Board. The new board would have no power to recommend, but would simply make a factual report to the top-level political Secretaries.

Admiral Burke warned that the Rubel plan posed a "danger of destroying the integrity of our military procurement." And he further declared that "integrity in military procurement is vital to the morale of the military and civilian experts in the Pentagon, and vital to the relationship with the industries that do business with the Pentagon."

A number of heads rolled at the Pentagon as a result of the civilian and military men's defiance of McNamara's ideas. Tough, cigar-chewing General Curtis LeMay, the Air Force Chief of Staff, was a semi-casualty; he had annoyed McNamara in the TFX controversy, and his appointment as Chief was renewed by the White House for only one year.

Admiral Anderson was ousted as Chief of Naval Operations. President Kennedy softened the blow by naming the Admiral as Ambassador to Portugal, but Admiral Anderson remained outspoken in his criticism.

In a speech at the National Press Club, he warned of the way the Pentagon was being run by McNamara. He declared that survival of the nation might depend on stimulating legitimate dissent in the Pentagon.[7]

The articulate retired Admiral, victim of his own dissent from McNamara's TFX decision, warned: "There are no infallible judgments with respect to national security. . . . Such self-deceptions are a preamble to defeat."

Admiral Anderson said he was well aware that high military officers must be responsive to the civilian authority. But he warned that civilian officials should not try to muzzle "the forceful expression of contrary views in proper channels or frank response to congressional inquiry. . . ."

He predicted that the Rubel proposal would be "to the ultimate detriment of our military services. . . . Ground rules for competitive procurement must therefore be clear, consistent and impartial," he emphasized. "The system itself must have integrity to protect people of integrity—both civilian and military."

Admiral Anderson forcefully attacked the "myth" that the admirals and generals are "villains opposed to progress and refugees from new ideas." He cited the warnings of Colonel Charles de Gaulle on the weaknesses in the Maginot Line; Admiral James O. Richardson's caution against leaving the U.S. fleet exposed at Pearl Harbor; and the case of Lieutenant William S. Sims, who, before World War I, took his case for gunnery reform directly to the President. He cautioned against stifling such creativity of the military.

"It is curious," the Admiral said, "that those who criticize the military as being backward tend to be . . . proponents of procedures and policies which would discourage a creative corps of military professionals."

Then, in an obvious thrust at the dogmatic and dictatorial Secretary of Defense, Admiral Anderson said: "All of us must shun reasoning based on unquestioned assumptions that become self-deception.

"Napoleon, the classic case, in his earlier years so precise and discerning, gradually became intolerant of criticism in his own command," Anderson went on. "Finally, he lost his battle, his campaign and his France."

Admiral Anderson stressed the dangers inherent in overcentralized structures, and concluded that Congress must be a constant check on the use of either civilian or military power in the Pentagon.

The controversies barely diminished the shine on Secretary McNamara's halo, since few persons could really follow the tangled details. Any criticism was drowned out by the sheer volume of homage paid to the Napoleon of the Pentagon by the Pentagon press-office claque, a few prostitutes of the press, the hero-worshipers, and the political parasites.

McNamara's boosters employed the first rule of huckstering—repetition—to create the public image of an administrative superman who knew all the answers on nearly all problems and was motivated by one-hundred-per-cent patriotism.

Few listened to such an experienced critic as Hanson Baldwin, the *New York Times* military analyst. Baldwin was not unmindful of a number of beneficial steps taken by McNamara, and he gave the Defense Secretary credit for having "instituted some much-needed management reforms, effected some economies."

Baldwin pointed out that by boosting spending from $42 billion to above $52 billion a year, McNamara had "added considerably to our strategic strength and our conventional war and general support forces."

But, while giving McNamara credit for certain improvements resulting from his "cost-effectiveness" studies, Baldwin stated that the Defense Secretary must also "share the blame" for creating a bureaucratic "over-centralized organization" that hampers new ideas and speedy development.

Among other cases, he cited the McNamara decision against the nuclear carrier, and pointed to testimony by Vice-Admiral Hyman Rickover criticizing the Defense Secretary's office for asking for "more studies, (and) more analyses: to the point that we don't build ships."[8] One of the Pentagon's cost studies was yet to show how seriously McNamara had blundered in deciding against the nuclear carrier.

On May 5, 1965, Representative William H. Bates (Democrat, Massachusetts) told the House that according to Department of Defense cost studies, a conventional carrier is more expensive than a nuclear carrier when the cost of oilers and protection for oilers are figured into the analysis. "This is borne out," he said, "in a detailed classified analysis submitted to the Joint Committee on Atomic Energy on January 13, 1965, by the Assistant Secretary of Defense, Mr. Charles J. Hitch."

By mid-1965, however, the construction of the carrier, now named the U.S.S. *John F. Kennedy,* as a conventional carrier had progressed too far to consider converting it to nuclear propulsion. Figures submitted to the House Armed Services Committee by the Defense Department indicated that conversion of the U.S.S. *John F. Kennedy* in 1965 would cost an additional $157,-800,000 and would delay the completion of the carrier at least a year.

Representative Mendel Rivers (Democrat, South Carolina),

chairman of the House Armed Services Committee, called Mc-
Namara's decision for a conventional carrier "an error in judgment" and reported that Admiral Hyman Rickover, though an
early and leading supporter of nuclear propulsion, "now feels that
the progress made on the U.S.S. *John F. Kennedy* now makes conversion to nuclear power too expensive."

Representative Chet Holifield, vice chairman of the Joint Committee on Atomic Energy, in an exchange of letters with Rivers
pointed out that "the only new surface warship authorized for our
naval striking force in the 1963, 1964, 1965 and 1966 programs is
the aircraft carrier, CVA-67, recently named the U.S.S. *John F.
Kennedy*." The California Democrat, usually an administration
supporter, termed it "a costly mistake for this great ship to be built
with conventional propulsion." But the damage had been done,
and the U.S.S. *John F. Kennedy* was destined to travel the seas in
the nuclear age dependent upon fuel from a fleet of oilers.

The Defense Secretary had produced virtually nothing new in
military weaponry during his administration, and he had rejected
technological advances. Yet he continued to be billed as the fore-
sighted defense genius who would produce a military establishment able to keep ahead of the Communist world.

McNamara preached on the horrible condition of U.S. defenses
when he took over the Pentagon, and soon the high degree of
readiness under *his* program was extolled. But after the Cuban
missile crisis, McNamara told of the sad state of our defenses to
meet that threat—which occurred nearly two years after he took
control.

McNamara broadcast whatever served the administration's purpose at the moment, whether it was foreign aid or the military
shoring up of Vietnam. He contradicted himself one minute and
reversed himself the next—and still was praised as a man with insight, grasp, and a forthright approach unusual in high government
office.

Much of the press reacted to criticism of McNamara in the manner of Pavlov's dogs slavering at the sound of the dinner bell.

When Senators and Representatives complained that McNamara was destroying our future defense posture, numerous writers automatically erupted in anguish, crying that the complaints came from old mossbacks who finally were being put in their place by an intellectual giant of the twentieth century.

And when experienced generals and admirals ventured to express alarm at McNamara's arbitrary decisions, some pundits of the editorial pages responded that at last a strong civilian authority was whipping "the brass" into line at the Pentagon. There would be no military dictator while Bob McNamara was around, the nation was assured.

When there were indications of leaks at the Pentagon that might prove embarrassing to McNamara's TFX decision, Assistant Defense Secretary Sylvester signed a brazen directive, setting up strict guidelines on what information was to be released about the TFX.[9] All comments to the press, Sylvester decreed, must stress that McNamara's decision would result in savings of millions of dollars to the taxpayers. Also, the press was to be instructed that the TFX was the plane the Air Force and the Navy wanted, and that it would represent a great advance in weapons systems.

Nothing at all about the TFX that ran counter to the McNamara-Sylvester line was to be distributed without clearance by Sylvester's office. It was an efficient—and autocratic—way to limit the dissemination of dissent and to spot the dissenters.

Senator Mundt, of the Permanent Subcommittee on Investigations, said the Sylvester directive would "force the Navy and Air Force to circulate a rather distorted version of the whole TFX affair." Glum John McClellan, chairman of the committee, disapprovingly characterized the directive as a ukase to Pentagon officials to "tell the public that black is white."

Criticism continued to be met with steps to silence or discipline the critics. During the Cuban crisis, Sylvester had issued a similar directive to all Pentagon personnel on October 27, 1962. It required that any talks with newsmen be reported to his office before the end of the business day, unless the talk had been monitored by a Pentagon information officer.

Despite complaints of censorship, Sylvester refused to retreat. With Alice-in-Wonderland logic, he argued that the directive was an "aid" to the flow of news from the Pentagon because it kept him abreast of all information any newsmen received. How this aided the "flow of news" critics failed to see. But Sylvester had McNamara's full backing, and he kept the October directive alive in the face of strong criticism for many months.

As late as May, 1964, Sylvester issued a reminder, in the form of a supplementary order, that the October directive was still in effect.

Weekly reports to Sylvester's office were to be made on all interviews granted by departmental personnel, including the Secretaries of the Army, Navy, and Air Force. The reports required a listing of the date of the interview; the name of the interviewer and his organization; the person interviewed; and the subject matter. Also required was a report on whether an information officer was present.

Many reporters complained that the Sylvester directives made news sources cautious about critical discussion of McNamara or the Pentagon political line. Others took consolation from the fact that their sources paid little attention to the directives, and Sylvester was ineffectual in trying to enforce it.

Still, the directive—whether enforced or not—hung over the heads of every Pentagon official, civilian or military, with the force of a department rule: To disregard it meant risking disciplinary action for violation of department rules. The resulting atmosphere made it politic for all Defense officials to keep in tune with McNamara's views, and to swallow their pride and hide their dissents.

McNamara himself might not insist on total loyalty, but the directive provided the means of identifying the dissenters. It also provided the teeth for disciplinary action against any official who carelessly forgot to report a meeting or a conversation with newspaper reporters, magazine writers, or other newsmen.

During the Kennedy administration, Hanson Baldwin had referred critically to the Pentagon as "McNamara's monarchy." There was no diminution of McNamara's power when Lyndon

Johnson became President, for the Defense Secretary had wisely catered to Texas.

To many observers it seemed miraculous that McNamara, who had played so close to both President Kennedy and Attorney General Robert Kennedy, could retain an equally advantageous position with President Johnson. But it was no more difficult to understand than his survival of the investigations of the X-22, the TFX, the nuclear carrier decision, and other controversial matters. Certainly, the Defense Secretary's predictions on the course of the Vietnamese War turned out to be as inaccurate and vulnerable as his arguments against the nuclear carrier. However, the continuing sparkle of his public image made some of his sharpest critics begin to doubt that there was a way to persuade the public to listen more than momentarily to facts contrary to the McNamara line. The huge public relations operation McNamara ran from the Pentagon seemed capable of drowning out or muffling nearly all voices of dissent.

CHAPTER 17

A Bug in the State Department

In February, 1963, a man named Otto Otepka was the Chief Security Evaluator for the Department of State in Washington. A law-school graduate, Otepka was a career civil servant with more than twenty-five years' service with the government. He had worked in the Internal Revenue Service, the Department of Agriculture, and the Civil Service Commission until 1953, when the Eisenhower administration shifted him to his sensitive and important State Department security job.

It can be fairly stated that the forty-seven-year-old Otepka was an exceptional civil servant. In 1958, when John Foster Dulles was Secretary of State, the Department gave him its Meritorious Service Award for his judicious handling of his duties as deputy director of the Office of Security.[1] In 1960, his departmental efficiency report commended his "long experience with and extremely broad knowledge of laws, regulations, rules, criteria and procedures in the field of personnel security.

"He is knowledgeable of Communism and its subversive efforts in the United States," the report added. "To this he adds perspective, balance and good judgment."[2]

Then, in 1961, after President Kennedy had come in and Dean Rusk took over as Secretary of State, Otto Otepka made a mistake.

He started worrying about the way the State Department, through a device known as "emergency clearance," was hiring personnel for high-level jobs involving security without a full F.B.I. investigation. He also became concerned over the shockingly casual way in which spies, using every method from subversion to sex, had penetrated the U. S. Embassy in Warsaw.

Then Otto Otepka made the additional mistake of cooperating with the Internal Security Subcommittee of the U. S. Senate, which was investigating the breakdown of security in Warsaw and elsewhere. In the course of events, one of Otepka's superiors testified under oath before the Senate subcommittee that Otepka had not been truthful about a certain fact.

Otepka was angry at being called, however it was phrased, a liar. He produced for the subcommittee, from his files, a memorandum signed by the boss who had said he lied. The memorandum showed that it was not he but his accuser who was giving untruthful testimony under oath.

From then on, Otto Otepka was in trouble. His office was "bugged," his telephone was tapped, he was put under tight surveillance. Security officers descended on him, ransacked his desk, his office safes, and then ousted him from his office. His secretary was transferred without explanation, and his private secretarial service was cut off.

He became known around the State Department as a man best not to know. Old friends shunned him—as if he were giving secrets to the Communists, instead of trying to do something about other State Department employees whom he suspected of having done just that.

Finally, the State Department tried to fire Otto Otepka for giving Congress the documents to prove he was telling the truth.[3]

The incredible thing about all this is the fact that it happened under an administration that spoke frequently and thrillingly of liberalism, of the rights of the individual, of the dignity of man. . . .

But let us go back to the beginning. Let us examine the facts in this remarkable case history of the vengeful and cynical persecution of a conscientious employee by public officials whose actions constitute a corruption and perversion of the spirit of fair play in a democratic society.

Prior to February, 1963, Chief Security Evaluator Otepka and a small group of career lawyers and investigators were in sharp disagreement with certain of their superiors over security procedures in the State Department. The Otepka group strongly opposed relaxation of security standards in the selection and handling of personnel. To Otepka, the fact that Nikita Khrushchev was talking like a good fellow for the moment, or the fact that Russia seemed to be falling out with Red China, seemed no proper reason for letting down the Department's guard.

Otepka was aware of the steady, unrelenting Soviet efforts to penetrate the State Department at the highest as well as the lowest levels. The Communists had been successful in subverting top-level officials in Sweden, England, and West Germany. The near total destruction of security in the United States Embassy in Warsaw was a frightening demonstration of how the Communists could effectively bore inside an American embassy.

Fortunately, intelligence from a Polish defector, Colonel Michael Goleniewski, made it possible for the State Department Security Division to remove more than a dozen persons who had been compromised by the Communists.

Attractive Communist women had seduced nearly all of the U.S. Marine guards in Warsaw. The Polish temptresses had free access to the Marine barracks as well as to the Embassy. The wife of one of the ranking officials in the Warsaw Embassy, while on a trip to Moscow, had been seduced by a handsome Russian agent. Efforts were being made to compromise this woman and her husband at the time the whole scandal was discovered.

Several code clerks in the Warsaw Embassy had been warmly entertained by Communist women. Irvin C. (Doc) Scarbeck, Second Secretary of the American Embassy, admitted he had been blackmailed after an affair with a Polish girl, and had subsequently passed secret papers to a Communist spy ring in Warsaw. Scarbeck was returned to the United States, tried and convicted, and sentenced to thirty years in prison.*

*Scarbeck's sentence was later reduced to ten years.

Even more disturbing to Otepka and some of his associates was the case of another official in the U. S. Embassy in Warsaw, who held a higher rank than Scarbeck and handled more secret information. Security officers finally concluded that he was a long-time Communist spy. Security Division and F.B.I. investigations appeared to corroborate Colonel Goleniewski's statement that this man had been an active spy for the Soviet Union for nearly twenty years while serving at a number of sensitive U.S. posts. Yet no charges were brought against him. He was allowed to resign quietly and live in Europe with no indication on the record that he had been other than an upstanding career Foreign Service officer.

Otto Otepka did not see a Red under every bed, but he felt that the sordid story of the U. S. Embassy in Poland should serve as a warning. Conditions in the Warsaw Embassy were not just the products of an active imagination; they were proven facts. Scarbeck had admitted his indiscretions and the passing of State Department papers to the Communists. The Marines admitted their activities with the Communist women in Warsaw. The wife of the high-ranking Foreign Service officer admitted she had been involved in an affair with the Russian.

There were many other breaches, even with the State Department's Security Division constantly on the alert. The problem of maintaining balance in the administration of a security program is a difficult one. After more than twenty-five years in government service, Otepka felt he understood the difficulty.

Otepka had witnessed the excessive zeal that had unbalanced the Republicans in their first months in power. Those were the days when the Republicans had tried to grab any scrap of evidence to dramatize their charge that the Truman administration had "coddled" Communists and Communist sympathizers. While he believed that there had been some general laxity and poor administration of security during the Truman administration, Otepka found himself to be a moderating force. He had insisted on sound evidence before challenging the loyalty or integrity of career State Department employees or political appointees.

It was Otepka who, in 1954, took the initiative in clearing Wolf

Ladejinsky, the U.S. agricultural attaché in Tokyo. Former Secretary of Agriculture Ezra Taft Benson had labeled Ladejinsky a security risk because Ladejinsky had been born in Russia and had two sisters living in Russia, and because his name appeared on the mailing list of the Washington Book Shop—an outfit identified in Congressional reports as a Communist-front organization.

The evaluation of Ladejinsky's record by Otepka had convinced him that Ladejinsky was not subversive. There were hundreds of loyal persons whose names appeared on the mailing list of the Washington Book Shop because they had purchased books there with no knowledge that the place was used on occasion for Communist meetings. It was the careful professional work of Otepka and others like him who brought the State Department through the frenzy of the McCarthy era, and established what Secretary of State John Foster Dulles regarded as a reasonably balanced—though admittedly imperfect—security program.

Otepka was not always pleased with the security clearances given at higher levels under the Eisenhower administration. But he was a career civil servant and lived within the framework of Big Government and the bureaucratic system. He made his recommendations, set out his reasons in a factual way, and registered his objections through channels when he felt there was reason for concern if he was overruled by superiors.

Politics and public opinion were facts of life that became involved in decisions on the political levels above Otepka, and Otepka understood his place. But, as a careful and experienced bureaucrat, Otepka demanded one thing. If someone up the ladder overruled *his* decision in a security matter, Otto Otepka insisted that the all-important paper record itemize all the steps taken, and contain the name of the person or persons taking responsibility for the controversial security clearance.

This knowledge of correct procedures and his insistence that they be carried out got him in trouble almost from the moment the Kennedy administration took over and Dean Rusk became Secretary of State.

The law provides for use of an "emergency clearance" for appointment of high officials where it is deemed essential to hire the man without a full F.B.I. background investigation. If the Secretary of State signs a so-called "security waiver," appointments can be made on the basis of a procedure known as a "national agency file check."[4] This is not a really extensive security check at all.

During the eight years of the Eisenhower administration, "security waivers" for emergency clearance were used only five times by the State Department. However, under Secretary Rusk the procedure was used with such frequency that Otepka became alarmed. By early 1962, Secretary Rusk had granted more than 150 security waivers to high-ranking State Department personnel.

Although complete background investigations were conducted later, this procedure meant that many officials were handling highly classified security matters before they had been subjected to a full field investigation. Also, once a man is hired and on the government payroll, it is often more difficult to dislodge him because of a questionable background than it would have been simply not to hire him in the first place.

To Otepka, this mass use of "emergency clearance" represented a substantial relaxation of security. But there were other problems that caused friction. He was involved in an investigation and evaluation of two major personnel security cases—those of John Stewart Service and William Wieland.

Otepka made a finding that Service was not a loyalty risk, though he questioned his judgment and conduct in turning over documents to Philip Jaffe, the publisher of the magazine *Amerasia,* identified in official reports as a pro-Communist publication.[5] Service was dismissed, but the Supreme Court ordered his restoration to duty on the ground that the Department had not followed proper procedures. Service subsequently was cleared, and served out his time until retirement as Consul General in Liverpool.[6]

Wieland was the State Department's highly controversial expert on Cuba. A key Department figure in the early Castro days, he was the subject of an official investigation on charges of being a Communist. Otepka concluded that the evidence did not support the charges against Wieland. But he did question Wieland's integrity on the basis of allegedly inaccurate and questionable testimony Wieland had given to security investigators. In Otepka's testimony before the Senate Internal Security Subcommittee, he stated that Wieland had given false and misleading information to security investigators.

"I think Mr. Wieland lied," Otepka testified before the Senate subcommittee. In his official reports to superiors, Otepka said he "did not use the term 'lie' but certainly the inference was plain."[7]

"There were such words as 'misrepresentation' and 'false statement,' " Otepka told the subcommittee.

Despite Otepka's finding, Wieland was cleared by Roger Jones, Deputy Under-Secretary of State for Administration.[8] However, plans to assign Wieland to a sensitive diplomatic post in Germany were later blocked by Attorney General Robert Kennedy.

The friction caused by these cases was increased by Otepka's opposition to certain changes in departmental rules and regulations. He believed the changes would weaken security standards further.

The Security Evaluator also refused to give approval for clearance for the appointment of several prominent persons to a high-level State Department committee. Otepka would not change his stand when requested to do so in a number of instances. He informed his superiors that they could overrule him if they saw fit, but that they should make a full record in writing of their reasons.

There was a continuing investigation of the State Department security procedures by the Internal Security Subcommittee, in 1962 and 1963, and Otepka was one of the witnesses. His superiors knew that he gave testimony criticizing what he believed to be a general relaxation of security, and the handling of certain cases.

In one instance, Otepka testified that he had given information on a security case to one of his superiors—Deputy Assistant Secretary of State John F. Reilly. The information had been passed on to Reilly by Otepka before the Department's decision was made. Otepka testified that he had given Reilly full warning of the particular problems involved.

Reilly was called before the subcommittee, and he denied that Otepka had given him this information.

The subcommittee's veteran counsel, J. G. Sourwine, who knew Otepka's reputation as a careful investigator, telephoned Otepka. Sourwine told him his testimony had been contradicted. Was he certain, he asked, that he was telling the truth? Indignantly, Otepka said that he certainly *had* told the truth, and that he could—and would—prove it.

Otepka went to his files at the State Department, where he obtained two documents he felt would prove his story conclusively. One was a memorandum he had written several months earlier to Reilly. It gave the details of the information about which Otepka had testified. That document had been initialed by Reilly, who said he had never heard of it.

The second document was a letter written by Reilly. This letter made reference to the information that Otepka had transmitted in the memorandum.

Otepka also passed along a third item. It was simply a sample personnel security case involving a young woman who had no derogatory information in her file, and who had been cleared without any problems. Otepka submitted this document to Sourwine to demonstrate how certain cases were handled under normal procedures.

Two of the documents proved that one of Otepka's superiors had lied under oath to the Senate Internal Security Subcommittee. When the full impact of what Otepka had done became known at the State Department, the smoldering antagonism against the security officer erupted into a full-fledged drive to get Otepka. He was their hair shirt, and certain State Department bureaucrats were going to strip him off.

The official record is not clear as to the identity of the highest-level officials who launched the "get Otepka" drive. But the activities of some of the participants are well documented in later testimony before the Senate Internal Security Subcommittee. In most instances, the facts were later described by the participants themselves.

Deputy Assistant Secretary of State John F. Reilly; David Belisle, an assistant to Reilly; and Elmer Dewey Hill, an electronics expert, met on March 13, 1963. Their purpose was to discuss ways of obtaining information about Otepka's cooperation with the Internal Security Subcommittee.[9]

The discussion touched on a wide variety of techniques that might be used to obtain anti-Otepka evidence. They discussed the possible use of a listening device on Otepka's telephone, a "bug" in Otepka's office to pick up conversations, and a close surveillance of his security burn-bag papers. (The burn bag is a receptacle for discarded material of a classified nature, which is picked up by an employee with security clearance and burned in an incinerator.) It might yield old typewriter ribbons, sheets of carbon paper, or scraps of paper that could give clues to Otepka's activities.

On Monday, March 18th, Reilly asked Hill, the bugging expert, to explore ways of eavesdropping on conversations in Otepka's office. Hill talked with Clarence Jerome Schneider, then chief of the Technical Operations Branch, Division of Technical Services. It was decided to modify the wiring in Otepka's telephone instrument to convert it into a secret listening device that would both pick up telephone conversations and other conversations in the room when the phone was not in use.

That evening, Schneider and Hill slipped into Otepka's office. They rigged the wiring in Otepka's telephone and arranged additional wiring to record the conversations. But, on testing the electronic trap, Hill found that he was unable to overhear regular conversations in Otepka's office because of an electrical interference that caused a loud buzzing sound. He could only eavesdrop on the telephone conversations.[10]

The next day, Hill reported the problem to Reilly, and with Schneider's help they sought—unsuccessfully—to obtain special equipment that would eliminate the buzzing.

About a dozen of Otepka's conversations actually were recorded, and Reilly told Hill he had a special interest in one of them.[11] However, the next day, March 20th, Reilly told Hill to discontinue the wiretap and recordings because he had found the type of information he was looking for "from an examination of Mr. Otepka's classified trash."

That evening, Reilly, Schneider, and Hill went to the corridor of the State Department where Otepka's office was located. Reilly and Schneider stationed themselves in the hall as lookouts. Hill entered the office and removed the planted connections from Otepka's telephone.[12]

A few days later, Reilly and Belisle conferred on the Otepka case. Belisle had just returned from a trip to Costa Rica with Secretary Rusk. Reilly brought Belisle up to date on the results of the Otepka telephone tap. He also told him he had had some success in obtaining information by rummaging through Otepka's burn bag. Reilly had found evidence, he said, that Otepka had supplied the Internal Security Subcommittee with a list of questions to ask State Department officials.[13]

In May and June, 1963, the Senate Internal Security Subcommittee questioned Reilly several times on the handling of a series of security cases. Tension heightened between Reilly and Otepka. It was intensified as Reilly found more scraps in Otepka's burn bag that he felt might be damaging. Reilly had continued to go through this after discontinuing the bugging.

On June 10th and June 18th, Reilly reported that he found facsimile copies of classified documents, and that the scraps of paper included parts of some documents with the national security classifications on them. Reilly judged this a technical crime of "declassification" or "mutilation" of classified documents.

The finding of these paper scraps in the burn bag was to be one of the grounds on which Reilly later would seek to have Otepka fired. But, in fact, persons other than Otepka could have discarded the scraps. Otepka later said in defense pleadings that he had nothing to do with the clipping of the papers that Reilly used as the basis for his charges. He contended that the clippings were "planted" in the burn bag in an effort to rig a technical charge against him when other methods failed.

On June 27th, Reilly and six Security Division officers walked into Otepka's office. They ransacked his desk drawers, obtained the combinations to the fourteen security safes in Otepka's office, and seized records. Then, in front of his secretary and other employees, they ousted him from his office. Reilly told him another office had been provided, that he was to go to it, and that he was not to return, under any circumstances, to the section of the State Department building in which the evaluation area was located. He was denied access to all his records, including personal papers.

When Otepka asked for an explanation, Reilly shook a finger at him and reminded Otepka that he had warned him earlier about "institutional loyalty."

Otepka snapped back that "My first loyalty is to my country.

"You're punishing me for telling the truth on Capitol Hill," Otepka declared. "I won't take back a word of it."

The new office—Room 38A05 in the State Department, outside the evaluation area—was a "little cubbyhole," Otepka found. It had bare walls, bare desk, and no files. He was given the job of writing a "new handbook on security matters," but was denied access to all information that had a security label on it. His secretary was taken away. When he needed secretarial service, he had to call Reilly's office and make arrangements for a temporary secretary assigned by Reilly.

No explanation of any sort was given him, except for Reilly's oblique reference to the need for "institutional loyalty" to the State Department.

Otepka told the Senate Internal Security Subcommittee that he placed loyalty to his country above loyalty to any departmental organization or political organization. He would continue to cooperate.

Many would have quit in disgust, or a more naïve man might have blurted out furious phrases that would have provided substantial grounds for charges of insubordination. Otepka kept his mouth shut, his ears open, and his instincts attentive to any evi-

dence that would support his suspicions that his office telephone
had been tapped. There had been peculiar noises on the line for
some time, and he had heard a report that Elmer Dewey Hill,
the department's electronics expert, had been in his office at night.
He passed this information along to the Senate Internal Security
Subcommittee.

On July 9, 1963, the Senate Internal Security Subcommittee
called Hill for questioning on reports that Otepka's telephone
had been tapped.[14] Chief Counsel Sourwine knew that Otepka was
in trouble because he had cooperated with the Senate subcommittee. He gave Hill an exhaustive, methodical interrogation designed to bring out the truth, without any equivocation, as to
whether Otepka's telephone and office had been bugged.

Over and over again, with variations, the counsel asked the
electronics man questions leading to the same point. Over and
over again, Hill denied everything.

Q. (By Sourwine): Do you know of any single instance in
which the department has ever listened in on the telephone of an
employee?

A. (By Hill): I cannot recall such an instance.

Q. Do you know of any instance where a listening device has
been placed in an employee's office?

A. Not to my knowledge.

Q. Specifically, did you ever have anything to do with tapping
the telephone of Mr. Otepka. . . .

A. No, sir. . . .

Q. Did you ever have anything to do with placing a listening
device in Mr. Otepka's office?

A. No, sir.

Q. Did you ever have anything to do with the search of Mr.
Otepka's desk or his safe or any of his files at night?

A. No, I had nothing to do with it.

Q. Did you have any knowledge if this was done, if it was done?

A. I now have knowledge of it. It was discussed with me by
Mr. Belisle.

Q. Did he [Belisle] tell you that this committee was concerned over the question of the tapping of Mr. Otepka's telephone?

A. Yes, sir.

Q. Do you want us to understand that you had no knowledge of either [the tapping or the search] until Mr. Belisle told you about this committee's interest?

A. Yes, sir.

Q. And . . . he did not indicate to you that there had been a tapping or a search?

A. That is right. Yes, sir.

Hill's flat denial of any knowledge that there had been a wiretap or any other "bugging" device placed in Otepka's office was contrary to the other information the Senate subcommittee had acquired. But there was more work to be done before Hill could be pinned down.

Senator Thomas J. Dodd (Democrat, Connecticut), vice-chairman of the subcommittee, called Belisle as a witness on July 29, 1963.[15] Again, Chief Counsel Sourwine pressed the questioning. He started by asking Belisle if he had ever investigated the State Department's rights to place a tap on an employee's telephone.

"Well," Belisle answered, "that would be a legal question, I guess, and inasmuch as I am not a lawyer, I don't know whether he [sic] has any rights or not."

The questioning continued:

Q. Do you have any information with respect to the tapping of the telephone of Mr. Otto Otepka?

A. No, sir.

Q. Do you know whether this was done?

A. No, I do not.

Q. Did you have anything to do with the placing of a listening device in Mr. Otepka's office?

A. I did not, sir.

Q. Do you know if this was done?

A. I do not.

A week later, on August 6, Deputy Assistant Secretary of State Reilly was summoned to a closed session of the subcommittee.[16] Sourwine asked:

Q. Have you ever engaged in or ordered the bugging or tapping or otherwise compromising telephones or private conversations in the office of an employee of the State Department?

A. No, sir.

Q. You never did?

A. That is right, sir.

Q. Specifically, in the case of Mr. Otepka you did not do so?

A. That is correct, sir.

Q. Did you tell Jerome Schneider [C. J. Schneider, then chief of the Technical Operations Branch] to install an electrical device to compromise Mr. Otepka's telephone?

A. No, sir.

Q. Did you know this had been done?

A. No, sir.

Q. Have any listening devices been installed in his [Otepka's] office?

A. No, sir.

Sourwine asked the State Department official other questions designed to cover all possibilities; then he asked the essential question again—whether Otepka's office had been bugged by anybody —to give the witness a chance to answer differently if he were so disposed. Reilly persisted in his flat denials that anything of the sort had been done, either on his orders or to his knowledge.

Then Sourwine informed the subcommittee: "You have a clear issue here on which we will have to take the testimony of other State Department employees. . . ."

Someone was lying. The Senate Internal Security Subcommittee intended to get to the bottom of it.

CHAPTER 18

"This Sordid Situation"

It was not exactly a surprise to Otto Otepka when, on September 23, 1963, he received formal notice that the State Department was going to try to fire him.[1] The only surprise was the timing. He had been led to believe that the move to get him was in limbo until the Senate Internal Security Subcommittee had completed its investigation.

Up to now, the investigation had been conducted behind closed doors. Any way one looked at it, the case was messy and reflected no credit on the State Department. Senator Dodd, vice-chairman of the subcommittee, who was deeply interested in the disclosures that had come out so far, thought he had the State Department's assurance that it would drop its efforts to take revenge on Otepka and would concentrate on tightening up its own security. This was all Otepka had wanted.

As it turned out, the Connecticut Democrat was overly optimistic.

Charges against Otepka were filed by Deputy Assistant Secretary of State John F. Reilly. But the charges were not Reilly's alone. They had the full backing of the State Department, including Deputy Under-Secretary of State William J. Crockett and Secretary of State Rusk.

The charge said that Chief Security Evaluator Otepka had made unauthorized delivery of State Department documents to J. G. Sourwine, chief counsel for the Senate Internal Security Subcommittee. Reilly contended that this was "insubordination" and conduct "unbecoming to an officer of the Department of State." Attention was called to a Presidential directive of March 13, 1948, which provides that:

". . . all reports, records and files relative to the loyalty of employees or prospective employees (including reports of such investigative agencies), shall be maintained in confidence, and shall not be transmitted or disclosed except as required in the efficient conduct of business."

The eleven-page notice of charges also stated that Otepka had prepared a list of questions for Sourwine to use in questioning Reilly and Belisle, and that he had clipped the security classifications from papers found in his burn bag of waste paper.

In his answer,[2] Otepka admitted he had prepared a list of questions for Sourwine to use after being apprised of "inaccurate and untrue" testimony from his superiors relative to the handling of certain security cases. Otepka also declared that he had delivered documents to Sourwine to prove that he was telling the truth.

He identified one of the documents as his memorandum of September 10, 1962, to Reilly. It "strongly recommended that certain of the prospective appointees not be cleared without further investigation."[3]

Otepka then pointed out that Reilly himself wrote a memorandum to higher officials on September 17th, referring to the fact that Otepka had warned against clearance of the appointees. Otepka went on to say that although the documents in question carried a "confidential" classification, none of the information he passed on to the Senate subcommittee involved anything that was not in the public domain. The documents were "completely innocuous and clearly not the kind that the [Presidential] directive was designed to protect," he said.[4]

The accused security officer argued in his reply that he had a right to produce records to defend himself, in view of the conflicts between his and Reilly's testimony.

"Mr. Reilly's testimony . . . seriously disparaged my performance of duty and impugned my integrity," Otepka stated. ". . . I submit that I had not only the right but the duty to defend myself, to correct the [sub]committee's record, and to support my oral testimony. . . ."[5]

Otepka pointed out that the law specifically prohibits officials from attempting to prevent civil servants under their jurisdiction from giving accurate information to Congress. And the Civil Service Commission's "Code of Ethics for Government Service," he further pointed out, states: "Any person in government service should put loyalty to the highest moral principles and to country above loyalty to persons, party, or government department."

"I believed then and I believe now that it was my duty to tell the committee the whole truth," Otepka stated. "By the same token . . . I would have been derelict in my duty if, by my silence, I had permitted untrue and inaccurate statements, of which I had personal knowledge, to remain unchallenged in the committee record."[6]

Otepka's anger at the charges was matched by that of members of the Senate Internal Security Subcommittee. The subcommittee condemned the "high-handed and irresponsible" actions in trying to fire Otepka for having furnished accurate information. Chairman James O. Eastland (Democrat, Mississippi) and Vice-Chairman Dodd were authorized to write a tough protest to Secretary Rusk. Their letter charged that the Department was engaged in a cover-up of "laxity" in the security program and a cover-up of "perjury" by State Department officials.[7]

Senator Sam Ervin stated that the attempt to fire Otepka was "an outrageous disregard for the law."

In a ten-page memorandum, the full Senate Judiciary Committee charged that a State Department clique used a telephone wiretap, room-bugging, and false testimony in an effort to oust Otepka. The committee memorandum to Rusk stated that it regarded Otepka as "the last old-line security officer in the [State] Department." It expressed concern over what it termed the "consistent effort" to fire Otepka and institute a softer line on security matters.

Rusk was informed that "although several State Department witnesses, including John F. Reilly and David Belisle, have denied it, Otepka's office has been bugged with an electronic listening device; his telephone was compromised by a State Department employee acting on instruction from the top level in the Office of Security."

The memorandum warned Rusk that the subcommittee knew "who ordered . . . [the bugging], who did the work, what mistake was made in the initial effort to connect an electronic device with Otepka's telephone line, who asked for help to correct the error—the whole story."

The State Department also had issued a blanket order forbidding any of its employees from testifying in the Otepka matter. This muzzling attempt infuriated some of the Senators, and the Judiciary Committee's memorandum noted that the subcommittee, "if permitted to call" certain witnesses, expected to be able to prove beyond reasonable doubt who was lying in the Otepka case.

Secretary Rusk himself was treated gently in the memorandum, for most Judiciary Committee members believed it was possible that the Secretary did not know the facts. The Judiciary Committee said it did not imply "that you, Mr. Secretary, have either done or intended to do anything improper."

"We have a mutual interest, I think, in getting this matter straightened out as speedily as possible," the committee added.

In its memorandum, the Judiciary Committee notified Secretary Rusk of evidence of a broad pattern of security laxity including the following:

1. Security-risk cases had been covered up and the security risks permitted to continue in service.

2. Security clearances had been granted for reasons other than sound evaluation of pertinent data.

3. State Department liaison with intelligence agencies had been improperly handled.

4. Incoming personnel security intelligence had not been related adequately to the personnel file.

5. Waivers of security clearances had been granted as favors or as a result of pressure.

The Judiciary Committee also was intensely critical of the use of six security officers to subject Otepka to "humiliating" treatment in front of other employees in removing him from his office in June.

In another letter on October 31, 1963, signed by all of its nine members, the Senate Internal Security Subcommittee, expressed concern over the "grave charges" filed against Otepka "growing out of his appearance as a witness . . . and his honesty in responding to the Subcommittee's questions." The subcommittee expressed "confidence in Mr. Otepka's integrity, capability, and professional skill."

"A committee of the Senate has a right to the testimony of any official or employee of our Government respecting any question of security or possible wrongdoing in any department or agency, if the subject matter of the committee's inquiry falls within its jurisdiction," Secretary Rusk was informed. "A Government employee who comes before a Senate committee and testifies truthfully should not thereafter be penalized or disciplined in any way for doing so.

"Mr. Otepka's testimony has been a valuable contribution to the Internal Security Subcommittee's current investigation of security in the State Department, and we feel he has performed a substantial service for his country. We would consider it a great tragedy if the services of this exceptionally able and experienced security officer were lost to the United States Government on the basis of alleged technical violations growing out of his cooperation with the Senate Internal Security Subcommittee."

On the Senate floor on November 5th, Senator Dodd said:[8] "I consider the dismissal of Otto Otepka . . . a serious challenge to responsible government and to the system of checks on which it is based."

The Senator declared that if Otepka's dismissal was allowed to stand, "it will become impossible or exceedingly difficult" for committees to get any information from employees of the Executive Branch, bearing on wrongdoing by their superiors.

Then he went on to tell his fellow Senators flatly that Otepka's superiors had lied under oath.

"They installed a tap on his [Otepka's] telephone," Dodd charged. "Although a State Department official has denied under oath that this was done, the subcommittee . . . has proof that the tap was installed."

Dodd's dragging the mess into the open caused a panic at the State Department. It was arranged for Reilly, Belisle, and Hill to meet at night in the office of Thomas Ehrlich, then an assistant to the State Department legal adviser, Abram Chayes.

The purpose of the afterhours conference was to try to arrange a way to save the Department from being embarrassed further, and, if possible, to keep Reilly, Belisle, and Hill out of trouble. Now began the most astounding and shocking part of the Otepka case—the backpedaling of the three officials to recant what they had told the Senate subcommittee under oath.

Each of the three men wrote letters to the Senate Internal Security Subcommittee to explain their sworn denials that Otepka's telephone had been tapped. The letters were prepared in the State Department's legal office, approved by Secretary Rusk, and sent to the subcommittee on the following day, November 6th.

Hill's letter to "clarify" his earlier denials was an admission that he, Schneider, and Reilly had wired Otepka's office telephone.[9] He said a buzzing sound interfered with listening on Otepka's wire and "the wiring connections which were made were removed without any conversations having been intercepted."

Belisle's letter was to "amplify" his denial of any knowledge of tampering with Otepka's telephone.[10] He admitted that "Mr. Reilly mentioned to me" the effort to tap Otepka's wire.

"I had, therefore, no first-hand information concerning these events, and it was for this reason that I answered Mr. Sourwine's questions as I did," Belisle explained.

Reilly's letter, also to "amplify" his earlier denial, said he had asked Hill and Schneider to "undertake a survey of the feasibility of intercepting conversations in Mr. Otepka's office.

"No conversations were intercepted as a result of the events described above," Reilly stated, adding that he had no knowledge that any of Otepka's conversations were heard or recorded.[11]

But the Otepka case was far from ended as a result of these letters of explanation and amplification.

In the first place, Subcommittee Counsel Sourwine viewed them rather dimly. He had information indicating that Hill, despite his "clarifying," had, in fact, listened in on Otepka's telephone; that several conversations were, in fact, recorded; and that several State Department officials—including Reilly—knew this.

In the second place, the State Department, instead of starting at last to investigate the alleged "untruthful" testimony by Reilly, Belisle, and Hill, pushed ahead with a new effort to oust Otepka. John Ordway, chief of the State Department's personnel division, sustained the Reilly-instigated charges of "insubordination," and Otepka was ordered dropped from his job. Only pressure from the Senate subcommittee induced the State Department to agree to let Otepka remain on the payroll pending a hearing.

Otepka decided to fight. On November 15th, he asked for a hearing. He notified the State Department that he would submit to a lie-detector test, and demanded that Reilly and Belisle also take such tests.

"Reilly and Belisle are unworthy of belief, and any finding against me based upon their testimony or upon evidence produced by them should not stand," Otepka declared in his answer.

While Otepka was girding to defend himself, the Senate subcommittee was preparing to question Reilly, Belisle, and Hill once more about their new stories.

In their appearances in mid-November, Otepka's three accusers retreated further from their previous testimony. Belisle now admitted Reilly had told him of the tap.[12] However, he contended he did not know there were recordings of Otepka's conversations. He insisted he had not intended to mislead the subcommittee in July; since his evidence was "second-hand," he argued that he believed himself to be excused from giving "hearsay" testimony.

Subcommittee members promptly branded Belisle's testimony as "an affront" to their intelligence. Some called him "evasive" and "untruthful" in his initial denials.

Reilly now admitted there had been a listening device placed on Otepka's telephone. He said he had the support of the Department and of Deputy Under-Secretary Crockett in his efforts to oust Otepka.[13]

It was Hill, the thirty-five-year-old bugging expert, who broke down completely on his reappearance. This time he admitted— his previous testimony and the letter that had been drafted for him by the State Department legal department to the contrary— that he had recorded about a dozen conversations from the tapped telephone.[14]

He made these recordings on general instructions from Reilly,[15] he added, noting then that Reilly expressed a special interest in one of them. Hill admitted that he had not been truthful in his earlier testimony. "I was trying to tell the truth, but to skirt the fact," he explained,[16] amplifying with: "I believe this was my obligation to the department to do as I did . . . to answer as I did."

"Either I or Mr. Schneider gave the recordings to another individual," Hill said when asked where the recordings now were. "I really do not know who that was."

"Why did you give these recordings to someone who was a stranger?" Sourwine asked.

"Mr. Reilly's request," Hill answered.

"Mr. Reilly knew about these recordings?" Sourwine asked.

"Yes."

"Had he heard them?" Sourwine continued.

"I do not know whether he had heard them or not," Hill replied. "I do know of one telephone conversation. I do not know how this knowledge came to him, whether he listened to the recording, but there was one telephone conversation which did seem interesting to him."

"He knew about, at least, one conversation," Sourwine asked.

"Yes," Hill replied.

The next day, Senator Dodd went on the Senate floor to charge that "perjury" had been committed by at least one high State Department official. "In a few days we will begin to present to the public the facts in this sordid situation," Dodd said.

That same day, the State Department announced that Reilly and Hill had resigned. The Department reported that Belisle's testimony still was under study.

Richard Phillips, the State Department press officer, declined to state whether Reilly and Hill had been asked to resign or to give the date the resignations would be effective, only saying it would be "at an early date."

Deputy Under-Secretary Crockett said he was unaware that Reilly and Hill had been engaged in tapping Otepka's telephone. They were "acting strictly on their own," he said.

In late December, 1963, the Senate Internal Security Subcommittee released transcripts of the testimony of Reilly, Belisle, and Hill. Senator Dodd said he was given periodic assurances that Belisle would resign, and that Otepka would be reinstated as Chief Security Evaluator and the charges dropped.

However, months after the exposure, Belisle still was in the State Department Security Division, and Otepka still was in quarantine.

On March 15, 1964, six men who had been Otepka's closest associates in the Security Division were assigned to a project in the Department's Bureau of Inter-American Affairs that carried a secret classification.[17] They were: Raymond A. Loughton, Harry M. Hite, Frank V. Gardener, John Norpel, Howard J. Shea, and Edwin A. Burkhardt. All six had been sympathetic to Otepka, and periodically voiced their views in defending Otepka against the charges filed by Reilly. All six had indicated they were willing to testify for Otepka.

As they examined the details of their new assignment, the men became convinced that the jobs did not require skilled investigators and evaluators; the new work could have been handled by clerks. As far as they were concerned, this reassignment was a demotion in status. In appeals filed with the Civil Service Commission, some of the reassigned men charged that they were being disciplined for their support of Otepka. They contended that they were assigned to a secret project to gag them and prevent them from disclosing just how insignificant the new duties actually were.

In his appeal to the Civil Service Commission, John Norpel, for example, declared that the State Department was using "falsely contrived" evidence to try to oust Otepka, and that he intended to aid Otepka in establishing that fact.

"I believe my reassignment is diametrically opposed to the basic defined concepts of the Civil Service merit system," Norpel stated in his appeal. "The morale and dedication of loyal Civil Service employees, who by their actions evidence the high standards in which they believe, are weakened by their observation of my recent experience. If a 'Code of Ethics' is to survive, it must be subscribed to by all Civil Service employees without fear of retaliation for telling the truth or recrimination for fulfilling a duty."

In May, 1964, more than a year after superiors had started their harassment of him, Otto Otepka still was barred from his regular State Department office—a room that still carried his name plate. He had been assigned to what he considered a make-work project on that so-called security brochure. He had no supervisory authority, but continued to receive his $18,200-a-year salary for work that could have been performed by a junior employee.

Otepka did not speak to old friends and associates when he passed them in the hall. He knew that to be seen talking to him could jeopardize a man's career at State. He was not invited to State Department functions. A few friends who had dropped in to see him in "the little cubbyhole" had been called on the carpet by their superiors and ordered not to visit Otepka again.

While the ordeal of Otto Otepka dragged on, the man who had sanctioned the original "get Otepka" move and who now was supposed to be in charge of settling the problem was put in line for a promotion. Deputy Under-Secretary of State Crockett was recommended by Secretary Rusk for elevation to the rank of career minister. President Johnson sent the nomination to the Senate Foreign Relations Committee.

Fed up with what he considered State's stalling, Senator Dodd finally went to President Johnson. Dodd urged White House intervention to correct what he called "an injustice in the Otepka case." Dodd also called for disciplinary action against those responsible for what he regarded as the "persecution" of Otepka.

Although there were repeated assurances to Senator Dodd that the injustice would be corrected, the Johnson administration seemed in no hurry to right the wrong. In fact, the evidence contradicting the assurances piled up. First, the charges against Otepka were not dropped. Second, the State Department denied Otepka's request for a hearing officer from outside the Department. He had argued that it was unlikely he would obtain a fair hearing from either a Foreign Service officer or an administration political appointee. Third, the unfriendly attitude at the State Department persisted toward Otepka, and he was left in agonizing isolation. Fourth, the State Department issued orders to burn the files of the twenty security field offices. This was explained as destruction of unneeded records, and as a step toward efficiency. In the opinion of Otepka and other seasoned security specialists, retention of the raw files in the field offices was an important part of the security apparatus, since the existence of those files made it risky to destroy information in the central file in Washington. Finally, the Democratic administration made a place for Otepka's chief tormentor—John F. Reilly. Despite the testimony Reilly had given in denying the wiretap on Otepka, he was hired by the Federal Communications Commission (F.C.C.) as a $17,000-a-year lawyer in the hearing division.

On the floor of the Senate, Senator Dodd had spoken of the Reilly testimony as "perjury," and the State Department had indicated that Reilly was forced to resign because of this untruthful testimony. Yet F.C.C. Chairman William E. Henry justified the hiring on the ground that there was no derogatory report in Reilly's State Department personnel file as a result of the wiretap or the denial that there was a wiretap.

"I felt it was a question of judgment rather than a question of perjury," F.C.C. Chairman Henry explained. "There were certainly some questions of judgment raised by Reilly's denials that he knew a listening device had been placed on Otepka's telephone. However, I was told by the personnel office that Mr. Reilly was an able trial lawyer and had a good record up to this [Otepka] case. I didn't believe that the judgment questions raised about Reilly in connection with the Otepka case would interfere with his doing a good job as a trial attorney in the Federal Communications Commission."

It was on this reasoning that the man who initiated the so-called "unauthorized wiretap" and then denied it under oath was rewarded with a government job. But Otepka, who told the truth to Congress, was still under charges in 1965—two years after the "get Otepka" moves started.

The Senate Internal Security Subcommittee, in March, 1965, repeated its unanimous support for Otepka and expressed concern over the signs that the State Department was still intent on disciplining Otepka for cooperating with the Congress. Whatever the final outcome of this case, the actions against Otepka represent a shameful blot on the record of democratic government. Otepka's grinding two-year ordeal held out little hope for justice for any career employee who believes in the right to dissent and who has the courage to act on his beliefs.

CHAPTER 19

The Protégé of L.B.J.—Bobby Baker

In many ways, Robert G. (Bobby) Baker was one of the best news sources on Capitol Hill. He was a veritable walking encyclopedia of knowledge, public or private, about everyone and everything in the United States Senate. And though he was very helpful in sharing his information with newsmen on Senate matters, Bobby Baker shunned personal publicity. He seemed to have a real passion for anonymity.

The young man from Pickens, South Carolina, had early been an employee of the Senate. He was hired first as a fifteen-year-old page.[1] By observing and emulating the operations of the men he served, he had learned the science of political power. Along the way, Bobby picked up knowledge of one of the most potent, if dangerous, formulas in the chemistry of politics—how political influence can be converted into wealth.

As he progressed up the ladder, Bobby Baker always was happy to accommodate all members of the Senate, regardless of whether they were Democrats (as he was) or Republicans. He was particularly attentive, of course, to the chairmen of the most influential committees, and to the Democratic leaders.

In 1955, Bobby Baker was named Secretary to the Democratic majority in the Senate. He was only twenty-six years old at the time, but he had some special friends in high places—the then Majority Leader Lyndon B. Johnson and Senator Robert Kerr, the late Oklahoma Democrat.

The Majority Leader came to regard Bobby Baker as "my strong right arm."

"He is the last man I see at night and the first one I see in the morning," Senator Johnson once said, in a statement that was to haunt him.

Baker was dedicated to building the power and prestige of Lyndon Johnson, and Senator Johnson apparently was appreciative. The Majority Leader even made speeches on the Senate floor about Bobby, extolling his virtues to the other Senators.

"There is a very simple formula that explains Bobby's success," Johnson orated on August 30, 1957. "He gives of himself unsparingly, and without regard to what he will get in return. . . .

"He is a man who truly serves his country, and I consider him one of my most trusted, most loyal and most competent friends."[2]

A year later, on August 23, 1958, Majority Leader Johnson gave Baker credit for "a great deal of the success of this Congress." Johnson said the smooth operation of the Senate was "due to Bobby Baker's alertness, his diligence, his devotion, his dedication, and his insistence that things be done right.

"He is a young man who has already gone very far and who is going much farther," Johnson said. "I believe he will reach much greater heights."[3]

In 1960, Baker boosted Johnson for the Democratic Presidential nomination. Although Bobby worked in a smooth, quiet manner, some liberal Democrats became irritated. They saw signs, during the preconvention period, that Johnson and Baker were manipulating committee assignments and other Senate matters to benefit Senators who were supporters of the Johnson-for-President movement.

In the Kennedy camp, there was resentment of Baker's activities. It was felt that the Senate employee was taking unfair advantage of a Democratic Senate post to push the man the Kennedy supporters regarded as their major opponent.

When the Kennedy-Johnson ticket was victorious in November, 1960, there were behind-the-scenes suggestions that Bobby Baker be given the White House job of maintaining liaison with the Congress. President Kennedy rejected the proposals and gave the job to one of his own men, Lawrence (Larry) O'Brien. No official reason was given. Some attributed it to friction between Baker and Robert F. Kennedy. Others said that, naturally, President Kennedy didn't want a Johnson man in such a key position in the White House. It also was said by some that the President had doubts about the wisdom of appointing a man who had the multifarious outside business interests of Baker.

Whether the President really said as much or not, the nation later learned that the outside interests which might have blocked Baker from an even more inside job had provided him a big financial return. Starting with a net worth of only about $11,000 in 1954, Baker had amassed a considerable fortune.[4] His net worth in 1963 was at least $1 million, and on some occasions Baker himself listed it as being in excess of $2 million.

The big question was how the young man from Pickens had managed to accumulate so much on his annual salary of $19,612 —even though his wife, Dorothy, brought in an additional $11,000 a year by working as a file clerk for the Senate Internal Security Subcommittee. True, Baker had obtained a law degree through night studies and was a partner in a law firm, but he never was seen in the law courts.

The first public indication of Baker's wealth emerged in the summer of 1962, when it was announced that Baker was part owner of a new million-dollar motel at Ocean City, Maryland. The Carousel was built by Baker, Mr. and Mrs. Alfred S. Novak and Mr. and Mrs. Donald J. Novak. The Novaks were in the construction business.[5]

The Carousel opened that summer with a lot of hoopla. It was advertised as a "high-style hideaway for the Advise and Consent set." Baker arranged with the Capital City Transit Company, of Washington, D.C., for charter buses with champagne bars to transport several hundred prominent officials to Ocean City for the opening of the luxury motel.

Among the guests, of course, were Lyndon B.—by that time, the Vice-President—and Lady Bird Johnson.

Many in official Washington were surprised at this sudden show of wealth by the South Carolina boy. But then, capital realists figured that Bobby might have just a small interest in the Carousel and that he was being carried along for his promotional potential.

After that one gaudy splash with the Carousel, Baker lapsed into obscurity so far as the public was concerned. But his office in the U.S. Capitol became an increasingly active center of feverish business and political manipulations.

In 1962, Baker talked with officials of Melpar, Inc., a Falls Church, Virginia, aerospace subcontractor, on behalf of another young man from South Carolina,[6] Ralph L. Hill, president of the Capitol Vending Company. Hill was anxious to obtain a contract to provide food-vending machines for the Melpar firm. After a good word from Bobby Baker, he was given the lucrative contract.

The relationship between Baker and Hill remained friendly until the summer of 1963, when the Melpar firm gave notice it intended to cancel its contract with Capitol Vending. Hill was told by a Maryland insurance man, Don B. Reynolds, that Baker had an interest in another food-vending firm and intended to take over the Melpar business for himself.[7]

After discussions between Baker and Hill regarding the deal, Hill said he intended to sue. Baker told his erstwhile friend he couldn't make a damage suit stick, and he could "ruin" Hill if he tried. But Hill didn't scare.

On September 9, 1963, Hill filed a $300,000 damage suit in the United States District Court in the District of Columbia in which Baker was named as one of the defendants. The codefendants were the Serv-U Corporation; its vice-president and secretary, Ernest C. Tucker; and Fred Black, a Washington public-relations "consultant" who included the North American Aviation Corporation among his major clients. Melpar was a subcontractor for North American. Tucker was Baker's associate in a Washington law firm.

Hill contended that Baker had used his influence as Secretary to the Democratic majority to help him land the Melpar vending contract.[8] Hill further said he had paid Baker $5,600 in cash for his help. This sum, he related, was paid at the rate of $250 a month from April, 1962, through March, 1963, and then was stepped up to $650 a month from April to August. Hill said he balked at Baker's request for a still larger sum.

The Capitol Vending president charged that Baker tried to force him to sell out to the Serv-U Corporation. And, when this effort failed, he alleged that Baker "conspired maliciously to interfere with the outstanding contract between Melpar and Capitol."

Hill claimed that Baker and Black conspired with the Serv-U Corporation to take over the Melpar business after his Capitol Vending Company was cut out.

The petition asserts that Baker was "able to interfere with the outstanding agreement between Capitol Vending and Melpar" because "Baker . . . was able to, and did, represent to defendant Fred Black that he was in a position to assist in securing contracts for North American Aviation Corporation."

Hill's suit charged that Baker and Black performed services for North American Aviation and that in return North American had entered into an agreement to permit the Serv-U Corporation to install vending machines in its California plants. It also was contended that Baker and Black helped Melpar acquire subcontracts from North American, and Melpar in turn placed its vending contract as Baker suggested.

Baker's law partner, Ernest Tucker, filed an answer denying that Black and Baker had conspired against Capitol Vending. He also stated that, to his knowledge, neither Baker nor Black had any financial interest in Serv-U.

Vend Magazine, a trade publication distributed from Chicago, carried a story in which it was stated that Baker did have an interest in the fast-growing Serv-U Corporation—a firm that had become the talk of the industry. This vending firm, starting with nothing, had in an eighteen-month period acquired franchises that would result in gross receipts of more than $3.5 million a year. Most of the sales were reported to be in the Southern California aerospace plants.

At the same time, Laurence Stern and Jack Landau, reporters for the Washington *Post,* reported that public records in Worcester County, Maryland, disclosed that Baker had engaged in a series of transactions with the Serv-U Corporation. Mr. and Mrs. Bobby Baker and their partners, the Novaks, had sold the Carousel motel to Serv-U for $1.2 million.

Friends of Baker reported his fury over the filing of the suit by Hill, but Bobby remained cool when he talked to reporters. Baker told them that he had no interest in Serv-U, and denied that he had received any money from Hill for using his influence on the Melpar contract. Hill simply was trying to "blackmail" him, he said.

The Secretary to the Democratic majority said he could not go beyond those basic denials in discussing the matter. He said he had been instructed by his lawyer, Abe Fortas, not to discuss any of his business transactions with Hill or any of the firms named in the suit. Fortas, a Democratic stalwart, long-time friend and confidant of Lyndon Johnson, and a former New Deal lawyer and Under-Secretary of the Interior, had become counsel of record for Baker in the $300,000 lawsuit.

"I would like to sit right down and explain the whole thing," Baker earnestly assured the reporters, sounding exactly like an aggrieved United States Senator who has been accused of some wrongdoing. "In the end, I know that you'll see that Hill has been spreading a pack of lies. I do have to be loyal to my attorney and follow his instructions.

"Some of these stories are so outlandish that I wouldn't believe them about anyone," Baker said. "I've made my enemies around here, and they are busy peddling a lot of filthy rumors. I hope that some of them get in print, because I'll sue."

Baker then discussed one of the rumors about his affairs. He said he had been lucky enough to be able to buy some of the so-called "MAGIC" stock in the Mortgage Guaranty Insurance Corporation of Milwaukee.[9] That was what had made him his money, he said. He said he bought the stock at two or three dollars a share, and that it had gone as high as $51 a share at one time.

"When it [the lawsuit] is all over with you will see there is nothing to it," Baker confidently declared.

He said he understood there would be political pressure on Democratic Senators because of his outside business activities, but he was not concerned. "If the Democratic Senators feel that I should go, then I'm ready to step aside. I feel that I've done nothing wrong, but I know politics."

Despite Bobby Baker's seeming confidence, a major political problem existed from the time the Baker case broke into the open. Democrats in the Senate had spoken of Baker as "little Lyndon," and he was identified closely with the Vice-President. Only a year earlier, Baker had named his baby son Lyndon Baines Johnson Baker. If Johnson and Baker were not a close political team, an overwhelming majority of the political observers in Washington were guessing wrong.

Vice-President Johnson was in Europe when the $300,000 damage suit was filed and the first rash of news stories appeared. The Vice-President cut his trip short by a day and hurried back to Washington. It was reported by his friends that the Baker problem was on his mind.

It was on the minds of the Justice Department and the Internal Revenue Service, at any rate. They were already in the process of approving full investigations of Baker after completing preliminary reports. Attorney General Kennedy was said to have directed that the Baker investigation be conducted with full vigor. No punches should be pulled, the President's brother ordered, because the investigation might embarrass the Vice-President or any other of Baker's political friends.

Vice-President Johnson was informed that there was to be a full-scale investigation of Baker by the F.B.I., but he was not asked if he approved or objected.

The Vice-President was treated courteously but coolly. The signs were ominous. It was known that many in the Kennedy inner circle—which didn't include Lyndon—considered the Texan expendable in 1964. Bobby Kennedy was said to be one of those who held this view. If Johnson were to be kept on the ticket, his political assets had to outweigh his liabilities demonstrably. Now the liabilities seemed to be piling up.

Evil days seemed to be ahead for Johnson's friends and political supporters. Some believed that the cumulative impact of the misfortunes might result in Lyndon's being dumped in '64. The Kennedy-Johnson ticket was only a marriage of convenience in 1960, with the obvious purpose of trying to take Texas and hold most of the South in line. It had worked, by the narrowest margin, and John F. Kennedy had been thankful. But President Kennedy was a cool and unemotional political strategist. Any trust and friendship that existed between the two men was limited to areas of mutual political advantage.

On the surface, Attorney General Robert Kennedy and Vice-President Johnson were congenial, but there were undercurrents of the old feuds from the preconvention campaign in 1960. Johnson had made abrasive attacks on members of the Kennedy family, including Joseph P. Kennedy, Senator Kennedy's father. Johnson had flayed the elder Kennedy's record as America's wartime Ambassador to Great Britain. He pictured him as a friend of Prime Minister Neville Chamberlain, author of the Munich pact which dismembered Czechoslovakia, and as one who opposed American entry into the war against Hitler.

"I was never any Chamberlain umbrella policy man," Senator Johnson had declared harshly. "*I* never thought Hitler was right."

The Texas Democrat also tried to link the Kennedys with "McCarthyism," in order to alienate the liberals from Kennedy.

"I was not contributing comfort to his [McCarthy's] thinking or contributing to his campaign," Senator Johnson said. The barbs were thrown at the Kennedys for their political contributions to and personal association with the late Senator Joseph McCarthy, arch-villain of the liberals.

Such slurs brewed bitterness in the Kennedy camp. Kennedy men struck back with ridicule of the drawling Texan. They called him Colonel Cornpone. The Kennedyites sniped at the L.B.J. Company's ownership of radio and television stations in Austin, Texas, which seemingly obtained their licenses from the F.C.C.

under circumstances suggesting favoritism. They also picked at suspicious circumstances in Johnson's past political career, including his highly controversial 87-vote victory in 1948, in his first race for the Texas Senate seat.

Once the Kennedy-Johnson partnership was formed and elected, many of the administration's political sore spots seemed to be linked with the Lone Star State and L.B.J. men.

These were, notably, the Billie Sol Estes case, in which Texans were involved up to the hilt, and the TFX-warplane contract, awarded to a firm with major installations in Texas and recommended by a Texas political appointee, Fred Korth.

Then there was an additional liability. An internal feud was stewing in the Democratic Party in Texas. This raised a question as to whether Johnson would continue to be a political asset in his home state. The long-smoldering rivalry between the "liberal" faction, headed by Senator Ralph Yarborough, and the Johnson group had erupted. It had resulted in a plea from Texas Governor John Connally, a Johnson man, to President Kennedy. Connally urged the President to fly to Texas to bind up the wounds and demonstrate Democratic unity. In Governor Connally's eyes, his friend Lyndon Johnson was essential to the success of the Democratic ticket in 1964.

To the Johnson supporters, then, Bobby Baker was one more big problem piled on top of a lot of other problems in September, 1963. Cartoonists and columnists had a field day with L.B.J. and his cronies Fred Korth and Bobby Baker. At Presidential press conferences, questions were aimed at ferreting out how President Kennedy felt about the "dump Lyndon" rumors. President Kennedy's answers were support, but far from a pledge, to Johnson.

The Democrats had hoped that the Bobby Baker problem could be handled as an internal party matter, since he was Secretary to the Democratic majority. Many Republicans probably would have accepted the wishes of the Senate Democrats and let them handle the Baker case as an internal problem. But there was one man who stood in the way.

Senator John Williams, a Republican senator from Delaware

and a tireless investigator of anything in government that smacked of wrongdoing, took a different view.[10] He did not regard Bobby Baker as the exclusive property of the Democrats; to him, the man was a $19,600-a-year paid employee of the entire United States Senate. Williams believed that the integrity of the Senate was at stake when a lawsuit charged that a Senate employee had used his influence in connection with a defense contract.

After reading the damage suit filed against Baker, the Delaware Republican asked his secretary to get Ralph Hill on the telephone. He wanted direct information about the proof available to support Hill's allegations about Baker.

Hill was cooperative. The vending-firm head knew of Senator Williams' reputation and had confidence in him—and Hill felt he was going to need all the help he could get in his dispute with Baker.

Baker's accuser came to Senator Williams' second-floor office in the new Senate Office Building. He spelled out his entire case with names, dates, and documents. As the story unfolded, there were other aspects of the Bobby Baker picture that bothered Senator Williams as much as the dispute over the vending-machine contract.

Hill said Baker had insisted that the $5,600 in cash be delivered in small bills, placed in a plain white envelope.[11] But the $5,600 Baker got from him, Hill said, was a drop in the bucket in the entire Bobby Baker operation. Hill told Senator Williams he had heard that the former page boy from South Carolina claimed a net worth of more than a million dollars.

Baker had made some tremendous profits on special purchases of the so-called "MAGIC" stock. That firm had two or three problems pending before governmental agencies, Hill said. He also related that Baker had recently purchased a $125,000 home in the fashionable Spring Valley neighborhood of Washington, at 5115 Van Ness Street, N.W.[12]

Baker, under the guidance of former Majority Leader Johnson, had been the major dispenser of Senatorial campaign funds for the Democrats. Much of this money was handled in cash, Hill said.

He gave Senator Williams the names of two other persons who might give more firsthand information on some of Baker's business deals that involved large amounts of cash—as much as $10,000 or $13,000.

Hill said Mrs. Gertrude (Trudy) Novak, widow of one of Baker's business partners, had direct knowledge of some of Baker's operations in large cash sums. He also related that Mrs. Novak felt she was treated unfairly by Baker in the sale of the Carousel to the Serv-U Corporation. Mrs. Novak, secretary for the Senate Small Business Committee, would be factual and cooperative, Hill told Senator Williams.

Hill also gave Senator Williams the name of another future key witness, Don Reynolds, a Maryland insurance agent, formerly from South Carolina. He had previously served with the State Department for five years.

Senator Williams telephoned Reynolds and asked him if he would come to his office for a talk. Reynolds did not know Senator Williams except by reputation, and he indicated he might drop by the office "just to get acquainted." He immediately called Baker, and told him Senator Williams had telephoned.

Later, when he came to see Senator Williams, Reynolds reported that Baker had warned him not to talk with Williams, that it might get all of them in trouble.

Reynolds was a former close friend of Bobby Baker. Although he had come to be disillusioned with Baker and several of Baker's business associates, this first conversation with Senator Williams was long on generalities and short on facts. Reynolds was cautious, and his conversation dealt with such prosaic matters as how long he had known Baker and the general nature of their relationship. Reynolds did state he was certain that Baker had a stock interest in Serv-U, and that the sale of the Carousel (in which Baker was a partner) to Serv-U (in which Baker was a stockholder) was not an arm's-distance transaction.

Reynolds also said that he and Baker had been engaged in one business venture that was backed by funds from James R. Hoffa's Teamsters' Union. In this case, Reynolds said he could speak from firsthand knowledge. He had dealt directly with Baker, and he had accompanied Thomas Webb, a Washington representative for the Murchison financial interests in Texas, to the Teamsters' headquarters for a discussion with Hoffa of a loan from the Teamsters' pension funds. He said Baker bowed out of that deal just before final acceptance of the Teamsters' loan by the group of promoters they had associated with in a firm called Wertco.[13] One possible reason for the withdrawal came out later as revelations occurred.

A few days later, Williams called Reynolds again. This time Williams had had time to check out some of the information Reynolds had given him, and it proved to be accurate. Reynolds had also been checking on what kind of person Senator Williams was.

The second meeting between Reynolds and Williams dealt with more specific information, but Reynolds was still wary. He wasn't sure that the mild-mannered Delaware Republican could really do anything to break Bobby Baker's power in Congress.

The attitude of the press toward Baker, as Senator Williams was starting his still-secret investigation, bears examination. Actually, there was only one newspaperman in Washington who had early knowledge of what Williams was doing; he was in Williams' confidence. Because the Senator, in his usual manner, wanted to have some ammunition before he started shooting, the reporter did not break the story.

Enough had come out to cast suspicion on Baker's activities, but the press walked on eggshells in approaching the story. Not convicting the man in the papers before he was formally charged and tried showed commendable restraint, but there was another reason, too. Generally, newspapermen were of the opinion that Bobby Baker would surmount the $300,000 damage suit and all the other rumors that were coming to the surface.

Many newspapermen and other observers reasoned that it would be impossible for the Democrats to take action against Baker because he knew so much about the public and private lives of so many Democratic Senators. Also, Vice-President Johnson was regarded as Baker's friend and mentor.

Senator Williams did not reason in the manner of many Senate "regulars." By now, he had progressed far enough in his investigation to feel that the honor of the whole Senate—not just that of the Secretary to the Democratic Majority—was at stake. He believed it absolutely essential that some explanation be pried loose as to why the Senate Democratic Majority Secretary kept large amounts of cash on hand, and had dealings in small-bill currency in plain envelopes. Maybe there was a satisfactory answer—if so, Williams wanted to hear it.

The Senator decided there was one direct way to get the answer. He picked up the telephone and asked for Bobby Baker. He was told the Majority Secretary would call him back.

Baker didn't call back. Williams called again, this time leaving word for the unavailable Baker that he wanted to see him. There was no response.[14]

Williams took his problem to Majority Leader Mike Mansfield, the Montana Democrat. As Lyndon Johnson's successor, Mansfield, in effect, was Baker's immediate boss. Williams told the Majority Leader he had heard some disturbing stories and wanted to talk with Baker about them. He related his difficulty in trying to reach Baker, and said he believed that any employee of the United States Senate should be available to answer questions put by any member of the Senate.

Mike Mansfield agreed. He explained that Baker was Majority Secretary before Mansfield became Majority Leader, and that he knew little or nothing of his outside business activities. But he said he would contact Baker and ask him to meet with a small group of Senators—Democrats and Republicans—on Friday, October 4th, to answer the questions Senator Williams had outlined.

A group of influential Democratic Senators, prodded by the activities of Senator Williams, was attempting to head off embarrassment by conducting its own investigation of Baker. Some of them suggested that Baker should submit his resignation, effective at the end of October, or at least by the end of the year. The fact that the Justice Department and the Internal Revenue Service were already conducting investigations of Baker prompted some Democrats to argue against any Congressional investigation of Baker's activities.

Some of the Senators were astounded when their good and faithful, always affable servant, Bobby Baker, failed to show up in answer to their summons for a chat on October 4th.

Initially, Senator Williams had planned to make a Senate speech that afternoon if Baker failed to answer his questions. However, the Delaware Republican, in a scrupulous attempt to be fair, wanted to be sure that the request for Baker's appearance had been relayed to him personally, and he wanted to give Baker an opportunity to explain his cash transactions.

Senator Mansfield agreed to make certain that Baker received personal notice that he was wanted at a meeting at 3 P.M. on Monday, October 7th.

Once again, the once friendly, now strange young man did not appear. Instead, he sent in his resignation.

In the denouement, the Senators—some of them—followed the courtly, old-fashioned rules of the "most exclusive gentlemen's club" on earth. Senator Mansfield issued a prepared statement accepting the resignation. It said that Baker had "discharged his responsibility to the majority with great intelligence and understanding.

"Developments during the past few weeks, however, have made it apparent to him that it would be best if he withdrew from office," Mansfield said. "He has acted, as was expected by those who know him, in what he believes are the highest interests of the Senate and the majority. I deeply regret the necessity for his resignation and the necessity for its acceptance."

The Democrats hoped that Baker's resignation would put the quietus on the unpleasant matter. That's what usually happens in such cases. The dominant press and political view was that all would blow over now so far as the Senate was concerned, and that all Baker—and his political mentors—had to worry about were the

Justice Department (maybe) and the Internal Revenue investigations.

But Senator Williams had different ideas, later to be supported by a few other Senators who became angry about the Baker affair. The Delaware man felt he knew how to, and should, force the United States Senate into an unprecedented investigation of itself, as well as of Bobby Baker.

CHAPTER 20

"Whispering Will"

His fellow Senators and reporters in the press gallery called him Whispering Will because his soft voice often was inaudible in the Senate Chamber. But what Senator John J. Williams said usually echoed with a roar throughout the entire federal government. From the time he entered the Senate in January, 1947, Williams retained the deceptive appearance of a bashful and timorous farm boy. He was slightly suspicious of the "city slickers" and sharp operators who manage to infiltrate and occasionally dominate the United States Senate. He did not barge into every debate, as some of his colleagues did, but waited until he was sure of what he was talking about.

John Williams, a grain dealer and chicken farmer in the small town of Millsboro, Delaware, was a self-made man. He was born in 1904, the ninth of eleven children. He was reared on the farm, and was accustomed to hard work. He quit high school to start working full time. When he was eighteen, he went into partnership with an older brother in a gristmill and feed store. The business was started with a $2,000 loan, and it flourished on long hours and attention to detail by the brothers.

When he decided to run for the United States Senate in 1946, the idea seemed preposterous. Williams had no political experience, and he lacked a commanding personality. He was given the Republican nomination because it was considered worthless against a popular Democrat. The country boy from Millsboro was to be the sacrificial lamb—or goat—in November's political ritual.

But the chicken farmer defeated the front-runner. Hard work, hand-shaking, and quiet talk were the success ingredients for Whispering Will. The election was considered a fluke, and shrewd political observers predicted that the man from Millsboro would be buried in the Senate and probably never be heard from again.

Senator Williams paid the same attention to detail in the Senate committees as he had in his business. He did his homework for hearings, and he learned that horse sense could carry you a long way. A farm boy from Delaware could be the equal of all the lawyers and college professors if he just worked hard and long enough.

Williams learned that some of the great reputations of the Senate were constructed on foundations of wind, and that a torrent of words often masked an absence of genuine knowledge. He learned that some of the reputations of the "intellectual Senators" had been fabricated from public-relations gimmicks. He learned that a man armed with facts gleaned through careful study could prevail over the roar and bellow of men who relied upon an auctioneer's voice or a pitchman's tactics.

It was 1950 before Senator Williams made a national impression with his revelations of major tax scandals in the Truman administration. From then on, the Senate knew that Williams of Delaware was no figurehead or straw man.

At first, Senate observers figured him as a party-line Republican with a partisan zeal for rooting out Democratic scandals. But then he showed equal aggressiveness in going after scandals or mismanagement in the Eisenhower administration. Applying the same yardstick of governmental ethics that he had applied to the Truman administration, he insisted that the unofficial "assistant president," Sherman Adams, hitherto an almost legendary untouchable of the Republican party, should get out. (Adams had become indiscreetly involved with Bernard Goldfine, a Boston industrialist with a propensity for giving away vicuña coats and costly Oriental rugs.)

Senator Williams' reelection by substantial margins in 1952, and again in 1958, demonstrated that the people of Delaware appreciated being represented by a man who was coming to be known as "the conscience of the Senate."

In late September, 1963, Williams started to work overtime, for he had concluded that the reputation of the Senate was at stake in the Bobby Baker matter. While many Republicans were willing to take what political advantage they could from the Baker affair, few viewed it as their responsibility to do the work necessary to start a Senate hearing. It was this attitude that the Democratic leadership counted on in first discounting the need for an investigation of Baker, and later in believing that his resignation would solve everything.

Thus, Senator Williams decided to move. On October 10th, three days after Baker's resignation, Williams introduced a resolution calling for an investigation by the Senate Rules Committee.[1] He told the Democratic and Republican leadership what he intended to do. He said he would agree either to a roll-call vote, so every Senator could be recorded as being for or against the investigation, or it could be a "voice vote."

Senator Mike Mansfield (Democrat, Montana) and Senator Everett Dirksen (Republican, Illinois), the respective leaders, opted for the voice vote.

As Williams introduced his resolution, he declared: "The integrity of the United States Senate is at stake.

"We in America are extremely fortunate in that we have one of the best forms of government ever conceived by mankind. But that form of government will stand only so long as its public officials respect the integrity of their offices and it can hold and maintain the confidence of the American people."

Williams voiced what all needed to hear. In recent weeks, "we have seen publicized rather serious charges of questionable transactions by an employee of the United States Senate.

"The Senate, which has never been reluctant to call to task officials of the Executive Branch when questions were raised concerning the propriety of their conduct, has an even greater responsibility to examine these charges that are being made against one of its own employees," Williams warned. "To ignore these charges would be a reflection on the integrity of the membership of the United States Senate."

He pointed out that "the Senate employee against whom the charges were made was given ample opportunity to appear in person and answer these charges but he rejected this invitation and instead submitted his resignation.

"The Senate and the country have a right to know to what extent public interest has been ignored," Williams declared.

Senator Williams said he would not repeat the "multitude of rumors circulating the capital." He added that none should be accepted as factual until proven, but that "none . . . are so unimportant that they can be ignored without being fully checked."

He said that all of the reports should be submitted to the Senate Rules Committee for examination. "The record must be made clear that the Senate does not consider this case closed merely by the resignation of an employee."

Mansfield and Dirksen dutifully praised Williams for his interest in the integrity of the Senate, and the resolution was passed by voice vote.

The resolution directed the Rules Committee to make a study of "any financial or business interests or activities" of any "officer, or employee or former officer or employee of the Senate" to determine if such acts "have involved conflicts of interest or other improprieties."[2]

In comments on the Senate floor, Senators Williams, Mansfield, and Dirksen agreed that the resolution was to cover Senators as well as employees. Williams said that Senators get their salary checks from the Senate, and in fact are listed as employees of the Senate.

With little fuss, Senator Williams had maneuvered the Senate into an investigation many people would have said was impossible to start.

Williams had started not only an investigation of Bobby Baker, protégé of Vice-President Johnson, but he had obtained a Senate directive that the Rules Committee should investigate any employee of the Senate. He did not request the investigation to embarrass his colleagues, but if they happened to fall in the line of fire as the investigation progressed, Senator Williams wanted the facts to come out.

Chairman B. Everett Jordan (Democrat, North Carolina) was not an aggressive investigator, and little progress was made in the first weeks. Then the tempo speeded up as newspaper reports covering the story started to document interesting new facets of the life and times of Bobby Baker.

Seth Kantor, of the Fort Worth *Press,* wrote that Baker had admitted that $50 a month was improperly withheld from the salary of a teen-age Senate employee, and that the money was paid to Walter J. Stewart, another Senate employee who worked under Baker. The young man, Boyd Richie, was a former beau of Lynda Bird Johnson. He complained to Vice-President Johnson about the $50 deductions, and they were stopped.[3] Apparently, no other action against Baker was stimulated by the Vice-President's direct knowledge of the incident.

Julian Morrison, of the Washington *Daily News,* broke the story of how Baker was able to make a windfall profit of nearly $28,000 on a stock deal in which he was not required to risk a cent. The influential Senate secretary had been permitted to buy that "MAGIC" stock in the Mortgage Guaranty Insurance Corporation at about $2 a share. It rose to more than $22 a share within nine months, after favorable actions by two government agencies. Other reporters followed up Morrison's lead, and shed more light on Baker's profits of more than $100,000 in this deal.

Then Erwin Knoll and Theodor Schuchat, writing for the Newhouse newspaper chain, reported that Baker had purchased a strikingly contemporary town house at 308 N Street, S.W., in Washington's southwest redevelopment area. It was occupied by Miss Nancy Carole Tyler, a onetime Tennessee beauty-contest winner, who was Baker's $8,300-a-year private secretary at the Senate, and another young Senate secretary.

The records showed that Baker made a $1,600 down payment on the four-bedroom town house located only a few blocks from the Capitol. The deal for the lavishly furnished town house came under some scrutiny by the Federal Housing Authority, which was involved in the financing of the redevelopment project, as the occupancy rules apparently had been violated. The house was purchased in Baker's name, and Miss Tyler was listed as his "cousin" in the application. The house was part of a cooperative housing development, and occupancy was restricted to owners or relatives of the purchaser. Miss Tyler was not his cousin.[4]

Soon, the *Des Moines Register* and the *Minneapolis Tribune* carried stories of an exotic 27-year-old German woman who was requested to leave the country in August, 1963, following an F.B.I. investigation that established her close association with a number of important government officials. The woman, Mrs. Elly Rometsch, was returned to West Germany as a result of her "personal misbehavior."

Mrs. Rometsch, the wife of a West German Army sergeant, had entered the United States on a diplomatic visa. Her husband was attached to the West German Embassy.

She was identified as a "party girl" who had visited the Baker-Tyler town house and participated in parties with some of the persons involved in the Baker vending-machine controversy. Her husband, Sergeant Rolf Rometsch, explained to reporters that his wife had worked as "a model" on occasion, to supplement their income in Washington, but that he had been unaware of any improper conduct on her part. However, within two months after they returned to Germany he divorced her on the ground that she had violated the marriage agreement.

On October 29, 1963, Senator Williams went before a closed session of the Senate Rules Committee to outline these disclosures and other general information.[5] He said it had been found that Bobby Baker had reported a net worth of more than $2 million in financial statements prepared for a Maryland bank. This and the other matters, Senator Williams said, merited detailed investigation by Chairman Jordan's staff.

In his characteristically quiet manner, Senator Williams refrained from making generalized accusations of wrongdoing. He merely spelled out the facts on a number of cases he felt should be pursued.

He said he wished to cooperate with Senator Jordan's committee, and promised to make all leads available as they came to him. Rules Committee members had the obligation to dig out all the facts, conduct the hearings, and arrive at their own conclusions. If Williams disagreed with their conclusions, he could say so later.

It was apparent to those who followed the story that the Senate Democrats were uneasy about what Williams might be holding back, and about the new information that was being brought to Senator Williams almost daily by newspaper reporters and magazine writers. It was almost as if Senator Williams had his own private F.B.I. Nearly all the rumors and all the bits and pieces of information that fell into the hands of the investigating reporters were made available to Senator Williams.

The introduction of the call-girl "angle" into the Baker investigation stimulated such rapid interest in good government that one national magazine assigned more than twenty reporters to the story.

Some treatments were unsubtle—but then the whole story was becoming more so. In its November 8, 1963, issue, *Life* ran a picture story titled "That High-Living Baker Boy Scandalizes the Capital." One page carried large pictures of Elly Rometsch and Carole Tyler. Opposite Carole and Elly was a full-page picture of a smiling Lyndon Johnson with his arm draped around the shoulder of Bobby Baker.

The *New York Times* investigations by reporter Wallace Turner linked Baker to business dealings with several Las Vegas gambling figures. Other stories traced Baker's initial involvement in the Florida land transaction that was eventually backed by Teamsters' Union money. Baker had withdrawn from this land deal shortly after the Teamster loan was approved, and it became clear that a public record would be made of those responsible for the loan.

Every story critical of Bobby Baker seemed to hurt the political fortunes of Vice-President Johnson. Johnson made no public statement critical of his former associate, nor did he take any step to disassociate himself from Baker. The Vice-President remained silent and unavailable except to those few reporters he could count upon to write that it just wasn't true that Baker was Lyndon's protégé.

In addition to any indirect problem the Baker investigation might have created for the Vice-President, there were also indications of more direct connections. Don Reynolds had given Senator Williams information concerning a $100,000 insurance policy he had written on Lyndon Johnson's life in 1957. He told Williams he was compelled to buy some advertising time on the Johnson-family television station in Austin, Texas, shortly after selling Johnson the insurance policy. Why an insurance agent selling policies in Silver Spring, Maryland, should want to advertise on a local station in Austin, Texas, was an intriguing question.

George Reedy, then press secretary to the Vice-President, contacted Reynolds in an effort to get the insurance man to quit talking about Johnson's insurance policies and related matters, Reynolds said later. By the time Reedy made his contact, it already was too late. Reynolds had already talked to several reporters. More to the point, he had given the full story to Senator Williams, together with photostatic copies of documents that he said supported his story.

Now the facts were closing in. On Thursday, November 14th, Senator Williams was back before the Senate Rules Committee for another two-hour session.[6] Again, the Delaware Republican made no sensational charges but quietly called attention to some transactions that had the potential for providing highly explosive political information. In an almost casual way, he mentioned the advertising time that insurance man Reynolds said he had been required to buy on the L.B.J. Company television station in Austin.

Then Senator Williams called attention to documents dealing with a story Reynolds had told him about a $585 stereophonic high-fidelity record player. Reynolds said he had been "persuaded" by Bobby Baker to give this expensive set to the Lyndon Johnson family in 1959, after selling Johnson the $100,000 policy.

It was a difficult period for the Kennedy administration. Problems involving dubious ethics and politics were crowding from many directions. By now, in addition to the Bobby Baker affair, there was the Billie Sol Estes matter, the Fred Korth matter, the

Roswell Gilpatric matter—all linked to Kennedy's Vice-President, Lyndon Johnson.

Although Senator Williams had made no public charges of impropriety, the newspapers were filled with stories, editorials, and cartoons. Bobby Baker had become a household word.

On November 21, 1963, Senator Williams told this reporter that he was going to push the Bobby Baker probe until he was satisfied it was being investigated properly. It probably would be his last big investigation as a Senator, he said. Senator Williams said he hadn't reached a final decision, but that he didn't believe he would run for reelection in 1964.

"Eighteen years in politics is a long time," Senator Williams said. "There are still a lot of things I would like to do, but I don't want to just stay down here and be another professional politician."

Senator Williams said he hoped that he would be able to force the Senate into a much-needed housecleaning before bowing out.

The story that Williams might retire from politics was printed in the *Des Moines Register* and the *Minneapolis Tribune* on the morning of November 22, 1963—a day that was to change the plans of many people.

CHAPTER 21

Testimony During Disaster— November 22, 1963

Worried by the dissension in the Democratic party in Texas, President Kennedy decided to go to Texas in November, 1963, on a goodwill mission. The President took along his wife, Jacqueline. The scheduled three-day trip was announced, in the deadpan American tradition, as nonpolitical in nature.

The first day of the trip, the Scripps-Howard newspapers reported, was "chock full of bad timing and highly political backfires."[1]

In San Antonio, the first stop, the liberal Democratic leaders didn't turn out in force to welcome their President because the conservative Johnson-Connally forces were in charge of arrangements. The leader of the liberal faction, Senator Ralph Yarborough, whose views were pro-Kennedy, declined to ride with Vice-President Johnson in the motorcade. Pointedly, he rode in a car with the liberal Texas Representative Henry B. Gonzales, one of seventeen Texas House members who flew to San Antonio at the President's invitation.

In Houston, Senator Yarborough again ducked a ride with Vice-President Johnson, and it was learned that Governor John B. Connally didn't even invite Yarborough to the $100-a-plate Democratic fund-raising dinner slated for Austin the next night.

Yarborough was quoted as commenting caustically: "Because

Governor Connally is so terribly uneducated governmentally, how could you expect anything else?"

Instead of a "fence-mending tour," as planned, it appeared that President Kennedy's trip in the first day had touched off more active feuds between the warring liberal and conservative elements of the Texas Democratic organization.

The outlook for the second day seemed just as dismal. Persons identified as "rank-and-file Democrats" complained that the 2,000 people invited to attend a Chamber of Commerce breakfast in Fort Worth were for the most part men who had voted for Richard Nixon in 1960. To soothe wounded feelings, Representative James Wright, the Democratic Congressman from Fort Worth, persuaded President Kennedy to give a ten-minute prebreakfast talk in a parking lot near the Texas Hotel, where the breakfast was to be staged.

In Dallas, there was a similar problem. The liberal Democrats, most of them staunch Kennedy supporters, were threatening to boycott a luncheon address because the 1960 "Nixon Democrats" had acquired most of the luncheon tickets.

During the breakfast meeting in Fort Worth, President Kennedy tried to make political capital out of the controversial TFX-warplane issue, which was almost a political plague in Washington. The President told the Fort Worth businessmen that Texas —and particularly the Dallas-Fort Worth area—was getting a large share of the defense dollar. He declared that Texas ranked fifth among all the states in prime military procurement contracts and second in the number of military personnel on active duty.

"I do not recite these facts for partisan purposes, nor are they the result of partisan efforts," the President said. He defended the TFX fighter plane as one that would "serve the forces of freedom in a manner no airplane on earth can match," and said: "There has been a good deal of discussion of the long and hard fought competition to win the TFX contract but relatively little discussion of what this revolutionary plane will be able to do."

In his recital of what the TFX would do, Mr. Kennedy made no reference to the fact that by placing the contract in Texas $100 to $415 million would be added to the cost of the plane. Nor did he mention, of course, that the less expensive plane, offered by the Texas firm's rival, Boeing, was "rated" superior by the military evaluation boards.

The TFX-warplane decision undoubtedly was a political asset in Fort Worth, where it would pour billions into the business community and would create thousands of jobs. But the reporters already were writing that the "nonpolitical" trip had turned into a fiasco which was hurting the Democrats and creating a situation that might turn Texas to the Republicans in 1964. If there was to be any political advantage from the Texas trip, President Kennedy recognized that he had to come up with something to give the appearance there was some harmony between the Johnson and Yarborough factions. Accordingly, he directed that Senator Yarborough and Vice-President Johnson should ride in the same car in the motorcade trip scheduled for Dallas at noon on November 22nd.

It was 11:37 A.M. (Central Standard Time) when President and Mrs. Kennedy and Governor and Mrs. Connally arrived at Love Field, Dallas. A few minutes later they entered an opentop car for a ten-mile motorcade tour through Dallas. They were in the first car, followed by a Secret Service car. The third car carried Vice-President and Mrs. Lyndon B. Johnson and Senator Yarborough as the reluctant symbol of a nonexistent unity in the Texas Democratic organization.

While President Kennedy was starting his fateful ride in Texas, the other half of the day's drama was being played out in a committee room of the old Senate Office Building in Washington, D.C.

At seven o'clock that morning (Eastern Standard Time), Don B. Reynolds, the insurance agent, awakened at his home in Silver Spring, Maryland, a suburb of Washington. It was a crucial day for him, for he was scheduled to go to the Hill for discussions with the Senate Rules Committee staff regarding the Bobby Baker investigation. He intended to keep his promise to cooperate, even though pressure was already being put on him by various political figures.

Some of the pressure was being applied by Reynolds' former friends—close associates of Bobby Baker—who were urging him either to "forget" the answers or to take the Fifth Amendment and refuse to talk. He was warned that he was tampering with the reputations of "big men" and that it could only cause him trouble if he talked.

The threatened trouble did materialize later, as promised. Before the investigation was over, strenuous efforts were made, through "leaks" of confidential information to the press, to blacken Reynolds' reputation and make him appear as a person unworthy of belief.

One of Reynolds' reasons for going through with his promise to Senator Williams was the desire of Mrs. Reynolds to make a complete break with Baker and his crowd. She didn't like the night life, the gay parties, the weekend trips to Miami and New York. She didn't like the "fast buck" attitude in the crowd her husband was running with—which included men like Baker himself; Fred Black, Jr., the big-spending "public relations" man; and Thomas (Tommy) Webb, Washington representative for the Murchison financial interests of Texas.

Mrs. Reynolds had met Senator Williams, liked him and trusted him, and urged her husband to cooperate.

Reynolds knew he had been careless in some of his business associations and activities, but was willing to cooperate with Senator Williams. As he got more deeply involved with the Delaware Senator, Reynolds was impressed by Williams' straightforward way of doing business.

Another factor motivated Reynolds. He believed that Attorney General Robert F. Kennedy would conduct a thorough investigation of Bobby Baker's activities, regardless of who might be involved. He knew the Attorney General had taken forceful action in indicting and convicting prominent Democrats in New York, Alabama, Maryland, and Indiana.

The Justice Department also had been involved in extensive

investigations of Teamster Boss James R. Hoffa. Reynolds felt
that Kennedy, Hoffa's avowed enemy, would have a special interest in following up the evidence that Baker and his associates were
involved in business dealings backed by a Teamster loan. This
loan had been arranged at the very time when a Congressional
committee, with Bobby Kennedy as chief counsel, had been investigating and exposing the activities of what the committee
called Hoffa's "Hoodlum Empire."

At 8:30 A.M., Reynolds arrived at the office of his attorney,
James F. Fitzgerald. They discussed the information he would
make available to the Senate Rules Committee, and then they
drove to the old Senate Office Building for the interview.

It was a few minutes before 10 A.M. when Reynolds and Fitzgerald were escorted to Room 312, where two staff members
waited. They were introduced to Lorin Drennan, an accountant
who was on loan from the General Accounting Office (G.A.O.),
and Burkett Van Kirk, a young lawyer from Lincoln, Nebraska,
who had been appointed as Republican minority counsel.

In the first two hours, the questioning ranged over the whole
scope of Reynolds' knowledge of Baker's financial operations.
Reynolds had listed Baker as a vice-president of Don Reynolds
Associates, Inc., which was his insurance business. The Maryland
insurance man said Baker was supposed to send prospects to him,
and that Baker had agreed to put up some money to become a vice-
president. The money never was put up, Reynolds said. He said
he and others found it difficult to get money out of Baker, although
Baker "always" was asking for money from them.

The staff questioned Reynolds about some payments Don Reynolds Associates had made to Baker that were written off as "business expense."

The Senate staff members stated that Baker had handled the
payments from Reynolds as loans, not taxable as additional income. Reynolds said these sums were not loans, and that he considered them as normal costs of obtaining certain business with
Bobby Baker's help.

Reynolds told how Baker had arranged for him to meet Matthew McCloskey at Baker's Senate office to discuss writing a performance bond on the District of Columbia Stadium construction project. McCloskey, a Philadelphia contractor, former Treasurer of the National Democratic Party, was then serving as U.S. Ambassador to Ireland. Reynolds went on to reveal that he earned $10,000 in commissions when McCloskey won the stadium contract and gave him the business of writing the performance bond.

Baker was cut in for $4,000 of the commissions, Reynolds said. He said he also paid $1,500 to William N. McLeod, Jr., who then was the clerk of the House District of Columbia Committee. He held back some details on the stadium-bond deal, and said later he did it because he didn't want to reveal his whole hand immediately.

Reynolds told of partying in Miami and New York. He named the political and business figures who were present at some of these parties and the business deals that were discussed. Reynolds told what he heard of Elly Rometsch, the German party girl whose name had been brought into the case as a visitor to the town house occupied by Baker's private secretary. He also named two other women who he said were "call girls" used by a defense contractor to entertain officials who were influential in the awarding of big defense contracts.

The sordid recital continued with Reynolds' disclosure that once he had called Baker's office to obtain a certain Capitol Hill telephone number. Through that number, he said, he was able to contact an abortionist (needed by a young woman he identified as a friend of a friend of his).[2]

He told the investigators of a conversation he had in the summer of 1963 with Ralph Hill, president of Capitol Vending, who was suing Baker and associates. Hill complained to him, Reynolds said, that Baker was trying to squeeze Hill out of the lucrative Melpar vending contract and deliver it to a firm in which Baker had an interest. Reynolds said that long before the lawsuit was filed, Hill had told him that he had been paying Baker $250 a month and later $650 a month to keep the Melpar contract, and that Baker was using his political influence to pull the contract away from him.

Reynolds said he was aware that Baker had been handling large amounts of cash, from $10,000 to $13,000 at a time, and that it didn't seem a normal way to do business.

Reynolds related that he had been involved in a Florida land-development project, in partnership with Baker; Scott I. Peek, the former administrative assistant to Senator George Smathers (Democrat, of Florida); Thomas E. Webb, the financial adviser for the Murchisons; and some Florida promoters. Reynolds said that he accompanied Webb to the Teamsters' Union building in Washington for discussions with James R. Hoffa of a loan for $150,000 for the Wertco land-development project near Jacksonville, Florida.

It was almost time for the usual noon luncheon break when the insurance man got started on his story of how he had been pressured into taking advertising time on the L.B.J. television station in Austin, and about the gift stereo which he said he had given the Johnsons at Baker's "suggestion." It was about 12:30 P.M., Washington time—11:30 A.M. in Dallas, Texas—when Van Kirk and Drennan suggested they send a girl for sandwiches and milk, rather than interrupt Reynolds' testimony by going out to eat.

The questioning and the discussion of the L.B.J. Company's affairs, as Reynolds knew them, went on.

About 1:30 P.M., Reynolds still was relating the details of how he had written two insurance policies for $100,000 each. The first policy was written in 1957, just two years after Lyndon Johnson's heart attack, Reynolds related. The second $100,000 policy was written in 1961.

Reynolds told the investigators he was required to make a gift of the stereo record player to the Johnson family.[3] For the next hour, he produced records to substantiate his story. There were the bills from the Magnavox Company, showing that he had paid for the stereo set. Because he purchased it wholesale through a friend, Reynolds said he had been able to get it for $585, but it had a normal retail value of about $900. It was the set that Mrs. Johnson had selected from a catalogue Reynolds said was sent to her by Bobby Baker.

Mrs. Johnson had insisted on quick delivery because she needed it for a musicale, Reynolds said, so he had directed that it be rushed by air freight. He explained that a mistake was made on the shipping orders, and the stereo set was sent to the Friendship Airport, in Baltimore. A Senate truck was sent to pick it up and deliver it to the Johnson home, then at 3921 Thirtieth Place, N.W., Reynolds said. Reynolds produced his canceled checks, in addition to the bills, proving he had paid for the set.

Reynolds went on to tell how he was pressured, in the aftermath of the insurance deal, to buy time on the L.B.J. Company station, KTBC. He emphasized that it was ridiculous for a Maryland insurance business to buy advertising on a Texas television station, 1,500 miles away. But, when he resisted, Bobby Baker prodded him, Reynolds said. He told investigators that Vice-President Johnson's administrative assistant, Walter Jenkins, also called and urged him to buy the TV time.

The insurance man insisted that it was not an illegal "kickback" arrangement made at the time he sold the insurance. He characterized it as "a shakedown" on his insurance commissions after the sale was made.

Reynolds said he called Jenkins and asked if it would meet his approval if he resold the time on KTBC to someone who might have some use for it. Jenkins, who was not only Johnson's administrative assistant but was listed as an officer of the L.B.J. Company, consented to this arrangement, Reynolds said.

Reynolds told the Rules Committee staff members that the law prohibits kickbacks on insurance, and he said he resisted making the stereo gift and the advertising payments as long as he could. He said that Jenkins referred to a letter from a man named Huff Baines—reportedly a Texas insurance man—in which Baines had agreed to a specific amount of advertising on the L.B.J. Company station if he handled Johnson's life insurance.

Although Vice-President Johnson contended, before and since, that he had no interest and no voice in the L.B.J. Company radio and television enterprises, Reynolds said it was the L.B.J. Company that paid for the insurance policy on the Vice-President's life. The company could not insure Johnson unless he was a person of such value to the firm that he would be regarded as a valuable, key man in the firm's operations, Reynolds suggested.

It was shortly after 2:30 P.M., Washington time, when Reynolds finished. He and his attorney were preparing to leave. Suddenly a woman secretary burst into the room. She was sobbing almost hysterically. As Reynolds and the interrogators looked at her in surprise, she cried: "President Kennedy has been killed!"

At first they thought it was a joke—a bad joke. Then, as they saw the woman's tears and her genuine distress, they knew it was no joke. Even as they had been talking, President Kennedy, riding with Mrs. Kennedy in the Dallas motorcade, had been killed by an assassin's bullet.

Reynolds was stunned. If President Kennedy was dead, then Lyndon Johnson, the man about whom he had been talking, was President of the United States.

Reynolds reached for the documents on the committee table which confirmed his story of the gift stereo set and the television advertising contract. He quietly pulled the documents toward him.

"I guess you won't need these," Reynolds said soberly. "Giving testimony involving the Vice-President is one thing, but when it involves the President himself, that is something else. You can just forget that I ever said anything if you want to."

Counsel Van Kirk replied that Reynolds should not concern himself with the problem of what should be done with the evidence.

"The documents on this matter are now the records of the Rules Committee," Van Kirk said. "The decision on whether we will use them is a matter that the Committee will have to decide. None of us can do anything about it."

At 3:39 P.M., Washington time (2:39 P.M. in Dallas), Lyndon B. Johnson was sworn in as the thirty-sixth President of the United States.

A disturbed Don Reynolds returned to his insurance office, and tried unsuccessfully to work. Later, he called Senator Williams for his assessment of the matter.

Senator Williams said that the facts and the documents had the same relevance they had had twenty-four hours earlier. He said he believed everything was so upset at the moment that it would be impossible to predict the future course of the Baker investigation.

"But I don't intend to let it drop, if I can help it," the Delaware Republican declared. Then it was that Don Reynolds knew he had passed the point of no return, and he had no choice but to stand firm with Senator Williams.

CHAPTER 22

The L.B.J. Company

When Lyndon B. Johnson assumed the presidency, attention was focused on the Johnson family's extensive interests in the government-regulated radio and television industry, which had helped make them multimillionaires. The Bobby Baker investigation caused discussion of the ethical problems present. Public hearings on matters that involved the L.B.J. Company's radio-TV holdings might make the matter an explosive political issue at any time.

For years there had been bitterness in the Austin, Texas, area because there was only one VHF (very high frequency) television channel available in that city of 200,000. The station, KTBC, was owned by the L.B.J. Company. In turn, Mrs. Johnson owned 52 per cent of the stock in the L.B.J. Company, and the Johnson daughters, Lynda B. and Luci B., owned another 31 per cent of the stock.

That acrimony increased in 1963 when it became apparent the Johnson family had an option to buy 50 per cent of the stock of the one community-antenna television company in Austin. (Community-antenna systems—called CATV—make it possible for paying subscribers to hook into a central antenna and receive network programs.) With the L.B.J. Company's new acquisition went the privilege of bringing by cable full programing from all three major TV networks. In short, it was a gold mine, estimated to be worth an additional $2 million to the Johnson family.

Mrs. Johnson acquired her first radio station in 1943, when Lyndon Johnson was a member of the House of Representatives.

The F.C.C. approved her acquisition of the only TV channel in Austin in 1952 when the then Senator Lyndon B. Johnson was a member of the Senate Interstate and Foreign Commerce Committee.

That is the committee which has jurisdiction over investigations and legislation for the Federal Communications Commission.

The Johnsons took the position that there was no problem of possible conflicts of interest when Senator Johnson was a member of the Senate Interstate and Foreign Commerce Committee, nor when he was the powerful Democratic Leader in the Senate from January, 1955 to January, 1961.[1] They saw no problem when Johnson became Vice-President either.

It was explained that Majority Leader Johnson owned no interest in any radio or television property, and had no voice in the operation of the radio and television interests the L.B.J. Company had acquired. It was all the property of the children and Mrs. Johnson. If they acquired a multimillion-dollar fortune in a government-controlled industry, it certainly was not because of his position as a public official, Johnson insisted. He contended he took no part in the radio and television business.

No one had paid much attention to the Johnson television interests in the period from 1961 through the summer of 1963. Then the Baker investigation came along, and the charges of allegedly pressured advertising-time sale created a new interest in the delicate questions of ethics involved. The public showed a lively curiosity in how the Johnson family acquired such valuable radio and television interests after Lyndon Johnson became prominent in the federal government.

Actually, the question of whether it is proper for members of Congress to acquire government licenses for TV and radio stations is an old one. Periodically, it has been raised in Congress and by the press. It had come up in the 1958 hearings before the House Subcommittee on Legislative Oversight. There had been such a press howl over one member of the House subcommittee owning a small interest in a television station that he sold his interest.

After the Bobby Baker investigation started, the editors of *U.S. News & World Report* asked Senator John Williams his views on members of Congress acquiring interests in businesses that are regulated by federal agencies.

The Delaware Republican said:

"The propriety of that would depend upon how such interests were acquired. It's not what you own or what you're doing; it's the background of how you got it.

"In my case, I did not own a television station before I was elected, my wife did not. I would certainly raise a question if we came out of here [the Senate] owning one. I think you have to go behind each instance to see the background."[2]

When President Johnson took office on November 22nd, his political advisers were on notice that a major political problem could build up over the radio-TV holdings. The November 22, 1963, issue of *Life* had a long article on "Morality in Washington." The November 25, 1963, issue of *U.S. News & World Report,* prepared before the assassination, had a cover story on "The Mess in Washington."

A week after President Johnson was sworn in to office as chief executive, Mrs. Johnson filed an application with the F.C.C. She asked permission to place the L.B.J. Company, with its television and radio interests, in a trusteeship.

Mrs. Johnson resigned as chairman of the board of the L.B.J. Company, and asked for a trust agreement that would give control of the property to two old Johnson friends and business associates—A. W. Moursand, general counsel of the Citizens' State Bank of Johnson City, Texas, and J. W. Bullion, also of Johnson City.

Mrs. Johnson stated that the trust would terminate only "at such time as the grantor's husband, Lyndon B. Johnson, shall no longer hold federal elective office or when said shares of the L.B.J. Company shall be disposed of, whichever shall occur first."

A Congressional watchdog, Republican Congressman H. R. Gross, of Iowa, chided President and Mrs. Johnson for setting up the trust to avoid a "conflict of interest" only after Johnson became President.[3] He questioned whether the trust arrangement actually would remove the possibility of a conflict of interest, and pointed out that new members of the F.C.C. would be appointed by President Johnson, and that some of the incumbents might be dependent on Johnson for reappointment.

Representative Gross declared that the "events of the last few weeks have dramatized a basic question: Should members of the House and Senate and officials of the Executive Branch be permitted to acquire or hold television and radio rights while serving in the Government?

"It should be apparent that the President, Vice President and others of high rank in Government should not obtain interests in a Government-controlled industry," Gross said. "There is either direct control of appointments to the Federal Communications Commission, as in the case of the President, or the troublesome situation where high officials have great influence that might be misused in associating with the F.C.C.

"It should also be apparent that members of the House and Senate have a position of some control over the F.C.C., through legislation, proposals of legislation, through appropriations, through investigation, and otherwise through political links. It is unreasonable to expect that all members of the F.C.C. can retain an absolutely objective posture in making decisions on radio and television involving the members of the Senate or House. This is particularly true if the television or radio rights sought personally involve key figures on the Commerce committees, Appropriations committee, or persons who are otherwise in position of leadership."

Gross pointed out to the House that although the L.B.J. Company's property had been put in trust for the duration of the period of time President Johnson was in public office, however "the profits accumulate for the family." Then he asked:

"Does the establishment of a trust in the case of the L.B.J. Company wipe out of the minds of the members of the F.C.C. the fact that the members of the Johnson family are the real owners of radio and television interests?

"I submit," Gross went on, "that every member of the Federal Communications Commission is going to be aware of the interest of the Johnson family in the field of radio and television. And I further submit that, in the case of the F.C.C., the chairman holds office at the pleasure of the President."

Representative W. J. Bryan Dorn (Democrat of South Carolina) applauded President and Mrs. Johnson for placing the L.B.J. Company stock in a trust.[4]

"This timely action on the part of the President and Mrs. Johnson, inaugurated by his own initiative, is most commendable and reassuring to the American people," Representative Dorn told the House on December 18th.

"The President specified that the trustees of his assets cannot accept any Federal subsidy. . . .

"This is an example of ethics and high moral standards in our President and our First Lady which will meet the overwhelming approval of the American people. . . . The times demand the very highest standards of ethics and the highest moral conduct by those charged with the administration of public affairs."

But Republicans persisted in asking why the same principle hadn't applied in all the years when Johnson was an influential member of Congress and Vice-President of the United States. Like Representative Gross, they continued to question whether placing the stock in trust would make the F.C.C. more objective.

Many Republicans sniped at the "trust" arrangement as a "phony" way to fool the public into believing that the possibility of a conflict of interest had evaporated. The sniping was aimed at the "L.B.J. Company." President Johnson's passion for branding everything with his "L.B.J." mark had created at last a major public-relations problem. It was difficult for him to disassociate himself and his family from the radio-television interests.

On December 20th, the Johnson-controlled broadcasting firm asked the F.C.C. for permission to drop the "L.B.J." brand and become the Texas Broadcasting Corporation. The stock ownership remained with the family, but the new name did not automatically conjure up an image of a tall Texas political figure in the White House.

This was a period of other adjustments by Johnson associates to accommodate President Johnson's new political position. In one such adjustment, the President's friend Abe Fortas, the Washington lawyer who had been defending Bobby Baker in the $300,-000 vending-machine suit, asked the federal court's permission to withdraw as Baker's attorney. Fortas told the court he wished to avoid any possible conflict of interest. He explained to the press that he was serving as President Johnson's liaison man with the Justice Department in the investigation of President Kennedy's assassination. The Justice Department, in turn, was investigating Bobby Baker.

Also, Walter Jenkins, special assistant to President Johnson, announced he had resigned as treasurer and director of the Johnson radio and television enterprises.

The President's problems, however, wouldn't stay buried. New developments began to break in the Baker case. A fresh row over community-antenna television service in Austin put the Johnson family's near monopoly back in the news.

The F.C.C., in a 6-to-1 decision, had rejected a petition filed by John Campbell, operator of TV Cable of Austin. Campbell had contended that the ruling of the F.C.C. would force him to delay rebroadcasts of programs for thirty days if the programs had been on the Johnson family TV station, but that his competitor, Capital Cable, would be permitted an unlimited immediate broadcast of all programs on all three networks.

What was particularly irritating to Campbell was the fact that the Johnson interests had an option to buy 50 per cent of the stock of Capital Cable at any time within a three-year period. Campbell argued that the Johnson-family television station already had a monopoly in VHF broadcasts in Austin, and it should not be permitted to have an additional competitive advantage through control of community-antenna television.[5]

A political scandal needs a good symbol that the public can associate with it. If the details are too abstruse, the scandal may soar over the head of the average citizen—and the press. The Truman administration had its deep-freezes, and the Eisenhower administration had Sherman Adams' vicuña coat—nice, easy-to-understand symbols.

On January 14, 1964, the new Johnson administration got its symbol—a stereophonic, hi-fi combination record player, which Don Reynolds, the insurance man, had purchased, allegedly at Bobby Baker's suggestion, as a gift for the Johnsons. Les Whitten, of the Hearst newspapers, and Paul Hope and John Barron, reporters for the Washington *Evening Star,* broke the news of the expensive "gift," which hitherto had been known only to the Senate Rules Committee—and, of course, the participants.[6]

Cartoonists, columnists, and editorial writers dealt critically with the hi-fi gift; also, with the disclosure of Reynolds' claim that he had been pressured into buying advertising time on the L.B.J. Company's Texas station, after he had sold the then Majority Leader a $100,000 life-insurance policy. President Johnson felt compelled to comment. He brought up the insurance matter at a brief press conference. He gave a quick explanation of the life-insurance purchase, said he considered the stereo a gift from Baker, and shut off the conference without giving reporters an opportunity to question him.

Said the President:

"The company in which Mrs. Johnson and my daughters have a majority interest, along with some other stockholders, were somewhat concerned when I had a heart attack in 1955, and in 1957 they purchased insurance on my life made payable to the company. And the insurance premiums were never included as a business expense, but they thought that was good business practice in case something happened to me so Mrs. Johnson and the children wouldn't have to sell their stock on the open market and lose control of the company."

The President added: "There is a question also raised about a gift of a stereo set that an employee of mine made to me and Mrs. Johnson.

"That happened some two years later [after the life insurance was purchased], some five years ago. The Baker family gave us a stereo set. We used it for a period. And we had exchanged gifts before.

"He was an employee of the public and had no business pending before me and was asking nothing and so far as I knew expected nothing in return, any more than I did when I had presented him with gifts.

"I hope that covers it rather fully. That is all I have to say about it and all I know about it."[7]

The answer didn't satisfy the press. At the next press conference, on January 25th, a reporter asked: "Mr. President, could you tell us generally how you feel about the Bobby Baker case and the way it is developing, whether it raises any serious questions about ethics in government?"

The President did not give a direct answer: "I think that is a matter the Senate is working on, and I told you the other day about the two matters that have created some interest among you. I spoke fully on them and said what I had to say."

"I am not talking about those matters," the reporter responded. "I mean in a more general sense."

"I understand, and I have covered your question as thoroughly as I know how," President Johnson replied.

Another reporter broke in:

"Mr. President, do you have any comment on the Republican criticism of the stereo set?"

That put the ball in his territory and Lyndon Johnson, experienced politician, replied with more gusto: "No, I have learned to expect Republican criticism and I have endured it for about 32 years," he answered. "I get amused by it once in a while, but I don't want to change it because I think that is kind of a hallmark of their party. You get accustomed to expecting it."[8]

There was further public controversy about the L.B.J. Company and the insurance transaction when the Senate Rules Committee released testimony disclosing conflict between the story told by Don Reynolds and a statement given to the committee by White House Aide Walter Jenkins.

Johnson's aide did not appear before the committee, either in public or private, but gave committee investigators a sworn statement denying "any knowledge of any arrangement by which Reynolds purchased advertising on the TV station."

Jenkins "emphatically denies ever suggesting to Robert G. Baker or to Reynolds the L.B.J. Company should get any sort of rebate from the commissions earned by Reynolds," the statement said.[9]

But Reynolds held to his story, testifying under oath that Jenkins, a director and treasurer of the L.B.J. Company, did take part in the advertising arrangements.[10]

The insurance man said that in addition to discussing the purchase of advertising time with him, Jenkins "discussed it directly with the President of Mid-Atlantic Stainless Steel Company, Mr. Albert G. Young." Reynolds explained that the advertising time on the Texas station was useless to him as a Maryland insurance agent, so he sold it to Young.

When Chairman Jordan was asked by reporters if he would call Young to verify Reynolds' story, the North Carolina Democrat said he did not intend to call either Jenkins or Young.

"We are not investigating tinware!" the Senator jabbed.

The Washington *Evening Star,* on January 26th, stated editorially that Jordan had given "a frivolous response to a pertinent question," and added:

"Unless Senator Jordan and his colleagues are ready to forfeit public respect and confidence, they had better investigate the issue of perjury which has cropped up during the pussy-footing probe of the Bobby Baker mess."

"Mr. Reynolds was testifying under oath," the editorial pointed out. "Mr. Jenkins . . . in a sworn statement denied any knowledge of the advertising matter. Thus it seems probable that one of the two men committed perjury."

The *Star* said that normally an investigating committee would try to get to the bottom of the conflicting stories, and would call all witnesses and examine the records of the TV station.

"Apparently the Senate [Rules] Committee does not intend to do this," the *Star* said. "It is trying to clamp the lid on what could be a very explosive (though legitimate) aspect of its inquiry. If it does, it can expect a vote of 'no confidence' from the American people. And this vote should come through loud and clear."

Under the pressure of public opinion, the Rules Committee heard Young's testimony, which corroborated Reynolds on many points. He said a man who identified himself as Jenkins had called him on the advertising matter. However, Chairman Jordan stubbornly refused to call President Johnson's assistant.

Meanwhile, a series of columns were written by Drew Pearson for the stated purpose of destroying Reynolds' credibility. The derogatory information purportedly came from secret files of the U. S. Air Force and other executive departments.

The subject of the Bobby Baker investigation came up again at the President's January 31st press conference.[11]

"Mr. President, sir," a woman reporter began. "I wonder what you think about a full-time Senate employee, or an employee of any Government agency, who would get himself involved in off-duty hours or in regular hours with consultants for defense contracting firms . . . with building motels, getting himself involved in deals with mortgage companies that are interested in pending legislation, and in visiting the Dominican Republic. . . . Do you think this is proper conduct for any Government employee?"

Again President Johnson avoided a direct answer. "The Senate committee is now making a study of the accuracy of some of the allegations you have made," he replied. "They will, in their wisdom, determine the accuracy of those allegations and, I am sure, render proper judgment."

"Mr. President," I asked, "do you feel that Mr. Walter Jenkins should go up to the Capitol and testify under oath to clear up the conflicts that are appearing in the testimony?"

"The general question was raised with me at my last meeting," President Johnson answered. "I spoke with candor and frankness on that subject about all I know about it. I said then that I did not plan to make any more statements, and I do not."

In the first week of February, Cabell Phillips, of the *New York Times,* wrote a story on the White House efforts to blacken Reynolds' character. He reported that "an important White House personage, but not the President," had called the publisher of a national news magazine and read excerpts from what was described as an F.B.I. file on Reynolds.

The *New York Times* reporter wrote that a number of editors and publishers and reporters had received similar calls. They were given part of the alleged information from the government files. The purpose was to show that Reynolds had brought "reckless charges" against persons in the past and allegedly had engaged in improper and immoral conduct while overseas.

Senator Carl Curtis, of Nebraska, the ranking Republican on the Rules Committee, told the Senate that the allegations being distributed by high administration officials were not relevant to Reynolds' testimony. Most of the testimony Reynolds had given before the committee was backed with canceled checks and other documentary evidence, he said.

On February 3rd, Senator Jack Miller (Republican, Iowa) said the Rules Committee had an obligation to "call all parties before it and to have it out" as to whether Reynolds or Jenkins was telling the truth.[12]

"Mr. Young stated that Reynolds came to him in 1957 and said he was 'obligated' to purchase $3,000 in advertising time on the L.B.J. Company station," Senator Miller said. "He wanted to have Young take over the advertising time for his own products," Miller explained. "Mr. Young stated that Reynolds told him he would have Walter Jenkins telephone Young about the matter, and that an individual identifying himself as Jenkins did call and confirmed the arrangement that had been made with Reynolds. Letters and checks in the committee files, I understand, substantiate Mr. Reynolds' payment of at least $1,208 for such advertising."

Said Miller: "The public has a right to know the truth about this transaction—not just half of the truth."

In a Senate speech on February 3rd, Senator Hugh Scott (Republican, of Pennsylvania) said he had received "veiled threats" for pushing the Bobby Baker probe.[13] The Pennsylvanian declared that he would push for a full investigation and calling of "all witnesses, no matter how many veiled threats may be conveyed to members of the Rules Committee."

For weeks, there had been reports of threats to witnesses who were to appear before the Rules Committee, as well as telephone threats to some Senators and staff members who were active in pushing the investigation. However, nothing was said publicly until Senator Scott's speech met it head on.

At a National Press Club luncheon, G.O.P. Chairman William Miller suggested a broad investigation of the considerable advertising revenues the L.B.J. Company reportedly had received from large defense industries.

"How many times did North American Aviation advertise over the L.B.J. station?" Representative Miller wanted to know.

(Reporters tried to get such information from the F.C.C., but the government agency that polices the communications industry would not release it.)

The G.O.P. chairman suggested that the President appoint a prominent Republican to head an investigation of the Bobby Baker case, advertising on the L.B.J. station, and other related matters. This, he said, would be following the precedent set by President Calvin Coolidge, a Republican, in appointing a Democrat to conduct investigation of the Teapot Dome scandals involving the Republican Harding administration.

The next day, Senator Scott again spoke of the "shocking" leak of confidential information about Reynolds. As some of the information allegedly came from Air Force secret files, he wrote to Defense Secretary McNamara:

"It is a matter of serious concern to me that such a leak could happen. I am doubly concerned that leaks of internal memoranda can apparently be used to destroy witnesses whose testimony becomes embarrassing. The situation is particularly serious when it's realized that this information was denied to proper officials of the United States Senate."

Rules Committee Counsel L. P. McLendon said the Defense Department had refused to give him the files on Reynolds because they were "classified."

In a House speech, Representative Gross charged that the Johnson administration had engaged in an "outrageous" attempt to "intimidate" Reynolds and other witnesses who might give testimony that embarrassed the White House.

The Iowa Congressman called upon President Johnson to demonstrate his good faith by punishing those responsible for the Reynolds "smear."

"If this 'leak' of information—if this attempt to intimidate a witness goes unpunished, then all who took part in it and all who condone it are equally guilty of outrageous conduct," Gross declared. "If the President disapproves of what has taken place in the peddling of this information, obtained from allegedly secret files, he should have taken immediate action to publicly denounce this despicable act."[14]

The *Army-Navy-Air Force Journal* declared that the leaking of the Reynolds file seriously "undermined" the confidential status of military files.

"As a result of what has happened, no service person can feel with unquestioning trust that the privacy of his official file will not be violated," the journal stated.

A Washington *Evening Star* editorial spoke of the "smear," and disclosed that persons connected with the White House had tried to peddle derogatory information and allegations about Reynolds to the *Star*.

The *Star* editorial related that, before it printed the first story on the gift stereo, representatives of the paper had consulted responsible officials as to Reynolds' reliability.

"There was, we were assured, nothing criminal in his [Reynolds] background," the *Star* stated.

"Two days later, however, these same government officials invited the *Star* reporters to inspect what purported to be excerpts from an Air Force intelligence report on Mr. Reynolds. . . . We, at the *Star,* decided against printing the derogatory charges. We could not disclose their source, they were not supported by any substantiating detail, and some of the material was libelous. We were impressed, too, by the fact that—whatever Mr. Reynolds' past performance had been—his testimony in this case was backed by clear documentary proof.

"On the day before our story appeared, we took it to the White House for comment. We subsequently received a telephone call from one of Mr. Johnson's associates, who did not attack Mr. Reynolds but did argue about some details in the *Star's* report. His objections seemed convincing, and the story was amended accordingly. We now think our account was accurate as originally written."

The editorial concluded: "The foregoing is offered as a sort of footnote to the news, illustrating the administration's reaction to one newspaper's handling of a sensitive story. Our experience leads us to the conclusion that there was indeed a rather clumsy and half-hearted effort to smear Mr. Reynolds and otherwise deflect the impact of his disclosures away from the President."

Despite the public pressure for continuing the investigations, the Democratic members of the Senate Rules Committee were set on ending it. The Democrats had a six-to-three majority on the committee. In addition to Chairman Jordan, the Democrats were: Senators Robert Byrd (West Virginia), Howard Cannon (Nevada), Claiborne Pell (Rhode Island), Joseph Clark (Pennsylvania), and Carl Hayden (Arizona). It appeared as if Chairman Jordan could count on all his colleagues to support him on most votes.

The three Republicans—Senators Scott, Curtis, and John Sherman Cooper (Kentucky)—made an effort to extend the life of the investigation to July 1st or September 1st. They were voted

down. They sought permission to send out their own investigator.
It was denied them. They had submitted a list of more than fifteen
witnesses, including Jenkins, who they felt should be called. Their
requests were steamrollered by power of numbers in early
March.[15]

Stirring public protest was the only alternative left to the dis-
sidents.

On March 16th, Senator Scott, moved to anger by the majority's
tactics, challenged the Democrats on the Senate floor. He urged
that the investigation be continued and that more witnesses be
called. He charged that the six Democrats on the Rules Committee
were lined up for a political vote to kill the investigations.[16]

"It is not an investigative decision," Scott declared. "It is a political decision. This investigation is embarrassing to members of the
Democratic party. The majority members of the Rules Committee are not watching facts; they are watching the calendar. The
November elections are approaching and they are determined to
put this skeleton back into the closet."

The Pennsylvania Republican taunted the Democratic members
for having "attached to themselves blinders for their eyes, plugs
for their ears, and handcuffs for their wrists.

"So equipped, they have stumbled into, through and around
one of the most sordid scandals in Washington in recent memory,"
Scott proclaimed. "The investigators have been directed to skip
evidence on party girls; they have been directed to skip evidence on
political contributions; they have been directed to skip evidence on
abortions."

The Pennsylvanian made a special point of the Democrats' refusal to call Walter Jenkins.

"The request to call Mr. Reynolds [in an open hearing] was
refused," Scott said. "The request to call an important witness, the
head of a telephone answering service, who would establish that,
in fact, Mr. Jenkins had made certain calls to Mr. Reynolds, was
refused.

"All the minority Senators," Scott asserted, "requested that Mr. Jenkins be called to testify."

The Republican resistance to the Democratic steamroller was taken up by Senator Williams, the Delaware crusader, in an appearance on the television program "Face the Nation," on April 5, 1964.[17] He said he regretted that the Rules Committee had ended the hearings "without pursuing some of the many leads . . . left dangling."

Williams pointed out that Reynolds had made his accusations "under oath," and that Jenkins should have appeared before the committee to answer in the same way. "Had I been Mr. Jenkins and had there been nothing to this charge I would have rushed down to the Rules Committee and almost demanded that I be given an opportunity to present my side of the case. I am very much disappointed that he did not do so."

The Delaware Republican called Reynolds "an excellent witness," and pointed to the documentary evidence supporting his testimony.

"There was . . . what appeared to be a determined effort to discredit him . . . based on some leads from some high sources. . . ." Senator Williams said, "I was suspicious that it may be an effort to intimidate any future witness that may want to testify before the Committee."

Williams said that Reynolds left the Air Force as a major with an honorable discharge, and he had "an excellent record" in the State Department "with 13 or 14 promotions."

"No one raised the question about discrediting this witness until after he gave some damaging testimony," Williams declared.

In March and April there was more critical comment in the House and Senate over the Johnson-family television interests. There were renewed demands for a Congressional investigation.

A *Wall Street Journal* series printed at this time described how the Johnsons had parlayed their $17,000 investment in the small Austin radio station into a multimillion-dollar radio and television complex. A number of helpful decisions by the F.C.C. had helped the Johnson television and radio interests soar to an estimated $7 million worth, if not more.

More recently, the F.C.C. decision rejecting the petition of a competing community-antenna firm, TV Cable of Austin, was reported to have added another $2 million to the Johnson-family interests. The decision forced TV Cable to delay for 15 days before rebroadcasting any network programs that had appeared on KTBC, the Johnson station. The Johnson family had an option to buy 50 per cent of Capital Cable, the competing firm that was permitted to operate without broadcast delays.

The President was questioned about this at his April 16th press conference. Specifically, I asked him to comment on the general ethical problem created when persons in government have interests in government-regulated industries.

The President said there could be no conflict of interest in his case "because I don't have any interest in government-regulated industries of any kind and never have had.

"Mrs. Johnson inherited some property, invested that property in the profession of her choice, and worked at it with pleasure and satisfaction until I forced her to leave it when I assumed the Presidency," President Johnson explained.

"As you know, and I want all to know, all of that stock [in the broadcasting firm] has been placed in trust, as has been the practice with other Presidents. And, although I own none of it, Mrs. Johnson has placed it in trust—an irrevocable trust that can be . . . disposed of, can be leased . . . can be sold at any time," the President said.

"Any of these actions would require action by the [Federal Communications] commission—even if you tried to sell, you would have to have their approval. But I see no conflict in any way. She participates in no decisions the company makes; it's entirely up to the trustees. And, in any event, if she did participate, the President wouldn't have anything to do with it."

The President said "we are perfectly willing to comply, and I'm sure the trustees would be, with any request . . . [the F.C.C.] did make" to make details of the option agreement public.[18]

The option agreement was made public a week later. It disclosed that the Johnson interests already had authority to examine the books of Capital Cable, to disapprove sale of assets, and to veto management decisions. It also still had a right to buy 50 per cent of the stock for the original investment cost. The Johnson television company had a large number of rights and considerable interest in the community-antenna firm.

John Campbell, of competing TV Cable, contended that the option agreement amounted to a "control" by the Johnson interests of Capital Cable and was against public policy. He previously had argued that the option agreement actually was better than an outright interest, for the Johnson family could wait to determine if it was going to be a successful venture before deciding on whether to buy in.

The F.C.C. disagreed with the Johnsons' competitor. It decided in May, 1964, that the agreement between the Johnson family firm and Capital Cable did not amount to a "control," and found there was no reason to interfere with a strong competitive advantage its ruling would give Capital Cable.

President Johnson was on record as insisting that he had no interest in any government-controlled radio or television station. Mrs. Johnson owned and operated the whole thing, he said. The President gave the impression that he never had played a role in the decisions or operation of the former L.B.J. Company and its affiliated stations.

But in a ten-column story in the Washington *Evening Star,* on June 9, 1964, the reporter John Barron gave a detailed account of Lyndon Johnson's participation in conferences and strategy moves in connection with the Johnson radio-TV purchases and sales. The story revealed how the young Texan, who had to borrow money to conduct his first campaign for a House seat, won public office, and emerged twenty-five years later with a fortune estimated at at least $9 million.

Life magazine's Keith Wheeler and William Lambert did even more extensive digging into the Johnson fortune. They estimated the Johnson family's accumulated wealth at approximately $14 million. In their carefully documented article, "How L.B.J.'s Family Amassed Its Fortune" (August 21, 1964) Wheeler and Lambert quoted men who said they had witnessed the aggressive personal role Lyndon Johnson played in the acquisition and expansion of the broadcasting holdings.

Republicans in Congress demanded an investigation of this accumulation of wealth. There were also demands for information on the advertisers who shifted their advertising budgets to buy time on the Johnson stations, and for close scrutiny of network decisions that often seemed to coincide with what was best for the L.B.J. Company interests.

But the Republican complaints fell on deaf ears in the Senate and in the House. The Democratic leadership had no intention of starting such an investigation in an election year.

There was little chance that the Bobby Baker probe would slip, even inadvertently, into the affairs of the Austin television operations. The Democratic leadership was firmly committed to cut off the investigation by May 31st, and, in the meantime, to resist all efforts to call Walter Jenkins or other controversial witnesses. Jenkins was not to be called, even when it forced Democratic Senators to go on record in a highly embarrassing roll-call vote against the continuation of the investigation.

This was power politics, and the Democrats had the powers of executioner and undertaker. The Republicans could only complain that Majority Leader Mike Mansfield, ordinarily a courteous and agreeable adversary, had become "a tyrant" in overriding minority rights because of "what he conceives . . . to be the political needs of a certain situation."

Senator Case called the attention of the Senate to a code of ethics passed in 1958, which he felt had proved rather ineffective. One provision of the code stated: "Never discriminate unfairly by the dispensing of special favors or privileges to anyone, whether for remuneration or not; and never accept, for himself or his family, favors or benefits under circumstances which might be construed by reasonable persons as influencing the performance of his governmental duties."

The then Senator Johnson, as Majority Leader, had the duty of formally presenting the resolution initiated by others in which all in the Senate pledged to "uphold these principles, ever conscious that public office is a public trust."

"It didn't go far enough to stop Bobby Baker," Senator Case said. "I suggest that no code will deter anybody except someone who doesn't need deterrence, unless there is some way to call to account those who violate its terms."[19]

CHAPTER 23

The "Gross Improprieties" of Bobby Baker

As the Senate Rules Committee counsel, Lennox P. McLendon, put it, Robert G. Baker was "a very versatile gentleman." Among the examples of his versatility that came to light in the Senate hearings were:[1] Interests in (a) a multimillion-dollar food-vending business in California; (b) the million-dollar motel in Maryland; and (c) two land-development schemes in Florida.

Baker also received commissions on a meat-import arrangement with a Murchison-financed slaughter house in Haiti. He was exploring gambling-concession arrangements in the Dominican Republic, and he drew those commissions, by report, from an insurance man in Maryland. In addition to being cut in on that lucrative stock buy from a Milwaukee mortgage-guaranty firm, he also was involved in a large bank-stock purchase in Oklahoma, and was allocated 1,500 shares of an oversubscribed issue of stock in a new bank in the District of Columbia.

Somehow, along with all of this private enterprise, Bobby Baker found time to arrange with contractors to construct a swimming pool and bathhouse at the Elms, shortly after that palatial Washington house was purchased in 1961 by Vice-President Johnson, and to look after myriad other interesting chores. He also had a job as Secretary to the Democratic majority of the United States. But Bobby Baker's basic business was politics, and his lesser businesses seemed to thrive in the back alleys of politics. He kept posted on the high life and the low life of Washington. His business associates ranged from known professional gamblers to United States Senators. His acquaintances could be found anywhere from the White House to the jailhouse.

There was no doubt about Baker's startling financial success, for his own financial statements indicated that his net worth had increased from $11,025 in 1954 to more than $2 million in 1963. During this period, his maximum Senate salary was $19,800 a year.

In a financial statement, Baker listed ownership of stock in 22 corporations, including six banks in six states.[2]

The Senate Rules Committee was charged with an important responsibility. It was to determine whether "conflicts of interest or other improprieties" by Baker *or any other employee of the Senate* (italics supplied) had figured in his sensational financial achievement. When it came to the showdown, however, the senators were reluctant to consider fellow U.S. Senators as "employees of the Senate" in pursuing their investigation.

It was relatively easy for Counsel McLendon and the staff of investigators to learn that many men in business and in politics had gone out of their way to help Bobby Baker make money. Officials of the aerospace and defense industries seemed almost ecstatically eager to do business with Baker's food-vending firm.

It was, however, more difficult to obtain evidence of why so many men of position and wealth wanted to be helpful to a young man with a Senate staff job. There were few written records explaining these matters, but the files of the District of Columbia National Bank produced one clue to the attitudes of those who dealt with Baker.

The bank clue was a memorandum, dated March 1, 1962, and signed by William F. Collins, executive vice-president of the bank. It stated bluntly:

"Mr. Baker's position with the U. S. Government recommends our serious consideration to the transaction as he is a gentleman with innumerable friendships and connections whose good offices in behalf of our bank could be very valuable to our group."[3]

There was no explanation in the memorandum as to how Mr.

Baker could use his innumerable friendships and connections on behalf of the District of Columbia National Bank. The Collins memo was written to justify approval of a $125,000 unsecured loan to Baker for purchase of a new house at 5115 Van Ness Street, N.W., in the fashionable Spring Valley section of Washington. The house was just around the corner from Baker's friends Vice-President Johnson and Fred Black, Jr., the Washington representative of North American Aviation. Mr. Johnson since has moved to the White House. Mr. Black, convicted of income-tax fraud, is appealing the conviction.

The Rules Committee investigators found a mathematical error of $300,000 in the $2.6 million net worth statement that Baker had submitted to Banker Collins in connection with the $125,000 loan.

This was an embarrassing thing to crop up in a document that was supposed to be checked by bankers. Collins admitted he had not checked the financial statement, and had not inquired about any of the assets or liabilities Baker listed. The banker told Senator Hugh Scott, the Pennsylvania Republican, that this was not at all unusual. The Senator disagreed.

It was brought out in Collins' examination that Baker was listed as the owner of 1,500 shares of stock in the District of Columbia National Bank. This was the first new national bank chartered in the District of Columbia in twenty-nine years. It received its federal charter in 1962. Its initial stockholders included such figures as Senator John Sparkman (Democrat, of Alabama), a member of the Senate Banking and Currency Committee; Mrs. Abraham Multer, wife of Representative Multer (Democrat, of New York), member of the House Banking and Currency Committee; and five Democratic congressmen from Alabama—Representatives George W. Andrews, George Grant, Robert E. Jones, Jr., Carl Elliott, and Armistead Selden.

Testimony further disclosed that Baker did not own all of the 1,500 bank shares listed in his name. He held some of them for Fred Black and for two Las Vegas gambling figures—Edward Levinson and Benjamin Sigelbaum.[4] The Senate Rules Committee called Levinson and Sigelbaum as witnesses. The two gamblers invoked the Fifth Amendment and refused to answer questions about their dealings with Baker.

Later, Representative Oliver Bolton (Republican, of Ohio) charged that "political influence" surrounded the granting of the federal charter to the bank. He asked for a Congressional investigation of the actions of Comptroller of the Currency James Saxon in giving the charter, but Representative Wright Patman, the Texas Democrat who headed the House Banking and Currency Committee, declined to follow up the suggestion.

It had been expected that the Senate Rules Committee would call all witnesses that any members believed could be helpful in exploring all possible improprieties. However, Chairman B. Everett Jordan was not a boat-rocker either by background or disposition. In fact, in fourteen years of following Congressional investigations, the author never has seen a more reluctant chairman of a Congressional investigating committee than the North Carolina Democrat. There is just one word for Everett Jordan—likable.

The sixty-eight-year-old textile manufacturer makes it a practice to get along with folks. He had been an "organization man" both in the textile business and in politics. He was chairman of the North Carolina Democratic Executive Committee from 1949 to 1954, and from 1954 to 1958 he was the Democratic National Committeeman from North Carolina. He was appointed to the Senate in 1958 to fill the vacancy created by the death of Senator W. Kerr Scott. The party, which appreciates "regulars" in North Carolina, elected him to fill out the remainder of the term, then reelected him in 1960 for a full term of his own.

From the time he entered the Senate, the amiable Tarheel had leaned heavily upon Bobby Baker. He was fond of the accommodating young man whom Majority Leader Lyndon Johnson had once described as his "strong right arm." Senator Jordan frankly admitted he set mighty high store on Bobby Baker's advice in legislative matters.

It was obviously painful for Jordan to conduct an investigation of his young friend. He seemed to want to sweep up the mess quietly, without making anyone angry and without creating distasteful problems for himself or anybody. One had the feeling that the kindly old Senator considered it just a sin and a shame that the U. S. Senate, which was composed of such fine fellows, had to mess around with such dirty business as slick business deals, abortions, and call girls.

Senator Jordan picked an equally venerable, seventy-four-year-old North Carolina lawyer, the ramrod-backed, courtly Major L. P. McLendon, as his chief counsel. The chairman started off the proceedings at such a grandfatherly pace that it appeared likely he would smother his own probe with charity and good will. He took the mass of information on Baker, provided by Senator John Williams, as if it were neither out of the ordinary nor out of line. Capitol Hill observers started speculating that the investigation might end without a single public hearing. Then the newspaper reporters and magazine writers took the initiative away from the Rules Committee.

The reporters began writing of Baker's dealings with gamblers; of his cut on meat imported from Haiti; of the $50-a-month held out from a page boy's salary; and of the $28,000 profit Baker made on the stock of Mortgage Guaranty Insurance Corporation (M.G.I.C.) without risking a penny.

The stories that first held national attention involved Baker's purchase of a $28,800 town house in Southwest Washington for his pretty secretary, Nancy Carole Tyler. Baker estimated he had invested an additional $6,500 in the lavender wall-to-wall carpeting, custom-made draperies, French wallpaper, special light fixtures, patio shrubs, and Philippine-mahogany panels for the recreation room.

Baker made a $1,600 down payment to River Park Mutual Homes, Inc., under a stipulation that the house was to be occupied only by immediate members of the purchaser's family. Records named the occupant of the four-bedroom town house as "Cousin, N. C. Tyler, age 23, administrative assistant, U. S. Senate."[5]

C. William Tayler, president and general counsel for River Park Mutual Homes, told the committee he was troubled about the matter after the Baker case broke into print. He said he talked with Baker about Miss Tyler and another Capitol Hill secretary who lived with her.

"It was implicit in our conversation that neither of these young ladies was a member of his immediate family," Tayler testified. "Mr. Baker was in violation of . . . the occupancy agreement."[6]

Miss Tyler's success story caught the attention of a sensation-craving public more powerfully than Baker's. The lissome secretary was earning less than $350 a month in 1961, just before she went on Baker's payroll. In 1963, she was earning $8,300 a year, had a new light-blue Ford, and beautiful clothes. She entertained at 308 N Street, S.W., in a fashion that delighted many powerful political and business figures.

Miss Tyler had something more than a pretty face and figure. Although people who knew her said she was not particularly skillful at typing and shorthand, she was bright and very discreet in dealing with the many confidential matters that took place in Baker's Capitol office. She quit her Senate job a few days after Baker resigned, explaining in her soft Southern voice that she was certain Baker's successor would want to hire his own secretary.

The press and public were even more titillated by the stories of Mrs. Elly Rometsch, the exotic German woman who had attended some of the parties at Nancy Carole's house and accompanied Baker and Miss Tyler on a business trip. Satisfying details were hard to come by. Mrs. Rometsch was not available for questioning in the late fall of 1963. As mentioned, the striking twenty-six-year-old brunette, wife of a German Army sergeant attached to the West German Embassy in Washington, had been requested to leave the country. An F.B.I. investigation had revealed alleged improper conduct on her part.

Reporters began digging deep for facts on the story of Elly Rometsch and some of her associates. Soon a picture emerged of *la dolce vita* in official Washington. Few names were mentioned in print, but it was apparent that Elly's charm and talent had landed her in the company of men of power and influence in the capital. She was reported to be bipartisan in her associations, and the possibility of Republican involvement in a party-girl scandal suddenly cast a new pall on the future of the Bobby Baker investigation. It was authoritatively said that neither political party dared press too hard for the full story of Elly Rometsch.

Fresh speculation that the Baker investigation would be smothered in the cradle suddenly arose when the name of a prominent Republican Congressman was injected into the proceedings. It was bruited about that Representative John Byrnes, of Wisconsin, had invested $2,000 in stock of the Mortgage Guaranty Insurance Company in September, 1960—a few months after he made inquiries and introduced legislation to help the firm with a tax problem that was crucial to the company's financial future.

The Wisconsin Republican was given a special price on the stock. He was permitted to buy it for $2.50 a share at a time when it was selling for more than $20 a share.

Byrnes was popular among Republicans at the Capitol, and he was mentioned in Wisconsin as a "favorite son" candidate for the Republican Presidential nomination. It was rumored that Republicans would rather drop the whole Baker probe than embarrass John Byrnes.

The choice was taken out of their hands when the Milwaukee *Journal* reported details of the stock purchase. Byrnes was lambasted editorially by many newspapers, and he shed tears as he rose in the House to defend himself. He said he did for M.G.I.C. only what he would have done for any home-state firm. The case involved a Wisconsin company "fighting for its life," Byrnes told the House. "As far as I was concerned the purchase [of the bargain rate stock] had nothing to do with the tax matter."

The Wisconsin Congressman admitted that "the company extended a preference to me" in the stock purchase that netted a $23,000 windfall profit, but insisted he had no knowledge of the favor until the fall of 1963.

"I swear before my God and this House, that had I known of these facts I would not have purchased the stock," Byrnes pleaded.[7] He then announced he was giving all the profit on the

M.G.I.C. stock to Scholarships, Inc., of Green Bay, Wisconsin, a charitable organization to provide money for college students.

Once the Byrnes stock story was out in the open, the Senate Republicans had their hands freed. All of a sudden they were clamoring along with Senator John Williams for investigation of "all improprieties," even if it included Senators or former Senators.

So it came to pass that there were hearings after all.

At the first hearing—an executive session, with the press barred, on December 6, 1963—Senator Scott tried to explore a possible relationship between two young women and a large defense contracting firm. Edwin M. Bostick, president of Melpar, Inc., an electronics firm that does about 99 per cent of its business with the government, particularly defense agencies, was on the stand. Scott asked Bostick, a social and business friend of Baker and Fred Black, if he knew a certain young woman, reputed to be a call girl.[8]

Chairman Jordan cut Scott off.

"Why are you asking that question?" he asked.

"I am prepared to tie it in later with other witnesses," Senator Scott replied. Naming another young woman, Scott asked if the defense contractor knew her.

Bostick balked at answering, and Senator Joseph Clark, Scott's Democratic colleague from Pennsylvania, observed that the questions appeared "entirely unconnected" with the investigation's purpose.

"I don't think we are interested in a fishing expedition into the private lives of young ladies," Senator Clark said.

"I would like to assure the senator this is not a fishing expedition," Scott retorted.

Democratic members did not want the questions asked, and after Bostick was excused, Senator Curtis objected to the Democrats' "theory that this investigation should be confined to business transactions alone."

Senator Claiborne Pell, the aristocratic young Democrat from Rhode Island, challenged him. "Are you suggesting that personal and sexual peccadillos would be within the framework of this committee?" Pell asked.

"Yes," Curtis replied bluntly.

"I would strongly disagree," Pell said.

Senator Curtis argued that the sexual peccadillos were in fact related to Baker's multimillion-dollar fortune.

"This didn't happen just by clever operations," Curtis said. "Party girls and entertaining were part of the business-promotion apparatus. The facts are available if we pursue it. . . . Girls were solicited on government telephone lines, taken to the place, entertained the prospective customers, and it is part and parcel of the transaction."

"The use of call girls for business promotion in my judgment is an impropriety," Senator Scott broke in. "Senator Williams feels the same way."

The Democrats had the votes to block hearings on the call girls, but there were other embarrassing issues that could not be hushed.

The first witness at a hearing to which the public was admitted was Mrs. Gertrude Novak, forty-three-year-old widow of one of Baker's business partners, Alfred Novak. She testified she "suffered tremendously" from financial dealings with Baker. She and her husband had $63,000 invested with Baker in the Carousel Motel. She complained that she had received no money since her husband's death, and had not received what she considered to be a satisfactory accounting.[9]

The blond widow, nervous and obviously worried over her financial problems, said that she received $7,800 a year as a secretary for the Senate Small Business Committee, but that most of her assets were tied up in her husband's estate. The estate was being administered by Ernest C. Tucker, Baker's law associate.

Mrs. Novak told how Baker and Tucker came to her home shortly after her husband's death and took the Carousel books away with them. Next, Baker suggested that she make Tucker administrator of the estate and sign papers surrendering her right to serve as executrix.

Mrs. Novak said she followed Baker's suggestion, thus giving Tucker full control of the estate, including her interest in the motel property. In return for her $63,789.62 investment, Mrs. Novak said, she received certain notes that "won't be delinquent for twenty years." It was her way of saying that the paper had a distant maturity date, and was of little value to her.

The Novaks had known Baker for about ten years, and Baker had given them some stock tips that, in the main, were highly profitable. The most profitable had been an investment in the Mortgage Guaranty Insurance Corporation stock.[10] Baker had persuaded her late husband that it was a sure investment, the widow said. Novak had agreed to advance $12,000 for a joint venture in which Baker would put up no money.

That stock deal paid off as predicted. Baker sold a major part of the stock a few months later for $66,889.86 and split the profits with the Novaks, thus giving them about $28,000 profit on their $12,000 investment. Baker's equal share of the profit was made without putting up a dime of his own money.

Baker persuaded the Novaks to plow the stock profits back into the Carousel, which they constructed as a joint enterprise in association with Al Novak's brother, Donald J., and his wife. Those were frantic days; Baker, the plunger, frequently revamped the already plush plans for the motel, adding a $100,000 night club and other costly innovations. This greatly worried the timorous Novaks.

On March 3, 1962, Al Novak was found dead in the garage of his home in Chevy Chase, Maryland, under mysterious circumstances. The coroner's verdict listed the death as both "accidental" and "suicide." After her husband's death, Mrs. Novak said, she found it futile to try to keep up with the dizzy details of the Carousel's operations.

Mrs. Novak said Baker told her not to worry, and assured her that he would be able to find plenty of money to take care of the Carousel obligations. Periodically, he asked her to come by the office to pick up envelopes containing large amounts of cash. She was to deposit the money in the motel account.

On one occasion, Baker gave her $13,300 in cash, and Carole Tyler counted it out for her in Baker's Senate office. Over a period of several months, Baker gave her more than $45,000 in cash. She said she didn't know the origin of the cash, and that it frightened her to carry such large amounts.

About this time, according to other testimony, Baker received an offer from the Tecon Corporation, an enterprise of the Murchison financial interests of Texas, to buy the Carousel for $1,500,-000.[11] According to Mrs. Novak's testimony, Baker did not tell her of this offer. Instead, he persuaded her to agree to the sale of the Carousel, in which she now had only a one-quarter interest, to the Serv-U Corporation for $1,016,566.27.

Serv-U was the vending firm in which Baker, at that time, had a one-third interest, Mrs. Novak said. Tucker, her lawyer—and Baker's partner—whom she had made administrator of her husband's estate, was chairman of the board of Serv-U.

(In the early phases of the investigation, Baker had denied that either he or Fred Black had an interest in Serv-U, and Tucker had said Baker and Black had no interest in the vending company to his knowledge. Later, in June, 1964, it was revealed that Baker had become virtually the sole owner of Serv-U, by adding to his own stock holdings the shares formerly owned by Fred Black, who had been convicted of income-tax evasion, and the two Las Vegas gamblers, Levinson and Sigelbaum.)

Mrs. Novak told the Senators it was "just shocking news" when she learned she had been persuaded to agree to the sale of the Carousel for nearly half a million dollars less than the offer the new owners had from the Murchison corporation. Tecon's offer to purchase was never accepted.

It was not until after the Bobby Baker case broke that Mrs. Novak hired another attorney to look out for her interests.

"I was very unhappy about it, knowing that Mr. Tucker was here as chairman of the board of Serv-U Corporation, administrator of my husband's will, and I was hoping to rely on him as an attorney," Mrs. Novak explained. "I thought there would definitely be conflict of interest, and I had to retain another attorney."

Among the several witnesses not called by the Democratic majority on the investigating committee to testify at the open hearings was Don Reynolds, the Maryland insurance man. The Republicans had many more questions they wanted to ask Reynolds, but the Democratic majority had other ideas about letting him return to the witness stand in a public session.

Ernest Tucker was called to testify in a closed session. Despite his earlier denials, the lawyer testified under oath that Baker and Black owned major interests in Serv-U—the food-vending firm that had become a multimillion-dollar business through its dealings with the aerospace industry. Baker's stock in Serv-U was valued at $1 million in some financial statements. It was held through Tucker.[12]

In open session, Max H. Karl, president of the Mortgage Guaranty Insurance Corporation, and other witnesses testified that Baker invested about $40,000 in M.G.I.C. stock. In a two-year period, Baker's stock jumped to a value of more than $400,000.

M.G.I.C. was having troubles with the Securities and Exchange Commission (S.E.C.) and the Treasury Department on problems that were vital to the firm's future. Those problems were ironed out in a few months, and M.G.I.C. stock soared to more than ten times its initial value.

Karl denied he had ever asked Baker to intervene with any government agency. The Secretary to the Senate majority was cut in on the lucrative stock deals out of pure friendship, Karl insisted.

Fred Black, Jr., expensively dressed and self-assured, also testified, but in closed session only. He said that Baker held stock in the District of Columbia National Bank for himself, Levinson, and Sigelbaum. Black also disclosed that Bobby Baker was an important contact in Black's operations as a Washington representative of North American Aviation and other defense contractors. He testified that a Baker introduction made it possible for him to establish a close relationship with the late Senator Robert Kerr, the powerful Oklahoma Democrat, who then was known as the King of the Senate.

Through Kerr, Black said he met James E. Webb, head of the

National Aeronautics and Space Administration (NASA). Webb formerly had been Kerr's administrative assistant.

Black insisted that Baker never called any government agencies to make appointments or to intervene for him. However, Baker provided contacts that were among the most important Black enjoyed in defense and space matters.

Majority Leader Johnson was head of the Senate Committee on Aeronautical and Space Sciences, and Kerr was a high-ranking member of the committee until 1961. When Johnson became Vice-President, Kerr succeeded him as chairman of that committee.

"Mr. Baker, Senator Kerr and I had lunch one day together, at which time I got better acquainted with him. . . . I played gin rummy with him lots of times after that," Black said.[13]

Black testified he borrowed $175,000 to buy stock in the Farmers and Merchants State Bank, of Tulsa, on Kerr's recommendation, and that he had an oral agreement to sell half of the stock to Baker.

After Kerr gave them the bank stock "tip," Black testified, he and Baker shared the information with the two gamblers, Levinson and Sigelbaum. He said he and Baker borrowed money from the Kerr-controlled Fidelity National Bank, in Oklahoma City, to buy the stock in the Tulsa bank. (James E. Webb, Administrator of the National Aeronautics and Space Agency was listed as one of the twenty major stockholders in the Fidelity National Bank. It was his agency that awarded the Apollo contract to North American Aviation.)

It also was through the Kerr-controlled bank, Black said, that he, Baker, Levinson, and Sigelbaum borrowed $100,000 to launch the Serv-U Vending Corporation. Almost immediately Serv-U was successful in landing a $2-million-a-year vending contract with North American Aviation. Baker made an investment of $28,000 in 2,850 shares of Serv-U stock; a year later, he listed the value of the stock at $1 million.

Reference to another U. S. Senator came out in the hearings when Milton L. Hauft, Baker's accountant, testified. Hauft revealed that Baker's tax returns disclosed $4,000 income from a joint business venture with Senator George Smathers, the Florida Democrat, and Scott I. Peek, the former administrative assistant to Senator Smathers.

Senator Smathers issued a statement confirming that he arranged for Baker and Peek each to buy one-eighth of his share in a land-subdivision project in Florida. Baker and Peek each invested $1,500, and each had received profit of about $1,000 a year for seven years.

The Florida Democrat, a close friend of Baker, said that Peek was having a difficult time financially and he wanted to help him make some money.

"Being apprised of the similar circumstances of Baker, who too had a young and growing family, I offered him one-eighth of my share of the investment," Smathers said.

At last, Bobby Baker himself was subpoenaed to testify in executive session on February 19th. Behind closed doors, he refused to answer any questions, on the ground that his answers might tend to incriminate him.[14]

Veteran Senators—sentimental about their institution—were rocked by the spectacle of the onetime impoverished page boy from South Carolina, who owed everything to the United States Senate, sitting in the witness chair and refusing to answer the legitimate questions of his former employers and benefactors.

The drama had to be played out. Baker was subpoenaed again to appear as a witness in a public session in the historic Senate Caucus Room—scene of such memorable investigations as the McCarthy hearings, the grilling of gangsters by the late Senator Estes Kefauver, and Chairman John McClellan's quizzing of Teamster Boss James R. Hoffa.

An overflow crowd jammed the hearing room to see Bobby Baker in the flesh. A balding, somewhat pudgy figure, he was noticeably ill at ease as he walked into the hearing room. He put on a good show, however, of waving and nodding to old acquaintances.

As an opening gambit, Committee Counsel McLendon noted

with severity that Baker had said he would not testify or produce records. The counsel then asked: "Have you changed your mind?"

"Major, whatever reputation I had in the Senate, my word is my bond. . . . When I told you I was not going to testify that ended it as far as I was concerned," Baker said imposingly.

After that statement, Baker declined even to enumerate his duties as Secretary to the Majority. He claimed the privilege of the First, Fourth, Fifth, and Sixth Amendments to the Constitution, and added: "I specifically decline to answer because of the privilege against self-incrimination."

He took the Fifth Amendment more than 125 times on questions dealing with the vending-machine business, Elly Rometsch, his association with gamblers, his dealings with Don Reynolds, his knowledge of abortion arrangements, and his part in the gift of the stereo set to Lyndon B. Johnson.

"Have you ever contacted . . . the Dominican Republic . . . concerning the securing of gambling concessions in that country?" Senator Curtis asked. Baker took the Fifth Amendment.[15]

"Have you rendered assistance to contractors, businessmen, and others, who may be doing business with the U. S. Government in . . . providing . . . entertainment facilities . . . including party girls?" Senator Curtis asked. Again Baker took the Fifth.

"Mr. Baker, did you ever urge or suggest that certain national advertisers buy time on station KTBC in Austin, Texas?" Senator Scott asked.

"I stand by my previous answer," Baker said.

A new note was introduced. Senator Scott asked:

"Mr. Baker, can you tell this committee whether or not you have had any business dealings whatsoever with one Joseph Fabianich, who is now serving time in Leavenworth Prison on white slavery charges?" Scott's question was met with the now familiar Fifth Amendment plea.

Senator Scott tried another tack: "Mr. Baker, did Mr. Fred Black give you $10,000 in cash in $100 bills in an envelope in the Carlton Hotel in Washington, these moneys to be delivered to one of the presidential candidates for his use [in 1960] in his campaign?"

Scott based the question on information from Don Reynolds that such a sum was delivered for the Johnson-for-President campaign. Another refusal was entered in the record.

Senator Curtis took up the interrogation again:

"Mr. Baker, did you, in company with Carole Tyler and Ellen [sic] Rometsch, leave Washington on Eastern Airlines on June 19, 1963, and fly to New Orleans and there meet Mr. Paul A. Aguirre [a Puerto Rican businessman]?"[16]

Baker took the Fifth Amendment, and Curtis continued: "And from New Orleans, did you proceed to Dallas, Texas, and from there to Miami, Florida, with your secretary [Miss Tyler], Ellen [sic] Rometsch and Mr. Aguirre?" Again, no answer.

Asking Baker these questions—even though he wouldn't answer them—was the only way the Republicans could force the issue, for the Democratic majority already had indicated it would disregard requests to call Aguirre, Fabianich, and more than a dozen other witnesses. The chances of having Reynolds and Black called for testimony in an open hearing also were regarded as almost dead.

A day later, button-cute Carole Tyler appeared before the Senate committee and the live television cameras, and softly invoked the Fifth Amendment.

First, however, Miss Tyler talked a bit. She complained of the great suffering she had experienced because of the "world-wide intimations and suggestions that I have indulged in improper conduct, to say the least.

"I have been investigated . . . by the Internal Revenue Service, by the Federal Bureau of Investigation, and by other federal agencies," she said in a demure voice.[17]

Although Miss Tyler claimed that a broad range of questions might incriminate her, she did not object to the television cameras. She wore a bright-blue coat and a high-fashion two-piece dress of bulky off-white silk, accented with large black buttons. She wore heavy, dark makeup, just right for the television cameras. Her embarrassment was well controlled most of the time as she turned smilingly and graciously to the right and left at the importunings of the television crews and the news cameramen.

Miss Tyler asserted that it was "an invasion of my right of privacy" to question her about the town house near the Capitol. She was not very helpful, but she wanted the public to think well of her. Looking earnestly at the TV cameras, Carole said in her soft Southern voice:

"I *pray* that the public will keep an open mind regarding me."

The fact that Baker and Miss Tyler claimed the privilege of the Fifth Amendment was interpreted by the unhappy chairman, Senator Jordan, as marking the end of the investigation—or nearly the end. He took the position that if the principals wouldn't talk, that had to end it.

The Republicans had different ideas. If Baker wouldn't talk, it simply meant that every witness should be called who possibly could give any information on the "improprieties" or "conflicts of interest."

In a Senate speech, Senator Scott explained that the Republicans wanted to call Joseph Fabianich, the convicted white slaver, who "was comfortably resting in the local jail in the District of Columbia until this investigation became hot.[18]

"What influence was used . . . to bring about this transfer from the District of Columbia jail to Leavenworth?" Scott demanded. "Mr. Fabianich was serving a nine-year [term] . . . on a white slavery charge. A brother of Joseph Fabianich, according to the notes of our investigation, had said, among other things— there was also the indication that Fabianich could testify to the fact—that Bobby Baker had on one occasion beaten up a young girl. That was regarded by the committee as not bearing on the fiscal irresponsibility of Bobby Baker, or any other impropriety, but [it was] regarded by me as a distinct impropriety.

"Before Mr. Fabianich could be produced, he was transferred to Leavenworth," Scott charged.

The Fabianich lead also had its sequel. Late in June, 1964, authorities in Maryland suburbs near Washington announced they had confiscated the card files of what was believed to be a call-girl ring. Some of the names were of "girls" who, on investigation, turned out to be supposedly respectable suburban matrons doing a little moonlighting on the side. Of more interest on Capitol Hill, the list included the names of some Congressmen, their committee staff members, lobbyists, and other prestigious Washington figures. The F.B.I. took over the list, and Senator Williams asked permission to scrutinize the files. Among those listed were at least five men who figured in the Bobby Baker investigation, including Fabianich.

The Democrats did not wilt under the scalding Republican criticism. Instead, they became even more determined to end the embarrassing hearings, pressing forward their plans to kill the Bobby Baker probe in the face of almost unanimous condemnation from the editorial pages of the newspapers.

On the Rules Committee, the Democrats had a six-to-three majority. They used it to reject Republican demands that more than twenty witnesses be called. The three Republicans—Curtis, of Nebraska; Scott, of Pennsylvania; and Cooper, of Kentucky—remained unified in their demand, but it was futile.

Chairman Jordan; Cannon, of Nevada; Clark, of Pennsylvania; Robert Byrd, of West Virginia; Hayden, of Arizona; and Pell, of Rhode Island, held like a fortress against further hearings. They said they knew all they needed to know about "conflicts of interest" or "improprieties." It was time to produce a code of ethics and some legislation to deal with reforming the Senate, the Democrats moralized.

Majority Whip Hubert Humphrey, of Minnesota, said it was time for the Senate to quit raking up all that dirt, and time to start thinking of constructive measures.

But Senator Williams, the Delaware Republican, said that the Senate had not completed its job. There were many more witnesses to be called to reveal the full picture of Bobby Baker's activities, and there was a responsibility to follow up other leads—even if they involved past and present Senators.

Senator Williams and Republican Senator Clifford Case, of New Jersey, jointly proposed a resolution expanding the jurisdiction of the committee. The wording of their resolution left no doubt that Senators were to be included in the Baker probe. Also, the resolution would have continued the hearings three more months past the May 31st deadline set in the earlier resolution.

Senator Williams called the attention of the Senate to an F.B.I. report stating that Baker had forged the name of his accountant, Milton Hauft, on tax returns of the Carousel.

The Democrats sought to minimize this deed by claiming there were only small changes in the returns on which Baker had signed the auditor's name. But the Delaware crusader said peremptorily: "Forgery is forgery."[19]

Senator Williams and other Republicans pointed out that Baker had obtained a federal small-business loan of $54,000 by listing, among his assets, a $100,000 deposit to the Carousel account in a Maryland bank. The truth of the matter was that Baker had arranged a short-term loan of $100,000, under an arrangement whereby he would be given a deposit slip but could not actually withdraw the money. It was a "fraud," said Senator Scott and Senator Williams as they pressed for Justice Department action.

Senator Williams said it was inconceivable to him that the Senate would authorize an investigation of its employees, and then balk at investigating Senators.

"A public office is a public trust and all public officials are servants of the people," Williams said. ". . . none of us are too big to be held accountable for our conduct. . . .

"Rejection of this resolution . . . can only be interpreted as indicating that the Senate feels itself above compliance with the same rules which we are seeking to impose upon our employees."

Senator Mansfield criticized the Case-Williams resolution for specifying an investigation of "illegal matters, immoral matters, improper activities, [or] campaign matters." The Majority Leader told the Senate the resolution unfairly implied "that the Senate and all within it are covered with dirt from rooftop to cellar."

Case, ordinarily one of the mildest of Senators, rose in anger to debate the fairness of the resolution. The political tension so apparent in every step of the Baker case flared into the open in a heated exchange between Senator Case and Majority Leader Mansfield.[20]

Case accused Mansfield of violating Senate rules by indirectly criticizing the motives behind the resolution. For approximately fifteen minutes, a shouting match developed between the two normally courteous senators.

Senator Edward Kennedy (Democrat, of Massachusetts) happened to be sitting in—to his obvious unhappiness—for the presiding officer of the Senate. The delicate parliamentary situation seemed to confuse him, but, acting on advice of the Senate parliamentarian, he banged his gavel and repeatedly ordered Case to take his seat. Fairly livid with rage, Case finally was forced to comply. Swiftly, the Democrats, by a vote of 42 to 33, killed the Case-Williams resolution to extend and expand the Baker probe.

Senator Case called it "one of the roughest and most unfair exhibitions" of overriding the rights of the minority of an individual Senator. Sadly, he told his fellow-Senators that Majority Leader Mansfield, usually "the gentlest and the most magnanimous man," had succumbed to "the political needs of a certain situation."

For days thereafter, Senator Case rose to his feet, quietly and briefly called attention to the Baker scandal, and entered into the *Congressional Record* page after page of editorials from all parts of the country, lambasting the Democratic leadership for its gag of the Baker probe.[21]

But, with all the inadequacies and omissions, the Democrats had not succeeded totally in covering up the Baker affair. The hearings had revealed far more than ever was expected that afternoon of October 10th, when Senator Williams had offered his initial resolution starting the probe. Even under the severe restrictions imposed by the Democratic majority, the Rules Committee record laid bare enough of the fantastic story for a unanimous conclusion that Baker was involved in many "gross improprieties."

With regard to Baker's concealment of his stock interest in Serv-U, the official report, on July 8th, stated: "His [Baker's] compelling reason for this concealment must have been that he was quite aware of the gross impropriety in his ownership of the stock under all the circumstances—one of the important circumstances being that the entire success or failure of the company depended upon whether he and Black could secure vending contracts with large corporations having defense contracts with the government."[22]

The investigation was far from exhaustive in trying to penetrate the "gross impropriety." The Rules Committee had raised more questions than it answered. One important question was: How important are "friendships and connections" in the awarding of the multibillion-dollar space contracts?

Power politics had prevailed over demands for a general housecleaning in the Senate, and the opportunity for the long-needed, thorough investigation of Congress was bypassed. This happened because many practical politicians in the Senate believed that, in time, most voters would forgive or forget a vote to kill the Bobby Baker probe. The party patronage-dispensers and the party disciplinarians in the White House would have much longer memories. However, a politically explosive arrest and the persistent work of Senator Williams were to dramatize again the Rules Committee cover-up in refusing to question two important Democratic political figures—Walter Jenkins and Matt McCloskey.

CHAPTER 24

Walter Jenkins

Quiet, unassuming Walter Jenkins was one man Lyndon Johnson had depended on for twenty-five years. They had been associated ever since 1939, when Jenkins went to work for Congressman Johnson. Their association continued through Johnson's rise to United States Senator, Majority Leader, Vice-President, and President.

Jenkins, forty-six, married and father of six children, was known as a devoutly religious man, a devoted family man, and a selfless government worker. As Johnson's No. 1 assistant, he not only handled the most sensitive political matters, but also managed the personal business transactions of Lyndon and Lady Bird. He acted as treasurer of the L.B.J. Company until Johnson became President.

Despite the vital spot he held in Lyndon Johnson's political and personal operations, Jenkins managed to keep out of the limelight until early in 1964, when his name came into the Bobby Baker case. From that time on, controversy raged over whether the Senate Rules Committee should call him to testify under oath. At issue was the statement Jenkins made which conflicted with testimony by Don B. Reynolds. Under oath, Reynolds had said that Jenkins had arranged for him to buy unneeded advertising time on the L.B.J. Company station in Austin, Texas.[1]

"They won't dare call Walter Jenkins," Reynolds told me a few days later. "Walter's a homo."

This was such a fantastic statement, I couldn't believe I had heard him correctly. It was, to be sure, injected into the conversation in the same casual way Reynolds had revealed to me other explosive information about life in the capital. I asked him pointblank what he meant, because I didn't want to be mistaken.

This time the husky insurance man said flatly that Walter Jenkins, the No. 1 assistant to President Lyndon B. Johnson, had a "record" as a homosexual.

If this were true, it would be one of the great masquerades in recent government history and a real political shocker.

"Are you sure you are right?" I asked, still unconvinced and wanting also to caution Reynolds against tossing out charges that might destroy his credibility as a witness.

"Walter is a homo," he repeated. "I know it is hard to believe, but it is true. I swear to God, Clark, it's the truth."

Don Reynolds had taken a risk in testifying about questionable activities of Bobby Baker and other men of great influence. I had been skeptical of many of his statements in the preceding fall, but the evidence accumulated by late February had already demonstrated that Reynolds had been telling the truth.

He had told the truth when he said Bobby Baker had a major interest in the Serv-U vending company, for Baker's law associate had later testified that he held about a million dollars' worth of stock for Baker. He had told the truth about the gift of the stereophonic set to the Johnsons, for President Johnson admitted receiving one that had been purchased by Reynolds. Bills and shipping orders showed that Reynolds had paid for the stereo set and that it had been shipped to the Johnson home. He had told the truth about being requested to purchase unneeded advertising time on the L.B.J. Company television station in Austin, Texas. Records and correspondence showed he paid for the time but didn't use it, and tried to resell it to another businessman in Silver Spring, Maryland.[2]

Against this background, I tended to believe Reynolds, but still I could not conceal my doubts. Reynolds had sufficient reason to be angry with Jenkins and other officials of the Johnson administration. The attempts to smear Reynolds with material from personnel files in the Defense Department and the State Department could have created a desire in him to strike back.

In addition, Reynolds had a specific reason to be angry with Jenkins, for it was Jenkins' statement that contradicted Reynolds' testimony. Moreover, he resented the favored treatment the Senate Rules Committee had given to Jenkins. Reynolds had told his story under oath, and therefore under threat of perjury, while Jenkins was simply interviewed at the White House.[3] Reynolds believed Committee Counsel Lennox P. McLendon and Investigator Ellis (Red) Meehan were intent on discrediting him.

I bore down on him. "Where is the police record?"

"I don't want to go into details now," he evaded, "but there is a record, and that's why they don't dare put him under oath. Too many embarrassing questions could be asked."

"But if Jenkins has a record as a homosexual, how could he possibly serve on the White House staff?"

Reynolds said he couldn't understand this either. He had heard, however, that there had been no full F.B.I. investigation of Jenkins since the homosexual arrest.

I questioned the idea that a Presidential assistant could hold a highly sensitive White House job without a full security clearance. How could there be such laxity in national security?

"Sounds like a cheap spy story," Reynolds conceded. "But if you knew some of these people as I know them, you'd ask yourself what is happening to our government. I *know* these people. I was running around with them, going to parties with them. If I told you all I know, you'd be even more shocked."

Reynolds wasn't yet ready to tell everything he knew, and I warned him not to discuss anything unless he could produce independent corroboration from records or from other witnesses. As I made signs of leaving, Reynolds told me simply to keep in mind that he had said Jenkins had "a record," and he suggested that I check Jenkins' security clearance.

A newsman doesn't ask the F.B.I. or the Justice Department about the security clearance of a man in high office unless he has substantial information behind him. Just asking the question can start a lot of talk. I therefore made only a preliminary survey of White House security procedures; it convinced me the information was so tightly held that I could be given false information without knowing it. The Johnson administration refused even to discuss the salary Jenkins received.

Since a question from a reporter might precipitate some changes in a record or file, I decided not to be too inquisitive and hoped the political winds would force the Senate Democrats to question Jenkins. Once he was under oath, the Republican committee members could get to the heart of the issue quickly. Either he had a police record or he didn't. If he did, he could be prodded for details.

While I waited to see what the Democrats would do, I read an old Senate report of December 15, 1950, entitled "Employment of Homosexuals and Other Sex Perverts in Government."[4]

"In the opinion of this subcommittee," the report said, "homosexuals and other sex perverts are not proper persons to be employed in Government for two reasons: first, they are generally unsuitable and second, they constitute security risks.

"There is an abundance of evidence to sustain the conclusion that indulgence in acts of sex perversion weakens the moral fiber of an individual to a degree that he is not suitable for a position of responsibility. Most of the authorities agree and our investigation has shown that the influence of a sex pervert in a Government agency tends to have a corrosive influence upon his fellow employees. These perverts will frequently attempt to entice normal individuals to engage in perverted practices. . . . It is particularly important that the thousands of young men and women who are brought into Federal jobs not be subjected to that type of influence while in the service of the Government. One homosexual can pollute a Government office.[5]

"Another point to be considered in determining whether a sex pervert is suitable for Government employment is his tendency to gather other perverts about him," the report continued. "Eminent psychiatrists have informed the subcommittee that the homosexual is likely to seek his own kind because the pressures of society are such that he feels uncomfortable unless he is with his own kind. Due to this situation the homosexual tends to surround himself with other homosexuals, not only in his social, but in his business life. Under these circumstances if a homosexual attains a position in Government where he can influence the hiring of personnel, it is almost inevitable that he will attempt to place other homosexuals in Government jobs."

The subcommittee had taken testimony from officials who were most concerned with security problems—representatives of the F.B.I., the Central Intelligence Agency, and the intelligence services of the Army, Navy and Air Force. "All of these agencies," the report said flatly, "are in complete agreement that sex perverts in Government constitute a security risk."

Although this report made it seem all the more unlikely to me that Walter Jenkins could have held his White House post with a homosexual record, my curiosity nevertheless was kindled by the severe resistance the Democrats offered to all Republican efforts to make Jenkins testify.

Reynolds was willing to appear for further testimony, and he urged Chairman Everett Jordan to subpoena Jenkins. The Democrats refused. In the official report (July 8, 1964) the Democrats contended that the conflicts between the stories of the two men had "no significant importance."[6]

"It is of no consequence whether Reynolds bought the advertising time at the request of Jenkins or of Baker or both," the Democrats stated, adding that "the only connection Jenkins had with the purchase of advertising time by Reynolds was to remind Reynolds that he had not complied with his agreement previously made with Baker, not with Jenkins, to buy advertising time."

The Republican committee members and most of the nation's editorial pages took quite a different view of the conflict between the statements. In their report, the Republicans said:

"As shown by the testimony . . . one of the requirements surrounding the original sale (of life insurance to Lyndon Johnson) was that Mr. Reynolds would purchase advertising time over radio station KTBC in Austin, Texas.

"Inasmuch as Reynolds could not benefit from advertising his Maryland insurance business in Texas, he, Reynolds, resold his advertising time to the Mid-Atlantic Stainless Steel Co. Albert G. Young, president of Mid-Atlantic Stainless Steel, confirmed that he did indeed buy this advertising time on station KTBC from Reynolds, but only after a man identified as Walter Jenkins acknowledged the station's connection with Mr. Reynolds."[7]

The Republicans then quoted the memorandum Jenkins and Counsel Lennox P. McLendon had prepared for the committee record. It said: "Nor does he (Jenkins) have any knowledge of any arrangement by which Reynolds purchased advertising time on the TV station."[8]

When the Republicans officially moved that Jenkins be called to "resolve this direct conflict in the testimony," the Democratic majority quickly defeated the attempt, 6 to 3, and thus erased hope of Jenkins' being questioned.[9]

I had almost forgotten the conversations with Reynolds when, on October 14th, my wife telephoned me in Denver, where I was covering the Presidential campaign. An informant had told her that Walter Jenkins had been arrested on a morals charge at the Washington Y.M.C.A. on October 7, 1964, at 8:35 P.M. The informant also reported there had been an earlier arrest in January, 1959, on a similar charge, that Jenkins was in the hospital and might resign before the day was over, and that people connected with the White House were trying to talk the Washington newspapers out of printing anything on the Jenkins arrests.

Several telephone calls to Washington sources verified the information for me. Don Reynolds had been telling me the truth. I could have found the corroboration for his story simply by running through the record of arrests by the District of Columbia morals squad.

The reports of a White House attempt (through Washington lawyers Clark Clifford and Abe Fortas) to suppress the story of the Jenkins arrests reached Republican Chairman Dean Burch on the afternoon of October 14th. He quickly gave the news media a statement.

"There is a report sweeping Washington tonight," it said, "that the White House is desperately trying to suppress a major news story affecting the national security."

Presidential Press Secretary George Reedy responded: "I don't know what he's talking about."

But even as Reedy was denying knowledge of the Jenkins problem, Merriman Smith, of United Press International, was preparing to break the story. Smith, the veteran U.P.I. White House reporter, had examined the records of the morals division at the District of Columbia police headquarters. Those records were clear. Walter Jenkins, 46, of 3704 Huntington Street, North West, had been arrested a week earlier on a charge of "disorderly conduct (indecent gesture)" in the men's room of the Y.M.C.A. at 1736 G Street.

Morals Division Detectives R. L. Graham and L. P. Drouillard had also arrested another man, Andy Choka, a 60-year-old timekeeper who resided at the Soldiers Home. Through a peephole in the Y.M.C.A. men's room, the plainclothesmen had observed Jenkins and Choka together in a toilet stall and had made the arrest on the scene.

In the lobby of the Y.M.C.A., the officers met their superior officer, Louis A. Fochett. Lieutenant Fochett accompanied the four to the police station, where Jenkins and Choka were booked at 8:35 P.M. and questioned. Jenkins identified himself as a "clerk" on the White House staff, and acknowledged an earlier morals charge in 1959. Jenkins put up a $50 cash bond, which he elected to forfeit rather than go to trial.

The police records also verified the earlier arrest of Jenkins—the one Reynolds had alluded to seven months earlier. The records stated that on "January 15, 1959, 10:20 P.M., Walter Wilson Jenkins (was) picked up at the Y.M.C.A., 1736 G Street NW, (on a charge of) disorderly conduct (pervert) . . . elects to forfeit." That time the bond was $25.

Once the United Press International broke the story, there was no holding the publicity flood. President Johnson, who was campaigning in New York, announced that Jenkins had submitted his resignation and that it had been accepted. Bill D. Moyers, thirty, was named to take over the job Jenkins had held at the White House.

President Johnson stated he had no knowledge of either morals arrest of Jenkins until a few minutes before he accepted the Jenkins resignation the evening of October 14, 1964. According to the White House account, the two Washington lawyers, Clifford and Fortas, both political intimates of President Johnson, had not talked with the President before trying to get the Washington newspapers to suppress the news of the Jenkins arrest.

James Reston, Washington Bureau Chief for the *New York Times,* said President Johnson's presidential campaign had been "seriously embarrassed." He viewed the 1959 arrest as "the most damaging aspect" of the Jenkins case because of the questions it raised about the administration of the national security program. Such questions were important, he said, even though "the evidence does not indicate that he (Jenkins) participated in the top secret discussions of the National Security Council.

"The fact that so intimate an associate of the President was involved in such a compromising situation," said Reston, "is probably the most embarrassing political situation since the Profumo sex scandal in Great Britain. . . . Walter Jenkins has revived and dramatized all the harsh feelings about morals, and political cliques, and the Texas gang in Washington, and this clearly can do the President no good."

Former Vice-President Richard M. Nixon was one of many Republicans who jumped into the Jenkins controversy.

"The question is why Johnson kept Jenkins in spite of an earlier apprehension on a morals charge in 1959," he said. The former Vice-President linked the Jenkins affair and the Bobby Baker case and told the press that President Johnson should appear on

television and explain why the two men closest to him in the past
ten years were both "bad apples."

Jenkins was ill, Nixon said. "But people with this kind of illness
cannot be in places of high trust."

Republican Chairman Burch tried to keep the nation's attention fixed on the "grave questions of national security. . . .
President Johnson, who talks about responsibility, now has the
responsibility to explain why he covered up for five and one-half
years—since January 15, 1959—that a top aide had been arrested
on a similar perversion charge. Knowing, as he must, the vulner-
ability of morals offenders to blackmail, the President should tell
whether Mr. Jenkins was permitted to sit in on meetings of the
National Security Council, and the meetings of the cabinet, and
otherwise given access to top military secrets."

Washington newsmen soon confirmed the obvious. Jenkins had
enjoyed the highest security classification possible—a "Q" clearance. He had attended Cabinet meetings, and he had attended
National Security Council meetings.

A White House offensive of sympathy was launched by the
First Lady. Jenkins' arrest, she said, was the result of "exhaustion
in dedicated service to his country. . . . Walter Jenkins has been
carrying incredible hours and burdens since President Kennedy's
assassination. He is now receiving the medical attention he needs.
I know our family and all of his friends, and I hope all others,
pray for his recovery. I know that the love of his wife and six fine
children, and his profound religious faith will sustain him through
this period of anguish."

The President joined the effort to arouse sympathy for Jenkins
and reassured the public by ordering an F.B.I. investigation to
determine if there had been any security leaks. "No man I know
has given more personal dedication, devotion and tireless labor,"
the President said. "For myself and Mrs. Johnson, I want to say
that our hearts go out with the deepest compassion for him and
for his wife and six children—and they have our love and prayers."
Privately, the President raged. The charges against Jenkins were
unjustified, he said, and he had probably been "trapped" into it.

By passing the responsibility to the F.B.I., the President successfully sealed off sources of information to the press. Several government agencies refused to talk to reporters on the ground that it would be improper during the F.B.I. inquiry. The press couldn't find out what person or persons were responsible for the fact that Jenkins had not been subjected to a full investigation when he became top assistant to the Vice-President in 1961, and to the President in November, 1963.

The F.B.I. had its difficulties too. Some of the agents told me it would be impossible to conduct an investigation of a man's activities for five years and arrive at any definite conclusion about security breaches through him.

But should the F.B.I. report indicate no evidence of a leak of security information, I was fairly certain it would criticize the laxity that had permitted Jenkins to retain access to highly classified information. The F.B.I.'s opposition to homosexuals in sensitive government posts had been set out firmly in the past.

D. Milton Ladd, Assistant to the Director of the Federal Bureau of Investigation, had testified that the Communists "have a program of seeking out weaknesses of leaders in Government and industry. In fact," he said, "the F.B.I. has in its possession information of unquestionable reliability that orders have been issued by high Russian intelligence officials to their agents to secure details of the private lives of Government officials, their weaknesses, their associates, and in fact every bit of information regarding them, hoping to find a chink in their armor and a weakness upon which they might capitalize at the appropriate time."[10]

Shortly after the F.B.I. investigation was ordered, I talked with Don Reynolds again about Jenkins.

"You didn't believe me," Reynolds chided. "Are you convinced now I was telling you the truth?"

I admitted to my earlier skepticism, and commented (or perhaps rationalized) that it was probably better that I hadn't pinned down the story on the 1959 morals arrest earlier. One morals arrest could be explained away as a mistake or a misunderstanding. Two such incidents, five years apart, could hardly result from some misunderstanding or "a trap," as the President privately maintained.

I asked Reynolds how and when he had found out about the 1959 arrest. He said he had learned about it in late 1959 or early 1960 from a Senate employee closely associated with Jenkins. "He wanted me to talk to someone about taking the arrest record out of the police-department files," Reynolds said. "I had a friend who had a good connection in the morals division, and he wanted me to use him to get the records destroyed. I asked my friend if he could do anything, and he said he wouldn't touch it. I let it drop."

According to Reynolds some important people had been aware of the Jenkins morals arrest and had been anxious to have that record destroyed. I now believed him.

Despite the complexities of an investigation that meant retracing the details of the public life of Walter Jenkins, the F.B.I. report was made in record time—on October 23rd, only nine days after the start of the investigation. It did not read like the usual F.B.I. report, but one had to keep in mind that the F.B.I. was acting under orders from President Johnson and Acting Attorney General Nicholas deB. Katzenbach. It said: "The F.B.I.'s extensive investigation of Walter W. Jenkins, former assistant to the President, disclosed no information that Mr. Jenkins had compromised the security or interest of the United States in any manner.[11]

"Every logical available source was contacted to determine whether Mr. Jenkins had engaged in indecent acts on other occasions; whether the national security had been compromised; and why, following a morals arrest of Mr. Jenkins in 1959, the then Majority Leader Johnson had not been notified.

"Mr. Jenkins was interviewed by the F.B.I. on Oct. 18, 1964, and admitted having engaged in the indecent acts for which he was arrested in 1959 and 1964," the report stated. "He (Jenkins) claimed that he had been 'enticed' by the arresting officer on the former occasion and that his mind was befuddled by fatigue, alcohol, physical illness and lack of food the latter time.

"Mr. Jenkins further advised that he did not recall any further indecent acts, and if he had been involved in any such acts he would have been under the influence of alcohol and in a state of fatigue and would not remember them.

"According to Mr. Hoover, the investigation which the F.B.I. launched last week has disclosed that Mr. Jenkins has had limited association with some individuals who are alleged to be, or who admittedly are, sex deviates. Mr. Hoover stated there was no information reported to indicate that Mr. Jenkins has ever engaged in improper acts with them."

The report gave none of the names of the other sex deviates with whom Jenkins had associated, nor the circumstances of these associations. It did not call anyone to task for the failure to request a full F.B.I. investigation of Jenkins. It reported simply that the F.B.I. had notified the Secret Service of the 1959 arrest record, but that the matter was "not checked further" by the Secret Service, with the District of Columbia police or anyone else.

"When he assumed office as President in November, 1963, Mr. Johnson still did not know of the January, 1959, arrest," the report said. "When questioned regarding his failure to order an investigation of himself, Mr. Jenkins stated that he thought he had been investigated in 1961."

It was ironic, then, that Jenkins should have been the man in control of the White House security program.

Only the month before his last morals arrest, Jenkins had signed a memorandum advising the tightening of preemployment security-clearance procedures in all government departments.

The memorandum said it would be "unfortunate if undesirable individuals were put on the federal payroll simply because sufficient precautions were not taken prior to their appointment."

In this memorandum Mr. Jenkins asked for a security "name check" before any individual was seriously considered for appointment to a federal post. "Those procedures can prevent considerable embarrassment both to the government and to the potential employee himself." The memorandum also stated, erroneously: "This practice is in effect at the White House and will be strictly adhered to in the future."

Senator Carl Curtis (Republican, Nebraska) charged that the F.B.I. report demonstrated President Johnson was "the greatest cover-up artist in all political history." He was "the first President to misuse the F.B.I. for blatantly political purposes," said the Senator. "Lyndon Johnson was quick to call in the F.B.I. for an ex post facto security check after the entire world knew about the Jenkins case, simply to protect his political security. He had not, however, called in the F.B.I. for security checks on his White House cronies to protect the security of the United States prior to the Jenkins revelations.

"In calling on the F.B.I. after the fact in the Jenkins matter, Lyndon Johnson submitted limited and restricted questions to that fine and respected agency and then released the desired results thus obtained," the Senator said. "No amount of manipulation of the great investigative agency can cover up the fact that had Lyndon Johnson not blocked a full investigation of the Baker case, the public would have long ago had the whole story of the Jenkinses and Bakers and others of their sort who infested this administration."

President Johnson tried to minimize the Jenkins affair. The Republicans had had "the same type of problem" in the Eisenhower administration, he said, but the Democrats had not made a political issue of it.

President Eisenhower replied that he had no knowledge of any such case in his administration, and other Republicans said that the case President Johnson referred to was not at all similar to the Jenkins affair. They explained that one man who was slated for a White House post early in the Eisenhower administration had been turned down because a preemployment investigation revealed the man's homosexual tendency.

Though the Republican candidate for President held his criticism of the Jenkins affair to the question of national security, campaign jokes about Jenkins spread like prairie fire. Despite its broad currency, the Jenkins case created no substantial political problem for President Johnson. Who can say if it was nullified or diminished by the ouster of Premier Khrushchev, the explosion of the nuclear device in Red China, the public uneasiness about Senator Goldwater, or something else?

Jenkins entered the hospital on October 14th, suffering from what his doctors described as "exhaustion," and he remained there under treatment until after the November 3rd election. He was not available for questioning by the press, and he certainly was not available for the long-delayed questioning by the Senate Rules Committee.

A month after the election, Senate Democrats announced that they would question Jenkins at some "appropriate time" in the future when his doctors agreed there was no danger from the "depressive reaction."

The Jenkins case, for all its embarrassing detail, represented a major public-relations coup for the Johnson administration. Although keeping a homosexual on the public payroll was not made to appear as a political virtue in the public media, it was rarely treated as a vice or a danger. Several columnists lavished sympathy on Jenkins, which, no matter how sincere and well-intended it was, nevertheless deflected the public's attention from the seriousness of the principle. The President's long-time friend, the nationally syndicated columnist William S. White, called Jenkins "one of the most honorable, most conscientious and most truly moral men I ever knew. Here is a man long suffering from combat fatigue as surely as any man ever suffered it in battle."[12]

Joseph Kraft described him as a victim of "the massive burden of tensions and fatigue that drove him to the ragged edge.

"The field will be wide open for desperate men to pose doubts and plant suspicions," Kraft wrote. "It will be possible to ask questions ad nauseam. What is the full story of all Mr. Jenkins' activities? Who cleared him? And when? Was his 1959 arrest known to the security officials? If not, why not? Did he answer a questionnaire about past arrests? If not, why not? If so, was there perjury?

. . . Those are just a few of the mysteries that can be worked up in order to foster the notion that some kind of dirty work or frame-up brought Jenkins to the White House in the first place."[13]

With this kind of sympathy going for it, the Johnson administration would never have any serious trouble. Thanks to a few legislators on the Hill, however, embarrassing questions were still being asked. The new target was another witness the Democrats had consistently refused to call for questioning—that Democratic fundraiser par excellence, Matt McCloskey.

CHAPTER 25

Money-Man McCloskey

Genial, white-haired Matthew H. McCloskey of Philadelphia, a general contractor, claimed to have raised between $30 and $35 million for his party over a period of thirty years, most of it in the late 1950's and early 1960's, when he served as Treasurer of the Democratic National Committee. He boasted of having developed the $100-a-plate dinner as a political fund-raising scheme, and President John F. Kennedy gave him credit for wiping out the $4.5 million Democratic campaign debt for 1960.

Using his shrewd business judgment, political friendships, and Gaelic charm, Matt McCloskey had also amassed a multimillion-dollar personal fortune. Public buildings were his speciality: schools in Philadelphia, state buildings, a Veterans Administration hospital, a building for the Central Intelligence Agency, a new office building for the United States House of Representatives, the District of Columbia Stadium. McCloskey & Co. did business totaling as much as $150 million a year, and 75 to 80 per cent of it was in public construction.

When the Bobby Baker investigation focused incidental attention on the McCloskey & Co. performance bond on the $15 million District of Columbia Stadium, Senator John J. Williams took an immediate interest. For years the crusading Republican had looked with suspicion on McCloskey's dealings with the federal government. The Democrats had, of course, refused to cooperate in any serious questioning of McCloskey. When the Maryland insurance man Don B. Reynolds told Williams that Bobby Baker had arranged with McCloskey for Reynolds to receive the performance-bond business on the stadium contract, the Senator was not surprised. Reynolds produced checks showing he paid $4,000 to Baker, as well as $1,500 to William N. McLeod, Jr., Clerk of the House District of Columbia Committee.[1]

Baker and McLeod had been active in the passage of the legislation that gave approval to the District of Columbia Stadium project, according to Reynolds. Under these circumstances, Senator Williams questioned whether it was proper for Baker or McLeod to have received any money that was directly or indirectly connected with the stadium project. It appeared to Senator Williams that Baker or McLeod, or both, might be using the prestige of official positions as employees of the Congress for private gain.

In his testimony, Reynolds related that Baker held a meeting in his office in January, 1960, with Reynolds, McLeod, McCloskey, and Congressman J. L. McMillan, the South Carolina Democrat who was chairman of the House District of Columbia Committee. At the time, it was revealed that McCloskey planned to bid on the stadium construction. Baker introduced Reynolds to McCloskey as his associate in an insurance business, and told him that if he received the contract, he would like to have McCloskey consider Reynolds as the insurance broker when it came time to purchase the performance bond.[2]

The records Reynolds produced seemed to support the story. McCloskey won the contract with a bid of $14,247,187.50, and McCloskey & Co. gave the performance-bond business to Reynolds. The premium on the performance bond was $73,631.28. Reynolds, as broker, wrote the bond through the insurance agency of Hutchinson, Rivinus & Co., in Philadelphia, in which McCloskey's son-in-law was a partner.[3]

Of the $10,031.50 that Reynolds received as a commission, $4,000 went directly to Baker by the previously mentioned check, dated October 15, 1960. The Baker payoff differed from the payments to McLeod in that Reynolds received two invoices for $1,000 each from McLeod for alleged "legal services." Reynolds paid the first $1,000 in full with a check, and paid $500 as "a compromise" on the second invoice. He described the total $1,500 payment to McLeod as a "sort of reward for his having tried to help me over a period of years."[4] (In an interview with the Rules Committee staff, McLeod indicated that he received the $1,500 for "legal services," but admitted it was a gift when questioned under oath. He explained giving misleading information to investigators by simply stating: "I was not under oath.")

Though these facts raised a question of propriety, there was nothing illegal in McCloskey's tossing the performance-bond business to Reynolds and Baker. Senator Williams sensed there were more questions to be asked. McCloskey had been the low bidder on the stadium, at $14,247,187.50. But what was the final cost of the project? The Senator learned that the contract price increased to $17,266,015.58 by the end of construction, as a result of 236 "change orders" issued by the D. C. Armory Board.

An extensively documented article in the *Wall Street Journal* for March 18, 1964, added further to the Senator's store of information. In it, the reporter Monroe W. Karmin called attention to the fact that in addition to the more than $3 million in "change orders" he had negotiated, McCloskey was asking the D. C. Contract Appeals Board to award yet another $1 million on the ground that bad weather forced the employment of "unusual and costly procedures not contemplated in the original contract."[5]

"Change orders" normally run from 6 per cent to 10 per cent on federal construction, the *Journal* learned from the Capitol Architect's Office. Other industry experts were quoted as saying that the 21 per cent jump in the McCloskey contract "just isn't normal." One losing bidder told the *Wall Street Journal:* "If we had known there were going to be that many extras, we could have shaved our bid lower than McCloskey's."

Dipping into history, the article revealed that during World War II, McCloskey & Co. was one of the chief beneficiaries of a concrete ship-and-barge program that cost the government nearly $170 million. With government help, McCloskey & Co. developed a yard at Tampa, Florida, originally estimated to cost $2.7 million. Before it was completed, the costs had soared to $7.5 million.

"McCloskey delivered 24 ships (most of which served in such uncelebrated roles as floating storehouses and training vessels) in 1943–44 that cost Uncle Sam $48,000,000, some $20,000,000 more than the contract price," the *Wall Street Journal* stated.

According to an official history of World War II shipbuilding, commissioned by the government, which the *Journal* now quoted: "The yards and the ships were built under contracts that guaranteed reimbursement of costs and payment of minimum fees, even when, as happened under McCloskey's contract, the cost proved much more than double the contract price. In such a case clearly the Government paid an outrageous amount compared to what it received."

Another government shipyard in which McCloskey appeared to have an interest came to public notice in 1962, when President Kennedy nominated McCloskey to be Ambassador to Ireland. Senator Williams, a member of the Foreign Relations Committee, requested that the nomination be held up pending a full investigation of two specific transactions: (1) the sale of a shipyard at Jacksonville, Florida, and (2) the $4 million repair job needed on a Veterans Administration hospital built by the McCloskey firm.

The Jacksonville shipyard had been sold in 1946 to a firm operated by Louis Wolfson. Williams said in a Senate speech that McCloskey had been associated with Wolfson in the bidding on this shipyard, and a man who worked for Wolfson had made a $25,000 payoff to a government official who was in a position to aid the Wolfson interests.

Senator Williams wanted McCloskey questioned under oath about his knowledge of the shipyard deal, but the Democratic-controlled committee settled for a letter of explanation. In his letter, McCloskey confirmed that he had been associated with Wolfson in the early bidding on the shipyard. He said, however, that he had severed his relations with Wolfson, prior to the final sale. He denied any knowledge of the $25,000 payment to the government official.

The committee's look into the Veterans hospital was equally cursory. The contract to construct this 1,000-bed hospital in

Jamaica Plain, near Boston, had been awarded to McCloskey during the Truman administration in 1950. McCloskey won the contract for $10,563,000. According to information that came to Senator Williams ten years later, there was need for several million dollars' repairs because of faulty construction. Less than a year after the hospital had opened, in 1952, the building reportedly had suffered major deterioration.

Senator Williams pressed the Kennedy administration to act to recover the millions the government stood to lose from the faulty construction. And he asked Foreign Relations Committee Chairman William Fulbright, the Arkansas Democrat, to hold up the McCloskey Ambassadorial nomination until an Army report on the hospital, then in progress, could be heard.

Without waiting for the report and without questioning McCloskey, the Foreign Relations Committee reported the nomination. Williams carried his fight to the Senate floor. There he moved to send the nomination back to the Foreign Relations Committee for further study. The move failed, despite the fact that 30 Republicans voted with Williams. There were 61 Democrats and a lone Republican, Senator Hugh Scott, from McCloskey's home state of Pennsylvania, voting against it. Ambassador McCloskey went to Dublin.[6]

Three months later, on October 10, 1962, Senator Williams made public the report of the Army investigation of the hospital. "Cracking, bulging and spalling of the brick surface had become evident," the report stated, as early as April, 1953, only six months after the construction was finished. Government patching efforts were futile. When consulting engineers made an inspection in mid-1961, their investigation "showed that more than half the limestone window mullions were cracked or broken; in some locations, there was evidence of major cracking, and the brickwork had moved away from the building frame to which it was originally fastened."[7]

The Army report also said "all windows have at times become inoperable and have required constant repair. Investigation disclosed that the aluminum windows, which were permitted under contract specifications as an alternate to rolled steel section windows, were not of a design adequate for a facility such as this hospital where they required constant operation . . . the windows are subjected to heavy duty but have only light duty capacity."

The building was in such bad condition, the Army report stated, that "steps have been taken to reduce accident hazards by limiting or eliminating personnel movement around the building in all but essential areas and by installing temporary protective covering over the roofs of entrances."

Because the Engineers Corps was short of persons qualified to inspect construction when the hospital was put up, the firm that designed the building had also been retained to inspect its construction. The consultants called in years later by the Army to evaluate the deterioration had recommended the replacing of the entire brick facing with insulated metal panels, and the replacing of all windows. The cost of the entire job was estimated at $4 million.

If the $4 million repair job was a result of faulty construction, as set out in the Army report, Senator Williams insisted the contractor should be held responsible. He sent the whole package to Attorney General Robert F. Kennedy with the suggestion that "the inspectors who approved this faulty construction in 1950 should likewise be called to account."

Under this prodding the Justice Department conducted an investigation, and on December 24, 1963, mailed demand letters to McCloskey & Co. and the architects and engineers asking $4,918,-577 plus interest by January 20, 1964, under threat of suit. The demand letters went to Shepley-Bulfinch-Richardson and Abbott, of Boston, the architects, and Charles T. Main, Inc., also of Boston, the engineers on the project. Additional damages of $2.5 million were sought from the Aetna Casualty & Surety Co., of Boston, which guaranteed that McCloskey would perform all conditions of the contract. The companies failed to pay, and the government filed its claim.

McCloskey & Co. and the architects and engineers were fighting the government claim when McCloskey's name came into the Bobby Baker investigation. This provided an opportunity for Senator Williams to refocus attention on McCloskey, and it gave Representative H. R. Gross, the Iowa Republican, the chance to raise some questions about still another McCloskey & Co. project—the huge, luxurious House office building known as the Rayburn Building.

The Democratic-controlled Congress had awarded the contract on the Rayburn Building to McCloskey in March, 1960, for $50,-793,000. By early 1964, the addition of a health suite, swimming pool, and other luxuries had boosted the cost to more than $70 million. This price excluded the cost of another contract with McCloskey & Co. for digging the hole and building the foundation for the building. The price of the latter started by contract at $6.66 million and was reported to have jumped to more than $9 million.

So far, all that had come out of the Bobby Baker hearings about McCloskey was the testimony by Don B. Reynolds on how McCloskey gave him the performance-bond business on the D. C. Stadium. A few weeks after this testimony, however, Reynolds confided to Senator Williams that there was a far more startling side to the performance-bond transaction than he had told. He said that a $35,000 payoff fund was created in connection with the stadium project by a planned overpayment on the cost of the performance bond.

The way Reynolds explained it to Senator Williams, Baker had arranged for McCloskey & Co. to pay him something over $109,-000 for the performance bond, although its actual cost was only $73,631.28. Under instructions from Bobby Baker, Reynolds submitted the $109,000 bill to McCloskey.[8] When McCloskey paid it, this created a surplus fund of about $35,000. Of this, Baker allowed Reynolds to keep $10,000 for serving as "bagman" (a sum comparable to the commission on the performance bond he would have received if he had not been required to write it through the Philadelphia insurance firm in which McCloskey's son-in-law was a partner).

Reynolds told Williams the remaining $25,000 was to be made

available in cash for the political campaigning of Baker's mentor, Senator Lyndon B. Johnson. His instructions from Baker were to deliver the cash in amounts of no more than $5,000 at any one time.

If Reynolds' allegation could be fully proved, then violations of income-tax laws and federal election laws might also be proved. Senator Williams recognized that he needed the fullest documentation possible before breathing a word about the explosive $35,-000 fund.

By this time a broad-scale effort to discredit and destroy Reynolds as a witness was in full swing. The most bitter attacks on Reynolds' character came from his old friends and business associates—men who had gone partying with him, helped him with business deals, and received money from him. These former pals had an obvious stake in creating doubts about the key witness against them.

When Senator Williams examined the records available to corroborate Reynolds, he knew he had to be exceedingly cautious. The key document was the check from McCloskey & Co. to Reynolds that included the alleged overpayment of $35,000.

Senator Williams moved very slowly as long as there was a chance that McCloskey might be questioned under oath. Under questioning by Republican members of the committee, McCloskey might be made to give some hint of the $35,000 overpayment.

While he waited to see if McCloskey would be called, Senator Williams reviewed the corroborative evidence already available and the means to obtain more. The established facts were numerous. Bobby Baker had been placed in charge of the Senatorial Campaign Committee by Majority Leader Lyndon B. Johnson in 1959 and 1960. Bobby Baker had handled large amounts of campaign cash through his Capitol office. He was a close business and social acquaintance of Reynolds, and had arranged for Reynolds to get the stadium-bond business. Certainly, the Senator reasoned, Reynolds himself was not in the position to command a $35,000 overpayment from McCloskey & Co. So, if there was proof of an overpayment, it was only logical that Bobby Baker had a significant role, and the fund might be for political purposes, as Reynolds claimed.

The Republicans failed in their efforts to have McCloskey called home for questioning. The Ambassador was merely questioned by the staff in a transatlantic telephone call. Reynolds, by contrast, was questioned under oath, and belligerently. The subsequent report of the Democratic majority Senate Rules Committee (July 8, 1964) stated that McCloskey admitted he had given the performance-bond business to Reynolds as a result of a conversation with Bobby Baker but added: "He (McCloskey) said the purchase of the bond was his own exclusive responsibility as a private businessman and that he could purchase it from anyone he wished to, since the rates were the same, no matter who the broker was. Thus selection of the broker did not in any way affect the cost of the project."[9]

Since the Rules Committee counsel, L. P. McLendon, and its investigator, Ellis Meehan, had clearly demonstrated their reluctance to ask certain hard questions, Senator Williams stepped up his efforts. Through someone who had seen a microfilm of bank records, he received confirmation in late July that there had been a $109,205 check drawn from McCloskey & Co. to Reynolds. The Senator's source could not obtain a photostatic copy of the check, so Senator Williams tried other avenues.

Meantime, on July 27, 1964, the Senate engaged in a debate on the reforms needed to protect it against such gross improprieties as those committed by Bobby Baker, which the Democratic Majority now admitted did exist. In the course of the debate, Senator Williams renewed his complaint about the Rules Committee's failure to question McCloskey and other important witnesses. He also urged Chairman Jordan to examine more closely the performance-bond transaction.

"What the committee does not have and which the committee should have and which I hope it will try to obtain," Senator Williams said, "is a copy of Mr. McCloskey's check to Mr. Reynolds as payment for this stadium insurance. I think it would be very important to have that information."[10]

Chairman Jordan didn't get the point. "I think Mr. Reynolds' record shows what the amount is," Jordan said. "The report shows what he paid for the performance bond. But I shall not argue that point."

"It shows," Senator Williams replied, "that Mr. Reynolds was to get $73,631.28." Williams reviewed the payment of $63,599.72 from Reynolds to Hutchinson, Rivinus & Co., the $10,031.56 commission Reynolds deducted, and the $4,000 and $1,500 payments to Baker and McLeod, and then added: "While it may be merely routine, I should like to see the $73,631.28 check (from McCloskey to Reynolds) to see if that is exactly what was paid. I would suggest that even now the committee could obtain a copy of that check. It may be interesting."

Neither Chairman Jordan nor Counsel McLendon took the suggestion. For this reason, and also because he felt he had served sufficient warning, Williams took matters into his own hands. On August 17, in the room off the Senate cloakroom, Senator Williams told me he had obtained the vital document, a photostatic copy of the check, but that he needed a few more days to put the case together.

Congress recessed for the Democratic convention from August 23rd to August 29th. When it returned on August 31st, John Williams was ready to unload. That evening he met with Reynolds for one last review of the important facts.

The next day, on September 1st, Senator Williams shook the Senate with the "new evidence," which he said involved "an additional kickback of over $35,000 which was made by Mr. Matthew McCloskey on the Washington stadium contract."[11]

"Of this extra kickback, $25,000 was scheduled through Bobby Baker for the 1960 Democratic campaign fund," said Senator Williams. "The rest represents payments to the individuals handling this transaction. . . . Mr. McCloskey was never asked to testify either in executive session or in public session, and the Democratic majority of the Rules Committee by a strictly party vote rejected the request that he be called as a witness to explain his arrangements with Bobby Baker in the payoff on the Washington stadium contract. Perhaps after today's report," the Senator said scathingly, "it can be more readily understood why someone in the high command ordered these hearings closed."

Williams charged that "in this conspiracy to channel this additional $35,000 into Washington several laws were violated." He called it a "payoff" and declared it "was arranged for the express purpose of channeling a $25,000 potential contribution into the Democratic campaign fund and to charge this $25,000 contribution as a business expense item on a government contract."

"By so doing," Senator Williams explained, "Mr. McCloskey could (1) circumvent the law which prohibits political contributions in excess of $5,000, (2) charge this item off on his books as an expense of doing business and thereby deduct it for income tax purposes, and (3) in effect charge it to the American taxpayers by adding this on a cost item of a government contract."

"According to Mr. Reynolds," Senator Williams told the Senate, "$25,000 of this $35,000 was turned over to Bobby Baker to be used as a contribution to the Johnson-Kennedy campaign fund of 1960."

Senator Williams said Reynolds brought the information to him because of a lack of confidence in the Rules Committee staff. He quoted Reynolds as saying: " 'I had hoped that the Senate Rules Committee would have provided this cooperation and assistance. It had been my intention to call this to their attention and to ask their assistance in getting certain documents; however, after my official interview with Major McLendon and the ex-F.B.I. agent (Ellis Meehan) who tried to intimidate me in his questioning I decided otherwise.' "

Senator Williams further told the Senate that the Rules Committee staff investigators had tried to get Reynolds to state that it was Bobby Baker, not Walter Jenkins, who discussed the purchase of the unneeded television advertising from the L.B.J. Company (see Chapter 24). Reynolds said to the Senator: " 'At two subsequent appearances before the Rules Committee I soon learned that the majority of the committee was more interested in discrediting me as a person and as a witness than it was in developing the actual facts of the case.'"

Senator Williams said that "Mr. Reynolds frankly admits that his part in this [stadium bonding] transaction was wrong. He (Reynolds) now recognizes his error and is cooperating in helping to develop the necessary information and documents to establish what really happened. Mr. Reynolds has again asked that he be called to testify under oath before any Congressional Committee which is interested in developing all the facts.

"The United States Senate has no choice," Senator Williams concluded, "except to re-open the Baker investigation and show the American people that the United States Senate does have the courage and the integrity to expose any case of wrong-doing regardless of how close the culprit may be to the Administration in power. I repeat, the United States Senate has no choice now but to re-open the Baker investigation and call Mr. McCloskey, Mr. Baker, and Mr. Reynolds as its first witnesses."

Other Republicans joined in the pressure for an immediate hearing, and Senator Karl Mundt, the South Dakota Republican, referred to the "colossal blunder" that had been made by Chairman Jordan and the Democrats on the Rules Committee in refusing to call McCloskey earlier.

Majority Leader Mike Mansfield defended Chairman Jordan and the Democrats. "I think they are entitled to our confidence and good will," he said.

But Senator Mundt declared that the Democrats, by refusing to call Jenkins and McCloskey earlier, had used their power "arrogantly" and denied the minority its right to call witnesses.

"The committee refused to call Mr. McCloskey," Senator Williams said bluntly. "I told the Senator from North Carolina (Jordan) plainly, in colloquy on the floor of the Senate, not a week or so ago, but back in July of this year that this particular check of Mr. McCloskey's should be obtained by his committee. The Senator from North Carolina took no action whatever."

Despite Democratic assurances that the investigation would move forward quickly, none of the key witnesses was called in the first few days of hearings. In a Senate speech on October 2nd, Senator Williams told the committee to "stop dodging around the issue, and call the witnesses, McCloskey, Baker and Reynolds." He said the Rules Committee Democrats were acting like "schoolboys delaying the trip to the woodshed in the pious hope that something will happen to the principal before they get there."

Towards one objective the Democrats did act. They did their utmost to defeat Senator Williams, who was then running for re-election. The tremendous effort to unseat the crusading Republican was backed by more than $200,000, and an army of imported Democratic speakers representing Cabinet and sub-Cabinet posts in Washington. Even President Johnson showed up in Dover, Delaware, to help eliminate "Honest John" Williams.

Senator Thruston Morton, the Kentucky Republican, called the drive "to get Williams" one of the "most shocking" developments of the campaign. "Senator Williams is the Democrats' Number One target in the country," Morton said, "because he had the courage and sense of duty to expose the notorious Bobby Baker case."

Republican prodding for action in the Baker and McCloskey affairs was useless. On October 13th, Chairman Jordan announced that the hearings would be recessed until after the election. The Republican Presidential candidate, Senator Barry Goldwater, burning with indignation, called the whole thing a political "cover-up" which he claimed was directed from the White House. Certainly, the White House could have had a full investigation if it had pushed for one.

Senator Williams survived the Democratic landslide victory for the Johnson-Humphrey ticket, and on December 1st, the Baker hearings resumed once more, with the Delaware Republican present and prodding. This time under oath, Reynolds told the story he had already privately revealed to Williams. He did not try to paint himself as an innocent party, but admitted that he had been wrong in many of his dealings with Bobby Baker and others. Senator Williams had persuaded him he should give testimony rather than take the Fifth Amendment, and Reynolds said he was keeping his word to the Delaware Republican.

Bobby Baker's testimony was not helpful. He claimed the Constitutional right of the Fifth Amendment not to testify, on the ground that his testimony might tend to incriminate him, and for good measure he tossed in the First, Fourth and Sixth Amendments.

Matt McCloskey, however, did testify. He entered the huge hearing room on December 2nd, a picture of suave confidence. The Ambassador enjoyed an obvious rapport with Chairman Jordan and Counsel McLendon. In explaining the $109,205 check, he admitted there had been a $35,000 overpayment. But McCloskey said he was as surprised as anyone when Senator Williams had first called attention to it. He insisted he had never noticed the overpayment on the $73,000 bond, and he denied he had ever had any discussion with Baker and Reynolds to plot the overpayment as a payoff fund. He had assumed that the extra $35,000 in the check to Reynolds was for general liability insurance. "Somebody in our organization goofed," McCloskey said. "We make goofs like that every once in a while."

Then the Democratic fund-raiser declared that Reynolds was "a liar," and that he would never have engaged in any such manipulation to get business expense money into the political-campaign funds. He also insisted that his firm had given the government good performance on contracts, and that he had never resorted to political favoritism to win contracts or to have the contracts increased by "change orders" after a bid was won.

Senator Williams said he doubted if such a shrewd businessman as Matt McCloskey would be so careless as to permit a $35,000 overpayment on such a standard item as a performance bond.

The question presented by the conflicting testimony was this: Was the overpayment of $35,000 a conspiracy payoff, as Reynolds testified? Or was it, as McCloskey claimed, a $35,000 "goof" that he and his auditors had overlooked for four years?

McCloskey had a big stake in picturing Reynolds as a liar, and he ripped into the Maryland insurance man with fury. Chairman Jordan also seemed intent on raising doubts about Reynolds.

And Committee Counsel McLendon went out of his way to question the truthfulness of Senator Williams on a point involving the investigation of McCloskey. Senator Williams was raising a question about some of the several government contracts of McCloskey & Co. when he commented that he had offered a "rather complete file" on these contracts to McLendon. The committee counsel, reported the Senator, had said he wasn't interested in the file.

"Senator," roared McLendon, "you're absolutely and unalterably untrue in your statement. You ought to at least tell the truth."

Senator Williams then detailed some McCloskey matters he said he had called to McLendon's attention. They had not been followed up, Senator Williams said, but he was willing to let it pass as "a misunderstanding" and to assume that McLendon had not heard what he had said.

Instead of making peace with Senator Williams, McLendon continued to question his truthfulness. Senator Williams asked for apologies from McLendon and the committee. Failing to get them, he walked out of the hearings. He would, he said, continue to develop evidence on his own, and would present his facts on the Senate floor.

Under this pending threat, the reopened investigation pushed through two weeks of hearings that opened up dozens of new leads on questionable activities by government officials. The first testimony was given about Bobby Baker's "partying" in New Orleans. Investigator Samuel Scott testified that Paul Aguirre, Baker's Puerto Rican business associate, had told Scott of a trip to New Orleans in May, 1963, with Baker's secretary, Nancy Carole Tyler, and the German model and party girl, Mrs. Elly Rometsch. On questions dealing with the "several days of partying" and on questions relating to his dealings with Baker on a Federal Housing Administration matter, the handsome Aguirre took the Fifth Amendment.

The committee also heard testimony on Baker's $5,000 fee from an ocean-freight-forwarding organization that was seeking legislation, the $30,000 windfall profit Baker received in a stock transaction with a union official, and the fact that Baker had cashed a $5,000 check paid as a commission for help in chartering a new bank in California.

Despite all the new information, the center of attention continued to be Don Reynolds. The early efforts to destroy Reynolds' credibility had failed because records and other testimony supported the major elements of his statements. However, late in 1964 he told his full story in a closed session of the Rules Committee. What he told then could wreck the political futures of many persons who still held important office. It was not hard to understand why the Rules Committee Democrats now renewed their apparent aim to destroy him and left dangling the many leads that could expose Baker or other employees of the Senate, Senators or former Senators.

In time it became evident they also meant to try to discredit Senator Williams. In the spring of 1965, before the Rules Committee had issued its report on the Baker investigation, word of its contents was leaked to the press. The story rolled from coast to coast that the McLendon report (it was named for the counsel who drafted it) would be very critical of Senator Williams. Republican Senators roared with indignation at this "underhanded" effort to "smear" the man who started the investigation.

Once he learned what the report was going to say about him, Williams took to the Senate floor and challenged the six Democrats to repudiate the report or stand up and debate him on its merits. He declared it was filled with provable errors. The effort to start a debate was futile. Chairman Jordan and his five colleagues stayed off the floor or simply refused to discuss the inaccuracies Williams documented. They had the votes to continue to do as they pleased.

On June 3, 1965, Senator Williams rose to challenge the Democrats again. And again the Democratic committee members refused to appear to debate. The tall Delaware Republican characterized their silence as comparable to a witness' pleading the Fifth Amendment.

The undefended McLendon report, said Williams, "is far more critical of the Senator from Delaware (himself) than it is of Mr. Baker or any of his associates. As I read it they really seem to pity Mr. Baker and almost apologize for having to criticize him at all."

Then he lashed out at committee efforts to discredit witnesses who "agreed to give testimony rather than take the Fifth Amendment. I am not carrying the torch for Reynolds," Williams said. "I never knew the man until this case broke in September or October, 1963."

Reynolds, he reminded the Senate, was involved in the investigation because of his dealings with Baker, other Senate employees, and Senators.

"Mr. Baker and his associates thought highly enough of Mr. Reynolds that they decided to go in business with him," Williams snapped. "In his testimony before the committee, Mr. Reynolds admits that he did wrong. I give him credit for such an admission. He admitted that he had allowed himself to be used as the bagman, handling political payoffs for Mr. Baker and his crowd in Washington."

"He [Reynolds] was considered to be reputable enough so that the man who was then serving as the majority leader of the U. S. Senate selected him as the person from whom he bought life insurance policies totaling about $200,000. . . .

"Mr. Reynolds was considered an honorable enough citizen so that the man who was serving as majority leader and who later served as Vice President accepted a stereo set from him as a gift. Likewise, Mr. Reynolds gave proof of the television time he purchased from the L.B.J. Company as a kickback on this insurance. . . .

"I did not buy any insurance from him. . . . I never accepted a stereo set from him. I think it is improper for a member of the Senate to accept a $600 or $800 gift from anybody. Let us get the record straight—Mr. Reynolds was Mr. Baker's and Mr. Johnson's associate, not an associate of mine, as this committee report would imply.

"When did Mr. Baker and his other associates suddenly decide that Mr. Reynolds was such a disreputable character?" Senator Williams asked. "It was after I and some others persuaded him to appear before the committee and not take the Fifth Amendment. . . . When he refused their suggestions that he take the Fifth Amendment before the committee they began their attack on his credibility. . . .

"Certainly, the man did wrong. I do not defend what he has done, but let us make it clear that those who have been pointing the finger of scorn at him in recent months are the ones who were in business with him, accepting gifts, and letting him serve as their bagman for political payoffs."

Senator Williams declared that the Justice Department had grounds to prosecute Bobby Baker and that any other citizen would have been prosecuted for similar action.

"If these are the standards of morality being established by the Great Society," he said, "then God help America."

To Senator Williams, one of the most significant leads still demanding investigation was the large amount of unexplained cash handled in Bobby Baker's Capitol office. A key figure in the big cash mystery was Miss Nancy Carole Tyler, for testimony indicated she had handled as much as $50,000 to $100,000 in cash. Although the pretty Tennessee girl took the Fifth Amendment on questions dealing with the cash, Williams remained hopeful that she would change her mind and cooperate in unravelling the source and disposition of the mysterious cash.

On May 9, 1965, the hope of obtaining cooperation from Carole Tyler ended forever. The small plane in which she was riding with pilot Robert H. Davis, 43, of Huntington, West Virginia, crashed in the ocean near Bobby Baker's Carousel Motel. Both were killed in the tragic crash that took place after Davis swooped low to buzz the Carousel, and was unable to pull the plane out of the dive.

Although aware of the investigation problem resulting from the death of Miss Tyler, Senator Williams was convinced there were still ways for the Justice Department, the Internal Revenue Service and the Rules Committee to obtain the evidence to prosecute Bobby Baker and some of his associates. He had more than five years remaining of his fourth term in the United States Senate, and he was pledged to continue the investigation regardless of the obstacles.

CHAPTER 26

How Much Decay?

"Truth provides the only solid foundation for achievement in our nation, and the same goes for all other nations."

Speaker John W. McCormack, May 9, 1965, on receiving the Veritas Medal from Providence College.

Measuring the extent of corruption in government today is like taking account of an iceberg. Every actual corruptionist, every premeditating thief who accepts payoffs or gives bribes or otherwise preys illegally on government is supported by a mass of persons who do not actively participate in wrongdoing, but who tolerate it one way or another.

We may feel some compassion for the Army officer who falsifies records because he is ordered to do so by his superior and fears being meted a bad fitness report. His perjury, however, serves the cause of the active corrupters and undermines the public's faith in the integrity of its government.

We may be understanding of the harried Cabinet officer who, unaware of unwise or improper decisions of his subordinates, inadvertently approves of their actions. But if that Cabinet officer permits his name to be used to justify improper actions after he has learned about them, or if he tries to hide the facts or actually condones illegal or unethical acts of his subordinates, he, too, contributes to the decay in government.

We may want to believe the self-serving statements of a Cabinet officer who claims great economies in his department's budget.

But we must ask ourselves what is happening to the integrity of his department's purchasing system when three different investigations disclose that expert, nonpolitical technical advice has been swept aside for vague "rough judgment" or arbitrary conclusions in the awarding of million-dollar contracts?

What is happening to our country when men are punished for giving truthful testimony? When one examines the costs to Jerry Jackis, N. Battle Hales, Otto Otepka, and Don Reynolds for having told the truth, one recalls with foreboding the statement of Edmund Burke: "Among people generally corrupt liberty cannot long exist."

Having given testimony that was critical of his superiors in the Department of Agriculture, N. Battle Hales was passed over for a regular in-grade advancement, and his secretary was carried off to a mental ward, stripped of her legal rights as well as of her clothes, and left to sleep on the floor in a locked room for five nights. Mr. Jackis, who discovered that American products were being used to build a Communist hospital in Cambodia and thus embarrassed a superior who hadn't been attending to his job, was demoted two grades and eventually forced out of government service while the superior advanced to a better job. Because he gave truthful testimony that showed laxity in the State Department's security program and embarrassed his superiors, Otto Otepka was harassed with wiretaps and other police-state techniques. "To get" Otepka, State Department officials went so far as to lie under oath before a committee of Congress.

Such contempt for truth and disregard for individual rights and liberties can discourage the most upright of government employees from volunteering information about laxity or wrongdoing. Consider, then, a man such as Don B. Reynolds, who has admitted to a less-than-perfect past and who decides to turn over a new leaf. After his experience, who else like him will be encouraged to make a clean break with an unsavory past?

After Reynolds testified at a closed hearing of the Senate Rules Committee on December 1, 1964, the forces against him went into high gear. Though he knew that his testimony hung like a sword of Damocles over the careers of many powerful figures in Washington, and he anticipated reprisals and pressures, he nevertheless became alarmed. "I might as well be in Nazi Germany," he said. "They are out to get me, and they are using every government agency and every dirty trick in the book to wreck my business. . . . I was no angel, and I expected to be investigated, but I didn't think I would be harassed to the point that my business would be wrecked and my wife would become ill."

He revealed that he had been questioned many times by the F.B.I., by tax agents, and by the Senate Rules Committee staff, and that the pattern of questioning made it appear *he* was the target of major emphasis, not Bobby Baker or others. He said his telephone was tapped, and he knew efforts were made to persuade some of his major insurance clients to take their business elsewhere. He lost his license to sell insurance in the District of Columbia after admitting the gift of the stereo set and the purchase of unneeded advertising time on the L.B.J. Company television station. He was the only one in the transaction to be penalized, however, or sharply criticized, despite his testimony that he was required to make these "kickbacks" in order to write the life-insurance policies.

While Reynolds' business foundered, Bobby Baker's flourished. North American Aviation, a firm with government contracts in the billions, continued to do business with the Baker-dominated Serv-U vending corporation and continued to pour dollars into Baker's pockets every week. In the few interviews he gave to the press, Baker indicated that business was fine, and he expressed confidence that there would be no prosecution of him resulting from the Johnson administration's investigations of his activities. One could assume that Baker's confidence was well founded from the fact that riding in the car with President Johnson in the Inaugural Parade on January 20, 1965, in the seat of honor usually occupied by the outgoing President, was the Senator from North Carolina, B. Everett Jordan, chairman of the Baker investigating committee.

Though he can view it from his own living room today, it has become increasingly common for the decent, well-meaning person to shrug off evidence of bad government. "There just isn't anything I can do about it," he laments. Another response, usually offered in an attempt at sophistication, is to wink at the evidence: "Corruption has always been with us, you know, and always will be."

Whether people honestly care but don't know what to do about it, or whether they think it's smart not to care, none can afford to forget what happened in Hitler's Germany, Mussolini's Italy, or Perón's Argentina.

Lured by Mussolini's promises to get things done and to build a better society, the Italian people embraced his authoritarian rule unawares. They permitted him to destroy the legislative check on his power and to impose such severe controls over the press that they heard little but praise of him and his programs.

German businessmen, labor leaders, and even church leaders did not heed the clear warnings of the authoritarian regime Hitler was about to impose on their country. The destruction of the legislative check was accomplished with a minimum of public protest despite warnings from men who were aware of it. The German press and radio accepted a "handout" routine in which essentially all information came from the government propaganda office.

As Secretary of Labor and Social Welfare, Juan Perón pushed social reforms that captured the people. They accepted his yoke without bothering to examine the fiscal soundness of his policies. Before the country got rid of him, he had wrecked the economy with fiscal irresponsibility and corruption.

I do not want to convey the idea that destruction of our democratic form of government is imminent. But neither do I want to give any reason for Americans to assume that their liberty and freedom are secure in perpetuity and that the corruption and governmental mismanagement cited in this book are not significant and indicative.

This nation has been fortunate that no administration has

grabbed all the power that is available to the President and maneuvered control of the legislative branch, the press, and other
communications media. Instead of pushing our luck, we would do
better to strengthen our defenses.

The size and complexity of the federal bureaucracy (the budget
now runs beyond $100 billion a year), and the secrecy that sur-
rounds so many of the decisions, make it virtually impossible for
the average citizen, or even a civil servant or a newspaperman,
to successfully challenge the bureaucracy. This is particularly true
when officials are trying to hide something. The only recourse the
reporter or the citizen has is through a proper committee of Congress. With its subpoena power, its lawyers, accountants, and special investigators, the committee can piece together the story of
what has taken place behind the closed doors of bureaucracy.

When a military contract is in question, the Defense Department could have a perfectly valid reason for claiming that "national security" interests make it impossible to give the public
detailed information. Though this kind of secrecy may be justified,
it may also cloak political favoritism, incompetence, or downright
dishonesty. The only way the public will know is to have a proper
committee of Congress conduct closed hearings based on investigations carefully conducted by investigators cleared to examine
classified defense information. The presence of both Democrats
and Republicans on all investigating committees assures a bipartisan check on the thoroughness of the probe, on the accuracy of
the report, and the fairness of any editing done for security reasons
on the published transcript.

This all-important power of the Congress to investigate is, like
all human institutions, unfortunately subject to abuse. Contrary
to what the critics of Congress would have the public believe,
however, the abuse is perpetrated no more often by Congressional
publicity seekers or malicious persecutors than it is by legislative
whitewashers who are protecting a cozy relationship between
themselves and officials of the agencies they are supposed to be
investigating. Like vice-squad detectives, Congressmen and Senators sometimes find it beneficial to get close to those they are sup-

posed to police. A committee chairman receives favored treatment at the agency for himself, his friends, and his constituents. In return, the agency officials are permitted to make decisions by any standards that suit their whims, and with little or no fear that either corruption or mismanagement will be questioned. Thus the independence of Congress is lost, and that particular area of governmental activity is left without an essential check.

Despite several notable examples of thorough Congressional investigations in recent years, I regret to say that the trend is in the other direction. Congress is losing its independence and becoming too willing a tool of the executive branch.

Presidential power over political appointments has always had some disciplinary effect on House and Senate members. But up to now it has been counterbalanced by the powerful independence of many committee chairmen.

Because the White House now, in the current political situation, has the votes to override the committee chairmen in their own committees as well as on the floor, it can disregard them. It can stop or limit investigations in some committees. Though the White House objectives are sometimes laudable, they are not always so. It is a bad omen when party discipline can kill an investigation before it is started.

The larger federal budget and such federal programs as the Area Rehabilitation Administration, the Domestic Peace Corps, and other parts of the war on poverty give the White House ever larger clubs to hold over the legislators. Congressmen and Senators are becoming increasingly reluctant to investigate, or even to speak on the floor, when to do so would offend an administration that controls the placement of multimillion-dollar contracts, the location of new facilities, and other largess. The recent dispute over the abandonment of many military bases pointed up the tremendous power the White House wields over local prosperity.

It is not difficult to imagine circumstances under which an extremely clever President could use the power over military contracts, social programs and political appointments to bring an end to the independent Congressional investigation as we have known it. Congress might resist any direct action to curb or abolish its investigations, but it is unlikely that direct action would be necessary. The attitude of most of the press and much of the public today is so antagonistic to Congressional investigations that the power could be whittled away with little notice. Whatever the motivations of its managers, the massive propaganda of recent years that has been aimed at discrediting Congress, and specifically at discrediting the Congressional investigation, has been regrettably successful.

The decline in the independence of Congress has been accompanied, unsurprisingly, by a parallel decline in the independence of the American press. As we have already noted, when the power of Congress is emasculated, the ability of newsmen to obtain accurate information from government suffers. When the threat of a Congressional investigation is removed or severely limited, the press loses its power to force disclosure of information by the executive branch. Then the newsmen can get only what the agency officials want to reveal, unless there is an inside source willing to risk his job to cooperate.

Without the Congressional power to investigate behind them, the reporters in Washington could be reduced pretty much to the level of the German newsmen who gathered at the Propaganda Ministry in the 1930's to receive their handouts from Dr. Goebbels. Limit the available information to handouts from the White House or any agency, and you will find it dominated by the theme of the incumbent administration's glories. Congressional committees, with all their faults, usually represent a diversity of political views.

Take away the hearings of Congress on the controversial subjects, and the radio and television industry will be even more susceptible to government influence than it is now. Television is without doubt the most powerful of the media today. Its independence is also the most qualified, for these reasons:

First, there are only three major networks that supply most of the nation's stations with news and public affairs programs. This necessarily limits the diversity of viewpoints.

Second, all radio and television stations are subject to government control through the Federal Communications Commission. Though the control over networks and programing is limited, it could be broadened. If not, there wouldn't be so much uneasiness about it throughout the industry.

Third, two of the three networks have direct or indirect interests in government contracts in the communications and defense fields.

Fourth, the mechanics and paraphernalia of television require an access to government offices and a degree of cooperation from high government officials that newspaper reporters and magazine writers do not need.

Fifth, the vast public interest that has grown, or been stimulated, in the President and his family places the Washington bureaus of the major networks in a delicate position. The pressure on the bureaus is great to obtain exclusive film of the President and his family, and the White House has complete control over cooperation on such special shows. There is obviously a distinct competitive advantage in being regarded as friendly to the White House and the administration generally.

The combination of all of these factors makes it unlikely that the television networks will be very aggressive in presenting critical material about any incumbent President or his political appointees. The exception will be the straight news reports on the charges of a political opponent or the criticism that originates in Congressional hearings.

Newspapers and magazines have also become more dependent upon cooperation from the administration. On-the-spot coverage by television has forced newspapers to look more and more for colorful detail, inside information, and exclusive interviews—all of which require special cooperation. The very size of government makes the Washington correspondent increasingly dependent upon the agencies' public-relations offices. When the functions of an information office are, in turn, restricted by an overall centralized information office, such as exists at the Pentagon, where Assistant Defense Secretary Arthur Sylvester has clamped down on the separate Army, Navy, and Air Force information offices, the threat to freedom of the press grows.

Despite the inroads, the government does not control the press today. One can say, however, that the conditions under which it could control the press have become a lot riper.

Different ways for dealing with decay in our government are suggested periodically: a comprehensive conflict-of-interest law, a new code of ethics, a federal crime commission or ethics commission to rule on questions of propriety and legality in all three branches of the federal government. From time to time, a special Congressional committee is created that does, in one manner or another, deal with some aspect of the governmental ethics problem.

All of these solutions are meritorious insofar as they focus public attention on the problem. However, a close examination should make it apparent that none of these approaches assures long-time solutions. A new law will be no better than the enforcement authority. Aggressive enforcement of present laws could have prevented nearly all of the scandals described in this book. A code of ethics is no better than those appointed to administer it, and an ethics or a crime commission is likely to be no better than the appointing authority. Nearly always, the appointment of the policing authority becomes bound up in the partisan or personal politics of men in the White House or Congress, or both.

The only real cure for the decay in our democracy is public interest, public understanding, and a public determination to demonstrate that "the people are the masters." No President has described any better what this means than Grover Cleveland, the Democrat. When he took his oath of office on March 4, 1885, Cleveland said:

"He who takes the oath today to preserve, protect, and defend the Constitution of the United States only assumes the solemn obligation which every patriotic citizen—on the farm, in the workshop, in the busy marts or trade, and everywhere—should share with him.

"The Constitution which prescribes his oath, my countrymen, is yours; the Government you have chosen him to administer for a time is yours; the suffrage which executes the will of freemen is yours; the laws and the entire scheme of our civil rule, from the town meeting to the State capitals and the national capital, is yours. Your every voter, as surely as your Chief Magistrate, under the same high sanction, though in a different sphere, exercises a public trust. Nor is this all. Every citizen owes to the country a vigilant watch and close scrutiny of its public servants and a fair and reasonable estimate of their fidelity and usefulness.

"Thus is the people's will impressed upon the whole framework of our civil polity—municipal, State and Federal; and this is the price of our liberty and the inspiration of our faith in the Republic."

Many American presidents have spoken forcefully on the importance of integrity in government, but in recent years few have matched their words with forthright actions. On May 9, 1965, in the aftermath of the Bobby Baker scandal, President Johnson said in an executive order:

"Where government is based on the consent of the governed, every citizen is entitled to have complete confidence in the integrity of his government . . . It is the intent . . . that employees avoid any action, whether or not specifically prohibited . . . which might result in, or create the appearance of . . . using public office for private gain."

The Johnson order is as broad a pronouncement as any ever issued on ethical standards in government. Whether it will be enforced depends ultimately on the average citizen.

In order to fulfill his responsibility today, the citizen must understand the relationship between the independence of Congress, the work of the free press, government information policies, and standards of integrity in government. The first step is to recognize that there are always enormous pressures for abandoning proper standards in the awarding of government contracts and other government decisions. The pressures will be there whether a Democratic or Republican administration is in power. The potential for bribes, payoffs, or plain political favoritism will increase as the budget increases and as the federal government assumes more and more functions. And the danger will be compounded whenever "national security" considerations make it necessary to set specifications, accept bids, and negotiate contracts in secret.

Therefore the power of Congress and the press to serve as a check on the executive branch must be preserved and actively supported. Though it is surely desirable, it is not essential that the judgments and motivations of the Congress and the press be consistently high-minded. What is important is that the Congress and the press maintain and exercise their rights as the counterforce. American citizens must understand the importance of this balance of power and be ever on guard against any threat to it.

If the public doesn't care about its Congress—or doesn't show that it cares—and if it continues to shrug its shoulders over arrogant administration and shoddy favoritism, as well as outright corruption, then one day the house of democracy may fall. For, in the end, the responsibility for good government rests with the people. America will get as good a government as Americans demand.

NOTES

CHAPTER 1

1. *Washington Coverup*, Clark R. Mollenhoff, Doubleday, 1962.

CHAPTER 2

1. The primary printed source for most of the material in this chapter is "Commingling of United States and Communist Foreign Aid," 87th Congress, 2nd Session, unanimous House Report No. 1907, Nineteenth Report by the Committee on Government Operations, June 25, 1962.

CHAPTER 3

1. "United States Aid Operations in Laos," 86th Congress, 1st Session, House Report No. 546, Seventh Report by the Committee on Government Operations, June 15, 1959.
"United States Aid Operations in Peru," 87th Congress, 1st Session, House Report No. 795, Fourth Report by the Committee on Government Operations, July 26, 1961.
2. Availability of Information from Federal Departments and Agencies, progress of study, July–December 1960, 87th Congress, 1st Session, House Report No. 818, Fifth Report by the Committee on Government Operations, July 28, 1961 (pages 155–194).
3. Availability of Information from Federal Departments and Agencies, progress of study, January–August 1961, 87th Congress, 1st Session, House Report No. 1257, Eleventh Report by the Committee on Government Operations, September 22, 1961.
4. Report 1257, pages 166–167.
5. Supreme Court of the United States (No. 26, October Term, 1960), United States, Petitioner, v. Mississippi Valley Generating Co., etc., January

9, 1961, 364, U.S. 520, 562 (1961), Mr. Chief Justice Warren delivered the opinion.

6. Supreme Court of the United States, 364, U.S. 520, 562 (1961), pages 10, 11, 12, 13 of the printed decision of January 9, 1961.

7. Military Cold War Education and Speech Review Policies Report by the Special Preparedness Subcommittee of the Committee on Armed Services, United States Senate, 87th Congress, 2nd Session, transmitted to the Armed Services Committee on October 19, 1962.

CHAPTER 4

1. The primary source for this chapter is "Illegal Actions in the Construction of the Airfield at Fort Lee, Virginia," 87th Congress, 2nd Session, House Report No. 1858, Seventeenth Report by the Committee on Government Operations, June 20, 1962.

CHAPTER 5

1. Draft Report of the National Stockpile and Naval Petroleum Reserves Subcommittee of the Committee on Armed Services, United States Senate, 88th Congress, 1st Session, transmitted to the Armed Services Committee on October 24, 1963, in connection with the Inquiry Into the Strategic and Critical Material Stockpiles of the United States.

2. Stockpiling of Copper by Office of Defense Mobilization, speech by Senator John J. Williams, of Delaware, Congressional Record, May 27, 1955, page 6131.

3. Windfall to Banner Mining Co. by General Services Administration, speech by Senator John J. Williams, of Delaware, Congressional Record, June 23, 1955, page 7728.

CHAPTER 6

1. Audit of General Services Administration Contracts DMP-49, 50 and 51 with The Hanna Mining Company, Hanna Nickel Smelting Company and The M. A. Hanna Company of Cleveland, Ohio, by the Comptroller General of the United States. Report to the Congress, April 26, 1961.

2. Stockpile report, October 24, 1963, page 97.

3. Stockpile report, October 24, 1963, page 74.

4. Stockpile report, October 24, 1963, page 74.

5. Stockpile report, October 24, 1963, pages 74–75.

6. Hearings (Part 6) before the National Stockpile and Naval Petroleum Reserves Subcommittee of the Committee on Armed Services on "The Hanna Nickel Contracts" in the Inquiry Into the Strategic and Critical Material

Stockpiles of the United States, 87th Congress, 2nd Session, August 13, 14, 15, 16, 17, 1962, page 2154.

Also, Stockpile report, October 24, 1963, page 76.

7. Stockpile report, October 24, 1963, page 92.

8. Stockpile report, October 24, 1963, page 80.

9. Stockpile report, October 24, 1963, pages 80–81.

10. Stockpile report, October 24, 1963, page 82.

11. Stockpile report, October 24, 1963, page 84.

12. Stockpile report, October 24, 1963, page 85.

13. Stockpile report, October 24, 1963, page 87.

14. Stockpile report, October 24, 1963, pages 87–88.

15. Stockpile report, October 24, 1963, page 89.

16. Stockpile report, October 24, 1963, page 91.

17. Stockpile report, October 24, 1963, page 92.

18. Stockpile report, October 24, 1963, page 98.

19. Congressional Record, speech by Senator Clair Engle of California, August 22, 1962, pages 17307–17323.

20. Stockpile report, October 24, 1963, Individual Views of Senator Strom Thurmond, pages 111–117.

21. Stockpile report, October 24, 1963, Individual Views of Senator Strom Thurmond, page 117.

22. Stockpile report, October 24, 1963, Statement by Senator Clifford P. Case, pages 120–121.

23. Stockpile report, October 24, 1963, Statement of Senator J. Glenn Beall, pages 118–119.

CHAPTER 7

1. Operations of Billie Sol Estes, Report prepared by the Intergovernmental Relations Subcommittee of the House Committee on Government Operations, 88th Congress, 2nd Session, October, 1964, pages 19, 20, and 21.

2. Operations of Billie Sol Estes, House Report, page 16.

3. Department of Agriculture Handling of Pooled Cotton Allotments of Billie Sol Estes, Report of the Committee on Government Operations of the United States Senate by its Permanent Subcommittee on Investigation together with individual, supplemental, and additional views, Senate Report No. 1607, 88th Congress, 2nd Session, September 30, 1964, pages 6, 7, and 8.

4. Senate Report No. 1607, page 72.

5. Senate Report No. 1607, page 77.

6. Senate Report No. 1607, pages 86, 145, and 146.

7. Senate Report No. 1607, pages 83–84.

8. Operations of Billie Sol Estes, House Report, pages 310–315.

9. Senate Report No. 1607, page 107.

10. Senate Report No. 1607, page 118.

CHAPTER 8

1. Transcript of Press Conference, United States Department of Agriculture, Friday, May 4, 1962, 12:00 noon.
2. Senate Report No. 1607, page 107.
3. Senate Report No. 1607, page 195, additional views of Senator Karl E. Mundt and Senator Carl T. Curtis.
4. Congressional Record, speech by Senator John J. Williams of Delaware, "Government Employee Railroaded to Mental Institution," May 17, 1962, page 8717.
5. Transcript of Press Conference, United States Department of Agriculture, Friday, May 4, 1962, 12:00 noon.
6. Transcript of Press Conference, Secretary of Agriculture Orville Freeman, May 3, 1962.
7. Senate Report No. 1607, page 113.

CHAPTER 9

1. Senate Hearing, Part 1, on "Pooled Cotton Allotments of Billie Sol Estes," pages 6 through 9.
2. Senate Report No. 1607, pages 116, 118, and 126.
3. Operations of Billie Sol Estes, House Report, pages 328, 329, and 330.
4. Senate Report No. 1607, pages 77 and 165.
5. Senate Report No. 1607, pages 148 and 195.
6. Senate Hearing, Part 2, on "Pooled Cotton Allotments of Billie Sol Estes," pages 622 through 627 and Exhibits 45 and 46.
7. Senate Report No. 1607, page 149.
8. Senate Report No. 1607, pages 192 and 193.
9. Operations of Billie Sol Estes, House Report, page 389.

CHAPTER 10

1. "Award of the X-22 (VTOL) Research and Development Contract," Report by the Preparedness Investigating Subcommittee of the Senate Committee on Armed Services, 88th Congress, 2nd Session, as transmitted to the Senate Committee on Armed Services on January 31, 1964, page 1.
2. "Award of the X-22 (VTOL) Research and Development Contract," Report, page 3.
3. "Award of the X-22 (VTOL) Research and Development Contract," Report, pages 3 and 31.
4. "Award of the X-22 (VTOL) Research and Development Contract," Report, pages 2, 3, and 7.

5. "Award of the X-22 (VTOL) Research and Development Contract," Report, page 9.

6. Hearings on "Award of X-22 (VTOL) Research and Development Contract," before the Preparedness Investigating Subcommittee, of the Senate Committee on Armed Services, 88th Congress, 2nd Session, on June 12, 13, and 14, 1963, pages 5 and 6.

7. "Award of the X-22 (VTOL) Research and Development Contract," Report, page 10.

CHAPTER 11

1. TFX Contract Investigation Hearings, Part 1, before the Permanent Subcommittee on Investigations of the Senate Committee on Government Operations, 88th Congress, 1st Session, February 26, 27, 28, and March 5 and 6, 1963, pages 3 and 4.

2. TFX Contract Investigation Hearings, Part 5, pages 1253 and 1254.

3. TFX Contract Investigation Hearings, Part 5, page 1271.

4. TFX Contract Investigation Hearings, Part 10, pages 2657 and 2658.

CHAPTER 12

1. Congressional Record, 88th Congress, 1st Session, February 28, 1963, speech by Senator Clifford Case of New Jersey, page 3051.

2. "The McNamara Monarchy," by Hanson W. Baldwin, *Saturday Evening Post*, March 9, 1963, page 8.

3. TFX Contract Investigation, Part 2, page 307.

4. TFX Contract Investigation, Part 2, page 400.

5. TFX Contract Investigation, Part 2, page 401.

6. TFX Contract Investigation, Part 2, page 439.

7. TFX Contract Investigation, Part 2, page 445.

8. TFX Contract Investigation, Part 2, pages 445 and 446.

9. TFX Contract Investigation, Part 2, page 446.

CHAPTER 13

1. TFX Contract Investigation, Part 2, page 523.

2. TFX Contract Investigation, Part 3, page 616.

3. TFX Contract Investigation, Part 3, page 768.

4. TFX Contract Investigation, Part 3, page 744.

5. TFX Contract Investigation, Part 3, page 726.

6. TFX Contract Investigation, Part 3, page 699.

7. TFX Contract Investigation, Part 3, page 700.

8. TFX Contract Investigation, Part 3, pages 775, 776, 777.

9. TFX Contract Investigation, Part 3, page 779.

10. TFX Contract Investigation, Part 3, page 792.

11. Robert S. McNamara, speech before the American Society of Newspaper Editors, April 20, 1963.

12. TFX Contract Investigation, Part 5, pages 1186 and 1187.

13. TFX Contract Investigation, Part 5, pages 1203 to 1207, including the Blackburn Memorandum of March 1, 1963.

14. TFX Contract Investigation, Part 3, letter on page 881 and 882.

15. TFX Contract Investigation, Part 3, page 883.

CHAPTER 14

1. TFX Contract Investigation, Part 2, page 419.

2. Nomination of Roswell L. Gilpatric, hearing before the Senate Committee on Armed Services, 88th Congress, 1st Session, January 17, 1961, page 2.

3. TFX Contract Investigation, Part 2, page 416.

4. TFX Contract Investigation, Part 2, page 421.

5. TFX Contract Investigation, Part 4, pages 1015 and 1016.

6. TFX Contract Investigation, Part 4, pages 1092 and 1093.

7. TFX Contract Investigation, Part 10, pages 2683, 2684, and 2685.

8. TFX Contract Investigation, Part 10, page 2622.

9. TFX Contract Investigation, Part 10, page 2622.

10. TFX Contract Investigation, Part 10, page 2655.

11. TFX Contract Investigation, Part 10, page 2657.

12. TFX Contract Investigation, Part 10, page 2711.

13. TFX Contract Investigation, Part 10, page 2714.

CHAPTER 15

1. TFX Contract Investigation, Part 7, page 1877.

2. TFX Contract Investigation, Part 7, page 1883.

3. Nomination of McCone, Korth and Harlan. Hearings before the Senate Committee on Armed Services, 87th Congress, 2nd Session, January 18, 1962, page 4.

4. Committee on Armed Services hearing, January 18, 1962, pages 6 and 7.

5. TFX Contract Investigation, Part 7, page 1881.

6. TFX Contract Investigation, Part 6, page 1472.

7. TFX Contract Investigation, Part 4, chart and testimony on page 1038.

8. Congressional Record, speech by Representative H. R. Gross of Iowa, July 24, 1963, page 12585.

9. Congressional Record, speech by Senator Milward L. Simpson of Wyoming, July 28, 1964, pages 19768–19770.

10. Presidential Press Conference of August 20, 1963. See *New York Times,* August 21, 1963.

11. Congressional Record, speech by Senator Wayne Morse of Oregon, October 31, 1963, page 19770.

12. Presidential Press Conference of October 31, 1963. See *New York Times,* November 1, 1963.

CHAPTER 16

1. Nuclear Propulsion for Naval Surface Vessels, Report of the Joint Committee on Atomic Energy of the Congress of the United States, 88th Congress, 1st Session, December, 1963, page 3.

2. Nuclear Propulsion report, page 5.

3. Nuclear Propulsion report, page 13.

4. Nuclear Propulsion report, page 16.

5. Nuclear Propulsion report, page 17.

6. Congressional Record, speech by Representative H. R. Gross of Iowa, August 1, 1963, pages 13072 and 13073.

7. National Press Club Speech by Admiral George Anderson, September 3, 1963.

8. Hanson W. Baldwin, "Slow-Down in the Pentagon," *Foreign Affairs,* January, 1965, page 262.

9. Defense Department Directive by Assistant Defense Secretary Arthur Sylvester, March 4, 1964.

CHAPTER 17

1. "The Office of Security," State Department Security Hearings before the Subcommittee to Investigate the Administration of the Internal Security Act and Other Internal Security Laws, of the Committee on the Judiciary, 87th Congress, Part 2, page 207.

2. Otto F. Otepka performance rating, "The Office of Security" Hearings, Part 2, page 208.

3. Department of State "Notice of Proposed Adverse Action" against Otto F. Otepka, served September 23, 1963, signed by John Ordway, Chief, Personnel Operations Division. Also, see the 12-page "answer" filed by Otepka with Ordway on October 14, 1963.

4. "State Department Security" Report of the Subcommittee to Investigate the Administration of the Internal Security Act and Other Internal Security Laws of the Committee on the Judiciary, 87th Congress, 2nd Session, October 4, 1962, page 5.

5. "Institute of Pacific Relations" Report of the Senate Committee on the Judiciary, 82nd Congress, 2nd Session, Report No. 2050, of July 2, 1952, pages 72, 127, 145, 146, 148, 155, and 171.

6. "Office of Security," State Department Security Hearings, Part 2, Otepka testimony, pages 195–200.

7. "State Department Security" Report of October 4, 1962, pages 183–184.

8. "State Department Security" Report of October 4, 1962, page 188.

9. "Resolution and Pertinent Data Relative to Security in the Department of State," 12-page pamphlet printed by the Senate Committee on the Judiciary, 88th Congress, 1st Session, dated November 8, 1963, page 11.

10. "Resolution and Pertinent Data," November 8, 1963, page 5.

11. "Testimony of Elmer Dewey Hill," State Department Security Hearings, by the Internal Security Subcommittee, on November 18, 1963, page 88.

12. "Resolution and Pertinent Data," November 8, 1963, page 5.

13. "Resolution and Pertinent Data," November 8, 1963, page 8.

14. "Resolution and Pertinent Data," November 8, 1963, page 3.

15. "Resolution and Pertinent Data," November 8, 1963, page 7.

16. "Resolution and Pertinent Data," November 8, 1963, pages 9 and 10.

CHAPTER 18

1. Department of State "Notice of Proposed Adverse Action" against Otto F. Otepka.

2. Otto F. Otepka's "Answer," filed October 14, 1963.

3. Otepka's "Answer," October 14, 1963, page 4.

4. Otepka's "Answer," October 14, 1963, page 5.

5. Otepka's "Answer," October 14, 1963, page 6.

6. Otepka's "Answer," October 14, 1963, page 11.

7. Judiciary Committee letter to Secretary of State Dean Rusk, dated October 5, 1963.

8. Congressional Record, speech by Senator Dodd of Connecticut, November 5, 1963, page 20031.

9. "Resolution and Pertinent Data," November 8, 1963, page 8.

10. "Resolution and Pertinent Data," November 8, 1963, page 11.

11. "Resolution and Pertinent Data," November 8, 1963, page 12.

12. Testimony of David I. Belisle, November 14, 1963, pages 8 and 9.

13. "Testimony of John F. Reilly," November 15, 1963, pages 72 and 73.

14. "Testimony of Elmer Dewey Hill," November 18, 1963, page 88.

15. "Testimony of Elmer Dewey Hill," November 18, 1963, pages 89, 90, 91, and 92.

16. "Testimony of Elmer Dewey Hill," November 18, 1963, page 93.

17. Civil Service Commission appeal records, including the appeal letter of John R. Norpel, Jr., filed April 6, 1964.

CHAPTER 19

1. "Financial or Business Interests of Officers or Employees of the Senate," Report of the Committee on Rules and Administration of the United States Senate, 88th Congress, 2nd Session, Report No. 1175, July 8, 1964, page 15.

2. Congressional Record, August 30, 1957, page 16722.

3. Congressional Record, August 23, 1958, page 19573.

4. Report No. 1175, page 16.

5. Report No. 1175, pages 22 and 28.

6. Report No. 1175, page 25.

7. Report No. 1175, page 26.

8. Report No. 1175, page 25.

9. Report No. 1175, page 32.

10. Congressional Record, Senator Williams of Delaware, speech on the Bobby Baker matter on October 10, 1963, pages 19181–19185.

11. Report No. 1175, page 25.

12. Report No. 1175, page 30.

13. Report No. 1175, page 48.

14. Congressional Record, Senator Williams' speech of October 19, 1963, pages 19181–19185.

CHAPTER 20

1. Congressional Record, October 10, 1963, pages 19181–19185.

2. Report No. 1175, page 5.

3. Hearings on "Financial or Business Interests of Officers or Employees of the Senate," March 3 and 9, 1964, Part 16, page 1535.

4. Hearings on "Financial or Business Interests of Officers or Employees of the Senate," January 23 and 24, 1964, Part 9, testimony of C. William Tayler, pages 884, 885, 886, 887, and 888.

5. Hearings on "Financial or Business Interests of Officers or Employees of the Senate," Part 21, pages 1793–1854.

6. Hearings on "Financial or Business Interests of Officers or Employees of the Senate," Part 21, pages 1855–1899.

CHAPTER 21

1. Seth Kantor story in the Washington *Daily News*, November 22, 1963.

2. Hearings on "Financial and Business Interests of Officers or Employees of the Senate," January 9 and 17, 1964, Part 1, page 71.

3. Report No. 1175, pages 40–45.

CHAPTER 22

1. President Johnson's press conference, April 16, 1964.

2. Transcript of interview in *U.S. News & World Report*, November 25, 1963, pages 43–47.

3. Congressional Record, December 12, 1963, page 24304.

4. Congressional Record, speech by Representative W. J. Bryan Dorn of South Carolina, December 18, 1963, page 24900.

5. Federal Communication Commission records on the Capital Cable Company application for microwave permits in connection with a community-antenna television business.

6. Washington *Star,* January 12, 1964, story by Paul Hope and John Barron.

7. President Johnson's press conference, January 23, 1964.

8. President Johnson's press conference, January 25, 1964.

9. Hearings on "Financial or Business Interests of Officers or Employees of the Senate," Part 1, pages 93, 94, and 95.

10. Hearings on "Financial or Business Interests of Officers or Employees of the Senate," Part 1, pages 96 and 97.

11. President Johnson's press conference, January 31, 1964.

12. Congressional Record, Senator Jack Miller of Iowa, February 3, 1964, page 1709.

13. Congressional Record, Senator Hugh Scott of Pennsylvania, February 3, 1964, pages 1710–1711.

14. Congressional Record, Representative H. R. Gross of Iowa, February 13, 1964, pages 2747–2748.

15. Report No. 1175, page 82. Also majority report, page 54.

16. Congressional Record, March 16, 1964, page 5200.

17. C.B.S., "Face the Nation," transcript of questioning of Senator John J. Williams of Delaware, on April 5, 1964.

18. President Johnson's press conference, April 16, 1964.

19. Senator Clifford Case testimony, May 26, 1964 before the Senate Rules Committee, page 1935 of the hearings.

CHAPTER 23

1. Report No. 1175, pages 17, 18, 19, and 20.

2. Report No. 1175, pages 22 and 23.

3. Report No. 1175, page 30.

4. Report No. 1175, page 29.

5. Hearings on "Financial or Business Interests of Officers or Employees of the Senate," Part 9, page 890.

6. Hearings on "Financial or Business Interests of Officers or Employees of the Senate," Part 9, page 882.

7. Congressional Record, speech by Representative John Byrnes of Wisconsin, November 21, 1963, pages 22634–22642. Also, see Report No. 1175, page 34.

8. Hearings on "Financial or Business Interests of Officers or Employees of the Senate," Part 6, page 498.

9. Report No. 1175, pages 28 and 29.

10. Report No. 1175, page 35.

11. Report No. 1175, page 29.

12. Report No. 1175, pages 26 and 27.

13. Hearings on "Financial or Business Interests of Officers or Employees of the Senate," Part 5, page 450.

14. Hearings on "Financial or Business Interests of Officers or Employees of the Senate," Part 14, page 1311.

15. Hearings on "Financial or Business Interests of Officers or Employees of the Senate," Part 14, page 1348.

16. Hearings on "Financial or Business Interests of Officers or Employees of the Senate," Part 14, page 1355.

17. Hearings on "Financial or Business Interests of Officers or Employees of the Senate," Part 14, pages 1369 and 1370.

18. Congressional Record, March 16, 1964, page 5198.

19. Congressional Record, speech by Senator John J. Williams, April 23, 1964, page 8655.

20. Congressional Record, comments of Senator Clifford Case of New Jersey, May 14, 1964, pages 10567, 10569, 10638.

21. Congressional Record, insertions by Senator Case on March 31, 1964; May 13, 14, 15, 19, 20, 21, 22, 25, 27, 1964.

22. Report No. 1175, page 46.

CHAPTER 24

1. Report No. 1175, page 42.

2. Report No. 1175, page 44.

3. Report No. 1175, page 92.

4. "Employment of Homosexuals and Other Sex Perverts in Government," Interim Report of the Committee on Expenditures in the Executive Departments by its Subcommittee on Investigations, 81st Congress, 2nd Session, Document No. 241, dated December 15, 1950.

5. Report on the employment of homosexuals, page 4.

6. Report No. 1175, page 44.

7. Report No. 1175, page 91.

8. Report No. 1175, page 91.

9. Report No. 1175, page 93.

10. Report on the employment of homosexuals, pages 5 and 6.

11. Text of F.B.I. report on the Jenkins case, *New York Times,* October 24, 1964.

12. "A Graveside Marked Despair," by William S. White, Washington *Star,* October 16, 1964, page A-13.

13. "The Tragedy of the Jenkins Case," by Joseph Kraft, Washington *Star,* October 16, 1964, page A-13.

CHAPTER 25

1. Report No. 1175, page 38.
2. Report No. 1175, page 39.
3. Report No. 1175, page 38.
4. Report No. 1175, page 38.
5. *Wall Street Journal,* March 18, 1964, "McCloskey's Story."
6. Congressional Record, speech by Senator John J. Williams of Delaware, July 12, 1962, pages 13330–13344, 13346, 13347, 13350.
7. Congressional Record, speech by Senator John J. Williams of Delaware, October 10, 1962, page 22933.
8. Congressional Record, speech by Senator John J. Williams of Delaware, September 1, 1964, pages 20576–20584.
9. Report No. 1175, page 40.
10. Congressional Record, comments by Senator John J. Williams of Delaware, July 27, 1964, page 16458.
11. Congressional Record, speech by Senator John J. Williams of Delaware, September 1, 1964, pages 20576–20589.

APPENDIX A

The admittedly erroneous "Memorandum for the Record," dated November 21, 1962, to justify the decision to award the TFX contract to General Dynamics: (From Part 2 of the TFX Contract Investigation hearings, pages 350 through 353).

EXHIBIT NO. 2

DEPARTMENT OF THE AIR FORCE,
OFFICE OF THE SECRETARY,
Washington, November 21, 1962.

MEMORANDUM FOR THE RECORD

We have reviewed the source selection evaluation for the TFX (F–111) most carefully.

This evaluation is by far the most comprehensive source selection evaluation in our experience, and we have great confidence in the details as well as the general conclusions. The magnitude of completed work provides a reliable indication of the quality of both the proposals and the evaluation. Requirements of the work statement have been met in practically all areas by both contractors; where any deficiencies exist, adequate provision has been made to comply with the work statement. All the necessary information is available for selecting a contractor.

The evaluation has produced an advanced aircraft operationally acceptable to both the Navy and Air Force users. It will be a true biservice aircraft, providing for both the Air Force tactical fighter mission and the Navy carrier-based fighter mission.

As both services agree, the TFX design represents a significant advance in the state of the art and results in a weapon system superior to those now in the inventory or in production for either service. The TFX can provide target coverage at a higher mach number than present aircraft and approximately five times the range in performing a typical mission profile. The following is a

comparison of the TFX and the F–4C, using the General Dynamics version
of the TFX as an example.

	TFX	F–4C
Ferry range		
Takeoff distance		
Landing distance		
Range at altitude (supersonic)	Deleted	Deleted
Range at sea level (supersonic)		
UCI	for security	for security
Airframe R. & D. costs	$503,000,000	$468,000,000

In its design the TFX has unusual flexibility and growth potential. Improvements in powerplants, weapons, and special equipment can be anticipated, followed by new techniques and new missions. Growth potential is an
important consideration, because the life of the aircraft should be long to
justify the high cost.

It is apparent from the evaluation that the Boeing and General Dynamics
proposals, although possessing strong dissimilarities, are rated equally. In the
raw score comparison, General Dynamics received 175.6 points and Boeing
172.1, a difference of less than 2 percent.

The Air Force gives a significant edge to the operational characteristics of
the Boeing aircraft, because of its longer ferrying range, greater firepower,
and the provision of thrust reversers for increased maneuverability. The
Navy also favors Boeing's operational features but to a lesser degree, at-
tributable in part to the lower number of Boeing aircraft which could be
accommodated aboard a carrier [deleted]. In the Navy version the Boeing
proposal has a speed restriction which would require additional weight to be
added. The General Dynamics aircraft is slightly inferior in weapon selectivity and carrying capability; however, its superior supersonic performance
and lack of a speed limitation are considered to be basic advantages which
can overcome the deficiencies.

Inasmuch as either of the proposed aircraft can perform the mission required by both services, and the evaluation of the proposals provides no
overriding margin between the competitors, it is necessary to consider other
factors in evaluating these aircraft.

The first of these is the degree of commonness. A high degree of commonness will initially provide a larger number of identical parts and their
required tooling, and a future higher rate of common maintenance and operating spares. General Dynamics has a distinct edge in this area, and more
closely adheres to the Secretary of Defense guidelines to "reduce weapons
system costs by maximizing similarities of Air Force and Navy versions and
by maximum use of common equipment and structures."

On a reasonably comparable basis, 85 percent of the parts in the General

Dynamics version are identical, contrasted with 60 percent in the Boeing proposal. This factor, we believe, will become increasingly important as the development program of the aircraft evolves. Furthermore, it is doubtful that, in the normal course of development, Boeing can maintain their degree of commonness. This conclusion is reinforced by the fact that Boeing contemplates separate static test programs for their two versions. As stated in the evaluation, Boeing "is, in effect, proposing two different airplanes from the structural point of view."

It is significant that General Dynamics' integrated program for the two versions of the aircraft showed a reduction of $623 million, in comparison with their cost of developing the two versions separately. The saving in the Boeing proposal was only $397 million, emphasizing the degree to which Boeing's version are (sic) less similar than General Dynamics'.

Another factor concerns the reservations expressed by the Navy regarding the structural aspects of the Boeing proposal.

It is believed by Boeing that components used in the Air Force aircraft can be manufactured by the same tooling and reduced for the Navy aircraft by machining. It seems reasonable that if the Navy reservations as to the adequacy of the Boeing design turn out to be sound, necessary modifications of the structural design will further reduce the degree to which the Boeing versions will be common. In addition, if the Navy's reservations as to the structural integrity, the fatigue problem, and the introduction of titanium in structural members are well founded, further manufacturing problems may be introduced which are not envisioned by Boeing at this time.

Another factor to which we gave consideration was the cost proposal of the two manufacturers. It is hard to understand the optimism of the Boeing estimates for engineering, tooling, and manufacturing. With respect to tooling costs, it appears from the estimates and the rationale used by Boeing that they are approaching the development of this aircraft on a very simple basis. Boeing has reduced its man-hour estimates for manufacturing by as much as 30 percent below the industry average and has based much of its estimating on experience with B–52, KC–135, B–47, and BOMARC costs. It is not believed that this experience is directly applicable to a high-density, complex fighter aircraft. Boeing provided for acquisition of duplicate tooling in the production program, which reduces the R.D.T. & E. cost estimate. Sustaining tooling man-hours have been reduced to a most unrealistic level and sustaining engineering has again, through bookkeeping, been costed in the production program rather than in the R.D.T. & E. program. This implies that there would be no manufacturing difficulties due to engineering change proposals during the research and development program.

We conclude that the Boeing formula for estimating the cost of the aircraft resulted from an overoptimistic impression of the complexity of the TFX in relation to Boeing-produced bombers. Boeing's estimates for the total research and development program are so low that, in our opinion, they have seriously misjudged the difficulties to be expected in this aircraft of new concept.

There are additional examples of excessive optimism in the Boeing proposal—the apparent belief that thrust reversers can be developed without major problems and engineering changes; the view that the variable sweep wing can be quite easily applied to the TFX concept; the use of titanium in structural members; and the unique design for the propulsion installation. These examples suggest, if our experience is any guide, that much redesign and testing would be necessary, contrary to the reduced engineering estimates and cost indicated in the Boeing proposal.

Conversely, it is noted that the General Dynamics proposal applies extensive engineering and test effort to the development program and could be considered as being conservative. It is felt that this approach is more likely to meet the development milestones and cost goals than the Boeing proposal.

In analyzing the summary of ratings in the evaluation, it is pertinent to note that the General Dynamics evaluation exceeds Boeing's in the technical areas of air vehicle, propulsion, flight control, secondary power and environment control, mission and traffic control, aerospace ground equipment, crew provisions, and personnel subsystems. These favorable areas, in our opinion, outweigh the deficiencies in offensive systems, reconnaissance, and penetration aids.

Further, the favorable rating in production program planning and cost realism provides much credibility to General Dynamics in areas with which we are particularly concerned.

The final consideration stemmed from the fact that the General Dynamics/ Grumman team has extensive experience in the development and production of high performance, tactical, and carrier-based aircraft. It is thoroughly familiar with all the problems of stability augmentation and supersonic operation. This experience is not obtained in developing and producing bombers and subsonic jet transports, which have been the major portion of Boeing's experience in recent years.

It is our opinion, therefore, in view of the fact that both aircraft proposed are acceptable and offer a capability far beyond present-day aircraft, we should accept General Dynamics' proposal on the basis that it proposes the greater degree of commonness, contemplates the use of conventional materials, provides the higher confidence in structural design, and offers the better possibility of obtaining the aircraft desired on schedule and within the dollars programed.

> FRED KORTH,
> *Secretary of the Navy.*
> EUGENE M. ZUCKERT,
> *Secretary of the Air Force.*

Approved:

> ROBERT S. MCNAMARA,
> *Secretary of Defense.*

APPENDIX B

The Statement of Chairman John L. McClellan on March 13, 1963, pointing up the "substantial financial errors" in the Defense Department's memorandum of justification on the TFX contract:

STATEMENT OF SENATOR JOHN L. MCCLELLAN

The request of Secretary McNamara that he be permitted to insert into the record, at this stage of the proceedings, a sworn statement for the purpose of refuting some testimony that the committee has received and to explain the reasons for his decision to award the TFX plane contract to General Dynamics has been granted, and his affidavit is now in the record and has been released to the press.

Later, at an appropriate time in the course of further hearings, Secretary McNamara will be called before the committee to testify, at which time he will be interrogated relative to statements contained in his affidavit and also with respect to other questions and issues that have been raised by testimony the committee has received from other witnesses.

The committee would have gladly permitted Secretary McNamara to testify personally to the contents of his affidavit at any time—since the hearings began. It was my understanding, however, that he did not wish to testify until after other witnesses had been heard. Mr. Adlerman, chief counsel of the subcommittee, was so informed by a representative of the Secretary before the hearings started, and I, as chairman, directed that the hearings proceed accordingly.

When the Secretary felt, however, that testimony the committee had received reflected derogatorily on the Defense Department and requested that he be permitted to submit a statement, permission was promptly granted him to do so.

I know of no better way to begin a hearing and develop testimony on the issues involved than to start and move from the ground up. It is, of course, impossible to put all of the evidence into the record in one day or even in a few days. Thus, there is no way to avoid what some have termed a "fragmentary" release of all the facts. The only way that this could be prevented would be to release nothing to the public until full hearings are concluded.

We have had a very short time in which to examine a 32-page statement submitted by the Secretary. A hurried reading of it, however, would indicate that there are some discrepancies between it and exhibit No. 2—the memorandum of justification for the awarding of the contract to General Dynamics—which was prepared by Secretary Zuckert and Secretary Korth and signed by Secretary McNamara on the 21st day of November 1962.

The testimony from the Defense Department witnesses so far shows that the Source Selection Board, the commanders in the Air Force and the Navy, and the Chief of Staff of the Air Force, Gen. Curtis LeMay, and the Chief of Naval Operations, Adm. George Anderson, recommended that Boeing be selected as a source of procurement for the TFX plane. The testimony of the Defense Department witnesses shows that the Government evaluated Boeing's design as superior in operational capacity in that it had a 1,100 mile greater ferry range, more than 50 percent greater weapon carrying capability, and the ability to land at low speeds on carrier flight decks and on short airstrips. The record also shows that Boeing would perform its contract according to the Air Force's own estimate for some $100 million less than General Dynamics.

However, the testimony also revealed that there were substantial financial errors, $31,800,000 in the stated research and development cost of the General Dynamics plane, and a further error of $29 million as a stated figure of the Boeing's estimate if it was required to produce two separate planes. In addition, it was shown that there was an error committed of $77 million in stating Boeing's cost which apparently was not corrected until the middle of November and presumably after a decision had been made by the Secretary to award the contract to General Dynamics. Mr. McNamara's statement is silent as to these basic facts in arriving at the decision to make the award to General Dynamics. Perhaps these would not be persuasive or controlling facts. Nevertheless, I think it important that we have further explanation with respect to how decisions can be arrived at when there are such large errors in the financial figures that were presented for them to consider before making an award.

Thus, the committee will of necessity have to pursue all these matters further and proceed with the hearing of other important evidence of witnesses who have very material and pertinent information that the committee will require for a fair and "judicious rendering" of its findings and such recommendations as it may deem proper.

APPENDIX C

The "Memorandum for the Record" by Albert W. Blackburn on March 1, 1963, on McNamara's TFX decision:

OFFICE OF THE DIRECTOR OF DEFENSE RESEARCH AND ENGINEERING,
Washington, D.C., March 1, 1963.

MEMORANDUM FOR THE RECORD

Subject: TFX program.

On September 1, 1961, the Secretary of Defense made the decision to proceed with TFX weapon system as a joint Air Force/Navy development program with the Air Force acting as the executive agent. This decision was made after more than a year of study and analysis of the pros and cons of such a program. Neither service wished for the program to proceed as a joint development because it would deny them the privilege of autonomously developing their own weapon system. Moreover, there was a feeling that it would be unwise to have the entire high performance spectrum for the next generation of tactical aircraft covered by a single development effort. Finally, there is a strong feeling held by many of the "old pros" in the weapons system development business that competition between the Air Force and Navy tends to generate better, more effective weapons. Throughout the exercise these points were never formally voiced by the services but rather they chose to argue against the biservice development program on the grounds of technical infeasibility. This was at a time when the Air Force was making a decision to buy into the Navy F–4H program and indeed to supplant much of the F–105 scheduled production with the Navy-developed F–4H. Thus, this outstanding Navy-developed aircraft will be the backbone of both Air Force and Navy tactical airpower until introduction of the TFX. The question of technical infeasibility is indeed difficult to substantiate under these circumstances particularly when one contemplates the very much greater flexibility of operations offered by the incorporation of such TFX innovations as the variable sweep wing and the afterburning turbofan engine.

In his September 1, 1961, memo to the services the Secretary provided certain guidelines under which the development was to be undertaken. The Air Force SOR—183 was to be the basis for the work statement that would go to industry. On top of this SOR there were added restraints to weight, length, mold line for accommodating an adequate radar dish, bomb/missile bay capacity, conventional weapons carriage capability, and Navy mission capability. These restraints were negotiated with and approved by General LeMay and Admiral Russell prior to the final signing of the September 1 memo.

On October 1, 1961, a request for proposal was submitted by the Air Force to industry which RFP incorporated the above noted guidelines. This work statement was reviewed by O.D.D.R. & E. and certain modifications thereto were made early in the period for proposal submissions which changes related primarily to carrier compatibility features. Prior to the presentation by the Air Force of their evaluation of the proposals, it was recommended to Dr. Brown that because of the potential magnitude of the TFX program and because of the inherent lack of competition, it would be a good idea to select the two top proposals and proceed through a further design refinement period wherein both of these contractors would be funded for their efforts. One precedent for this was the WS–110 (B–70) competition wherein Boeing and North American were carried on a funded basis for more than a year during which very large and significant improvements in the design proposals were effected. This recommendation to proceed with two contractors was, in fact, implemented, and on February 1, 1962 it was announced that Boeing and General Dynamics would be awarded a $1 million contract each and given 90 days in which to refine their respective design for the TFX. The second proposals were submitted May 1, 1962, and the evaluation thereof was completed June 1, 1962.

Subsequent to evaluation of these two designs, although the Air Force was satisfied, the Navy felt that their requirements could be met by neither proposal. A memo was prepared for Secretary Korth's signature stating that the Navy could not use the aircraft and recommending that the Air Force be allowed to proceed independently with its development for their unique use. When it was learned that such a memo was in preparation, it was pointed out to Admiral Pirie that such a position could only result in delays to the program since the Secretary had already decided to proceed with the joint development. Admiral Pirie then took it upon himself to get with the Air Force and convince them that greater attention should be paid to the unique problems of Navy fleet air defense. As a result, instead of the memo being signed by Mr. Korth, Secretary Zuckert requested additional time in which to attempt a satisfactory solution to the Navy's problems. It was decided to give the contractors an additional 3 weeks to remedy the deficiencies in the Navy version of their design proposals.

At this point some discussion of the original work statement and the Navy deficiencies is appropriate. Originally the Navy argued very strenuously for restrictions on size and weight because of the unique requirements of carrier operations. The original guidelines were based on these very real problems.

When the satisfactory goal of [deleted] pounds was established, it was done so with a view to using the GE engine which at that time was in great favor. When the GE engine was found to have an unrealistically optimistic development program, it was eliminated from consideration and the Pratt & Whitney engine was selected for the TFX. This selection was accomplished after the first design competition. The selection of the P. & W. engine which is slightly larger than GE engine and has a greater thrust rating meant that the TFX would be a larger aircraft and the [deleted] pounds weight limitation for the Navy could not be met using this engine. Subsequent to the second evaluation in order to crystalize the Navy's reservation about both design proposals there was added to the Navy performance requirement an ability to perform a [deleted] maneuver at 35,000 feet altitude, at combat design gross weight and at loiter mach number without buffet onset. Buffet onset was further defined as a (plus or minus) .05g perturbation. This requirement, which is a very difficult one indeed to meet, had further impact on the weight of the aircraft. In effect, with this additional requirement the Navy was saying we are less concerned about weight and size per se than we are with total operational utility. The impact of this added requirement was that the Navy aircraft would require considerably greater wing area than any proposal submitted to date.

The response of the competing contractors to the Navy deficiencies as identified in their second proposal and clarified by their additional requirements was vastly different. On June 16, 1962, their proposals were submitted to the BPO, WPAFB. General Dynamics presented their proposal in the morning, and it was clear that an atmosphere of complete panic and confusion prevailed with the result that they presented not one but four solutions to the Navy problem out of which they selected two as being the most desirable. In one of these the Air Force fuselage was used with a brandnew Navy wing and in the other the Air Force wing was used with a brandnew Navy fuselage. Upon conclusion of this presentation the impact on those who had received it was generally that the whole concept of a biservice TFX development had been completely lost. It was as though the Navy had at last found and succeeded in having accepted an additional requirement which would indeed make a biservice development technically infeasible. That afternoon the Boeing Co. presented their answers to the Navy problem and a more workmanlike and professional approach coupled with real imagination applied to the Navy problem could not have been asked for. Not only was a common design preserved but it appeared even to the most critical of Navy technical observers that for the first time one of the competitors had come to terms with their problem and offered realistic solutions. What is even more interesting is the fact that not only was the Navy airplane superior to earlier design proposals given by the Boeing Co. but the Air Force airplane also profited from the proposed improvement. This gain in Air Force performance was reflected in greater local carrying capability, shorter takeoff and longer ferry range. The cost for these improvements was in a somewhat higher gross weight and greater supersonic drag.

At this point in time there was no doubt in anyone's mind as to the relative competence of the two competing companies. However, there was brought to light at this juncture a difference in procurement philosophies of the Air Force and the Navy. Although the Navy was perfectly willing to admit that Boeing represented the most acceptable source for procurement of the TFX as now defined in the work statement, they took the position that the estimated effects of the rather substantial exchanges to the Boeing wing, particularly with regard to the high lift devices that had been added, had not been adequately validated by analysis and test because of the very short period of time allowed the companies in correcting the Navy deficiencies. The Navy insisted that before they would commit themselves to the development of the Boeing aircraft, the company must be given time to validate their latest design proposal and the Navy must be given time to evaluate the validating data.

The Air Force on the other hand was perfectly happy to commit themselves to the Boeing Co. as a source and refine the design as necessary as the development proceeded.

Thus another impasse was reached wherein a full and free commitment by both services to the favored design could not be established. Failing to get a commitment from the Navy to this WS development Secretary McNamara made it known that he would not permit the continuation of the program with a single contractor and elected to continue the competitive nature of the exercise for another 90 days, giving each contractor an additional $2.5 million to further refine their design proposals and validate their data. The Air Force and Navy would have 60 days to evaluate the contractor submissions. The Secretary evidently was also concerned about the large variance between contractors cost estimates and the much higher cost estimated by the Air Force. At the start of this next round, Secretary Zuckert instructed the BPO to treat each of the competitors as though they were a prime contractor and work directly with them to assist in correction of their deficiencies.

As might be expected, the failure to reach a decision at this point had a severe impact on the morale of both the evaluation team of the Source Selection Board and of the design teams of both contractors. In order to alleviate the morale problems a letter to the heads of the competing companies was prepared for Mr. Gilpatric's signature which outlined the reasons for the continuation of the competition. In general, this letter stated that adequate technical validation of the Navy fixes had not been submitted, that substantiation of cost estimates was inadequate, and that satisfaction that either submission represented a truly common design was lacking. He went on to say that not only must the TFX weapon system be acceptable to both services but that it must also represent a demonstrably significant increase in effectiveness over the systems it would replace.

Some comments relative to the difference between contractor and Air Force estimates of program costs should be made. The contractors cost estimates are based on accomplishing the specific work as set forth in their proposals.

They include no money for changes to these specifications and schedules which changes invariably occur in a program of this magnitude. The Air Force estimate of the costs are historical and are based on the actual cost of similar programs which without exception have experienced very significant changes in the total scope of the programs as they have evolved. These changes are costly but in many cases they represent a change in scope of the program which, in fact, will yield a more effective weapon system as an end item.

During the 90 days following the three submissions by the contractors two very different types of activity were taking place at Fort Worth and Seattle. The General Dynamics engineers were desperately seeking to evolve a satisfactory configuration whereas the Boeing engineers were carrying their design into detailed wind tunnel analysis for both subsonic and supersonic performance and were identifying such detailed design problems as optimum location of all the various stores, the problem of a satisfactory pitot boom location, small improvements in wave drag, and the detailed aerodynamic design problems associated with handling qualities, etc. All the imaginative aerodynamic fixes devised by Boeing in their third submission to satisfy the very difficult Navy maneuver requirements somehow found their way into the final General Dynamics design to a degree of similarity that would hardly be coincidence. With the aid of these devices, the General Dynamics design was finally brought together in a single aircraft for the Navy and Air Force but with an empty weight approximately 2,000 pounds greater than that of the Boeing design. In their effort to refine their designs and to meet the Navy's often expressed concern for weight, the Boeing engineers departed from commonality to reduce weight. However, those uncommon items could have been restored to the Navy airplane to give it the same speed envelope and same skin gages as applied to the Air Force aircraft at less than the 2,000 pounds difference between their two proposals. In fact, with the additional loiter afforded by the Boeing design, this aircraft which would be structurally identical to its Air Force counterpart would still have a 2,000-pound lighter mission weight if identical missions were to be flown.

The final presentations were given to the evaluation team of the Source Selection Board on September 11, 1962. The General Dynamics presentation was inspired. Histrionically it could not have been better paced or more interestingly presented. Their design was essentially a new one, the lines were smooth, and the data appeared to be well validated. They did not present detailed information as to their external stores location nor such fine points as handling qualities. The Boeing presentation followed that afternoon and was dull by comparison. The Boeing engineers had gone beyond the broad considerations of base drag, range, and maximum mach number and had gotten into the fine details of working on very small drag items and problems of stability and control. There is an interesting comparison to be made here between the AH–1 aircraft which was the predecessor of the F–4H and the F–4H as it finally evolved. The AH–1 was a very clean and slick appearing aircraft whereas the F–4H with all its odd bumps, cranked wing tips, sawtooth leading edges and drooped stabilizer is a very homely and awkward appearing airplane; however, the things that were done to the AH–1–which never was built–to arrive at the F–4H configuration are the kinds of things that are necessary to evolve a useful weapon system from an aerodynamicist's design. The General Dynamics engineers were still in the early phases of their configuration evolution with lines still straight and eye appealing, whereas the Boeing designers had begun to identify the detailed problems of the final configuration resolution and were clearly much further down the line in coming to terms with the total design problem.

When the announcement was made that General Dynamics would be given the development program, it was clear to all those involved that this decision could be justified only on the basis of a broad, high-level policy of the administration, and could not in any way be associated with the merits of the two proposals on either an operational, technical, management, or cost basis. The operational commanders were the strongest in their support of the Boeing design; however, the depth of technical development of the Boeing design and its imaginative innovations such as thrust reversers, high-lift devices (later adapted by General Dynamics) and top-mounted engine inlets clearly pointed in favor of their proposal. From a cost point of view it is a well recognized fact that between two aircraft of generally the same performance requirements, the lighter empty weight aircraft should be the cheaper. From the management point of view the handling of such major Air Force weapon systems as the B–47, B–52, and the Minuteman as well as the KC–135/707 development must be considered superior to the management given the F–102, F–106, and B–58 series and the notoriously poor management exercised in the General Dynamics jet transport program. If *Fortune* magazine articles are to be read into the record of the McClellan committee investigation, the articles of January and February 1962 on General Dynamics management would hardly support the case for that company on a cost-realism basis.

Probably one of the most critical features of the whole TFX exercise is the damage that may have been wrought on our entire design competition structure. It is difficult to imagine that several hundred top technical experts from Wright Field and the Bureau of Weapons would again with such seriousness of purpose and over such a long period of time, including many 7-day weeks, so enthusiastically seek to accomplish the choice of the superior weapon system proposal in another such competition when the total effort expended by them is from their point of view completely negated by an executive decision. This is especially true if the reason given for this decision is that they had not done their job well and that their recommendations are invalid. The impact on the morale of this highly professional and well-motivated group would be much less if it were announced that though their recommendations were within the scope of their considerations, higher level problems of depressed areas, geographical spread of so large an effort and the importance of the outstanding Fort Worth facility caused a reversal.

A final word on the protection of a common design. In 1951, the Navy decided they needed a Navy version of the F–86. This was built in prototype at the North American Los Angeles plant (Air Force) and designated the FJ–2. Production was shifted to the North American Navy plant at Columbus. Subsequently the airplanes were reengined and in their final configuration the FJ–4 with a Curtiss Wright J–65 engine and the F–86H with GE J–73 engine didn't even have a common rear view mirror. The point is that if we are really concerned about retaining a maximum degree of commonality, there may be a better case for building them all at the same plant than can be made from a comparison of design proposals.

In summary, the Secretary of Defense laid on a task in the TFX which was not popular in concept with either Air Force or Navy. Nevertheless, the two services turned to with an unprecedented and very real spirit of cooperation, and carried the Secretary's desires through an agonizing year of very productive appraisal and reappraisal. The Secretary chose to make a decision on the basis of information different from that evaluated under the established ground rules. That is certainly his prerogative, but there is no real, supportable case to be made for his choice on the grounds of operational, technical, management, or cost considerations. As a matter of loyalty to his own organization, a different rationale for the TFX decision should be found.

A. W. BLACKBURN.